Isherwood's Australia

An Autobiography

First published in Far North Queensland, 2023 by Bowerbird Publishing

Copyright @ 2023 Alan Isherwood

All rights reserved. Apart from any fair dealing for the purpose of private study, research, criticism or review, as permitted under the Copyright Act, no part of this book may be reproduced or transmitted in any form or by any means, electronic or mechanical, including photocopying, recording or by any information storage and retrieval system, without prior permission in writing from the publisher. The moral right of the author to be identified and to have his text preserved is asserted. Enquiries should be made to the publisher. Images copyright, individual owners.

ISBN 978-1-7638746-2-6 (paperback)
ISBN 978-0-6457433-6-4 (hardcover)
ISBN 978-0-6457433-3-3 (digital)

Isherwoods Australia
Alan Isherwood

First print edition: 2023
4th print: 2025

Edited by: Alan Isherwood and Bowerbird Publishing
Cover Concept & Design by: Crystal Leonardi, Bowerbird Publishing
Interior Design by: Crystal Leonardi, Bowerbird Publishing

Front Cover Image: Alan Isherwood
Title Page Image: Taken by Richard Darby, 1962. The author on a hitchhiking trip from Ringwood, Victoria, leaving Echuca enroute to Maude in the Riverina, NSW.

All images used with permission.

Distributed by Bowerbird Publishing
Available in National Library of Australia

Crystal Leonardi, Bowerbird Publishing
Julatten, Queensland, Australia
www.crystalleonardi.com

Events, documents, images, personalities, institutions, products, equipment and organisations are mentioned as the author recalls them and are published in good faith. Aboriginal and Torres Strait Islanders are advised that this book may contain names and images of people who have passed away.

For my family and friends.

Isherwoods Australia

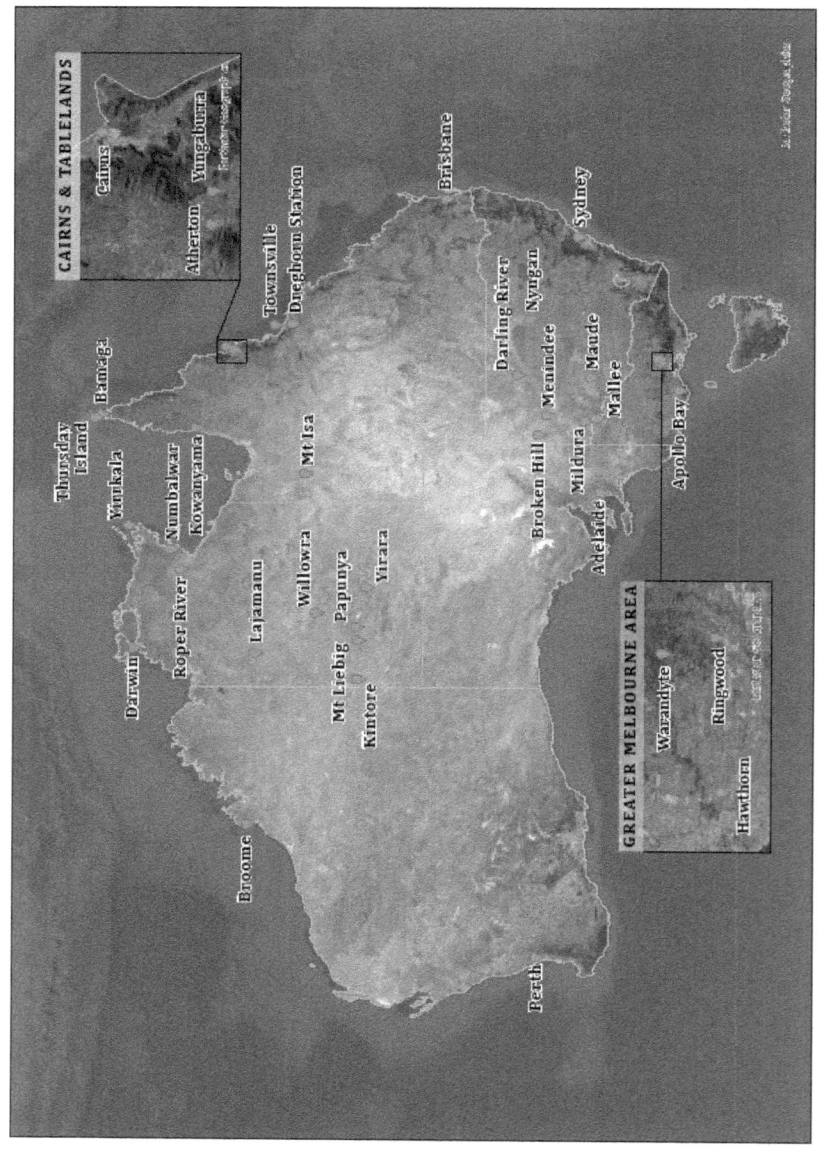

CONTENTS

Map of Australia	Page I
Preface	Page XIV
Bradshaw & Isherwood Coat of Arms	Page XVI
Isherwood Family Tree	Page XVI
Prologues by Rev. John Woodley & Werner Sattmann-Frese	Page XVIII
Foreword by Jim Varghese AM	Page XIX

Chapter 1
Foundations

A Colonial Past	Page 1
The Early Years	Page 6
Ireland Street, Ringwood	Page 8
Goings on in the Backyard	Page 11
Family Relations	Page 17
Mum	Page 18
Dad	Page 19
Grandpa and Apollo Bay	Page 22
Aunty Lil and Uncle Jack	Page 27
Guy Fawkes Night and Other Exploits	Page 28
High School Days	Page 32
Adolescent Affairs	Page 38
Growing Up	Page 39
Turning and Fitting	Page 45
A Zephyr Six	Page 48
Bush Fires	Page 50
The Balwyn Experiment	Page 51
A Raft on the Darling River	Page 53
Darby	Page 62
The Incident at Yarra Glen	Page 63
Time out and a Return to Nature	Page 64
Darby gets Married	Page 65
Leaving Home	Page 65
Alan is Starving in Broken Hill	Page 66
The Train Crash, West of Nyngan	Page 68

CONTENTS

Chapter 2
On the Move

Sydney	Page 69
Newcastle	Page 70
Home Hill and the Inkerman Sugar-mill	Page 71
Townsville	Page 74
A Super Rocket	Page 74
Saturday Night in Ayr	Page 76
A Land Rover Series 2	Page 77
The Fight at the Malpass Hotel	Page 78
Life in Townsville	Page 79
Rose and I got Married	Page 81
To Victoria via Central Australia	Page 82
Back to Ringwood	Page 83
A New Series 2A	Page 83
Vietnam War	Page 84
Across the Nullabor and on to Perth	Page 85
Mount Pleasant, Palmyra, and Maylands	Page 85
Methodist Overseas Missions (MOM)	Page 87

CONTENTS

Chapter 3
Darwin to North East Arnhem Land

From Perth to Darwin	Page 88
Yirrkala	Page 90
First Impressions	Page 91
Settling In	Page 92
Work at the Mission	Page 94
Community Gardens	Page 96
Turning the Other Cheek	Page 97
Terry Parry	Page 97
Flying Again	Page 98
ELDO Tracking Station	Page 98
A Buffalo on the Ridge	Page 99
Bush and Beach	Page 101
Spear-fishing	Page 102
King Fish	Page 104
Strange Phenomena	Page 104
Caledon Bay	Page 104
A Rich and Complex Culture	Page 107
Ranga at the Water Hole	Page 109
Goings on at the Mission	Page 110
Aunty's Cat	Page 111
The Gove Land-rights Case	Page 112
Out of Arnhem Land	Page 114
Reflections	Page 120
Further on Down the Road	Page 121

CONTENTS

Chapter 4
Brisbane Building Connections

Appleby Road	Page 122
Wertz and Hiller	Page 123
Goings on at Appleby Road	Page 124
Thank God for Lifesavers	Page 125
Fernberg Road	Page 125
A Governor's Gardener	Page 126
Michelle and Christine	Page 127
Moving in at the end of the Hall	Page 128
Rosco	Page 129
The Rolling Stones	Page 130
The Demise of Kirwin	Page 130
Richard and Jill, Maxine and Shane, and Peter Marsh	Page 131
From Fernberg Road to Indooroopilly	Page 131
Jim Varghese	Page 132
Anne and Errol Klibbe	Page 133

CONTENTS

Chapter 5
A Return to the Northern Territory

Lajamanu (Hooker Creek)	Page 135
A Remote Government Settlement	Page 136
A Dependence on Air Services	Page 138
Life on the Settlement	Page 139
Business	Page 141
Baptist Church Mission	Page 142
Aboriginal Welfare	Page 142
The Works Manager	Page 142
The Tanami and the Granites	Page 146
Warnabari	Page 149
Mums Visits to Lajamanu	Page 150
Death at the Admin. Office	Page 152
Cultural Studies	Page 155
Lifelong Learning	Page 157
Nurses are Flown out	Page 158
A Brief Return to Far North Queensland	Page 159
Flying Again	Page 160
Born Free	Page 161
Mount Peter Road	Page 162
Numbulwar	Page 163
Willowra Station	Page 195

CONTENTS

Chapter 6
Papunya & Beyond

Atomic Bombs	Page 209
Working at Papunya	Page 210
Alistair Burns	Page 211
Petrol Sniffing	Page 212
TAFE	Page 213
Life Outside Work at Papunya	Page 213
Grandpa has Passed Away	Page 214
Standing Orders	Page 214
The Derwent is up	Page 215
Neanderthals in the Mist	Page 217
Local Characters	Page 218
A Used Car Industry	Page 220
More Land Rovers	Page 220
Japalyi and Twinkle Toes	Page 222
South Australia	Page 223
Church	Page 223
The Fox and the Chooks	Page 224
Uwe and Cathy	Page 224
Joe Lane	Page 225
Flying Again	Page 225
Holidays	Page 226
Back at Papunya	Page 227

CONTENTS

Chapter 7
North Queensland

Ingham Special School	Page 231
Townsville	Page 232
Other Goings On	Page 234
Kirwan High	Page 235
Atherton Tablelands	Page 238
Friends and Neighbours	Page 241
Glenwood Close	Page 243
A Queenslander	Page 244
Fiji	Page 250
Up the Cape, Torres Strait & Across the Gulf	Page 254
Back on the Tablelands	Page 258

CONTENTS

Chapter 8
Politics

Brisbane	Page 267
The Party	Page 268
A Party Response to the National Competition Policy	Page 271
Back Home to the Tablelands	Page 273
Copenhagen	Page 274
England – A Sense of Place	Page 275
Facing Reality on the Tablelands	Page 278
Further Progress	Page 280
Press Releases	Page 281
Under Attack	Page 282
Interference and Undermining	Page 282
Targeting to Harvest Votes	Page 283
Visit to Lajamanu	Page 284
Branch Website Up and Running	Page 285
National Conference	Page 286

CONTENTS

Chapter 9
Beyond the Party

Restoration	Page 289
Sar Chung	Page 291
Lajamanu and Nhulunbuy	Page 291
Yirrkala Revisited	Page 292
ARDS and Richard Trudgen	Page 294
Courthouse Observations and Other Things	Page 296
Farwell to an Old Friend - A Homeland Funeral	Page 298
Witjiwitji is at Gapuwiyak	Page 299
Daliwuy Bay	Page 300
Helping Out	Page 300
Crocodiles and Birany Birany	Page 301
Back in Court	Page 302
From Nhulunbuy to Roper River	Page 305
Mum has Passed Away	Page 307
Environmentalism in Practice	Page 309
Cairns House	Page 310
Back to England, via Sursee	Page 310
England	Page 311
Back on the Tablelands	Page 313
An Easy Two	Page 315

CONTENTS

Chapter 10
Consolidation & Progress

Werner Sattmann-Frese	Page 318
Other Goings On	Page 319
Psychopathy	Page 320
Cyclone Larry	Page 321
Law 6 - Control of Nuisances	Page 322
Reactions to Injustice	Page 323
Bella is Born	Page 323
Poultry	Page 330
Classic Motorcycles	Page 331
Land Rover	Page 333
Bingginwarri to Launceston	Page 334
Death of a Friend	Page 334
Back to the Northern Territory	Page 336
Ilpirli	Page 340
On a Queensland Railway	Page 342
Byron Bay Bluesfest	Page 344
Home Again	Page 345
Life is a Piece of Cake	Page 346
Cyclone Yasi	Page 347
Other Goings On	Page 348
Possible Future Scenarios	Page 349
Silas is Born	Page 351
Rats	Page 351
Hoyte has Died	Page 352
England with John Humphreys	Page 354
With Pia and Franz	Page 354
Paris	Page 355
English Idiosyncrasies	Page 356
Wybersley Hall	Page 357
It's Cold in Penzance	Page 358
From Oxford to Hong Kong	Page 360
Back to Atherton	Page 360
Dehydrated	Page 361
A New Years Eve	Page 362
Classic Racing at Hampton Downs	Page 363
Home to the Neoliberals	Page 364

CONTENTS

Chapter 11
A Return to Politics

Grassroots Politics	Page 367
Birth of a Community Group	Page 367
The Tablelands Action Alliance (TAA)	Page 369
Active Support - Thin on the Ground	Page 371
A New Approach	Page 373
An Invitation	Page 377
The #STOPADANI Campaign	Page 377
Old Friends Come to Visit	Page 379
Family Matters	Page 380
Politics in the Pub	Page 382
Judith has Passed Away	Page 383
More Campaigning	Page 383
A New Allegiance	Page 385
School Strike for Climate (SS4C)	Page 387
The Socialist Alliance (SA)	Page 393
Front Line Against Coal (FLAC)	Page 393
Christmas 2021	Page 399
Federal Elections	Page 401
Conclusion	Page 405
Acknowledgements	Page 407
About the Author	Page 409
Praise for Isherwood's Australia	Page 411
From the Publisher	Page 412

Preface

Our acreage, near Atherton on the Tablelands in Far North Queensland, has served as a sanctuary and home for me and my family and an inspiring place from which to write this book.

Isherwood residence, Atherton, Queensland. A painting by friend and former Senator Woodley.

Given the opportunity, I'd live my life all over again, and in a sense, I am by telling stories of adventure and evoking positive and spirited responses. Many of the stories were recorded in letters, diaries, and on film, with the view to writing this book. But, to be perfectly honest, I think it's just meant to be.

I started to work on this autobiography on Friday, the 28th of November 2003. It was a sporadic affair, with gaps of months and even years, between bursts of enthusiasm while also dealing with the necessities of daily life. Nevertheless, this work represents more than a series of chronological events; it radiates vitality and is a true account.

My parents encouraged the exploration of my identity and connection to the past. On my father's side is John Bradshaw, who was heavily involved in the English Revolution. My account of my mother's ancestry was based on notes that were recorded during genealogical discussions with her, building on Australia's colonial past.

The book is divided into eleven parts, portraying childhood dreams and expectations, colourful escapades in Hawthorn, and later in Ringwood. Finally, the story unfolds, revealing a tumultuous adolescence full of activity, joy, exhilaration, and upheaval.

The book characterizes my life in the mid-1960s to mid-1980s with Rose in far-flung corners of the Northern Territory, places and cultures distant in space and time.

Personal challenges came into play in our quest for deeper understanding.

Turning the pages, the avid reader is transported to another realm, a rollercoaster of attempts to transform society through vigorous campaigns against climate change and a global system that nurtures corporate greed and exploitation, threatening almost everything we stand for. Another Australia is possible.

I invite you to read on.

Marple Hall, a sketch by Mrs. Isherwood in the 1880s.

Bradshawe and Isherwood
of Marple and Wybersley

Bradshawe and Isherwood Coat of Arms.

FAMILY TREE

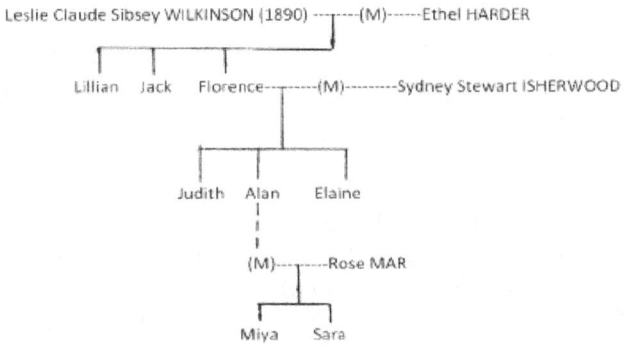

Isherwood Family Tree

Prologue

My initial contact with Alan was during my time as a Senator in the Australian Parliament from 1993 to 2001. Alan and Rose lived and worked in various communities around Australia.

Alan was more than just a member of the Democrats. After learning of his extensive talent, I engaged him as a staff member in North Queensland. He built a profile and promoted the Australian Democrats in North Queensland. Alan worked full time as a staff person although I could only pay him for a few days each week.

Alan and Rose worked for First Nations people early in their working years through the Methodist Overseas Missions in the remote Northern Territory. They have maintained contact and continue to support Aboriginal and Torres Strait Islander people.

I commend this Autobiography to anyone who would like to read about an exciting, adventurous life, a committed family man, concerned for, human rights, social justice and how to make a positive difference for our future.

Rev. John Woodley
Uniting Church Minister and former Senator

It was 17 years ago that I received a phone call from a man called Alan Isherwood. Alan had seen my name in a list of sustainability educators, and, following his curiosity, he determined to contact this man with a German name, me.

The rest is history. It wasn't long after our initial brainstorming on the phone, I found myself in Far North Queensland and met a most remarkable person. Through his fascinating stories about his life in the Australian outback, I got to know some of this country through the eyes of a man passionately dedicated to engaging First Australians, social justice and empowerment of the disenfranchised and exploited citizens of this remarkable country. I heard many of these fascinating stories while watching diapositives - 35mm slides over gin and orange juice and often listening to African American blues Swing, Rock and Ska classics by the open fire in the backyard.

There were adventures that I am now sharing with our boys and granddaughters. The scariest of those was when Alan and his wife Rose were swimming at Etty Bay. I lay dozing on the soft sandy beach, wondering whether or not swimming in waters inhabited by crocodiles should be called Australian Roulette and whether or not I would see them again. I felt a strange movement and opening my eyes, came face to face with a cassowary staring at me. I propelled myself a metre to the side. The big bird was as startled as I was and loped away, all in a split second. Ever since, I am not so sure what precisely Australian Roulette could be.

I agreed with Alan that he should make his life story available to the public. It turned out to be an epic tome about the fascinating life of an extraordinary man - a young scallywag, adventurer, and committed family man, dedicated to sustainable living. During his later years, Alan moved on to progressive politics, rainforest rehabilitation, garden and chooks and biodynamics. I have seen him stirring 500 in the big pot on the full moon.

But now, 'a shadow of his glorious former self' he has failed to prevent the current multiple crises, it was not his fault. Alan casts a far-reaching shadow, still working to make a positive difference, as many people in Far North Queensland and beyond will attest.

In closing, I would like to thank Alan for allowing me and my family to be part of his life. It is my pleasure and honour to write this prologue for his book. I am sure that we will finally work out what Australian Roulette means. If we keep stirring our pots in the right direction, we will all enjoy a sustainable future.

Dr Werner Sattmann-Frese
Wagstaffe, NSW, August 2023

Foreword

I have known Alan Isherwood, affectionately known as the "Great White Hunter" and his wife Rose since 1970. Alan respected my drive and energy in creating the Revitalisation of Christianity movement which supported student activism against apartheid and the war in Vietnam.

When we first met he used to live opposite Government House and we formed a good anti-establishment think group generating new ideas on peace, animal welfare, indigenous rights and the environment.

Alan loved plants and animals including snakes, venomous and non-venomous.

At the time Alan and I were both bold activists - Alan was blessed with an inquisitive personality and a questioning mindset combined with a bold and adventurous streak.

I met Alan's wife just three years after they were married – she was the perfect partner for Alan and provided love, emotional stability and the platform for authentic adventures of heart, mind and soul on all the issues that challenged him.

Rose was of 4th generation Chinese origin Australian and my new partner (and later wife) Pauline was an Anglo-Celtic fifth-generation Australian. Both Alan and I defied the then white mindset and married outside of our tribal clans.

My brother Matthew and I shared a house in Indooroopilly with Alan and Rose for over a year. We enjoyed some great times with them particularly when Alan's pet snake appeared and tested guests' reactions!

After this period Alan and Rose went on to have two beautiful daughters who also embraced an adventurous spirit and a commitment to social justice and the environment.

Alan and Rose worked all over Australia, including remote and isolated First Nations communities in Northeast Arnhem Land, the Central Desert of NT, Cape York and Torres Strait in FNQ. Alan became adept at speaking and understanding some of the indigenous languages and even taught in the Guadalcanal language of the Solomon Islands.

Alan, Rose and their family managed to visit the Pacific Islands, China, USA, Europe and England including the ancestral homes of Marple and Wybersley Halls in Derbyshire and Rose's ancestral village of Sar Chung in Canton province of mainland China.

After moving to the Atherton Tablelands in 1989, Alan resigned from teaching in 2008 to embrace his passion for political activism.

He became a Liaison Officer for the Australian Democrats and ran the Far North Queensland Senate office of Senator John Woodley. He contested the seat of Kennedy in the 1998 Federal elections and again as an independent candidate for the 2001 Queensland State Elections. Alan founded the community group, Tablelands Action Alliance or TAA in 2014.

Alan and his family are still front-line activists supporting the Socialist Alliance including campaigns such as the #NOT4SALE campaign, and #SCHOOLSTRIKE4CLIMATE among others. Alan continues his active support for Climate and Social Justice, Refugee rights, the natural environment, and a sustainable future for his grandchildren, future generations, and the planet.

As a senior citizen Alan enjoys long-distance swimming, connecting with nature and organic gardening.

I can personally attest to Alan's love of music - he lives and breathes Mendelssohn's Songs Without Words, Rachmaninoff, the Melbourne Ska Orchestra, 1950s Classic Rock and Roll, African American Blues, Reggae and 1940s Swing. Not surprisingly, Alan loves to play the role of DJ and also to engage in conversation with friends and family. Alan has managed to achieve fulfilment through the interdependent harmony of what he feels, thinks and believes – a subset of my interacting three-frames philosophy.

I commend this book for your enlightenment and enjoyment- it is an opportunity to expand your perspective on what truly matters in your life's journey.

Jim Varghese AM
Chairman
The Leadership Company Qld Pty Ltd

Isherwoods Australia

Chapter 1
Foundations

A Colonial Past

My father was born in 1905 at 120 Humphreys Street, Ballarat East.

Sketchy as it may be, I hope this brief history, transcribed from the inscriptions in the Isherwood Family Bible, will shed some light on my ancestral beginnings. A Lancashire Bellringer, Dad's grandfather, Joseph Isherwood, was born on Easter Sunday, the 7th of April 1822, in Salford, Manchester, Lancashire, England. His father was John Isherwood, and his mother was Ann Newton. He first married Jane Ann Pearce on 5th November 1843 in Retford County, Nottinghamshire. Their daughter, Georgiana, was born on 21st May 1848. Georgiana's sister, Ann, died on 3rd April 1854, aged three years.

Joseph was 43 when he came out to the colonies in 1864 alone. His wife, Jane Ann, died at Oldham on 6th January 1866 before she could join him. Georgiana followed her father out on the ship HMS Gresham in 1869. Joseph became the Publican of the Raikes Hotel in Smeaton in the gold fields in Victoria. He was 46, on his 2nd marriage to 29-year-old Elizabeth Healy from Clunes, County Kilkenny, Ireland, on 8th February 1871. Their first child, Elizabeth Ann, born 26th May 1872, survived to age 24.

Tragedy struck again soon after their twins, Joseph Ramsen and Mary Helen, were born on 1st March 1874. Joseph died six months later, and Mary Helen at 12 months old. Then my dad's father, Sydney Stuart, and his twin sister were born on 4th January 1877. Unfortunately, Sydney's twin sister died soon after birth. As if that wasn't enough, another set of twins was stillborn, causing the death of their mother on 27th February 1880. They were all buried at the Smeaton cemetery on the 29th of February that year.

Over one hundred years later, in 1984, during our visit to the old gravesite, our daughter Miya, seven years old at the time, suffered an unusual nosebleed, forcing us to retreat away from the place. We couldn't guess what forces were at work, and fortunately, the bleeding stopped after we had left. Only a couple of months before my Great Grandfather Joseph died on 1st October 1889, his daughter Georgiana wrote him a letter. She was 41. He was 68.

I never met my Grandparents, Sydney Stuart, and Florence Henrietta, and know very little about them. They once lived at 77 Melville Street, Hawthorn. Sydney was born at Smeaton and was only 12 when he lost his dad in 1889. He spent four years at Broken Hill. Pictured - Grandparents, Florence Henrietta & Sydney Stuart with son, my father, Sydney Stuart Jnr., 1906.

Grandparents, Florence Henrietta & Sydney Stuart with son, my father, Sydney Stuart Jnr., 1906.

The family arrived at Broken Hill in 1918. Sydney suffered from chronic lead poisoning when he was employed at the mines.

Records of the family are held at the Family History Centre. It is a story of hardship and struggles during the prolonged Miner's strike in the early 1920s. Unions around Australia contributed to a fighting fund and kept the Miners going. Dad's sister, Aunty Merle, said she got a peg doll for Christmas because the family had no money during those dark days of the Great Depression. Sydney died early when my dad was 21. Florence died when Dad was 26.

The Isherwood Family Bible inscription, including the reference to Marple Hall, would indicate that the Isherwoods have a direct link in connection to John Bradshawe, President of the High Court. He presided over the trial of King Charles 1st in 1649, during the English Civil War. The author, Christopher Isherwood, also part of this connection, was raised at Wybersley Hall in Derbyshire. I remain optimistic that this brief outline of the history of the Isherwoods will, one day, serve as an enticing starting point to take up the next step of this journey by referring to the readily available relevant publications and documents about the Bradshawes and Isherwoods, which are held in my estate. The direct links with our ancestors can be re-established and documented as a separate publication.

The following account is based on notes I took during genealogical discussions with Mum from the late 1980s to 1991.

Mum's grandfather on her father's side was John Wilkinson. I understand that he was Jewish. John and his brother, Sam, and sisters, Minnie and Lottie, were born in Skellingthorpe, Lincolnshire, England. They embarked for the colonies from Lincoln.

According to Mum's account, John was in the rag trade, owned a clothing manufacturing business in Richmond in the colony of Victoria, and lost everything in the Great Depression during the 1890s. Sam became a Tranter and bought 5 acres of land in Burwood. He had a carrying business where he moved general goods via horse-drawn carriage into Spencer Street, Melbourne.

John married Sarah Larter, born in Ipswich, Queensland, in 1862. Sarah became a school Teacher, and her father was a Physician. According to Mum, Sarah was raised by aunts and disapproved of Mum's mother, Ethel.

John and Sarah Wilkinson had three children. There was Leslie Claude Sibsey Wilkinson, my grandfather, Olga, and Muriel. Olga eventually married Archibald Maconochie. Olga died in 1978. Muriel was born at least six years after Les and died at 60.

Grandpa (Les) was born in Dorcas Street, Hawthorn. The house was elevated and close to the Yarra River.

The family lived at number 19 Denmark Street, Kew. Les's mother, Sarah, lived there well into her 80s. Les attended Hawthorn Central School. After school, he took up photography and commercial travel. He played the pipe organ at St. John's Church in Kew before enlisting in the armed forces to fight in France in WW1. He spent nine months in the trenches before being wounded and discharged.

At 23, he married Ethel Harder in 1913. Ethel, a pianist, practised for six hours per day and tutored Dame Nelly Melba's daughter. Mum and Aunty Lil were born before he went to the War. Uncle Jack was born in 1918. On returning from the war, Les became an Advertising Manager at George's Department Store in Collins Street, Melbourne. After further study, Les won a higher-status position at Buckley and Nunns in Melbourne.

Grandpa gave up Buckley and Nunns for the Mallee wheat at one pound a bag. Grandpa acquired 804 acres at Yirara of virgin Mallee scrub. The place was named Lone Pine after one native pine tree. Les was to acquire another 3000 acres under the Returned Soldier Settlement Scheme.

My Mum, Florence, turned eleven on April Fool's Day in 1926.

My maternal grandmother, Annie Butler, was born in England, and her father was a Watchmaker. Annie came from England to NZ with her father to settle there at about 19 years old. Annie met Heinrich Harder, a Sailor, born in Germany to Danish parents in Schleswig-Holstein. 'Henry' Harder had run away to sea at 14 due to the German invasion of Denmark. Henry was a Sailor for 20 years after that.

Mum's grandma, Annie Harder's (nee Butler) family, fled the French Revolution to settle in the UK. Annie died in December 1941 at age 89. Henry was ten years older than Annie and died at 68 in 1914. Their address was 3 College Street, Hawthorn.

According to mum's account, Annie cared for six children; her own four children; Lena, born 1875; Florence, 2.5 years younger; William, and Charles. She also cared for Jessie (mum's aunt) and Ethel (Mum's mother). I recall going to Lysterfield with Mum and Dad to visit Mum's aunty, Jessie, and her partner, Nova.

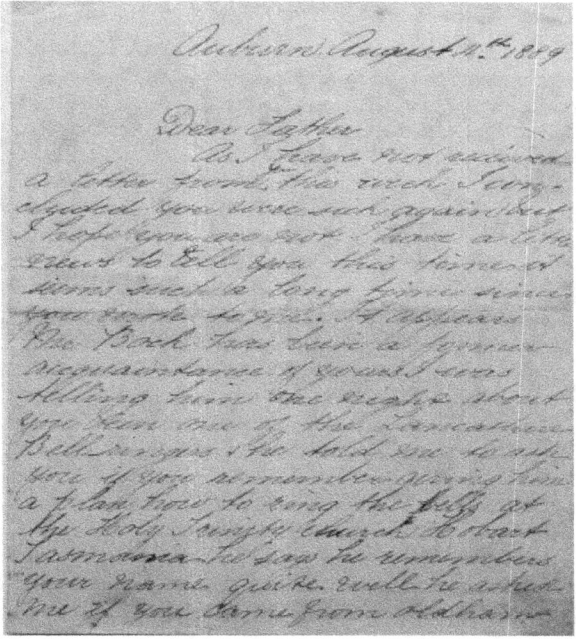

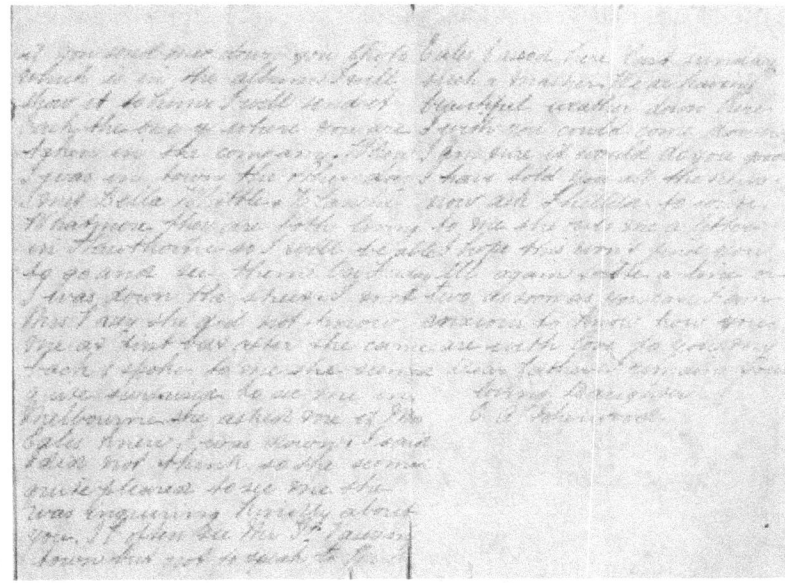

Above - Pages 1 & 2 of letter written by Georgiana, 1889.

The Early Years

44 Power Street, Hawthorn

It was not until the late 1940s, when I was three, that my memory kicked in with a bit of prompting and sketchy visions aided by the odd black-and-white photo. For example, our backyard at 44 Power Street, Hawthorn, was enclosed by a high wooden fence. I remember climbing the back fence to peer out along the narrow cobblestone laneway.

Me, Mum and Judith, Christmas 1949

For Christmas in 1949, my older sister, Judith, got a big inflatable rubber ball with different coloured panels. Mum made her a complex doll house with an open back so she could arrange all the furniture in the various rooms. Judith was about six, my younger sister, Elaine, was not yet born. I got a shiny red cart and a cast aluminium racing car, which I used to skate on.

The house was a red brick Edwardian place with heavy bluestone window sills. It had a narrow frontage and was dark inside. Mum and Dad spoke of buying 44 Power Street but didn't, and we eventually relocated to Ringwood, fifteen miles to the east of Melbourne CBD.

Life in the 1950s was a world away from what it is now. The Australian population was around 7 million, excluding First Nations people, who, at the time, were not included in the census. Ringwood was a rural mixed dairying and fruit-growing area, and a ride on the train to Melbourne was a big undertaking. Dad was still recovering from Tuberculosis, and Mum would take us to the Museum and Art Gallery, Botanic Gardens, and the annual Melbourne Show, or we'd visit relatives. I always had a nasty headache after a trip to the city. There was a social connection between the city and the countryside.

Many city people had relatives in the country. The city folk enjoyed the opportunity to engage in the rural goings-on. They understood rural families' issues through conversations around a Sunday roast during weekends, holidays, etc. With the more recent exodus from the country to the city, this tradition had been broken, and relatives were forced to visit each other in some far-off city, some even overseas, more than likely involving travel by air, train, or a very long drive.

Farming in rural Australia was a stable, protected, and viable option for income generation. For example, 50% of a working household's income went to food. Choices in everyday consumer goods were limited. For instance, if you wanted a plug for the kitchen sink, you didn't have to look far because there was only one brand, and the price was the same in any shop.

On Show Day, free sample bags were full of good quality confectionery, toys, and whistles for the kids. In addition, food items like fresh milk in returnable bottles, fresh bread, ice for the ice chest, and fresh veggies were delivered to the door, often by horse-drawn cart into the early 1960s.

It was safe to play on the street; as teenagers, we hitchhiked everywhere.

Our family doctor made home visits. I remember that in the late 1950s, there was a newspaper report of a murder in Perth. It was a major front-page report that everybody talked about for ages; murder was rare in those days. In the evenings, before the arrival of television, we would sit in the living room by the fire to listen to the news on the radio, programs, and serials like the 'Air Adventures of Biggles,' 'Night Beat,' 'Randy Stone Continues his Story,' 'Dad and Dave,' and 'Blue Hills.'

Ireland Street, Ringwood

We moved out to Ringwood from Hawthorn when I was five. Mum and Dad felt it would be a healthier environment for the family.

There was open bushland dominated by eucalypts – stringybark, messmates, tea trees, and sawgrass on clay soils. Peter Marsh lived a few houses up the road, and we became close friends. It was a dirt road, quite uneven, but because of the yellow clay, it never seemed to get muddy.

We would make trips out to our half-acre block where the building of the house was in progress. It seemed to take ages to build. The hardwood frame stood there for many months before the roof tiles were laid. Finally, the weatherboards were on, and the red brick chimney, fireplace, and septic tank were finished on 31st December 1949. The floorboards, hot water service, wiring, and plaster work were completed by 17th April 1950. It was on 11th August 1950 that we made the final trip out to move into 18 Ireland Street, Ringwood. The wooden paling fence surrounding our ¼ acre house block was erected on 25th January 1951. Mum and Dad had also bought the quarter-acre block next door. Our phone number was WU 6796.

Judith and me at 18 Ireland Street, Ringwood, 1949.

Mum and Dad bought our first car on 22nd June 1953, a grey 1949 Ford Prefect with 8742 miles on the clock. From the outset, nobody seemed all that impressed. It was noisy and uncomfortable with fumes inside. It was top-heavy and felt like it would topple over on the corners. I got car sick a lot.

Dad and Elaine in the dreaded Prefect, 1953.

We gradually met more neighbours. Laurie Ryan was next door, and the Marshes and McCubbins were across from them. Lorna Harkensee and Charlie Martin also lived in our street. Lance, John, and Leslie O'Reagan lived on the farm on City Road. Lindsay Hobbs and Beth Roberts were up on City Road too. Peter Bouroudale, Trevor Shearing, John and Mervin Robbins, and Bev lived in Ireland Street. Mrs. Kramer and Mrs. Kimberley were across the road. Everyone knew and helped each other. Mum and Dad eventually sold the block next door to a Pommy family.

I used to have many dreams. When I was about six, I used to have nightmares. There were two main themes; one was about falling. Luckily, I always managed to wake up before hitting the ground. The other was about being chased by savage animals. I tried to scream for help but could only whisper.

Again, I would manage to wake before being set upon.

In those early days, I shared a room with Judith. I had somehow developed a fear that there was a lion lurking under the bed or in the cupboard. I never shared this fear with the rest of the family. I systematically checked for lions under the bed and in the cupboard every night before bed. Once satisfied that all was clear, I had no trouble sleeping.

Christmas was a special time for me, even though I never got many presents. There would be one main one and top of the range, including a fabulous red Cyclops scooter with a large wooden foot-well and a foot brake at the back, an upright polished brass donkey engine, a Meccano set, a clockwork Hornby train set, a skittle set, a pirate pistol that you stuck in your belt and a leather cowboy outfit with cap-gun and holster to match. English Clockwork tinplate toys were great, the most impressive being a big clockwork Mettoy 1950s-style racing car. One year we all got a Triang clockwork tinplate toy. Judith got a green London bus, Elaine, a steam roller, and I got a Rolls Royce in British racing Green with black mudguards, doors that opened, a dash, a steering wheel, and a clear windscreen. Another year I got a royal blue Malvern Star bike.

I'd lay awake all night on Christmas Eve, anticipating what the morning would bring. It was usually around 3 am that I'd get up and sneak into the dining room and try to establish, in the dim light, what the presents were that Dad was putting around the tree. By then, the stockings were hanging from the mantelpiece, bulging with nuts, dried fruit, lollies, and balloons, with an orange and some nuts left close by for Father Christmas. Then I'd scurry back to bed to lay awake and speculate until dawn when there was sufficient light to check in more detail. We were up early to start unwrapping the presents and taking them in to show Mum and Dad, who were still in bed. We were never disappointed.

Straight after breakfast on Christmas morning, I'd be off to Peter Marsh's and others to share and compare presents, ride the new scooter or bike, then get home for a roast lunch with aunties, uncles, and cousins, then out again for the afternoon.

A memorable little experience springs to mind that I'd like to share too… One day, I went to Melbourne with Aunty Lil, who bought me a doughnut to eat on the train. I was about five and had never seen a doughnut. She explained that you don't eat the hole with doughnuts because if you do, you'll swallow the air, causing extra air in the stomach. So, to the amusement of everyone on the train, I chewed carefully all around the hole in the middle and threw the hole out the window.

We loved our special train trips to the Melbourne Show too. The Melbourne show was a highlight of the 1950s. We went on the show train, a train set aside, especially for the event. The showgrounds were vast, including the pavilions, equestrian events, displays of the latest farming equipment, and everything else imaginable. The sample bags were the best part. They were free and full of quality samples of what companies had to offer, such as soap, chocolate, and other confectioneries. In addition, the bags included toys for kids, like wooden whistles where you pulled out a piston to change the tune, balloons, and other things.

(L-R) Judith & me out the front at 18 Ireland Street, 1951.
Judith & me playing cricket on the block next door, 1951.

Moomba was another family affair. We went by train to Melbourne's annual Moomba Festival, and the biggest attraction was the noisy and colourful parades and marches along the streets. Just about every organisation was represented there. There were schools, Councils, Government Departments like Primary Industries, Hospitals, local manufacturers, the armed forces, and the Police. There seemed to be an enormous amount of energy and expense put into spectacular floats in which local manufacturers and traders exhibited their products.

Back at Ireland Street in Ringwood, a lot was going on.

Goings on in the Backyard

Mum and Dad bought two quarter-acre blocks, one adjoining the house block where we cleared some bush and ran goats. We bought our goats and chooks from the Croydon markets. Petal was our first goat. She was old, brown and white, with big horns. Snowdrop was a white pedigree Swiss Saanen and our main source of healthy milk for quite a few years until she was struck down by a virus or snake bite just outside the pen. Judith was about ten when she took on the responsibility of milking Snowdrop. I used to ride Snowdrop and the other goats and tease them. When I wasn't looking, they would rear up and butt me from behind, and I got many hours of pleasure playing with the kids. Nobody wanted billy goat kids, and we had to get rid of two of them. Mum approached Laurie Ryan, the builder next door, to dispatch them. He must have cut their throats and buried them. We loved the kids and were suspicious and horrified when we saw part of an ear near where they were buried.

Our backyard at 18 Ireland Street, Ringwood during the late 1950s.

There was a tall messmate gum tree down the back, and by the time I was around twelve, I had attached a rope high up on a limb of this tree which served as an excellent swing with a stick tied to the end. It had a long travel, ending over a heap of tree branches to break the fall. I climbed it often with the occasional rope burn to my hands, but it seemed worth it. We'd compete for the longest drop, and at other times, I'd set myself records of how far I could dive to catch hold of the stick to swing. During one of these occasions, I dived, missed the rope, and slammed into the ground, skidding along on my stomach. I got winded and badly bruised and that was the end of that.

At around the same period, a new arrival in the district was Gary Pearce, who lived in Heathmont and had introduced us to new adventures. Gary organised the breaking into the back of the Heathmont Lolly Shop under cover of darkness to steal soft drinks to enjoy in his hut in his backyard. The tree house served as a base from which operations like raiding the apricot, peach, and cherry orchards would be planned and implemented. Being shot with pellets of saltpetre was discouraging.

Another thing we were introduced to was the art of possum hunting. The hapless ringtails slept during the day in nests usually suspended high up in blackberry vines along Dandenong Creek. The possums were challenging to get at, and we got some bad scratches, but it seemed worth it. First, we made spears to poke right through the nest. Then, if there was a possum in the nest, we'd dry the skin to use for the lining of the walls of our new tree house near the creek.

One afternoon we found a baby possum. I kept the baby as a pet and called it 'Elvis.' He ate tender new gum leaves from the bush across the road, oranges, and other fruit. He lived happily in my bedroom, and I carried him around in my shirt everywhere, even to school. Elvis was nocturnal, romping around and feeding during the night. Mum refused to come into my bedroom to make my bed and collect clothes for washing because she said she couldn't stand the smell of the possum urine. I became very close to little Elvis, whom I had come to know and love until he crawled into bed under the blankets one fateful night for warmth. In my sleep, I rolled on him and awoke the following day to find him flattened. I was greatly disturbed by this tragedy, and this episode marked the end of Gary Pearce and possum hunting for me.

Some months later, I heard that Gary was out with some other boys one day looking for possums. They were walking, single file, along a narrow track through a large thicket of blackberries. Gary was behind Graham Turner when he tripped on a blackberry vine across the path. The rifle discharged as the butt hit the ground, the bullet hitting Graham in the back. Graham died.

I heard that Gary, under instruction from the Police, had to go and tell Graham's parents what had happened. Gary showed little remorse. I never saw him again.

By the mid-1950s, I spent much of my spare time in the bush across the road on weekends. On one occasion, I'd caught a brown snake. I wanted to milk the venom from its fangs. It was about two and a half feet long, and wasn't particularly happy. I left the snake in a shoe box out the back and hurried up the road to get Peter Marsh to come down and see it. Alas, by the time we got back to see the snake, it was in bits on the lawn. I was devastated and couldn't fathom what had happened until Mum, still agitated, told me she'd chopped it up and not to bring dangerous snakes home again. Poor Mum must have been watching the proceedings in terror and took advantage of the opportunity when I left, rushed out and dispatched the snake before my return. I also brought blue-tongued skinks home from the bush, and Mum had no objection to these quiet, harmless things. I often took one to school in my jumper and even had a whole family in a small pile of rocks in the backyard.

I wanted to fly as well. When I was seven, my first attempt at flight was from the top of the six-foot fence with Dad's big black umbrella. I was ecstatic about being suspended in the air initially until, halfway down, the umbrella collapsed inside out, and I hit the ground heavily with the umbrella on top of me. The experiment had been partially successful to the extent that further unmanned attempts were made using a rock suspended from a large square piece of cloth thrown from the garage roof. The seed was set, and by the time I was around sixteen, I had begun a new and enduring career in control line aeroplanes. During the mid-1970s, I was to return to manned flight when introduced to hang-gliding. I'll talk about these episodes in more detail later.

By the time I was around 10, I was often out of hearing range when Mum or Aunty Lois would call me home for Sunday roast. My boundaries usually expanded into the bush, defending the hut against Lesley O'Reagan, hunting, raiding the orchards, and other activities. As a result, I would often be home late and locked out while everyone else enjoyed the Sunday roast lamb. This happened a lot, and if I didn't want to miss out, a cunning plan would have to be devised. The problem was solved when one afternoon during the season; I brought home some ripe, juicy peaches and nectarines from the nearby orchard. Holding them up at the dining room window was enough to bribe them into letting me in, but not without a stern warning about stealing and being late. However, I got away with it and would be absent again when it came time to help with the dishes.

Moe was a very clever and articulate 50-year-old Sulphur-crested cockatoo given to the family when I was ten. I spent a lot of time with him. Unfortunately, he'd been injured and couldn't fly. He had a highly unpredictable temperament, was noisy, and very destructive.

During the day, he could be found talking and jigging on the clothesline, grabbing at anyone who ventured near the line. He bit me occasionally, drawing blood, so I'd roll his cage with him in it, sending him hurtling down the backyard.

When mum would call me for lunch or dinner, *"Aaaalan,"* Moe would repeat it. He'd also stroll along the tops of the high wooden neighbourhood fences, stopping to talk to people. At night time, he was in his cage in the woodshed.

Me with cockatoo 'Moe,' at Bring Your Pets to School day, 1959.

He was a constant companion and spent much time sitting on my shoulder, going everywhere with me on the bike. Careering downhill at breakneck speed, he'd hang on with his beak to the handlebars, spreading his wings and screeching in a spectacular show. He'd chase us around on the lawn, and one day, he was playing on the lawn with the dog Peggy when Dad accidentally trod on his head. He was blind in his left eye after that incident. There was a 'Bring and show your pet day' at school in 1959. Some kids brought white mice, rabbits, guinea pigs, cats, dogs, etc. Moe stole the show with his crest and his repertoire of antics. After Mum sold Ireland Street, she gave Moe to Charlie Martin. Charlie told me later that Moe had died of shock when Charlie's house burned down about 25 years later.

Peter Marsh was a friend living up the road. Peter's father, Mr. Marsh, was a Carpenter, and the family had migrated from England. Mr. Marsh, a tall, lanky, jovial man, enjoyed the odd beer at the Pub after work. He'd fall asleep on the train on his way home, ending up at Ferntree Gully, having to do the circuit back to Ringwood. I collected tall beer bottles, which were stacked up against his wall. We got a penny per bottle.

The Marsh's lived in a little fibro shed while Mr. Marsh was building their three-bedroom weatherboard bungalow. It was similar to ours and also seemed to take forever. Mrs. Marsh was a Nurse but worked at a Hosiery Factory in Melbourne.

The Marsh's were always friendly and accommodating, and I spent a lot of time up there. One day, Peter and I were playing on the lawn, under a bed sheet from the clothesline, when I got the shock of my life. I was on the receiving end of a misdirected kick up the bum. Mr. Marsh was apologetic, explaining that it was meant for Peter, who had been told about playing with bed sheets. He even went and apologised to Mum.

I was conscious of the Marsh's different standards during those early days. On a weekend, for instance, Mrs. Marsh would clean Peter and his younger brother David's canvas tennis shoes with white paste. I enjoyed the pungent smell and the bright white sand shoes. They were always placed neatly outside the back door in pairs, ready for the boys. She seemed to do everything for them, and they never did the dishes or other chores I was accustomed to.

One day, Peter and I were discussing our parents' age, and he said his mother was 32, which I thought was getting on. She was always very kind and concerned and seemed to spend much time on a weekend, during the summer, in bathing togs, getting a sun tan. Mrs. Marsh also cared for her appearance with bright red fingernails and make-up. My mum never wore nail polish.

It was during 1955 when I spent a fair amount of time at John Robins' place. It was interesting. John's father and brother, Mervin, were mechanics. There were always motorcycle, car, and truck parts and engines in various stages of repair out the back. I don't remember seeing much of his mother, and I'll mention his sister, Jolene, a bit later. At one stage, I couldn't wait to get there after school, to hook into a thick slice of fresh soft white bread smothered in tomato sauce. But, unfortunately, the attraction was more the novelty rather than nourishment. Mum had reservations about the Robins,' and I never told her about the bread and tomato sauce.

John had a lot of white mice running around in a big cage, and they had eaten out the inside of a stale loaf of bread and were breeding in it. I was fascinated by all this and loved the smell of them, infused with the bread, and would sit and watch as I ate my bread and sauce. One day, Mervin offered me a couple of mice, and Mum reluctantly agreed to have them on the proviso, that I took full responsibility for them. I was enthusiastic about them and set up a cage under cover outside, near the back door. They were a breeding pair and soon began to multiply in the loaf of bread. Within no time, there were nine mice, breeding exponentially.

Mum was soon complaining about the smell. One afternoon when I'd got home from school, she gave me the ultimatum of either shifting the mice as far down the back as possible or she'd get rid of them. While I couldn't understand how she didn't like the smell, I set them up against the fence down the back, near the chook pen. At first, I fed and watered the mice diligently, but the novelty gradually wore thin, and they eventually died of thirst and starvation.

We had a lot of relatives too.

Family Relations

The relatives we saw the most of were Dad's sister, Aunty Meryl and Uncle Roy and their kids Lois and Janice. There was Mum's sister, Aunty Lil and Robert and Janet, and their father, Uncle Gordon, who had contracted cerebral malaria from the war in New Guinea. Then there was Dad's cousin, Uncle Jack Hankin, and his wife, Eileen, from Mossman, Sydney. There was Mum's aunty Jessie and cousin Harry Martin, Mum's brother, Uncle Jack and Aunty Gwen Wilkinson, and cousins Wendy and Reg. Grandpa was Mum's, father. Mum's cousin Fred Archer and his wife Sue, with Kenny, Robyn, Pam, and Rodney, our second cousins.

We had many visitors, primarily relatives from the city. My cousins would bring their tomahawks, help cut winter firewood, and do everything that country kids did. For example, we'd take them down the bush to the hut, collect wildflowers, blackberries, and mushrooms from the bull paddock, and get chased back under the fence by the bull. They'd help pluck a chook or milk the goat, and I'd take them fishing for eels in the creek and possum hunting. We'd build a fire, skin the eels, and fry them in butter. When in season, there were raids on the cherry orchard. We'd play in the backyard with the cockatoo, Moe, Peggy and the guinea pigs in the wood pile.

As mentioned earlier, there was a lot of contact between the city and the country, which meant that people from town understood life in the countryside well. For the kids, it was all hands-on. For the adults, Sunday roasts and simply sitting and talking over afternoon tea and scones were enough to keep them abreast of what was happening.

Mum

Mum and her brother, Jack, 1940.

Mum's closest friends were Gwen Kimberley, Polly Perkins, and 'The Kramer Dame,' a Swiss immigrant. Mum was highly influential in my appreciation for the natural world. She drew my attention to delicate details like the fringes on the tiny purple fringed lily, or chocolate flower, as she called it, because of its perfume. As a result, I spent a lot of time across the road in the bush and became connected to the natural environment.

Mum also told us about her family picnics on the banks of the Murray River near Red Cliffs, in the Victorian Mallee district after Grandpa returned from the First World War. She discovered human remains in the form of exposed and sun bleached bones and skulls.

Mum could never accept the rationale of surrounding landholders that the site was a gazetted cemetery. This burial site inspired my later investigations into the site as one of many mass graves along the Murray River.

Mum had a few expressions that she would use in conversation. These expressions were English in origin.
Here are a few examples;
"The woman was putting on airs and graces, and standing on ceremony." (pretentious and ritualistic).
"He was cracking hardy." (hiding anxiety and fear).

"She was done up like cake." (overdressed).
"He had no gumption." (showed no initiative or commitment).
"They were like little tin gods." (shallow and narcissistic).
"They were nothing but cheap tarts." (rough and promiscuous).
"A little Lord Fauntleroy." (a child who gets away with 'murder'). For example, after a Sunday roast with visiting relatives, the job of doing the washing up was a shared chore. Pretty well without exception, though, Mum would ask, *"Where's Alan?"* Someone else would explain that I had gone; I was out entertaining friends. Indeed, Mum sometimes referred to me as a *'little Lord Fauntleroy.'*

These expressions have subtle differences –
"A Society Dame." (a well-heeled woman who was conceited and took a dim view of the working class).
"The Kramer Dame." (the neighbour across the street by the name of Mrs. Kramer, who was conceited).

Years later, Mum was to visit and share many experiences with me and my wife, Rose. Dad was different.

Dad

Dad, right, on the apron of the loco, western Victoria, 1925.

Peter Marsh and I built a hut down the bush under one of our favourite stringy bark trees. The floor was soft barked logs, with a rudimentary frame covered with branches, making it dark and cozy inside. One day, Dad was so furious at something I did or didn't do that he chased me around the orange tree, down the driveway, across the road, and down the bush track, where I escaped by shimmying up the tree. Poor Dad was huffing, puffing, and conceded that he wouldn't climb up there after me. I knew that climbing was way beyond him. He told me, as calmly as he could, that he would wait until I got home to face the razor strop. But, as usual, he didn't follow through with the threat.

Dad was born in 1905 and was ten years older than Mum. Such age gaps were commonplace during and immediately after the war.

Dad was an older man of fifty years when I was a lively ten-year-old. Unfortunately, he wasn't healthy, and I don't recall doing much with him, like fishing and other things that may have developed a bond between us. However, I was never really conscious of it.

I remember Dad sitting in his fireside chair with a tall beer and a roll-your-own cigarette, watching the news or cricket. I was always bemused by his having his egg poached in milk for breakfast.

Before Ringwood, Dad was recovering in the 'san,' as Mum referred to the sanatorium in Heidelberg, from an operation that left him with only one and a half lungs due to tuberculosis, a common debilitating disease of the period. I recall the enormous crescent-shaped scar that ran from Dad's chest to his back.

I didn't see very much of him. He used to make all sorts of useful things in leather, like a scabbard for his cutthroat razor, a stylish imitation croc skin black handbag for mum, and soft, warm sheep-skin moccasins for the family. We went by train to visit him regularly, and sometimes he would be well enough to come to the park in Hawthorn to spend time with us.

I never got the opportunity to get close to Dad as a father because of his illness and long recovery, and later, his shift work. However, I remember him studying for his position as Power Operations Engineer in the Victorian Railways. Mum always told us to be quiet, go outside, or *"you'll wake your father."*

Years later, I remember a serious discussion between Dad and my sister, Judith, who, at the time, was a feisty young Student Teacher, ready to knock the colonial Brits at every opportunity. Dad responded, saying, *"Well, I'm a British subject and proud of it."*

Dad was a big, well-framed man; you could tell he wasn't of convict stock. He was also a Socialist, a staunch Labor man, probably with affiliations with the Australian Communist Party. He was an accomplished musician and played Strauss, Sweet Irish Songs (his mother was Irish), the Volga Boatman, Delibes Copellia Ballet, and more often, towards the end of his life, the heavy and powerful Rachmaninov's Prelude Opus 3 Number 2.

Dad was a Mason; the regalia and ritual were a mystery to me. Occasionally, he would share stories of his childhood with us, and one story was about his journeys between Wentworth and Broken Hill. He travelled by horse drawn Cobb & Co. coach from Wentworth along the Silver City Highway, then a rough, sandy bush track to Broken Hill. His father was a Miner then and eventually died young from lung-related problems that most miners would have suffered.

While Dad was still in recovery, his sister, Aunty Lois, and Uncle Les would often come out to give Mum support. In the early days, they would arrive in a baby Austin Seven and later a grey Austin A 40. Aunty Lois was a kind and gentle soul. She never forgot our birthdays, and even in 1967, when I married Rose in Townsville, she sent a beautiful set of high-quality Actil bed sheets. Later, Rose and I continued to travel and work as lay missionaries in remote North East Arnhem Land and all over Australia. She tracked us down and never missed sending birthday cards. I deeply regret not being able to show her our appreciation due to her untimely death from cancer.

Dad had enlisted in the army when WW2 broke out. He was rejected on the discovery that he had a spot on the lung, which turned out to be tuberculosis. The subsequent long illness must have been terrible for him, feeling dependent and powerless. Old family photos reflect happier times in his youth, living a bright and vibrant life, camping with mates, good-looking girlfriends, etc.

Judith got married in April 1962. She was 19 when she left home. My first niece, Andrea, was born in September of that year. Dad died at age 57 from a heart attack on 12th December 1962. He was travelling home on the train after the night shift. He had been painting the living room ceiling before heading off to work. At seventeen, I was devastated when the police came to our house with the news of Dad's passing. I cried all night. Judith told me that a friend of Mum, Eunice Woolard, witnessed Dads' death on the train that night. I remember someone later saying that while travelling on the train, they took a 'stiff' off the train at Camberwell. I was distressed at the insensitivity and lack of feeling or respect for this man and his family, my family. I felt alone and found solace in a friendly acquaintance with Robby, who lived on Wantirna Road and had also recently lost his father. Another friend, Darby, was to lose his father to cancer shortly after.

Grandpa and Apollo Bay

Some of the most important experiences during my early years are the Christmas holidays with Grandpa. His beautiful property was between the township of Apollo Bay and the Otway Ranges along the wild southern Victorian coast.

I greatly admired Grandpa (Mum's father) Leslie Claude Sibsy Wilkinson, born in 1890. Mum was always very close to him. She stayed with us at the remote Papunya settlement in the Central Desert in 1982. She described her dream to me when Grandpa passed away at 92 from a heart attack. She was trying to hold him from sinking into a whirlpool.

Apollo Bay was a special place for me and my family. At an early age, I recall travelling along the Great Ocean Road in our dodgy grey Ford Prefect. The worst thing was the petrol and exhaust fumes, mixed with the smell of vomit. It was a nightmare as the ugly old top-heavy machine lurched from one hairpin bend to the next, causing me to get car sick. We often had to stop by the side of the road for some fresh air and time to recover, preparing for the next episode of retching. It took

Grandpa's property, Apollo Bay, early 1960s.

me a couple of days to recover from the trip.

It was a relief for everybody as we pulled into Grandpa's driveway and up to the house. The house was on top of a hill about three miles from town. Mum would point out the cypress pines on a distant hill on the approach from Apollo Bay for the last three miles of the trip.

On arrival, we'd climb the front steps to the veranda, from where the view of the bay, nestled in the surrounding hills, had to be seen to be believed. Cypress pines surrounded the house and gardens for protection from the winds of the Southern Ocean. The garden was beautiful, with exotic and Australian native shrubs and small lawns in between. There were hedges to the front and side of the house, and I remember Grandpa talking to the blue wrens as they twittered away in the garden. During the 1950s and 1960s, Grandpa's place was an English garden oasis amidst an otherwise bleak and hostile environment of exposed hills rolling down to Shelly Beach.

The front door led into the living room, lined with warm timber panels and a broad shelf with the odd antique vase displayed.

There was an English oak dining suite next to the front window and the piano to the side against the wall with a bust of Beethoven and a metronome. Sheet music was stacked neatly on the what-not shelves adjacent to the piano. An open fireplace and mantelpiece were the central focus. The meat safe stood beside the door in the room next to the kitchen; there were no fridges then. A wood stove dominated the kitchen where everyone ate their meals at the table. The dining suite in the living room was reserved for special occasions. For example, when Aunty Lil, Uncle Jack, and all the cousins were there for Christmas.

Grandpa's father was Jewish but he never talked about it; I found out after

Grandpa at his piano, 1967.

he'd passed away. He was an accomplished musician. He played the organ for the Presbyterian Church in Toorak. His wife, Ethel, was a musician too, who died tragically of pneumonia in the Mallee.

One day, I asked Grandpa about a hole inside his right elbow. He told me that it was a bullet wound from the war and how it happened; he was in the trenches in France, ready to go over the top in a bayonet charge through no man's land towards the enemy trench. He'd only gone a few steps when he was struck by a machine gun bullet in the right elbow. He said it was as though someone very strong, had grasped him by the arm and flung him face down onto the ground. He was able to get back into the trench, and it was a week before he received medical treatment. The bullet had passed right through the elbow, and the wound had become gangrenous. The treatment was successful, however, and the doctor told him that he could save the arm only because Grandpa, unlike most other soldiers, was a teetotaller. The doctor explained that, as a general rule, in such circumstances, limbs were amputated due to the wounds failing to heal because of the levels of alcohol in the blood.

Grandpa took advantage of the post-war soldier settlement scheme on his return from the war. In the remote Victorian Mallee district, he developed a successful sheep and wheat property at Yirara, near Red Cliffs.

I remember that Ella was with Grandpa in the early days. My grandmother, Ethel, had already passed away; Mum said Grandpa then married Ella for convenience. I remember teasing Ella with the tea towel. I also had good times with her when I would go with her to milk the cow and separate the cream. I would help by turning the big separator handle and washing up afterwards. I'd squat down with my mouth open, and she'd give me a squirt of milk direct from the udder. I loved the taste of warm fresh Jersey milk and cream. The house kitchen had the pleasant aroma of sour cream as Ella also made butter.

There were always big blowflies around during summer, and at one stage, Mum had observed that Ella was complaining that the lamb chops on a dish in the meat safe were fly-blown. Grandpa just told her to scrape off the eggs; the chops were still fresh. He was right, but Mum wasn't impressed.

I learned to drive on Jackie Raymacher's Massey Ferguson tractor out on Grandpa's expansive front lawn. He was less than impressed with my doughnuts on the soft lawn after a shower of rain.

I was interested in horses, even though I wasn't familiar with them. Jackie insisted I take the quiet horse for a ride down to the ocean, along the track through the Otway rainforest; it wasn't far, and the horse knew the way. We got the horse ready with the bridle and riding bareback; I left the dairy, trotted up the road, and turned left onto the track through the forest. Suddenly, the horse took it upon himself to put on a bit of a spurt. I had no control over him, so I tucked my head down over his neck and enjoyed the ride. We were at full gallop as we approached the cliffs and a sheer drop into the pounding white foam and rocks below. I panicked, rolled off the horse onto the ground, and slowly got to my feet. I was surprised to see the horse standing before me, waiting for further instructions.

In ignorance, I had fully expected him to continue at full gallop down towards the cliff, where we'd be smashed by the enormous waves and rocks below. After a self-examination, there were no injuries. I climbed back on the horse and turned him around. He bolted for home. It was an important lesson in respect for horses.

That night I talked Jackie into coming for an overnight camp down on the beach. I never fully understood why a boy my age, around eleven, born and raised there in such familiar surroundings, could be so fearful of camping on the beach. Such was Jackie's fear when we camped down the back of Grandpa's at Shelley Beach. We lit a fire from driftwood and did some exploring. Poor Jackie didn't get any sleep that night.

Grandpa taught me a lot. He had rabbit traps and taught me where and how to set traps, kill, and skin rabbits early in the piece. He also showed me how to tie a fishing hook to the line.

I remember the brass binoculars that stood on the shelf above the wood stove in the kitchen. From the verandah, Grandpa used them to watch ships passing by on their way through the Bass Strait.

Grandpa handed over the farm in the Mallee to his son, my uncle Jack, when Jack returned from WW2. Grandpa relocated sheep, among other things, from the Mallee to Apollo Bay as part of this process. The merinos hadn't adapted well to the wetter climate and suffered greatly from foot rot. I remember him out on the hill slopes rescuing sheep that had gone down, heavily laden with fleece and unable to stand. I recall him bringing sheep back in the wheelbarrow to shear and nurse back to health in the shelter of the big cypress pines in the house paddock.

Judith and I would often rise at daybreak to check rabbit traps in the warrens along the gully that led down to the bull paddock and Shelley Beach. Then, on our return in the crisp early mornings, back up the hill to the house, we'd listen for the welcoming sound of Grandpa's practice of Mendelssohn's Flight of the Bumblebee and other pieces by Beethoven.

Jacki, me and Judith on Jacki's horse near the shearing shed, 1951.

The steep coastal hill slope district where Grandpa had relocated was, in the past, covered by temperate rainforest, which never recovered from the devastating Black Friday bushfires of January 1939. Instead, it became a dairy farming district with lush green feed all year round. The stark, grey skeletal remains of the giant mountain ash trees, still standing in this bleak landscape, were a dramatic reminder of what the country once looked like. Large flocks of English starlings competed against native birds for nesting hollows in the dead trees. In some sections of the property down towards the sea, bracken fern, ragwort, and other woody weeds had begun to take hold and, if unchecked, would quickly replace the pasture.

After breakfast, Grandpa would go down to clear the scrub with his Allen Oxford motor scythe. It seemed an endless task, and after visiting the old house some years after Grandpa had passed away, this impenetrable weed had indeed taken over the hill slopes and gullies.

Above all else, Shelley Beach, known only to locals then, was our first port of call on arrival at Grandpa's. We couldn't wait to get down there. It wasn't the swimming, because it was too dangerous with huge white-tipped waves crashing onto rocky cliffs. There was a spectacular blowhole that would spurt white water through a hole under the wave-cut rock shelf high into the air like a giant whale. We spent hours at a time collecting shells on the beach. There were various large and small shells, including a rare paper nautilus, cowrie shells, cones, and many others.

We explored wave-cut platforms, high vertical rock faces, and deep caves along this wild coastline and watched the forests of giant kelp in the ebb and flow of the monster swells in and out of small secluded bays. Then, at low tide, we'd sit and wonder at the diversity of marine animals that lived in small, perfectly round rock pools scarcely a couple of feet across. Permanent residents such as sea urchins, tiny fish, crabs, barnacles, and others lived there.

Aunty Lil and Uncle Jack

Some years there would be a clash of relatives staying at Grandpa's, and the house would be full. We always got on well with Robert and Janet. Aunty Lil seemed irritable around the Isherwood kids, so I avoided her. I only met Mums' brother, Uncle Jack, twice. Once at Apollo Bay for one of Grandpa's birthday celebrations and the other time at Dad's funeral at the Box Hill cemetery later in 1962. Jack and Aunty Gwen had two kids, Wendy and Reg, with whom I got on well and deeply regretted seeing only once. Aunty Lil would invite herself, Robert, and Janet to Jack's farm in the Mallee and stayed on many occasions.

Jack and Gwen never invited us to the farm, and Mum was too proud to ask herself, so all we saw of the farm were Mum's early black and white photos. I secretly resented being denied the opportunity of visiting this place that had been so important in Mum's earlier life. Strange mob in some ways – the Wilkinsons.

We revisited the house at Apollo Bay in the late 1980s, some years after Grandpa passed. I was saddened to see that it had fallen into disrepair. The cypress pines had grown too high and no longer afforded protection for the delicate and fragile garden, which had all but disappeared. Cold winds from Bass Strait reclaimed the hilltop, whistling through the ghostly pines. I'll return now to various exploits back at Ireland Street Ringwood.

Guy Fawkes Night and Other Exploits

Guy Fawkes Nights was a November tradition, and through the week preceding, in O'Reagan's horse paddock, the Isherwoods, Marshes, Harkensees, O'Reagans, Robins', Hobbs' and all the other neighbours would collaborate to build an impressive bonfire with dry eucalypt branches from the surrounding bushland. The structure was sophisticated and included an effigy of Guy Fawkes made from straw and old clothes positioned precariously on the top. This practice, however, was short-lived and later events went ahead without the effigy.

After dinner, neighbours would gather. When it was getting dark, the fire was lit and provided sufficient light for the distribution and setting up of the fireworks amidst all the excitement and loud crackling of the tinder-dry branches. Parents closely monitored activities, and I don't recall any injuries during these events; the injuries were to come later. Fireworks included the ever-popular Catherine Wheels mounted on a nail on a makeshift stand, sparklers, and an array of spectacular skyrockets, bangers, and sparklers. Guy Fawkes Night was a community event everyone looked forward to, bringing us together. By the following day, the only evidence of all the drama and activity the night before was the smouldering ashes and red bits of paper scattered over the paddock. There were spent skyrockets everywhere, and we made bombs out of the ones that hadn't gone off.

A range of surplus fireworks, especially the bangers, were in demand and on sale after Guy Fawkes night, and kids extended the fun over the following days. For us, this surplus provided endless opportunities for developing an innovative career in fireworks. Penny Bangers was preferred over the smaller Tom Thumbs. The more extensive and less frequently available Three-Penny Bangers were reserved for more serious projects, which I'll describe later.

One short-lived activity that Darby, Peter Marsh, and I had created was Shanghai banger fights. From your fortification behind a tree, you'd light the wick, quickly load it into the leather and fire the banger straight at your opponent, who would take cover behind a tree. The idea was to get the timing such that the banger would explode just before it hit the tree or immediately on impact, causing no harm.

One day, I lit a banger that had a particularly fast-burning wick. I had the rubber stretched to its limit and was about to let go when the banger exploded in my right ear, tearing flaps of skin from my hand and leaving extensive bright red and black wounds over the inside of my thumb and forefinger. I thought I'd lost my hearing. We ran home to my place, but Mum was out shopping, so we went to Peter's. Mrs Marsh was horrified and rushed to dress the injuries. We discontinued the Shanghai component of the banger career.

Another, probably more risky banger activity was to light the penny banger, holding it by the bottom with the tips of the forefinger and thumb, high above your head, allowing it to explode harmlessly. It was a sensation to feel the blast at such close quarters and not end up with injuries. Unfortunately, the smaller bangers were less reliable. They were sometimes prone to fizzing, failing to explode, and acting like a skyrocket into your hand, causing a severe and painful burn. The wound was light in colour, like pork crackling. There was no future in it, and we soon abandoned the handheld idea for something safer and more predictable.

Another innovative way to use these bangers was to light them and quickly place them under a tin on the ground, which, if the position were correct, would be propelled straight up high into the air. You could also stand on the container and be lifted nearly a foot off the ground on a good day.

Letter boxes became a prime banger target. There was plenty of them around the town. The steel ones were the best, and there was no mess; you lit a banger, slid it into the slot under cover of darkness, and ran a safe distance to watch the blast. Walking home from school, you'd know the ones you'd done by their rounded bulging sides.

I must have been temporarily relieved of my senses when one afternoon, Peter and I decided to do the same on my Dad's homemade wooden letterbox. The letterbox, shaped like a little house, was white with a red chimney, roof, and little windows. It was mounted on a sturdy post to the side of the double front gate. We used a three-penny banger, and I latched the door. We were alarmed at the explosion's size and the extent of the damage, which blew the entire letterbox into splinters, scattering them in a radius of 30 feet to the other side of the road. Turning towards the house, I saw Mum standing with arms crossed, looking down the driveway from the living room window. She had seen the letter box blowing up and said, *"You wait til your father gets home, my lad."*

We set about repairing the letterbox, collecting what we could of the splintered remains, and putting them in categories. The splinters with red paint were part of the roof, white for the walls, and there were painted windows. We recovered the chimney intact, and the floor was still attached to the post.

The three-inch nails we found in the shed would have to do, and we spent the rest of the afternoon nailing it all back together. It was the worst repair job imaginable. When Dad got home, Mum told him what had happened. He felt we'd suffered enough, left it at that, and got a new letterbox.

Spud guns were crude makeshift firearms made from a length of water pipe. We recognised the potential of these, especially when loaded with marbles. So one afternoon down at the Robins,' we put a marble projectile straight through one side of the shed and out the other and then abandoned anything further to do with spud guns.

By emptying the explosive powder from bangers and gunpowder from Lindsay Hobb's brother's 12-gauge shotgun cartridges, you could make a powerful bomb. By sealing the outer plastic cover and extended wick, you could end up with waterproof bombs for blowing things up and even stunning fish. It was at the Jumping Creek Road swimming spot that Darby appeared on the scene. We made a particularly large device to blow up the big gum tree on the river bank, which, as planned, was used as a diving platform.

We dug a hole under the tree, buried the bomb, lit the extended wick, ran to a safe position further up the hill, and watched and waited. It was fantastic. In an enormous explosion that echoed over the hills and valleys, in the dust and flying debris, we saw the tree rise vertically, as if in slow motion, about three feet clear of the ground, dropped back into its original position, and slowly keeled over into the river with an enormous splash in the perfect place for diving off. The only downside of this was the disappearance of Dad's new shovel. We searched everywhere, but alas, it was nowhere to be found. I never mentioned it. Dad sometimes wondered aloud about its mysterious disappearance.

During the summer, on the weekend, We'd hitchhike to the Jumping Creek Road turn off on the approach to Warrandyte, walk up the hill, get over the fence, and down the other side to the swimming spot on the river.

One afternoon on the way back, I did a bit of tightrope walking on the top wire of the fence. It was barbed wire. Things went well until I lost my footing, tearing my jeans and sustaining a nasty flesh wound three and a half inches long down the side of my right buttock. Mum was out shopping when we returned home, so Mrs. Marsh came to the rescue and dressed the gaping, stinging wound.

Lindsay always seemed old for his age and had a surly grin, and because I was a bit wiry or skinny, he nicknamed me Bones or Bonesy, which I had no alternative but to accept. White-backed magpies used to build on the outer branches of the big tall radiata pine trees on his place, and one day, I decided to brave the dive-bombing of the parent birds, climb out along the high branch, get the young ones from the nest and take them home to keep as pets. The parents followed me home, dive-bombing all the while. I put the young ones in the chicken coop to teach them to talk. The parents fed them until they could fly. I lost interest, and they all eventually dispersed.

It was John Robins' idea - the ball bearings for the billy cart wheels – they went a lot faster. John's older brother Mervin had plenty of ball bearings. The billy-cart was basic, with a steering rope attached to a front swivelling axle and no brakes. The new bakers' shop was on a sloping part of Wantirna Road, just up from the City Road turn-off. The new concrete footpath made an ideal billy-cart runway. One afternoon after school, I'd started a run from up the top of the hill to coast past the bakers and other shops.

The timing was wrong, and unfortunately, the fat baker, dressed in white, emerged from his shop, laden with a huge basket of freshly baked bread on his way to his van. There was nothing I could have done to avoid the collision.

He was struck side-on, causing his legs to give way, and when I looked back, he was flat on the footpath amidst loose loaves of fresh bread. I kept going to the bottom, grabbed my billy-cart, and took off across the horse paddock toward home. I never mentioned the incident to anyone, carefully avoiding the baker's shop afterwards.

While uncomfortable about it, I feel compelled to mention primary school.

The Ringwood State Primary School was on Greenwood Avenue. My first day at school was a non-event. I was most impressed by Mr. Reid's expertise with the leather strap, which I managed to avoid. One particular boy seemed to be a frequent target, and I would wince when he got the belt because it would flip around his wrist as he attempted to pull his hand away, irritating a large cyst on the top of his wrist.

I also remember standing to attention on the bitumen out in the quadrangle, enduring assembly, and being bored stiff. But it wasn't all bad.

My fondest memories are embedded in the school playground. There was a period during the middle years dominated by the "Redex Trials," where cars were tested by being driven through the most arduous conditions around Australia. We emulated these events by carving intricate tracks in the dirt in the shade of the old school-yard pine trees near the back fence. We'd flick marbles which would follow the tracks until there was a collision or other calamity, and then it was someone else's go.

I met new friends at primary school, including Sandy Allen, a Scottish immigrant. Sandy and his family arrived at Regina Street, just a short distance from us. I used to walk to school along the dirt road and up the big hill with Sandy and occasionally, just for fun, drop Peter Marsh along the way. I went over to Sandy's sometimes after school. Their place was a bit grimy, and I wasn't impressed by how Raja, their big Dalmatian, dominated the porch out the back. But Sandy was fun, and we remained friends through adolescence.

I moved on to Form One at Ringwood State High School. I always seemed to have other, more important things on my mind. However, I did enjoy riding my Malvern Star to school and couldn't wait to get back on it to ride home again.

High School Days

The Ringwood State High School (RSHS) was the antithesis of an inspiring or stimulating place of learning, a state facility with most classrooms of the drab grey prefabricated style. Grey school uniforms with blazers, caps, ties, and long socks with green and purple stripes reflected the school's ambience. The uniforms were mandatory and to be worn at all times. The school logo read 'Ringwood State High School - Culture and Service.' It wasn't long before I saw high school as a complete waste of my time. I could have picked up what I learned in one year rather than four years. A typical end-of-year report noted that "Alan could do better if he tried harder." Another midyear report indicated that "Alan's presence is disturbing," I was soon condemned for life as a failure. I must have often been the focus of conversation in staff rooms all over the school. I may even have been one of their scapegoats. I was later to become a teacher.

Soon after my first days at high school, I learned that football was seen as a virtuous undertaking at RSHS, and all the able-bodied boys were encouraged to become involved. At first, I cooperated so enthusiastically that Mum and Dad bought me a beautiful pair of football boots. They were my pride and joy, and with the long football socks, I felt proud and invincible. The football boots were lace-up leather with big stops nailed to the soles. I polished them and even took them to bed with me. Soon though, I found that the aggressive competition wasn't for me, so I discarded my beloved football boots and took up the more appealing challenge of tennis. By Third Form, a friend and I would take the afternoon off to go to his place and listen to music.

I befriended Klaus Wieneroider, a quirky Bavarian immigrant whom I nicknamed Hoyte. Hoyte and I started to wag school at lunchtime to go to his place when his mother wasn't home. Our route took us over the railway line, through the park at Ringwood Lake, and up through town to Munroe Street. I enjoyed the heavy German rye bread with Swiss cheese or honey and a cup of percolated coffee while listening to the Thunderbirds, Johnny Cash, and Kenny Ball on the radiogram in this exotic German environment.

One of the pleasant occasions I looked forward to was the long salad roll once or twice a week. We wasted no time in getting up to the shop to order our long rolls and had them finished by the time we returned to the playground. On another rare occasion, we got to bring a pet to school. I brought Moe, my cockatoo. At other times, I had a ringtail possum, a snake, or a blue-tongued lizard concealed under my jumper and would get it out during boring lessons, inadvertently disrupting the class.

When I was thirteen, I had appendicitis and had my appendix removed. It wasn't long before I was back at school. Then, one day, I was wrestling with another boy in the school toilet when I felt a sharp, stinging pain. To my horror, on lifting my shirt, I found that I'd busted the stitches, and the wound had opened, allowing a short length of intestine to fall out. In fear, I ran out, holding my stomach, jumped on my bike, and headed home. Mum rang the Doctor, who wasn't in the least phased, and poked it all back in and re-sutured the wound, telling me not to exert myself for the next few days.

The best way to describe my piano teacher, Miss Thermer, was to liken her to Olive – Popeye's girlfriend. She was a humourless woman, must have been close to six feet tall with glasses, and always seemed intense when I was around. Miss Thermer would grasp my fingers individually, pressing them into the piano keyboard to get me to practice the scales and other exercise pieces.

Hoyte had chosen to learn the Cello and had special permission from Miss Thermer to take it home to practice on weekends. One Friday afternoon, we headed to his place on our bikes after school. The game on the way there was to force each other to jump the roadside curbing. Hoyte was carrying the Cello, in its bag, across his shoulder, gripping the neck with one hand, steering with the other, and trying to ward off my attempts to get him to jump the concrete curb. He did jump the curb, snapping the neck of the cello. It reminded me of a chook with a broken neck with its head flopping about. He was worried all weekend about how he would explain his misfortune to Miss Thermer.

In a phase of our ongoing experiments with explosives, we extracted match heads from their sticks, compressed them between two bolts and a nut in the middle, threw them spinning high into the air, and ran clear to hear the explosion as the device impacted the concrete cricket pitch. We rarely found the nuts or bolts. The inherent dangers of these practices were made clear during a later parade on the quadrangle.

We had water pistols at school too. Most kids acquired their water pistols from Coles. They were the shape of an automatic. Most kids left their guns at home, but my friends and I brought ours to school. We cherished these water pistols and were very discreet with their use until one idiot decided to take things too far by loading his gun with Indian ink. I only used watercolour.

Mr. Gormsby, the high school Principal, was generally referred to among students as Spot, a rounded, cigar-smoking man resembling Winston Churchill, who seemed determined to make an example of us. With military precision, Spot lined us up and ordered us to place our water pistols on the floor before us. He stepped on them and, with a deft heel swivel, crushed them into splinters under his enormous weight. It was around this time that Guwie appeared on the scene.

Peter Geuhenov used to harass me just about every recess time in the corridor, as a rooster might do to another chook in a chook pen, and it was relentless. I dreaded the recess bell when I had to leave the relative safety of the classroom until one day; I was determined to do something about it. It was out in the corridor when Guwie started pushing me in the chest. I was suddenly overcome with courage and, without warning, grabbed him by the shirt front and shoved him up against the steel lockers with all my strength.

There was no harm done; Guwie was surprised and shaken by my response and, from that day, became quite friendly towards me. He lived just down the road toward town, and interestingly, from his place, I had first heard the fabulous music of Little Richard - Lucille, Good Golly Miss Molly, Jenny Jenny, and all the others back in my primary school days. I had never actually visited him and have been eternally grateful to him for the music.

Mr. Maloy, the art teacher from Warrandyte, was a small intense man with a thin mustache, dark hair slicked down with Brylcreem, and orange tobacco-stained fingers. Hoyte and I sat up the front because I enjoyed art, but I didn't think he liked me very much and didn't seem to trust me. He was a snappy dresser and wore superb grey suede shoes. In one art class, he had planned an introductory lesson on the applications of Indian ink.

The desks at that time had ink wells inserted in them, and on this occasion, the inkwell had been charged with Indian ink for the lesson. Curious, I carefully lifted the little inkwell from its hole in the desk and accidentally spilled the black ink down onto Mr. Maloy's suede shoes. He immediately began whacking me around the ears, and I shielded the blows with my arms. It seemed to go on for ages to the amusement of the rest of the class.

On another unfortunate occasion, I was chewing, and Mr. Maloy must have noticed this earlier, gradually becoming irritated by it. Then, without warning, he was upon me, had me in a headlock, and hooking the chewy out of my mouth. His cigarette fingers tasted awful, and the experience genuinely shook me. We were deeply saddened to hear that his house in Warrandyte and others were burned down in the bushfires later that year.

Our Form Three Geography Teacher, Mr. Chambers, was one of the more colourful characters. He seemed to have a good sense of humour and would give us a friendly grin. Of all the subjects, Geography was one of my favourites, and I looked forward to attending classes. Mr. Chambers was immaculate. He had a big bony face, was over six feet tall, had a thick Scottish accent, a dense head of Brylcreemed hair, tan, and used to wear his white shirt and tie with sleeves tightly rolled up high, exposing impressive biceps.

I wasn't alone in my admiration of his powerful presence. However, it wasn't long into the year that things began to change. We were at the back and sometimes talked, especially when he was writing on the board with the left bicep (he was left-handed) presented at its best. On one occasion, when someone at the back was talking, Mr. Chambers ceased writing on the board, slowly turned, his eyes narrowing, and fixed a glare on the culprits at the back of the room and said he'd shot better men than them.

One of the worst experiences of my life happened during a lunch hour when I chanced to meet Mr. Chambers on the elevated walkway that went past the Manual Arts rooms. He was on playground duty. He grinned at me, and I gave him a grin in return. The next thing I knew, he struck me hard with the back of his hand, saying something like take that grin off your face and sent me flying off the walkway, and I landed flat on my back on the concrete path below. I struggled to my feet. I was so shaken that I took myself to the Principal's office. On my explanation of what had happened, Spot dismissed the event, saying that he didn't think Mr. Chambers would ever act in such a way, and I left with the sickening feeling of betrayal.

Mr. Roland was a heavy man, looking more like a farmer, and was my Form Three Woodwork Teacher. His son Doug and I were mates at this time. I used to spend time occasionally on a weekend at their place in North Ringwood, playing with Doug in their cherry orchard. In the season, Doug and I would ambush the goldfinches, which would descend onto the cherry trees to eat the fruit. Then, from our concealed position under the tree, we could shoot them from underneath at close range with a Daisey air gun, which you pushed down on the muzzle to load.

I never warmed to Mr. Roland, and I didn't think he liked me, particularly as a mate for Doug. So there was a good opportunity to punish and humiliate me by giving me the strap during our Woodwork classes. I didn't fully understand, but I felt the punishment wasn't always justified. Hoyte was also in this class with me and had embarked on what I thought was a project of great magnitude compared to mine. Hoyte was making a complete stereo hi-fi record player with speakers and all.

I found Woodwork wasn't my forte, like much of the other activities offered at this dreary institution. I never had a say in what subjects I was taught, and so was stuck with it and made the most of it. My primary project, in stark contrast to Hoyte's, was a possum club, something of a protest project. This bright idea came to me one afternoon after school when walking past the wood-heap on my way down to feed the chooks.

A discarded Queen Anne chair leg sticking out of the wood pile presented itself as the basis of the design. It had a beautiful already-made handle on the bottom end and increased in thickness and weight towards the square upper end. I knew that I'd never use it on possums because I'd never get close enough to them, but I was now committed for want of any other tedious Woodwork project. I took the material to school and explained my project to Mr. Roland, who was probably relieved that I would at least be constructively occupied. Tools required for this project were a vice, mallet and chisel, a wood rasp, plenty of sandpaper, and some varnish. I failed Woodwork, Hoyte, on the other hand, enjoyed celebrity status on completing his hi-fi unit and became a very competent Carpenter and Cabinet Maker.

Adolescent Affairs

Around this time, I began to take an interest in girls, and they seemed interested in me too. I was about 14 when I developed a crush on Gail Shaw. Gail was quiet and tall, with short darkish hair. Gail did very well academically. She shared my interests in nature, and other things about her set her apart from the others, who were boring by comparison. It was a short-lived affair after Gail invited me home to her place. Her parents didn't have much to say, and I knew they took a dim view of me as a suitable partner for their daughter.

Hoyte had a girlfriend called Julie Stratfield and I was amazed at how well-developed she was. Julie was a stunner. She was small, pretty, and seemed very mature for her age. She also took an interest in me, especially in my swimming togs at the Ringwood baths. Hoyte was intensely aware of this and initiated a pledge, which meant I was allowed to see Julie but not permitted sex with her. I was happy with this arrangement because, to be honest, I was a bit frightened of her and had never had sex. However, I did ask her if she'd like to come hitchhiking with me to the swimming spot on the river on Jumping Creek Road. She was delighted, and I ended up there alone with her. I was pleased to be back on the road, hitching home.

On other occasions, Hoyte and I would go to Julie's place after dark. She would be at her bedroom window along the side of her house. I'd climb a leafy tree, out of sight, on the nature strip and wait. Then it would be Hoyte's turn to wait, and she would tell me about a promise she made with Hoyte not to do anything with me, so we'd talk at the window. Hoyte and Julie remained a couple until he left school and joined the Navy.

I didn't have to venture very far for the company of girls; at home, John Robins' sister, Jolene, would leave letters for me in the new letterbox. She was good-looking with long wavy blond hair. It got to a stage where I became fearful of her whenever I went to the Robbins' place. Jolene would come up to me, rest her arms on my shoulders, get close, and sway side to side. Finally, it was too much for me, and I gave up going there.

Beth Robinson, older than me and a friend of Judith's, lived on City Road. Beth surprised me at a party when she came close to me and seemed intense. In hindsight, most of the girls seemed intense, and I was uncomfortable with them then and always conscious of their presence. On one embarrassing occasion, I had been playing up at home. It was pretty early on Saturday morning because I was still wearing my pyjamas. After mucking around in the kitchen one morning, Mum, laughing, chased me with a broom out of the house, down the driveway, through the front gate, and down the road in full view of the neighbourhood, girls included. During this time, I joined the Police and Citizen's Youth Club.

Growing Up

Mum and Dad must have thought I might benefit from attending the Police and Citizens Youth Club. It turned out to be a highly regimented club. There were organised activities, and we had to line up for everything. One evening, I was assigned to the trampoline.

I was working up to a summersault when the stitching along the middle seam of the giant canvas trampoline failed spectacularly. I went through the middle of the trampoline, feet first, hitting the floor lightly on my feet. It must have looked a treat; me standing through the ruptured seam up to my arms, dazed but luckily uninjured.

On another occasion, we were lining up for an activity, and I wasn't focused on the instructions and mucking around when the boy next to me saw fit to strike me across the face with the back of his hand. Apart from the shock of the assault, I was perplexed as to how and why this boy, my age, could have been given the power to exercise such violence and humiliate someone like that.

Also attached to the club was the Pastor, who took us on a trip in his Austin A40. He asked us where we'd like to go for the afternoon. We went to our favourite swimming spot on the Yarra River at Jumping Creek Road, where he watched as we undressed for a swim. He would also buy cigarettes and ice cream for us. We thought he could watch us as much as he liked, and we were on a good wicket while it lasted; I vaguely recall that he was removed from the club. I didn't last long at the club and preferred doing things at home.

I was about fourteen when we changed my bedroom from the temporary sleep-out on the back veranda to a proper room when it was built as an addition to the back of the house.

Over the years, the new bedroom became my space, a precinct. I painted the walls flame-red, doors and window sills in gloss black, and sky blue for the ceiling. Possum, fox, snake, and goanna skins were pinned to the wall. A stuffed and mounted Eastern Shrike Tit, Crimson Rosella, Yellow Wattle Bird, and Black Bird I had created as part of my self-taught taxidermy activities, adorned the walls.

Against the wall adjacent to my bed stood a varnished, step-shaped timber bookcase that displayed my bullet, rock, and skull collections. In addition, I had a tanned red kangaroo skin on the wooden floor. Eventually, I added a set of bullock horns as well. Later, I added a gun rack, holding a .303, a 12-gauge, double-barreled hammer gun, a .22 air rifle, an antique Winchester .32–20 saddle carbine, and a .22 rifle on to the wall. It was an excellent place to be. Incidentally, around this time, there was an unfortunate incident down in the chook pen that begs a mention.

Making and using shanghais, or slingshots, was an important pastime. It soon progressed from the rudimentary car tube to a hollow round section of surgical rubber and leather arrangement attached to a suitable timber fork from a tree. This advanced, formidable version, was loaded with a lead sinker or a glass marble. One afternoon after school, I could be seen in the backyard practising. The clothes-peg tin attached to the stem of the clothesline was a favourite target.

On one particular occasion, I casually took random potshots, and the rooster appeared. The rooster was being groomed for Christmas dinner in 1960, as was the custom in those times. I had no intention of damaging the bird. But, from a distance, the projectile, only a stone in this case, could be seen as it swerved through the air, went straight through the chook wire fence, and ricocheted off the side of the rooster's temple.

The blow to the head caused the big black bird to take on a drunken stagger around the yard, bumping into things and looking like it was in trouble. The thing I regret, to this day, is that Dad, on his return home from work a bit later that afternoon, had noticed the rooster staggering around, went back up into the kitchen for afternoon tea, and told Mum that the rooster was sick and he would have to knock it on the head and bury it. He didn't want to risk it for Christmas dinner. I never told anyone that I'd accidentally shot it with my Shanghai. It was around this period that Saturday matinees were becoming popular.

During the early 1960s, we looked forward to the pictures on a Saturday afternoon. We would arrange to meet at the Ringwood Picture Theatre for the British Movie-tone News, Mickey Mouse and Donald Duck, Tarzan, Batman, the Lone Ranger, or Superman, and a John Wayne Cowboy and Indian movie as the main feature. The girls usually sat separate from the boys. Then, at the risk of being chucked out by the Usher, we would roll jaffas down the aisle along the wooden floor. We didn't like kids up on the balcony throwing their chewy down on us and would report it to the Usher, who would be forever up and down the stairs to shine his torch in their faces and threaten to throw them out. And he did; you could see them being escorted along the aisle towards the front and out, where they'd have to sit and wait until the end, sometimes as long as a couple of hours, for their mates to emerge.

The next chapter in developing my self-directed career in flying opened with great enthusiasm, shared by all. Sandy, John Robins' brother Mervin, Darby, Peter Marsh, and some hangers-on were there. Our weekend runway and the flying circuit were just up the road in the cow paddock. Equipment included control line aeroplanes, which we constructed from balsa wood frames, covered with tissue and dope, all consistent with the principles of powered flight, including ailerons and horizontal and vertical stabilizers, trimmed and powered by a single-cylinder diesel engine fed by a fuel line from the fuel tank situated between the wings behind the engine.

There were two control lines from a round handle out about fifteen metres to connectors on the inside wing tip. The ailerons and horizontal stabilizers were controlled by a slight upward and downward wrist movement. The pilot stood in the middle of a thirty-metre diameter circuit. Once launched, the aircraft would fly around, control lines kept taut by the trim of the vertical stabilizer. Of the several planes I had, the first was of conventional aerodynamic features, powered by a 1.5 cc engine, and had a wide, deep wing section with plenty of lift. From the outset, though, there was a problem.

Charlie's son, Tony, who was considerably younger than us, was determined to make a nuisance of himself by getting in the way and refusing to cooperate. One day, out of desperation, I gave him a swift kick in the pants, telling him to bugger off home. He went home all right and came back with his father. Charlie, a nuggety man of short stature, came striding up the road, through the fence, and across the paddock. He was coming straight for me. Charlie demanded that I turn around so he could kick me in the pants. I refused, and he kicked me anyway, and we didn't see any more of Tony.

The novelty of flight would wear thin as a plane began to look tatty from repeated crashes with patches and other makeshift repairs. Aircraft were prepared in various ways, sometimes with a mouse strapped into the cockpit or set alight and launched into their final flight. One plane was shot down with shanghais; another came down in flames.

As flying skills progressed, we began to experiment. Towards the end of the life of any plane, a pilot would engage in powered stalls, dangerous loops, wing–overs, inversions, other aerial stunts, and finally, a nose dive at full speed.

The 'Swallow' marked the pinnacle of my flying prowess. This was a serious aeroplane, silver, and red, low swept-back wing configuration, and was fitted with a 6cc engine, four times the capacity it was designed for. Built for speed, there was no undercarriage; it was hand-launched. Provision was made for a larger fuel tank, strengthened wing frames and engine mountings, and longer control lines. The speed of this thing struck everyone. It was indeed spectacular - like a fighter jet. It wasn't aerobatic, just fast; we estimated it could do 180MPH. Inevitably, like the others before it, the 'Swallows' days were numbered. One Saturday morning, the 'Swallow' was fueled, a glow plug connected to the battery, and on the fourth flick of the prop, the powerful diesel engine burst into life. It began to scream after a minor carburettor adjustment.

In the air, straining at the end of the control lines, you got the impression that it was trying to break loose to wreak havoc above the surrounding countryside. The 'Swallow' was at its best that morning - low flying, straight and level, vertical climb, inversion, and recovery from manoeuvers. It was magnificent, and neighbours came to watch in amazement at the spectacle. Then came the rise to the apex and the final vertical dive. We dug the engine out of the ground – it had penetrated the earth's surface to about six inches, and I still have this engine on display in my current precinct.

The 'Swallow' marked the end of that chapter of flight. I wasn't to take up flying again until the mid-1970s when I graduated to hang-gliding, which I'll elaborate on later. I was seventeen when we began taking an interest in the old goldfields at Warrandyte.

At seventeen, on a weekend in 1962, Terry, Peter, Darby, Trevor, and I would set off on our push bikes and head for Warrandyte to explore the derelict gold mines in the surrounding hills. The landscape was what we'd imagined the aftermath of the battlefields of World War I in Europe might have looked like. The countryside was strewn with old shafts and tunnels and mullock heaps left abandoned after the Victorian gold rush of the 1850s. It was typically dry, undulating open forest country of the hill-slopes surrounding the old township of Warrandyte, about a five-mile ride east from Ringwood.

Whipstick Gully, an extensive maze of tunnels and shafts, was one of the most productive mines down Kangaroo Ground Road. It became a favoured haunt.

Equipped with a hanky over the mouth and nose and a candle, we carefully winched each other up and down shafts and crept deep into dark, rank tunnels through the rock, deep underground.

We used candles because someone said the flame was a good indicator of how much oxygen was in the air in the tunnels. There were never any concerns, and we spent hours in the blackness chipping away by candle-light at the bright pure white and brittle veins embedded in the sand-stone parent rock along the walls and ceilings, collecting what was supposed to be gold-bearing quartz. We agreed to only whisper or speak very softly for fear of triggering a cave-in. Darby had a passion for gold mining which remained with him. Back in Ireland Street, a new set of events was unfolding.

The Marsh's had finished building and had just moved into their new weatherboard house. Mr. Marsh converted the little bungalow into a workshop in which he would make furniture and other items. The workshop was meticulously organised, with large sheets of feature veneer leaning neatly against the wall and various grades of sandpaper stacked in their respective piles. An array of carpentry tools was hanging in their proper places on peg boards, which covered the other walls. There were benches and other equipment, all in a meticulously organised fashion, around the area. At a glance, you could tell that Mr. Marsh was a proud and accomplished carpenter. Such was the setting for the following afternoon's events.

The Marsh's tabby cat had been taking chickens literally from under their noses. Finally, Mr. Marsh had decided that the cat had to go. He'd got wind of my recent purchase of an antique Winchester 32.20 saddle carbine and had sent Peter down to engage my services in the dispatch of the cat.

I jumped at the opportunity since it would serve as a good test of the new rifle, and besides, I was never fond of cats because of their damage to native fauna. So we placed a wooden chopping block on the floor in the workshop. Peter gently got hold of the cat by the neck and carefully held the head against the side of the block. The plan was that the bullet would pass neatly through the cat's brain and harmlessly come to rest embedded in the wood block, killing the cat instantly and humanely.

In the bowels of the Whipstick Gully gold mine, Warrandyte, 1962. Photograph courtesy of Richard Darby.

Yes, the cat died instantly without suffering, but we failed to anticipate the following events. The cat's nervous system immediately kicked in. Jumping free of Peter's grasp, the cat sprung into a series of dramatic nervous reactions. The cat ran straight up the wall, across the ceiling, down the opposite wall, across the floor, and around, again and again, finally coming to rest, twitching under one of the benches. Tools were scattered everywhere. It was a hell of a mess.

I was fond of Mr. Marsh because he had a good sense of humour and was always understanding. His restraint on this occasion was no exception. We cleaned up the mess as best we could - Mr. Marsh cut his losses, the cat was gone, and the remaining chickens were safe. Finally, we buried the cat down the back and reflected on the afternoon's events. We had concluded that the combination of centrifugal force, inertia, and the nervous system characteristic of cats' fight versus flight phenomena had maintained the cats' uncontrollable revolutions around Mr. Marsh's work-shop.

It was time to leave school.

Turning and Fitting

Towards the end of the 1960 school year, it had become clear to everyone that I should leave school and do some trade or apprenticeship. So Dad organised for me to become a Turner and Fitter. An Engineer himself, he had recently been promoted to Power Operations Engineer for the Victorian Railways. He must have felt confident enough with the idea, even though I expressed no inclination toward the engineering trade. In hindsight, it was a wise decision on his part since I've never regretted gaining all the practical skills involved in the trade.

Dad introduced me to a firm called Jonson Tools in Box Hill. John, the boss, was a gruff middle-aged man in a grey dust coat. The company made a range of brass air-hose fittings, air-gun nozzles, and so on. They seemed accommodating, and Dad was content that things were working well. On Dad's occasional reconnaissance visits to monitor my progress, Ray, the Foreman, would be very conciliatory. Ray, a rather dapper man of average stature, paraded around the grimy shop floor in a well-ironed grey dust coat and tie.

I became friends with Dennis, the Toolmaker. I admired his methodical skills and was fascinated by the level of accuracy his work involved. Dennis taught me a lot. I made a complex hunting knife from a length of annealed spring steel. Machining involved milling the blood grooves, turned handle mount, and a hollow ground blade. The handle was constructed of leather sections with a turned bronze knob screwed onto the end. I made a scabbard for it from two pieces of solid wood encased in leather with provision to hang on my cartridge belt.

I was very proud of the knife. It was formidable and could have passed as a precursor to the knife featured in the film Crocodile Dundee. It was, however, so desirable that it was stolen from our Land Rover in Darwin some years later. Dick also took me hunting above the snowline for spotted fallow deer.

The boss's son came to start his apprenticeship about six months after I had arrived. He was a violent person who would threaten other workers. Fortunately, he left me alone, but I was terrified of him. One day, I saw Dennis at smoko time with two black eyes. He had been attacked and repeatedly bashed by the boss's son in the side of the head. The boss's son would also boast about his Saturday night exploits involving what he called 'poofter bashing.' He would go out with his mates' targeting homosexuals and violently attack them on the street.

Initially, I went to work by train, got bored, and hitchhiked. I became a regular, and a man in a Peugeot used to pick me up from a convenient spot along Canterbury Road. The man didn't say much – just puffed away at his pipe, listened to classical music, and never actually introduced himself. I imagined him to be an Accountant or Bank Manager or something like that. I enjoyed the fusion of the aromatic pipe tobacco mingling with the smell of leather, the classical music, and the exotic Peugeot – a cut above the cars I was familiar with. It had a lot of aluminium trim on the outside body-work and around the dash, including the column gear stick and nice red leather seats. I was later to abandon hitchhiking in favour of riding my motorcycle and always looked forward to knock-off time and the ride home.

About a year into my apprenticeship, I acquired my first motorcycle, a 1951 twin-cylinder, sprung frame 500 cc BSA Golden Flash, in part exchange for my alto saxophone. I had come by this bike through the Robins' and Johns' Uncle Rollie helped me restore it under a gum tree at his place in Wantirna Road.

I painted the bike with copper-based gold paint, which would turn green from the surface oxidation, and I had to polish it every week with a cutting compound to renew the gold colour. It wasn't long before I was riding the bike to work. One wet morning, I was approaching the main intersection on Canterbury Road when the bike skidded on the wet, greasy road, and I could see that I was going to overshoot the intersection. This called for drastic action, and I lay the bike over on its right side and, in a shower of sparks, came to rest right in the middle of the highway. I escaped injury, and there was minimal damage to the footrest. No cars were approaching at the time.

On the weekend, I'd be out on the bike meeting friends at Warrandyte, swimming in the Yarra River, and talking to girls. The bike was impressive in gold, with a large perspex windshield. To top it off, I wore a powder blue long-sleeved shirt with white gauntlets and a white helmet just for fun. I discovered pleasure in approaching cars at speed from behind - without exception, the driver would slow down, thinking it was the police after them. It was a personal secret pleasure, and I didn't discuss it.

On one occasion, I'd just left Warrandyte on my way home when a car pulled level with me and pointed below the seat, shouting, *"Your bike's on fire, mate."*

On looking down, flames had taken hold below the seat and spread. Finally, I could pull over to the side of the road, grab my towel, clamber down the bank to the river to soak the towel, and somehow extinguish the flames. The fire hadn't reached the fuel tank, but there was severe damage to the rubber seat, wiring, and fuel lines. I tied a length of rope around the front forks and had the bike towed back home. My Dad passed away in December of 1962, leaving me to take more control over my life.

It was in 1963 after I lost my Dad, that the Foreman at work tried to offer support through my grieving and organised my involvement in quizzes and other activities during lunchtime. However, I was bored with it. I was bored with the seemingly endless repetitive jobbing work on capstan lathes and milling machines. It drove me to use a transistor radio and ear plug on a lead listening to the Beatles and Rolling Stones during the long hours of repetition. The forman disapproved of my listening to music while working and one day, came up to me while I was sitting at the milling machine and snipped a small piece of wire with a pair of scissors right in my face, threatening to cut my earphone cord if I didn't refrain from listening to music. In a pent-up burst of anger and indignation, I jumped up from the stool, shoved him backward, and told him that I was leaving immediately and that my first port of call would be the Victorian Apprenticeship Commission. I packed my gear and left. The commission staff were accommodating and understanding and organised an immediate transfer to a new engineering place in Clarice Road.

The new Engineering firm was well-organised and professional. They produced precision form tools for the manufacturing of car

Me and the BSA Golden Flash, 1962.

parts. I was welcomed and respected there. Darby followed suit and was soon transferred from a heavy engineering works in Balwyn. We were allocated training tasks on various equipment, including lathes, milling machines, shapers, and surface grinders, and spent time in the projection room. The company understood our adolescent needs and tolerated our absenteeism, practical jokes, and other antics. They didn't even mind us taking the odd few days off from time to time to go pig hunting in the Riverina. There was Bob, the Foreman, George, Ennio, and other friendly staff who were supportive and accommodating. Ennio was an Italian precision tool maker and expert on the surface grinder. At work, he'd arrive in his sports car, a shiny Red Austin Healy Sprite. Ennio gave us rides in the Sprite.

A Zephyr Six

Compared with the old Ford Prefect, the Zephyr was at the other end of the spectrum. It was a grey 1955 Ford Zephyr Six Mark One - winner of several world rallies, including the East African Safari rallies, and could accelerate to over 60 miles per hour in 20 seconds. It had slab sides and red leather upholstery and, for the times, was a good-looking and racy machine.

I was seventeen and knew how to drive, so it wasn't long before I took the Zephyr for several short outings around the neighbourhood. While I failed to get permission from Mum and Dad to drive the car, I exercised great caution and responsibility, never went with friends in the car, and never ventured more than a few miles from home. It was an incredible thrill for me to drive. My job was to clean the Zephyr, carefully polishing the heavy chrome bumpers, grill, and other embellishments.

For me, the Zephyr was nothing short of a transformation in travel. Family trips, especially to Grandpas, now had a new meaning. Having put up with nausea and vomiting, the lurching, lumbering, top-heavy, dangerous, and smelly old Prefect became a thing of the past. True to its reputation, the Zephyr was fast and smooth, and with the static electric strap hanging from the back, travel sickness was history. We arrived at Apollo Bay in about half the time. I remember Dad taking Sandy and me for a trip to Walhalla.

On his way to work, Dad drove to Ringwood railway station, left the car in the car park, and continued the rest of his journey to Jolimont by train. Unfortunately, it was early in 1962 that the vehicle was stolen from the Railway Station car park. It was later discovered on the side of the road out toward Dandenong. The wheels had been taken and it was set alight and partially burned. The insurance company paid for the repairs, but it was always different. In hindsight, I suspect that this incident took its toll, placing much stress on Dad, who already had health problems and must have contributed to his early death in December of that year. Around this time, I bought an air rifle, and Darby got a shotgun.

I acquired a Gecado .22 air rifle. We'd hold a target in our hand while the other would shoot the target from a distance of about 30 meters. On one unfortunate occasion, Darby was shot in the base of the thumb and had to have the slug surgically removed. Darby had just bought a single-shot hammerless medium choke 12-gauge shotgun. The main feature he was excited about was its spring-loaded ejector mechanism, and he was keen to show me how a spent cartridge was ejected from the chamber automatically, as you broke the action after a shot was fired. We were at Darby's place, sitting on his bed, and he was showing me the gun. His mother was in the living room reading.

Darby loaded the gun with a live cartridge, and as he lifted the barrel, slamming the action shut, I intuitively leaned back out of the line of fire. The shotgun accidentally discharged, straight past me, through his bedroom door, through his Mums' vacuum-cleaner bag, and the shot ricocheted off the walls along the hallway, embedding themselves in the kitchen cupboards.

We were shocked, and poor Mrs. Darby was frozen in her chair, fearful that someone had been shot or killed. We investigated the damage. The bedroom door had a one inch hole in the inside panel and the plywood had split away, leaving a gaping hole on the other side. The vertical vacuum-cleaner bag had a lot of little tufts of lint sticking out of one side, indicating where the shot had passed through, and there were many lines, like heavy lead pencil marks, on the walls along the hallway.

We determined that what had happened resulted from a design fault where the firing pin had locked on, striking the cartridge percussion cap when the action closed, causing the gun to discharge.

A careful application of model aircraft fabric, dope, and a lick of white paint applied to both sides of the door disguised the hole perfectly. For Mrs. Darby, life gradually returned to normal. Mrs. Darby put their house on the market shortly after the shotgun incident. I worried about the disguised holes in the bedroom door if they were discovered.

Bush Fires

It was a scorching hot day on 14th January 1962 when the bushfires broke out. The east of Melbourne came under threat, and Ringwood served as an operational hub for the rural firefighters and their equipment. It was what I imagined a war to be like. Fires raged in the Dandenongs and threatened Kinglake, St. Andrews, Hurstbridge, and

Warrandyte. Hundreds of volunteers assembled on the main street to receive instructions and equipment. Some were issued with backpack sprays; others, like Hoyte and me, had a hessian bag secured to the end of a broom handle. Local carriers and other businesses donated transport for the firefighters, including water tankers.

Amidst the excitement and confusion, volunteers were assigned to the backs of trucks and utes, which would be sent off to the various hot spots and endangered towns. We jumped on the back of the Hurstbridge truck and were instructed to tackle a firefront threatening a goat farm.

We arrived at the farm to see a massive ball of orange smoke and flames billowing high above the surrounding hills. It looked more than a mile wide. The fire was fast approaching and we jumped off the truck to organise our gear when we heard an almighty roar and crackle. The terrifying thing was the wall of orange flames way above the tree tops on the ridge, was roaring up towards us. We felt the heat as though from a furnace.

The standard firefighting procedure was abandoned, and there was no thought of fighting anything, only survival and it was every man for himself. We ran to the other side of a tin shed and huddled against the wall under our wet hessian bags. We weren't game to look out when we heard the roar as the fire raced overhead, down over the dam, the paddocks beyond, and on through the valley. It was all over in seconds. We peeked out from our refuge. What we saw was like the aftermath of an atomic explosion. There was nothing left - the countryside was reduced to grey ash. Burnt, blackened goats and sheep dotted the landscape, hanging on the fences and floating in the dam. Roasted chooks were hanging up in the remains of the chook-yard fence and surrounding trees.

Raw intuition informed our seeking refuge from the flames behind the tin shed. It was this and the wet bags that saved us. I haven't entirely understood how close to death we were. Over thirty people were burned alive that day.

My sister Judith and Hilma were married on April 19, 1962.

(L-R) Hilma, Judith, Mum, Dad, me, and Elaine at Judith's wedding, 1962.

The Balwyn Experiment

It was in June 1963 that Hoyte, Darby, and I decided it was time to spread our wings, leave home and share a flat in the city. We chose Balwyn because it was far enough from home, and we were by now regular patrons at the Town Hall where the Saturday night jazz dances were held. We would meet girls and have a good time without parental constraints. Hoyte was still in the Navy, and Darby and I were finishing our apprenticeships. Darby had a Holden ute.

Saturday nights would find us in the thick of Melbourne's fertile trad jazz scene. We soon expanded our activity to the popular Gas Works at the Kew Town Hall with the vibrant Red Onion Jazz Ensemble. The dance movement was simple but effective. First, you would take up a position side-on, your partner facing in one direction and you in the other, holding hands. Then, you'd march on the spot, shake hands to the rhythm, regularly change positions, and repeat the movement. We were also great fans of rock and roll.

The Rendezvous at Mitcham was a good rock and roll venue. The Easy Beats and the Twilights played there. At one of these dances, I met Jan. Jan was tall and attractive. Jan's friend, Lyn (whom Darby would eventually marry), just tagged along for a while, and we'd bring them back to the flat to stay the night. Hoyte seemed to have difficulty getting a girlfriend; we concluded he was too intense around women, so he put them off.

We never went to rock and roll dances for fear of being bashed up by the rockers. We preferred to go to friends' parties and enjoy the safety of their homes or garages. I preferred the Rolling Stones over the Beatles. The parties we attended were usually dominated by music such as the Rolling Stones, Eric Burden, the Animals, and The Who.

An apprentice wage didn't go far; we never had enough money after paying rent. Milk soon became our staple diet since it was easily accessed in the early morning hours, immediately after delivery to the front steps of houses along the streets. We were reluctant to return the bottles for fear of being found out, so the milk bottles accumulated along the kitchen walls – dozens of them. Renting the flat at Balwyn also involved another sort of milking; milking petrol.

We couldn't afford to pay for the amount of petrol we needed. Petrol was readily available from cars parked in the dimly lit suburban streets during the early morning hours. Our kit, stashed in the back of Darby's ute, was a 4-gallon drum and a length of garden hose for siphoning. On a regular planned 'petrol night,' we'd leave the flat, usually around midnight, to milk the cars. A full drum lasted a couple of days. We'd worked out a roster system for the person on watch.

We milked a Vanguard with a rounded back one night in Surrey Hills. I wasn't comfortable with this choice, having had a bad experience running into the back of one on my way to school on my bike. We fed the hose into the tank, finished siphoning, and couldn't withdraw the hose. It was hanging on, stuck in one of the tricky tight bends. We pulled and pulled, and the car was rocking violently from side to side when the house lights came on. We fled the scene, hose left protruding from the car, and headed back to the flat.

Someone had recorded our registration number because it wasn't long before there was a loud rapping on the door. It was the police asking about Darby's registration number, where we were at 12.45 am that morning, and what we were doing. They told us to dress and come to the station to make a statement. They prepared the statement based on what we'd told them about the Vanguard and advised us of impending court proceedings.

I was terrified by the whole episode, but Darby seemed to be at ease. He was enthralled by the powerful police Studebaker. The police gave us a performance demonstration of the police car on the return trip to the flat. I couldn't make much sense of Darby's attitude and his adoration for the police. In hindsight, they could have bashed us up and thrown us into the clink if they saw fit. I was worried about the trouble we faced with having to go to court, and this incident marked the end of the few months of independence. It was September when we packed up and returned home to our parents. Our mothers engaged solicitors, and the day of the court hearing came. I was terrified.

The solicitor told the magistrate that we were young boys away from home and didn't mean any harm. We had run out of petrol, were afraid, and had no option but to milk the Vanguard for enough petrol to get home. The solicitor also told the magistrate that we were all very sorry, would never milk petrol again, and were now back home under the guidance of our parents and so on. To everyone's relief, we were released on a good behaviour bond with no criminal conviction. In the summer of 1963, I planned to sail a raft down the Darling River.

A Raft on the Darling River

The plan was to sail from Menindee to Wentworth on the Murray-Darling junction in northwestern Victoria. I made a preliminary trip to Wentworth to make contact with anyone who could give me some practical hints. I sought advice from an old man who had been the captain of a paddle steamer, shipping wool bales from the outlying sheep stations to Wentworth when the rivers were the dominant mode of transport.

The old man told me about things to look out for on the river; submerged rocks, fallen trees, and sand bars that could impede my progress. He advised that at the time of the year that I planned to go, December, the river would be low and likely to have little flow. Another man told me that the river bank behind the old Menindee Hotel would be an excellent place to launch a raft since they were refurbishing part of the Hotel, and there would be plenty of valuable materials to build the raft. So, I went to Menindee, and the Hotel people said I could have as much old flooring and other materials as I needed for the job. I was delighted at the prospect.

Now on four week's holidays from work, I packed my kit of two rucksacks full of oranges, pliers, hammer and nails, a folding canvas stretcher, a blanket, Winchester, shotgun, ammunition, a hand-line, bird book, and a Brownie box camera and film, and again, hitchhiked up to Menindee. The plan was to live entirely off the river with the oranges to supplement an anticipated meat diet. The raft building was easier than expected and was finished in a few days. It was about six feet square with four fuel drums serving as floatation, secured with fencing wire to extended floor joists, forward and aft. I used facia boards to enclose the deck and cut a V-shaped slot to take the paddle out the back and a mast for a sail.

    I was scared stiff and had little sleep for the first few nights on the riverbank. Having secured the raft, I unloaded my gear, set up camp on the high bank, collected enough firewood for the night, lit a fire, and had dinner before dark. I kept the shotgun loaded and against a nearby tree for easy access. There were sudden noises that broke the silence of the clear still nights. I wasn't familiar with this new environment. Dingoes howled nearby, and red kangaroos grunted and thumped their tails on the ground as they hopped across the black soil plains. I heard feral pigs squabbling in the distance and sudden splashes in the water down the bank. I'd keep the fire going; half the time, I'd have hold of the gun just in case. Occasionally, I'd fire a shot in the dark beyond the fire to scare things away.

    My fears were unfounded, though, and soon enough, I settled into a routine, became comfortable with the nights, and began looking forward to setting up camp by the end of the day on the river. I never saw a soul and enjoyed the solitude.

    A typical day found me awake at dawn to light the fire, cook breakfast, pack, load up, organise the deck, untie the raft, and push out into the river to start the new day. I became attached to this little raft. It was my home, and I felt safe out on the water. First, I'd shoot a duck – they were usually black ducks in flight. I'd heard that these ducks can reach speeds up to over 180 miles per hour, and I was pretty impressed with my shooting skills.

    Initially, I dived overboard and retrieved the duck from the water without a problem. After a while, though, I found that the hawks had associated the report from the shotgun with a lame duck and would dive in to pluck it from the river before I could get to it.

    On more than a couple of occasions, I had to off-load the gear onto the bank and drag the raft across a sand bar or fallen, partly submerged river gum. I had many groundings. Sometimes where the bank was even, I'd find it quicker and easier to walk along the bank, pulling the raft behind me. Then, one day while negotiating some rapids, I punctured the left-hand front floatation drum causing the raft to list badly and flooding a portion of the deck.

Old Menindee Hotel, 1963.

Launched - the raft became my home on the river for 16 days, 1963.

Campsite on the banks of the Darling River, 1963.

This was something that I wasn't prepared for, and luckily, about a mile or so downstream, I came across a well-used track that led to a homestead. Unloading the raft, I pulled it up the bank to see what could be done. It turned out to be a dint with a tiny hole on the underside of the drum. The homestead was about half a mile away. They gave me a wad of pitch to mend the hole, and I rewired the drum to the joists with the repair work on the upper side. It was mid-afternoon before the repair was finished, and I set off again with plenty of time to test my handiwork before setting up camp for the night. All went well during the following days, and I had time to explore exciting landforms along the Darling River.

It was approaching the third week on the river that things began to get tough. The days were getting hotter, with more exposed sandbars, rocky outcrops, and fallen trees to negotiate. So reluctantly, on the 16th day, I abandoned the remaining reach of the river into Wentworth, packed my kit, and made my way along a track to a sheep station. They gave me a bed for the night in the shearers' quarters, dinner, and breakfast the following morning. They were very friendly and listened with great interest to my life story on the river and assured me that if I ever wanted a job on a station after I finished my apprenticeship, I could work there. Finally, a station hand gave me a lift into Wentworth. I estimated that I had travelled about 130 miles on the river.

This wasn't the last I saw of the Darling River. My friend Hoyte was on holiday, and we drove to Wilcannia in an Austin A40 the following year.

Not long after Hoyte was discharged from the navy, I accompanied him to Sydney, where he bought a car, and we travelled across to Wilcannia on the Darling River in Western NSW. He purchased a black Austin A40, and the dealer told us that while it looked a bit rough, overall, for twenty-nine pounds and ten shillings, he could vouch for its reliability.

Hoyte drove through the city – I hadn't yet got my licence. The Austin was trouble-free as we arrived in Wilcannia. We stocked up with supplies and continued down into the southwest Riverina. One day while driving along the seemingly endless stretch of dirt road, we spotted a lone emu and gave chase across the open black soil plains. We had nearly caught up with the emu when there was a sudden, sickening crunch as the front right-hand side of the car collapsed. On investigation, we saw that the shock absorber had parted company with the wheel arch where it was once bolted and protruded through a big hole through the wheel arch.

At the Homestead before heading for Wentworth, 1963.

On board the raft, 1963.

The steering was now severely restricted to only half of its original travel, and you had to force the steering wheel to make a turn. We made it to Moama, and a mechanic at the service station welded the hole and shock absorber back into place. All went well, we were back on the road again, and we regained our confidence until the Austin began to run unevenly and lose power. We pulled over to the roadside to investigate the problem.

On my return from a pee, I noticed that Hoyte had the bonnet up, was standing with one foot on the front bumper, leaning over the radiator, and peering into the smokey, dark, oily cavity that was the engine bay. Hoyte slowly shook his head, exclaiming, *"However did they win the war."* It turned out that all that was wrong was a spark plug lead had come adrift – probably vibrated loose during the ill-fated emu episode or negotiating miles of rough dirt road. We drove the five miles into Echuca, where the engine began to lose power again, but it was more serious this time. The Austin A40 was clapped out. When poor Hoyte went to meet a girlfriend in the town to take her to the pictures, the Austin broke down and konked out for the last time. Hoyte was forced to abandon the Austin on the roadside in Echuca, and we hitchhiked the rest of the way back to Melbourne.

By the end of 1964, hitchhiking had become a significant part of our lives. Darby and I would venture only a few miles from home in the early days. The Yarra River at Warrandyte and our more private spot over the hill off Jumping Creek Road was a favoured destination. Soon we'd set off for distant, unfamiliar places like Warburton and Woods Point, Ballarat, Glen Rowan, Jerilderie and Kelly country, Echuca, Albury and Tocumwal on the Murray, and Maude to hunt feral pigs in the lignum on Vin's sheep station. Carrying a shotgun across your shoulder was never a problem.

We'd travel with a rucksack and sleeping bag, a rifle and something to drink, a few pieces of fruit, and enough cash to buy the odd pie. It wasn't long before we were hitching all over Victoria to Port Augusta, South Australia, and even Sydney – it seemed limitless – all within a single weekend. Apart from Warrandyte and the Yarra that I've already talked about, there were a few other trips worthy of special mention.

Hoyte - "However, did they win the war," 1963.

On one occasion, we were chasing a lift on the approach into Ballarat when a Kombie van pulled up. It was raining, and we were wet through. The bloke in the van explained that he had some accommodation for us if we wanted it and that we should get out of our wet clothes. He asked if we had eaten and invited us for dinner. He seemed all right, and we accepted his offer. He gave us a tour of his awe-inspiring museum collection. There were early gold mining paraphernalia and equipment, steam engines, stuffed birds and animals, and skulls, including human skulls and other relics. We enjoyed dinner, drank his wine, and talked about the history of Ballarat and the gold fields, among other things.

We had no idea that this generous, sophisticated gentleman was a rampant sexual predator who, after capturing our confidence, in the early morning, attempted to sneak into my bed with me in it. I awoke and kicked him out before he could have his evil way with me. We viewed his behaviour as a betrayal and left early in the morning before he got up. There was another incident too.

When a car pulled up on hitchhiking trips, there was often a contest over who would get the front seat. It was another Volkswagon – a beetle. Darby got to the door first, and I clambered into the back. In no time at all, the driver presented Darby with some pornographic pictures and put his hand on Darby's thigh. Darby reacted strongly, swearing and throwing the driver's hand away. The driver stopped the car, and we got out as quickly as possible.

On the way to hunt pigs on the sheep station at Maude, Darby and I would break the journey to enjoy the relatively dry exotic atmosphere of Echuca with its streets lined with ancient peppercorn trees, old stone houses, and shops.

Echuca had been an important river port on the Murray, with its massive jetty sitting atop what looked like a forest of enormous river-red gum logs. We spent a lot of time there, swimming with local girls. The Adelaide, another derelict paddle steamer, was moored on the river's opposite bank.

We camped in a cabin on the upper deck of an old paddle steamer moored at the jetty. This river steamer was in original condition, with equipment in place and fittings intact. The old Melbourne creaked and groaned through the night as we slept in our sleeping bags on sprung wire bunks by the open windows. I'll never forget waking up to the kookaburra calls at daybreak echoing along the river with its beautiful steep sloping banks lined with magnificent river red gums. We had an uninterrupted view of the morning mist slowly lifting from this noble and gentle river. We fished off the lower deck of the Melbourne, and saw a platypus there, and Murray Cod and Bream jumping.

Around this time, the focus was on pig hunting in the Riverina. Darby had acquired a jungle carbine, and I always took my double-barrel hammer gun. We'd pack our gear and hitch-hike up through Echuca, across the river, and out to Maude on the Murrumbidgee River.

We had previously contacted a sheep property owner at the Maude Hotel and were welcome to hunt the feral pigs – they were destructive and caused severe losses in the stock. A single pig would get in amongst the flock and rip their stomachs out. The farmer appreciated our help in eradicating what we could. The pigs spent their days in the lignum scrub, which grew on the broad river flats. The lignum was an almost impenetrable woody weed that grew in extensive thickets.

It served as a refuge for the pigs, emerging to wreak havoc among the sheep at night. You could walk in between the large clumps. Hunting expeditions through the lignum were intense and exciting. You didn't know what to expect. We'd be carefully following a pad through the scrub, and suddenly, without warning, a big black pig would break cover from just a few feet away, often too fast to get a decent shot. Occasionally we'd get a glimpse from a distance away and be able to stalk them. One afternoon, not far from camp, Darby shot a big boar with tusks, reminding us how dangerous it could be to be on the wrong side of one of these animals. My 12-gauge, loaded with SGs, was only effective at close range.

One quiet moonlit night, we were camped by a billabong under big river red gums on the edge of a lignum patch. The shotgun had both barrels loaded and leaning against a tree trunk within easy reach from the sleeping bag. I never slept soundly in the bright moonlight. It wasn't long before dawn when I spotted the sizeable bulky silhouette of the boar that had come out of the lignum and along the bank toward the edge of the billabong to water, only about twenty feet away. There was no wind, and it hadn't noticed me under the tree in my sleeping bag. Darby was sleeping on the other side of me and was dead to the world.

Hitchhiking, en route to Maude in April 1964. Photograph courtesy of R. Darby.

The Melbourne at the Echuca Wharf, 1963.

At a camp on the Murrumbidgee River. Photograph courtesy of R. Darby.

I was nervous at such close quarters that I thought the pig might even hear me breathing and come for me. We'd heard stories about pigs; they could attack while you slept and eat your face off, especially when your movement is restricted in a sleeping bag. I'd also heard domestic pigs could kill and eat humans under certain circumstances. I wasn't taking any chances and slowly withdrew my arms from the sleeping bag and reached for the shotgun. I slowly aimed, drawing back the left-hand hammer. Click. The massive feral pig started with a grunt, facing me head-on. I fired. The pig took off into the lignum, and I turned to see Darby bolt upright in his sleeping bag. We got up, lit the fire, and sat and talked about how close it had all been, why I hadn't woken him up earlier, and so on, until dawn.

Darby

In early 1963 Darby bought an Austin A70. It was heavy and slow and used a lot of oil. Towards the end of its' life, Darby would replenish engine oil with discarded sump oil from the garage more often than we would put petrol in the tank. It got so bad that plumes of blue-grey smoke would billow out from the back like a smoke screen and you couldn't see anything behind. Eventually, Darby decided that we'd conduct an experiment by running the engine full throttle with a brick on the accelerator pedal to see what might happen. Having done this, we moved out of harm's way. After some time the engine exploded causing a conrod to break out of the side of the engine block. What a mess.

Darby was now 18 and armed with a driver's licence. It was June 1963 when his Mum bought him a grey 1956 Holden ute. It was difficult for me to fathom why his mother would do this. It was in good condition, and safe. We went everywhere in this ute, Darby and I, often camping in the back.

Inspired by Del Shannon's song The Wanderer – *"Well I'm the type of guy who likes to roam around, where pretty girls are, well you know that I'm around"...* Darby got a sign writer to paint 'The Ringwood Wanderer' in large lettering across the rear tailgate. Things changed when Darby would go out cruising and getting speeding fines. I was sure that the police were targeting him and his ute. But Darb seemed to enjoy the attention it brought, and my outings with him became fewer as I was being replaced by his girlfriends. One trip of a different kind springs to mind.

Darby in his 1956 Holden ute, 1963.

The Incident at Yarra Glen

It was in 1964 when we were shooting rabbits near the river at Yarra Glen. On our return to the car park, there was a carload of people just arrived. There was a small group of young men who began talking to each other and insulting us as though we were encroaching on their territory. They were hostile, watching us like a pack of savage dogs about to attack. We withdrew slowly and Darby drove off slowly up the road. They jumped into their car and were now in pursuit and nudging right up, almost against the back of the ute.

At first, Darby maintained a slow pace. They were after us. Frightened as we were, we agreed that our lives were at risk and the circumstances called for drastic action. As we drove slowly along the remote dirt track, I put two cartridges into the shotgun and climbed out of the window and into the back of the ute. Darby picked up speed as I raised the gun and pointed the barrel straight at the left front tyre of the car, and fully prepared to fire in self-defence. We were relieved as the car broke away and we couldn't see them for dust. We never spoke to anyone about this incident. I was worried about reprisals afterwards but we never saw them again.

Time out and a Return to Nature

Darby was a fan of the Beatles and one day during a cruise, all excited, he told me about their new song that was just about to be played on the radio. It was 'A Hard Day's Night' and I enjoyed this new experience with him. But I felt that this new lifestyle wasn't me. It seemed repetitive and shallow and I gradually withdrew, returning to my interest in the natural world. I spent more quality time in the local natural environment. I did some research on taxidermy.

As a first project, I prepared and mounted a yellow wattlebird, then a blackbird, eastern shrike tit, and finally a crimson rosella. I passed them all onto Darby on my departure from home and he has kept them to this day. During these experiments, I always had my bird book – Neville Cayley's 'What Bird Is That.' I made a lot of observations of birds and their behaviour and anatomy. First I carefully skinned the bird, using formaldehyde to preserve the skin. Then manipulating the materials such as cotton wool which was bound with string to form the correct body shape, over which I stretched the treated skin and stitched it along the breast under the feathers. It was around that time that Ringwood was undergoing a transformation as a rural district being swallowed up by urban sprawl. I was resentful.

The developers were bull-dozing my beloved bushland across the road, to make way for streets and rows of houses. As a protest, I threw mud at the white undercoated weatherboard houses with the result that the police come knocking on the front door with threats against us. A putrid landfill was established just up on the rise from my old childhood haunt. I felt that there was something sinister about the blue-black sludge oozing along my pathway through my beautiful open stringybark forest. I gradually withdrew, never to return, and felt a personal loss of a place I had cherished. This made a deep and lasting impression on me. I had become conscious of the reckless destruction of nature that I was to experience time and time again into the future.

Darby Gets Married

Darby and Lyn were married at the Ringwood Methodist Church on 16th March 1965 – Lyn was pregnant, I was the best man, and Darby was late. We had the reception and party at Judith's place in Bayswater. Judith was running a childcare centre there at the time. The party was organised by my girlfriend Jean. I was the photographer but regrettably, I'd forgotten to put film in the camera. Darby never forgave me. It wasn't long after the wedding that I was making preparations to leave home and travel.

Leaving Home

In hindsight it would have seemed a bit strange to my friends that I left when I did – all those opportunities squandered and so on. I remember clearly, the disappointment my boss, Bob, at Summit Engineering, had expressed. By leaving, I was throwing away a lifetime career in precision tool making. I didn't even wait for my apprenticeship indentures and other paperwork to arrive.

My girlfriend at the time, Jean, was English. She was a stunner and some years older than me, fun-loving, and had two small children. She seemed intensely keen on me and eager to share in my future. I felt I was getting into a relationship I didn't understand and suffered some anxiety at the time. I have no doubt that in part, this predicament informed my decision to plan my departure.

It was in December 1965 when Mum and Elaine dropped me and my big leather suitcase off, on the Hume highway, just out of Melbourne. I was heading North and my first port of call would be a job at a sheep station that I'd arranged earlier, during my rafting days on the Darling River. It wasn't until I was talking to Elaine much later that it struck me, how Mum must have felt as they waved goodbye to their only brother and son with no idea of when they would see him again. How must Mum have felt as she had her last glimpse of me, left standing alone there on the highway? Elaine said that Mum cried and cried. I understand now, as I write, of the powerful emotional trauma a mother suffers as they inevitably let their children go.

I heard later on that some of the family took a dim view of my leaving home when I did. Mum never let on to me how distressed she was that day. She wanted me to depart happily full of excitement and wild expectations as I began my adulthood adventures. She didn't want me to feel any guilt or obligation to step into the breach left by Dad's sudden death a few years earlier. Many years had passed before I heard that I'd been roundly condemned by Mums' brother, Uncle Jack, her sister Aunty Lil and cousin Robert who said, *"you disappeared off the face of the planet."* Grandpa wrote to Mum saying *"it's a shame that Alan walked out on you. It was his responsibility in the circumstances to fill the vacancy left by his father. Young people seem to be selfish these days."*

I also heard much later that I'd been irresponsible in leaving home and leaving my mother in the lurch. I never suffered any guilt over leaving home though, and often wrote to Mum about my adventures. She kept all my letters. I loved Mum and we saw a lot of each other over the years. I'll be talking about these happy times as they unfold.

Alan is Starving in Broken Hill

I remember Dad's stories of travels from Adelaide to Wentworth and finally Broken Hill, by Cobb and Co's horse-drawn coaches via the soft sandy wheel ruts called the Silver City Highway. I was determined to see Broken Hill and find out what it was like. I soon ran out of cash and worked chopping wood and cleaning, for an Italian woman in a run-down boarding house for a bed and mutton sandwiches with stale bread with no butter.

After a couple of days, I went to the police station. I was hungry and pleaded with the policeman to lock me up where I would at least have some decent baked beans or whatever they fed prisoners. Judith later told me that Aunty Lois had a dream about "Alan starving in Broken Hill". While sympathetic, the policeman said that they weren't able to do much for me, but rang Mum for me to arrange some money to be sent up from home. I returned to the boarding house and they let me stay on until my money came through. Of the many letters I wrote to Mum, here are a couple of examples, from the mind of a twenty-year-old - a product of his time.

Tuesday 11/1/1966
98 Argent Street, Broken Hill. NSW

Dear Mum,
I didn't get a job on any of the stations around Menindee. Things are too dry. I ran out of money when I reached Menindee. I met the Menindee timber mill boss in the pub and got a job for this morning on one of the saws and made 2 pounds.

It's 6.45pm now and I've been back in Broken Hill for about half an hour. I have a room at the lodging house for two nights costing 30/- leaving me with 10/- til I find a job here if I find one.
Could you please send some money up here in a hurry so if I don't get a job here I can take off to Queensland. I'll send it back as soon as I get a job.

I hope all is well down there.
My regards to everyone.
Love
Alan
PS. send the money to me c/o 98 Argent Street Broken Hill.
Could you find out Veronica's address for me, just the house number will do. Her phone number is 87 3304.

Thursday 13/1/1966
Broken Hill

Dear Mum,
How are you, and is Elaine behaving herself? I spent yesterday hunting for a job but there is no hope here... Did you hear in the news about the old red gum tree on the bank of the Darling River which burned down a couple of days ago at Menindee? I was among the locals watching it blaze away on Monday night... it was the tree under which the unfortunate Burke and Wills had camped on their journey north. But the more interesting fact is, that it is also the tree under which I built my raft. It was about 300 years old.

When I get the money Mum, probably tomorrow, I'll have to get the train across to Parkes and hitch on to Sydney from there, as no cars travel from here to Sydney at this time of the year. I could possibly catch a lift up to Wilcannia, and get stuck there for days and run out of money again. Actually being stuck here at Broken Hill is quite a lesson I've learned and it will never happen again in a hundred years.

I've written to Jack Hankin to let him know I'll be dropping in for a few days. In Sydney, I'll make arrangements for a job in Brisbane or Surfer's Paradise for a while then try for a station job in the Northern Territory... Mum, could you ask Darby to ask Summit Engineering to do something about my apprenticeship indentures, but don't send them up to Broken Hill as I will be leaving as soon as the money comes through? I'll let you know where I am in my next letter.

The people here at the lodging house are letting me have the room until the money comes through. I'll last out on milk, cantaloupe and grapes, so I won't starve. Give my regards to Judith and Hilma and everyone else.

Love
Alan

The Train Crash, West of Nyngan

There were only two of us in the carriage and I soon made friends with the girl also travelling to Sydney and we talked into the night. It was around midnight, west of Nyngan when the train lurched and ran off the rails. We came to a squealing grinding halt leaving our carriage and others listing badly to the left side. I looked out from the window towards the front and saw lights shining down and under the diesel loco. I climbed out of the window, slid down to the ground, and made my way through the dark toward the front of the train. The railway workers were checking the damage and it was then that I understood how much damage had been done.

There were men in overalls crawling on their backs looking underneath the loco, which had slid off the rails. The wheels of the loco and forward carriages had chopped through the middle of the wooden sleepers for a long distance along the track and gouged a deep furrow into the blue-metal base. The crash had disturbed scorpion nests and there were dozens of the big orange things scurrying around. It was a frightening sound as they scuttled over the stones under the spotlights. It gave me the creeps and I was concerned for the safety of the men but so scared that I ran back along the train and climbed up into the safety of my carriage to wait out the rest of the night. At daybreak, the Salvos turned up with sandwiches and cups of tea. Later in the morning buses came to pick us up and take us the rest of the way to Parkes and Sydney.

Chapter 2
On the Move

Sydney

On my arrival in Sydney, I found a boarding house on the north side in Crows Nest with a strange couple. At breakfast, the man drank his tea from a bowl with a tablespoon. I got a job for a few months at a nearby Lapidary workshop. They made lapidary equipment like tumblers and polishing discs and jewellery from gemstones like agate, amethyst, and golden tiger-eye that they collected from as far afield as the Northern Territory.

There were shelves with wooden trays full of rough rocks only revealing their exquisite figuration after being cut with a diamond saw and polished. There was no challenge in assembling the little machines and I soon took to discretely cutting and polishing my own pieces. Gus, the man in charge, was big and fat. One day I watched him having an accident. Gus nearly electrocuted himself by snipping through a live electric extension cord that was plugged into a power point.

Gus was thrown backwards, air-born, about a metre, hit the wall and slid to the floor. Miraculously, he recovered quickly and didn't seem to suffer any injuries. There was a quarter-inch hole burned in the blade of the dress-making scissors he used to cut the lead.

Gus was keen to show me the city lights and took me to a strip joint in Kings Cross. I was less than impressed especially when he kept calling to the strippers "take your hat off - take your bra off" during the performances. It wasn't long after that that I went to stay with my Uncle Jack Hankin – Dad's cousin. Jack and his wife, Eileen, lived in an imposing elevated octagonal red brick house. The top floor reminded me of a lighthouse with sweeping views over picturesque Mossman Harbour on Sydney's North Shore.

I felt welcome, Jack showed me around and I helped him with work on his boat. Jack was planning to take me on a scheduled flight in his Beaver, a prewar 12-cylinder radial engine bi-plane, out west, to Lowth, a Darling River town, where he had a mail run. Jack was something of a rough diamond and seemed very proud of me, eagerly introducing his young and promising nephew to his mates at the pub. I admired him and saw him as a bit of a surrogate Dad.

We seemed to be getting on really well until one morning, out of the blue, Uncle Jack asked me *"how long do you think you'll be staying?"* Shocked and assuming that I was no longer welcome, I said, *"actually I was planning on leaving today."* I felt betrayed and straight after breakfast, I packed up and left them and was never to see them again. It was much later that I discovered that their marriage had ended. I caught a train to Newcastle that day.

Newcastle

I found a place to live in Newcastle and decided to work at the BHP steelworks as a fitter. Someone said that I should investigate the idea of taking the paid, one-year full-time in-house marine engineers' course. My perceived romance of a ship's engineer, swanning around in a smart white uniform and wining and dining the girls was appealing. I applied and was enrolled the following day. The study and the practicums were interesting and challenging.

I also looked forward to body-surfing at Nobby's Beach on the weekends. The waves were so big that you had a view across the hinterland from up on the crest. There were dumpers too. I couldn't tell the difference and after falling from the crest and pummeled into the bottom, nearly breaking my neck.

There was one thing about the steelworks that I had difficulty coming to terms with, and that was, having to become one of eleven thousand faceless workers who flowed through the gates at the end of the working day. I felt that I had been reduced to a number and was increasingly disturbed by that. I was talking to a fellow student one lunch hour – Trevor Denman from Townsville and he told me all about life in North Queensland and that I should seriously consider contacting Inkerman Sugar Mill about work as a fitter.

Within a couple of weeks, I was on the road again on my way north. Hitch-hiking proved slow and being keen to get started at Inkerman, I caught the train from Brisbane, arriving at Home Hill two days later.

Home Hill and the Inkerman Sugar-mill

The train pulled up at the Home Hill station at about 3 am. I collected my suitcase and made my way over to the sugar mill. I had nothing to do but wait until dawn. So I sat myself down on my suitcase under a street light at the front of the mill. Flying foxes were arguing and squealing in the mango trees and huge cane toads gathered around the base of the lamppost to gulp down the moths and beetles that came to the light. It was an exotic and exciting place.

Sunrise was like going to a movie because I'd been travelling north through the night during the last leg of the trip without being able to see the changing scenery outside. It was the middle of the crush and it wasn't long before I was signed on and allocated a room at the barracks. I ordered my basic tool kit and started work amidst the rumbling machinery, belching steam, turbines and centrifugals. There were huge valves, suspended grid walkways, sweet pungent smell of raw sugar juice pouring from the crushing rollers, and cane bins coming and going. The workers included locals and others who were seasonal, who stayed at the barracks.

Inkerman Mill barracks, 1966.

One wing of the barracks was allocated to the fitters whose role in the maintenance of the mill was held in high regard by management, and fitter positions were permanent. Another wing was allocated to electricians, another to plumbers, another to sugar chemists, and so on. There was a bell and we'd eat in the mess. There were about 15 workers, and I enjoyed the novelty of the military precision and routine, camaraderie, and good hearty meals.

The fitters were often called out at night, walking the one hundred meters or so from the barracks along the track to the mill. Everything about Inkerman and Home Hill was exotic and an exciting new adventure for me. One of the many stories I was told was the story about the 1954 cyclone and the shooting of a croc from the steps of the local post office. I often wrote home to Mum describing my experiences.

Work in the mill was really diverse and interesting. It was a highly unionised workforce. The foreman, Gordon Stockdale, and his mate, Fernsey, took a liking to me, taking me under their wing. There were routines that involved checking the glands on the valves throughout the mill, and tightening them as necessary. There was the welding of the toothed rollers which gripped the bagasse, carrying it along the line toward the boilers. Clad in a raincoat to protect against getting drenched with raw sugar cane juice, we'd crawl under the revolving roller to strike an arc and deposit beads of weld to aid the roller in its gripping function. There was work on the cane bins involving repairs to wheel bearings and welding. There was fitting the enormous keys that held the rollers from spinning on the shafts and so on.

Inkerman Mill, 1966.

I was proud of my own little room at the barracks to the extent that I painted it – green floor with footprints leading to the bed, pink walls adorned with a big map of Australia, and pencil sketches of bones and skulls I'd collected from the bush. I kept it in immaculate condition.

All the blokes from the barracks would spend a lot of time down at the Malpas hotel, drinking beer at the bar, after work. I spent my time doing drawings and later on a weekend, when I got my motorbike, down at Groper Creek. I could be found hunting in the mangroves for mud crabs and doing wildlife photography. Gordon, Fernsey, and the others were most amused at the big carpet python whom I named Harry. I got the python from a flying fox camp in the mangroves at Groper Creek. They often made jokes about it and I was the centre of attention. Harry normally slept in the cupboard in my room at the barracks and occasionally in my locker down at the mill. Harry ate small birds and reptiles that I collected. He was docile and easy to keep.

It was 1966 and North Queensland sugar mills were union strongholds. Inkerman was no exception. Fernsey, Gordon Stockdale, and other local fitters acquainted me with the politics and workplace issues of concern, like the recently graduated operations engineer – a sullen and belligerent bully, George Simpson, otherwise known as the boy bastard. I embraced the issues with enthusiasm. The engineer was soon onto me, and when he caught me alone, would threaten to dismiss me. I'd report back to Fernsey and Gordon and he would back off only to have another go later, like a savage dog – he gave up eventually and left me alone. Other fitters included Geoff Todman, Gordon (Bluey) Lowter and Dave Pearson. The other engineers were Fred Mocom, and Jimmy Lanane.

Harry the python lived in my cupboard.

It was the same year that Gough Whitlam came to talk to the workers during his election campaign. Whitlam spoke with us under the shade of a big mango tree. I was most impressed, especially by Labor's stance on the Vietnam War, human rights, First Nations and social justice issues.

This meeting informed my later decision to become involved in Federal Politics. Dad's long-term affiliations with Labor suddenly made sense. I also spent time in Townsville.

Townsville

My first introduction to Townsville was through a lift with a couple of workmates from the barracks. One of them had a powder blue 1962 XL Falcon – I was impressed by its power and enjoyed these beer-drinking trips to Townsville. I'd hang around waiting and return to the barracks with them. I was looking forward to another weekend trip in the Falcon.

We were riding along, just past Giru, when someone in the back suddenly screamed out to stop, and that there was a snake on the road. *"Snake, snake"* he screamed. As the car pulled up he jumped out, got an axe from the boot, and chopped up a traffic counter into one-foot lengths. They were all so amused by his drunken antics. I had just bought a motorbike.

Baby Square Tailed Kite at Groper Creek.

A Super Rocket

I'd accumulated some cash and felt that the time was right to get my own transport. I bought a motorcycle from a local worker. It was a 1962 BSA 650 Super Rocket – candy apple red with chrome tank and mudguards, and chrome crash-bars front and rear. In no time at all, I had the mufflers off to savour the sound of a straight-out exhaust from the big twin. It was a bit deafening and the barracks residents complained until I refitted the mufflers. I went for my licence at the Home Hill Police Station.

I arrived there one Saturday morning in thongs, shorts, and a tee shirt. The Policeman came out with me to view the bike and asked me to ride up the road, turn around and come back. I did this and by the time I turned to come back, he had disappeared. I parked the bike out the front and went inside to find him writing out the licence. He didn't see fit to query me about road rules or anything else, and the ten-year licence was free.

Now that I had a licence I was independent, transport-wise, and had Ayr and distant Townsville in my sights. I enjoyed the bike and spent a lot of time down at Groper Creek, Home Hill Beach, and other local spots. During a weekend, I could be seen cruising, feet up on the front crash bar, tee shirt, and no helmet, up the Bruce Highway through Ayr, Giru, Alligator Creek and finally into Townsville and back home later in the afternoon.

The BSA Super Rocket, 1966.

Saturday Night in Ayr

Sometimes, Saturday night would find me at the popular dance venue in Queen Street, Ayr. Populin's Hall was above the furniture shop in Queen Street and often patronised by the Italian and Greek cane cutters all reeking of garlic. Old-time dances included Gypsy Tap where you'd take three steps back, three steps forward, run to gather momentum and slide to the other end of the hall. There was also the Pride of Erin, Barn Dance, and Waltzes. The local girls would sit on chairs along the walls, while the boys would take up space in the middle of the hall and once a dance was announced, ask the girl of their choice for a dance. Student nurses, Rose Mar and Cheryl McLaren from Townsville were there one night. I went over and asked Rose for a dance and from then on, my life changed. Pretty well all my spare time was taken up either with Rose, thinking about her, or travelling to Townsville to see her.

At first, I'd cruise up to Townsville on the bike to pick her up at the nurse's quarters. Rose's colleagues seemed impressed with me and we'd chat in the lobby while I was waiting. Years later, Rose would tell our friends of the time she came down only to find that one of the nurses was trying on my corduroy jacket and from then on made sure that she didn't keep me waiting too long in the foyer in future. We often rode to Saunders Beach among other places on the bike and spent the night together at Civic House. We'd also go to the Hotel Allen where they sold Cairns draft beer in tall clear bottles. We listened to live music at the Seaview on the Strand in Townsville. Rose would come down to parties at Cheryl's place in Gray Street in East Ayr. Charming and romantic American servicemen from the USAF on R&R leave from Gaum would sometimes be there with their expensive gifts and flowers for the girls.

We were fishing on the breakwater in Townsville one day when one of Rose's friends insisted on sitting next to me. I had a one-hundred-pound breaking strain line with a big heavy sinker because it was rocky and the line would often snag on the rocks. It wasn't once but twice that on yanking the line off a snag it would let go suddenly – the sinker catapulting into the unfortunate girl's stomach with a thud. It was lucky that no one was injured.

I had another girlfriend at the time too. I was actually engaged to Julie from Vermont near Ringwood. I asked her on several occasions about coming to join me in my adventures. I thought that her parents had reservations about me and she said that they wouldn't allow her to come. She wouldn't give me the engagement ring back and that was the end of that.

A Land Rover Series 2

I traded in the Super Rocket for a 1958 Series 2 petrol short wheel-based soft top 2.25cc Land Rover in bronze green. I was pleased to part with the bike since the novelty had worn thin and besides, the clutch had begun to play up. The Land Rover, Little Patti we nicknamed it from the number plate, was superb. It was my first car and the first of four Land Rovers that Rose and I were to own. Home Hill beach was a favoured destination and I'd take off the canvas top, and take some of the barracks blokes with me to the beach. We'd ride along the beach at speed. I'd drive with the ratchet hand throttle on while standing on the floor, with the others hanging on to the hood frame.

It wasn't long after I'd met Rose when I introduced her to Harry the python who was often asleep under a blanket in the middle seat of the Land Rover. On looking down as I carefully lifted the blanket to show her, she was alarmed but put on a brave face. I wasn't aware of this until she mentioned it sometime after we were married. We were eventually to drive this Land Rover all the way through Central Australia and down to Melbourne and I'll describe that trip later.

An incident occurred at a local hotel that I should mention.

Rose and our new Series 2 Land Rover, 1966.

The Fight at the Malpass Hotel

I normally didn't drink at pubs. It was a Friday afternoon when some of my co-workers convinced me to join them for a few beers at the Malpass Hotel. They saw drinking at the pub as an important social responsibility. After a couple of beers, one of the itinerant workers, a moody, aggressive sort of bloke, accused me of deliberately running over a bump while he was riding in the back of the Land Rover at Home Hill Beach, causing him to bump his head on the overhead tubing.

In jest, I told him that he owed me an apology for damage to the Land Rover - a big mistake. He took it seriously. Spoiling for a fight, he demanded that I step outside. I thought he was joking and went along with it. We were out on the footpath when he threw a swing at me and I still refused to take it seriously. He was much older than me but wasn't very strong. Another wild swing connected on the side of my head and it now dawned on me that this bloke was serious.

During the return to the barracks from the beach one day, he had temporarily knocked himself out by hitting his head up against the hood frame. It was then that I found out that he had suffered an earlier head injury in an accident at a bench grinder where the wheel had disintegrated with a section lodging itself in his skull, some years previously. He was so feeble that I had time to figure out how I was going to manage this situation. It was important that I prevent him from not only hurting me but more importantly, himself, given that he had a steel plate in his head as a result of his previous injury.

I grabbed him and as gently as I could, lowered him to the pavement where I could immobilise him. His arms were still flailing about as he tried to land a punch and I copped a couple of light blows to the side of the face before I could finally pin him down by hanging onto his wrists. He eventually settled and agreed to give up. I gradually loosened my grip on him, finally releasing him so he could continue his drinking back in the pub with the others. I wasn't used to fighting and, was a bit shaken by the experience. I walked on back to the barracks. He never apologised, I never had anything else to do with him and I never went back to the Malpass Hotel.

Life in Townsville

It was in August 1966 that I proposed marriage to Rose on the beach at Hell Hole and not long after that, relocated to Townsville. Rose and I rented a flat in Gilbert Crescent North Ward with Harry the python. I got a job as a maintenance fitter with the Commonwealth Works Dept based in Garbutt. Rose was still nursing at the Townsville General.

My job was focused on the RAAF base in Garbutt, and I enjoyed the work. My assistant, Bob Hall, a Londoner, and a buffoon, was fun to be with except for example, when he would question my professional ability while doing maintenance work on aircraft jet fuel installations. On one occasion, at the end of the year, Bob and I drove back to the flat after the work Christmas party. I ended up driving the Land Rover into the stone wall at the flat, bending the front bumper. I didn't remember driving home from the party and we had apparently fallen out of the Land Rover onto the ground where Rose found us in an intoxicated, delirious, and dehydrated state on her return home from work late in the afternoon.

On the odd occasion in Bob's absence, I was allocated the services of a young bloke from Camooweal in Western Queensland near the Northern Territory border. I was intrigued by his short nuggety stature and lispy drawl, which made me wonder if Camooweal people were all like that. He used to drive the Department's big orange International ute on our trips to the RAAF base to work and to the army base at Macrossan on the way to Charters Towers.

Of the characters I met in Townsville, Kel Stuart, from South Australia warrants some special mention. Kel, an older man, somewhat eccentric, had come to us from work at the new manganese mine on Groote Eylandt. Without warning, in the middle of tightening up the bolts on a flange or other job, Kel would break into little risqué songs – he seemed to have a repertoire of dozens of them - and if you were lucky he'd throw in an Irish jig as well. We bumped into Kel again a year or so later on our travels in Darwin, in his "Min-min Motel" a white Morris mini-van that he used as a camper van.

Bob Hall and I became friends and he introduced Rose and me to his wife Veronica and her family. We also became lifelong friends with Veronicas' parents. Jim and Nora Hull lived in North Ward on the slopes of Castle Hill overlooking Magnetic Island. Jim was an engineer at the Stuart Cement works. Over a "rough red," Jim and Nora often told us stories of their travels and work in India, Burma and other exotic places like Dares Salaam, Tanganyika, Botswana, and Kenya. He told us stories of the Mau Mau nationalist movement and their attacks on the white settlers in the 1950s.

Jim was a British railway engineer and once told us about having to keep the fires alight through the night to stop the lions from taking the workers from their tents, dragging them off and eating them. They had developed a taste for the workers. Jim and Nora also told us about their opulent lifestyle with African servants and frequent encounters with high-ranking people from the British Colonial Office at various functions. I was always amused and impressed by their sophistication and always pictured Jim, going about his business in colonial Africa in white or khakis and a pith helmet, and they had the accent to match. The whole idea of life in remote and exotic places struck a chord with me and Jim and Nora were influential in our later decisions to work in remote North East Arnhem Land and the Central desert in the Northern Territory.

We met Arthur Gleeson and his mates through Trevor Denman. Arthur lived with his family in an elevated 1930s Queensland house in Hermit Park. Both Arthur and Trevor were keen on Rose but were apparently no match for me. I used to enjoy the innocent fun of mucking around with the fantastic model electric train set with tracks, going in all directions, covering half the area under the house. One thing that we had in common was motorbikes. Arthur raced a Vincent Rapide sidecar outfit at the local race circuit during the sixties and restored a number of classic British bikes over the years.

Rose and I got Married

Rose and I got married on 19th May 1967 at the Townsville Registry Office and our witnesses were Ron Lee, from the RAAF Base, and his Malaysian wife, Marina. I was amazed at how Marina used to eat ripe red birds' eye chillies straight off the bush.

Rose and me - Married in Townsville, 19th May 1967.

We shifted from Gilbert Cresent and shared a flat with another couple in Gregory Terrace. Rose knew her from nursing and Ian was a dodgy customer claiming to be a ringer from out west. One evening we returned home to find that the couple had disappeared, owing rent and taking other gear. Rose and I were to head off soon after.

To Victoria via Central Australia

By mid-June, we were heading across the Barkly on our way to Victoria via Central Australia. On the black soil plains, the Barkly Highway was only partially sealed, very uneven with loose rocks and big pot-holes. But the Land Rover was solid and stable and we soon developed confidence in it.

At the end of a tiring day of driving, we set up camp well off the road and into the bush. We slept in the back with the back flap open, our heads out the back. We'd wake up to the mournful call of the crows and Rose got worried after I told her a story about people who had become blind as a result of crows coming down and pecking their eyes out.

A camp on the Gibber Plains, northern South Australia, 1967.

Through Hughenden, Richmond, Mt. Isa, Camooweal, and across the border into exotic and remote Northern Territory we came, making camps along the way. We drove south from Ti Tree towards Central Mount Stuart where we camped the last night before getting into Alice Springs. It was a cold and sleepless night. In an attempt to stave off the freezing cold, I shovelled red hot coals into a large hole I had dug in the sand beneath where we were sleeping. The warmth only lasted a couple of hours.

We also travelled to Hermannsburg where we first met desert people who were making artifacts to sell to tourists. They carved goannas, snakes, and other animals from mulga wood. From Alice Springs we continued south to Adelaide and finally to Ringwood, Victoria, and my family home in Ireland Street where we stayed with Mum.

Back to Ringwood

I found a fitting job in a wire products firm in Bayswater and Rose worked as a bookkeeper for Community Aid Abroad at Camberwell. We had decided to stay 6 months and work to save some money to continue our travels. We had also agreed that the Series 2 SWB Land Rover wasn't big enough and that we should investigate the idea of buying a bigger one.

A New Series 2A

I was still working at the same place in Bayswater. In response to my inquiry, a salesman drove a grey LWB series 2A out for me to check. It was a beautiful diesel and being so sluggish and noisy compared to the series 2, I declined and instead, we bought a 1964 Petrol hard-top – grey and cream, in mint condition. Rose and I planned some modifications we'd make to it, for bush travel. Darby was excited and had a drive of it over bush tracks around Warrandyte.

I fitted the new Land Rover with army rear shackle plates to lift the back and a spring steel bullbar on the front which also held two jerry cans. With some advice from Laurie Ryan next door, I built cupboards along the top sides in the back with sliding doors, mounted a sink in the back corner connected to a water tank underneath, and stainless steel mirrors at the back on either side. We had mats on the front footwells to stop the engine noise and made a complex roof rack. John Robins helped me make a hatch in the forward part of the roof.

    Mum was getting increasingly concerned. She'd asked me to paint the house and I'd agreed but we hadn't agreed on when this might happen. Of course, preparations for travel were our priority and for Mum, it seemed that the painting wasn't a likelihood, and thought that we should leave. When the Land Rover was finished, Rose and I packed up and went to live in East Ringwood in an attic flat overlooking the Dandenong Ranges. This flat belonged to Terry Clark, was on the top floor with great views over the town of Ringwood and across to the Dandenong Ranges.

    The place had a bohemian ambiance and we had a good time there having parties and catching up with old friends. There was Terry Clark, Peter Guhenuf, Peter Marsh, Terry Reilly, Hoyte and Darby and a number of others. I'd known Terry Clark since before I left home and had worked with him in a camera shop in Ringwood. Terry introduced me to professional-level SLR photography and I eventually bought my first SLR, a Pentax Spotmatic from him to record our future adventures. Terry also introduced us to some of the finer things in life including Coonawarra Cabernet Sauvignon and oysters accompanied by live classical piano music at the Bird and Bottle restaurant in Croydon.

    There was something sinister that I should mention too.

Vietnam War

A number of people whom I knew from Ringwood were called up and came to visit while on leave from training. We discussed the ethics of the Vietnam War and whether or not Australia should be involved. I had concluded before leaving home, two years previously, that I was opposed to the war, would refuse to comply if called up, and was prepared to be imprisoned for two years as a conscientious objector. Such was the law at the time. Our six months in Victoria soon came to an end and we were ready to go. We left Melbourne much better equipped than we had been in the past.

Across the Nullabor and on to Perth

It was late 1967. The Nullarbor Highway was wide, unsealed, and in places, very rough. There were enormous wash-outs and other holes scattered along the way. Makeshift indicators of wood from the bush were stood in a conical shape over deep depressions to alert drivers so that they could avoid falling into them. It was very hot and it took several days to make the trip, camping off the road at night. We spent time at Kalgoorlie and Coolgardie before going on to Perth.

Nullabor Highway, 1967.

Mount Pleasant, Palmyra, and Maylands

My first job was as a labourer in a wool shed at Fremantle. The foreman was called Jock. Jock was of small stature and wore big work boots. My jobs included scraping the putty from around glass window panes and moving things about. After a couple of weeks, I got bored and used to go and climb up in between the wool bales where I could be out of sight and sleep to pass the time. One afternoon, I was sitting on a stack of timber, chatting to one of the other workers, when Jock came over to me and told me that I was finished and to go down and collect my pay. I pleaded for one more chance but alas, there was no second chance. I got the sack from James Hardy too, because of my outspokenness on union issues. Rose continued to work at a Real Estate Agency in Saint Georges Terrace in the city.

We rented a room in a 3 bedroom house in Mount Pleasant, Hugh Fisher had another room. The landlord was a Spanish man called Manuel. Manuel, his wife Sylvia, and little Manni slept in the 3rd room, and the rest of the house was a shared arrangement.

We became friends with Hugh and on one occasion, on arriving home from a party at 3 O'clock in the morning, Hugh was so drunk that he used the laundry sink as a toilet and was evicted the following morning. Not long after Hugh's departure, Rose and I were also evicted. I'd caught a small carpet snake during a trip to Yanchep and I decided to keep it in a shoe-box as a pet. On returning home late one night, Manuel was waiting up for us to tell us to leave the following morning. Manuel explained that the snake had escaped from its box in our room, made its way into the living room and was on the top of the bookcase beside him watching TV. He saw it and must have panicked, although he did manage to get the snake back into its box. It was all too much for poor Manuel and we had to go and find somewhere else to live.

Hoyte was in Perth at the time and following our eviction from Mount Pleasant, we stayed with him and his wife Diane at their house in Maylands. It was early in 1968. Hoyte was self-employed and installed fake brick panels on houses. Hoyte offered me work as an assistant and we did installations at Moura and Morawa, north of Perth.

While Hoyte and I were away working, a strange thing happened. Rose reported that one evening on her return home from work, she discovered Diane with Hoyte's clothes laid out on the bed and she was pretending to shoot poor Hoyte. On another occasion, she turned up at our worksite and accused me of taking Hoyte away from her. It was all a bit disturbing, and we were concerned for Hoyte. It was around that time when Rose and I went for an interview at the Methodist Overseas Missions (MOM) office in Perth, in response to an advert in the paper.

Methodist Overseas Mission (MOM)

The job description was to participate in a variety of ways, in the dismantling of a mission station north of Port Hedland. The panel felt that we were too young for the task but, advised us of a more suitable position coming available in North East Arnhem Land.

It so happened that there was a lay missionary vacancy at Yirrkala Mission. We would need to be able to demonstrate our suitability as lay missionaries. The first of a series of interviews found us seated with a panel of experienced missionaries. We were interviewed on several occasions and I was filled with admiration for these men who had travelled hundreds of miles in dugout and outrigger canoes with head hunters in remote inaccessible places. Their mission work took them to places like the upper reaches of the Fly River, deep in the jungle, and other isolated places in PNG and the remote islands of the Pacific.

The MOM was concerned about Rose's Catholic background and my Presbyterian beginnings. We assured them that we were able to adapt. The missionaries encouraged us to come to church where we were introduced to their colleagues and we learned the relevant aspects of the MOM ritual. I discretely bought a new bible. It was a soft-covered black book with gold edging. I dog-eared the corners, giving it a well-used look, and carried it everywhere. After three months of mentoring and other preparations and having the enviable status of lay missionaries bestowed upon us, we were ready for Darwin and beyond.

Chapter 3
Darwin to North East Arnhem Land

From Perth to Darwin

We were well prepared for the trip up the Western Australian coast. The route took us through Meekatharra, Marble Bar, Port Hedland, Broome and on to the Northern Territory. We had instructions to stay with an MOM missionary based in Broome. The Reverend Trevor Foote and his family gave us an official welcome. The large old colonial timber house was cool and dark inside with wide, fly-wired verandas all around with sea-grass matting on the floor.

The Reverend Foote taught me how to say grace – something that I'd need to know on arrival at the mission – it went like this:
"For what we are about to receive, Lord make us truly thankful, amen."

Boab tree – Kimberleys, Western Australia, 1968.

And you had to have the intonation right. We were to catch up with the Reverend again in 1995 at Graceville in Brisbane which I'll talk about later. There had been rain north of Broome and we did a fair bit of wading through flooded creeks through the Kimberleys to Old Hall's Creek, across to the Northern Territory border and on to Darwin. The trip took several days. Before dark, we set up camp by the side of the road at the end of an arduous day's drive. On arrival in Darwin, we duly reported to the MOM headquarters in Knuckey Street.

We met the chairman, Gordon Symons and stayed in the visitor's house on site. It was a large and busy complex where all the mission supplies came and went to the wharf to be loaded onto the eastbound barge for the far-off mission stations scattered along the remote Arnhem Land coast. The missions had exotic Yolngu names like Galiwinku, Milingimbi, Maningrida, Ramingining, and Yirrkala. Rose and I had a few days to familiarise ourselves with HQ and Darwin, pick up last-minute supplies and arrange for the Land Rover to be shipped to Yirrkala by barge – there was no road to Yirrkala.

It was 6th March in 1968. My first flight ever, to Yirrkala on the milk run was in a Connair (Connelan Airways) wartime vintage DC3 plane that was in service in the bush at the time. It was slow, rough and noisy - a sort of aerial Land Rover. The flight took us east along the Arnhem Land coast to Yirrkala mission.

The tropical savannah lands ended abruptly in the Arnhem escarpment stretching out towards the east. Looking north towards the Arafura Sea and Papua New Guinea, endless freshwater flood plains stretched out into the distance. Vast coastal mud flats blended into meandering saltwater estuaries lined with mangroves and seething with saltwater crocs and hammerhead sharks. Long white sandy beaches were broken by wide mangrove-lined tidal estuaries. One of the missionaries had seen a large croc cruising about 10 miles out to sea during a flight into Darwin. We landed with a bump on the old wartime airstrip, twenty-five kilometres from the mission.

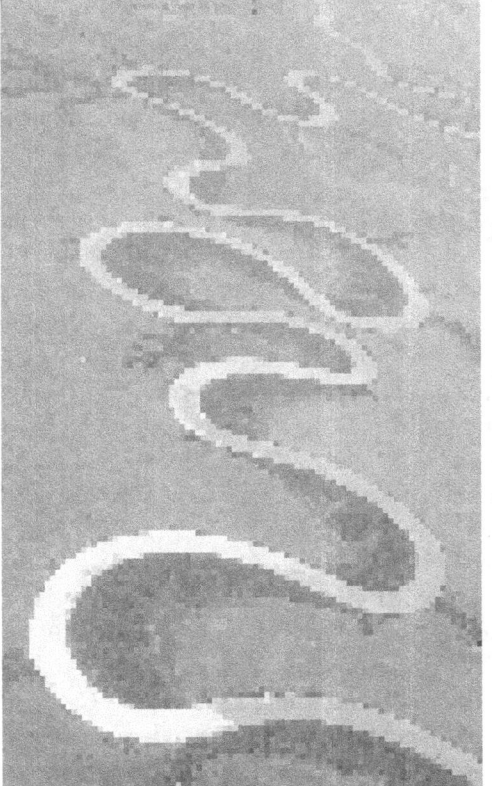

A view from Connair - Alligator River, Northern Territory, 1968.

Yirrkala

The Beach Camp - Yirrkala - where the fresh water meets the sea, 1968.

Yirrkala mission is located on the Gove Peninsula in North East Arnhem Land. During the late 1960's there was a population of approximately 800 people.

Traders from Macassar, (now Sulawesi), in the northern Indonesian islands, made seasonal voyages to the northern coast of Australia for hundreds of years. Among other things, they fished for trepang or sea cucumber for the Chinese market. There was vigorous trade between the Macassans and the Yolngu (the name used for people of Arnhem Land). They traded a variety of goods and materials such as steel and other commodities. The Macassans contributed to the language, art, and Yolngu economy. Cultural exchange and intermarriages occurred and the contact has left its legacy on both sides of the Arafura and Banda Seas.

Mainstream Australians had little or no interest in North East Arnhem Land until several attacks occurred there in the early 1930s. Late in 1932 a small group of Yolngu men attacked and killed five Japanese fishermen. The incident became referred to as the Caledon Bay Crisis. In 1933 two white prospectors and two beachcombers were attacked and killed. A member of the police party that was sent to arrest those responsible for the attacks was also killed.

In the interests of avoiding further conflict, the Methodist Missionary Society, in consultation with the Commonwealth Government, provided a buffer between the Yolngu and intruders by establishing Yirrkala Mission in 1934.

First Impressions

My first impression of Yirrkala was punctuated by isolation with only radio contact with the rest of the world. There were regular radio schedules with Darwin HQ. There was the mysterious and exciting Yolngu culture. There were camp-fires dotted around the hill-side in the evening where people sat to sing their folk songs to the rhythm of the yidaki or drone pipes and clap sticks – songs about their ancestors, connections with the country, the sulphur-crested cockatoo, kangaroo, and crocodile.

The sea was turquoise with white sandy beaches where turtles laid their eggs. Beyond the beaches were open tropical savannahs with pockets of dark monsoon rainforests. The estuaries were home to flying foxes, crocodiles and mangroves, mud crabs and mosquitoes. There was the morning mist over fresh water billabongs in the dry season and the drama of the monsoon storms, in a place where English was a second language. To me, it was a mystical paradise - a magical place. We felt privileged to be welcomed there.

There was the legacy left after the 2nd world war – the wartime airstrip, the Catalina air base and the wreckage of warplanes resting in the quiet bush. The beheading of Missionary Rupert Kentish onboard a Japanese warship just off the Wessel Islands was still fresh in the memory of older Yolngu. Wilbur Chaseling and his wife selected this place called Yirrkala where the freshwater creek flows through a small patch of rainforest and out to the sea, and set up camp there, back in 1934.

Our mission house, as with other buildings, was built by the missionaries from local hardwood and it had termite-resistant native cypress pine floors. We had a view from the kitchen and dining room overlooking the blue Arafura Sea. At mid-tide, Yolngu kids played on a rocky outcrop, sliding down over the slippery rock into the water. The mission office, which was perched on a small cliff overlooking the sea, was next door.

Settling In

It was 6th March 1968 when we were picked up from the Gove airstrip. The Land Rover and our food and other supplies were to follow by barge. As was customary, for the first two weeks, we were billeted for all meals with the missionaries. There was Doug Cole, the carpenter, and his family from Warnambool. David Kingham, the hygiene supervisor. Jonatani Rika the agriculturalist and his wife Lossa from Fiji, and Wally Fawell, the superintendent and his wife, Jill, from Perth. There was Alan the electrician and his family, Colin the plumber, and Malcolm Bray, who was my work supervisor.

Our house at Yirrkala, 1968.

It was fortunate that the Reverend Foote had mentored me in the art of saying grace during our stay with him at Broome. I suffered a bout of anxiety on learning, one afternoon that we were due at the Brays' place for dinner that evening and in preparation, practised the Reverend Foote's grace.

There were other missionaries there for dinner as well and it all started off pretty well with everybody quietly seated at the table in anticipation. My anxiety turned into full-blown terror and I would have done anything to have someone else say the grace, but already versed in basic Methodist protocol, I slowly began this brief yet critical speech.

Mindful that this was very much a first impression of us, I began thus - *"For what we are about to receive"* - then came the mental block — I couldn't think of the next part to complete the grace. About half a minute went by in complete silence. You could have heard a pin drop. It seemed like half an hour until I was able to regain my composure by coughing as though something was caught in my throat and blurting out *"For God's sake. Amen."* God all bloody mighty, I thought - I've murdered grace.

Foreground - Church left, Shop right, background - gardens and school, Yirrkala, 1968.

As Lay missionaries, Rose's job was general office duties and mine was to assist in general maintenance at the workshop. Under the Welfare system, the mission was largely self-sufficient. Items that couldn't be produced locally were imported via Perkins' barge, the Arafura, based in Darwin, and the Warawi from Cairns and Brisbane.

It was at the Administration office, that Superintendant, Wally Fawell, first shook my hand. His thumb was missing – torn off by a lawn mower, he explained later- I was alarmed when I felt a horn-like stump - like something stabbing into the palm of my hand. It triggered a violent reaction, my suddenly pulling my hand away, flicking it as if something was embedded in my right hand.

Rose worked with Yinyindjurr who introduced the mission system to her. She taught Rose how to read and report on the weather.

Rose taught her typing and office procedures. The MOM chairman Gordon Symons would have lunch with us on his regular visits. We thought that he was relaxed in our company and perhaps saw us as a breath of fresh air, in contrast to other stodgy missionaries. Gordon laughed at my jokes and we got on well.

MOM missionaries were only paid a sort of pocket money and in our case, all our needs were catered for, that is food, rent and payment on the loan on the Land Rover. As new recruits, we would have limited contact with the Yolngu until our mandatory two weeks crash course in Gupapuyngu language was successfully completed.

The regional MOM linguist was Beulah Lowe who visited all Arnhem Land missions and our resident linguist was Joyce Ross. Joyce conducted ongoing language lessons for missionaries from beginners to the more advanced. I personally welcomed the challenge, quickly mastering the basic sound system enough to communicate in a basic way and even have the odd juvenile joke. I continued to practice my Gupapuygnu at every opportunity at work and on weekends. Language ability among the missionaries varied widely however and most made only limited attempts to speak or write Yolngu matha. I remember a sign roughly painted on the top of the mudguards of the Hygiene tractor reading "Yakka nina duwala" meaning "don't sit here."

It wasn't long after we arrived that we had a surprise visit by a small group of Yolngu musicians led by Djamputjawa. They had come to play a series of folk songs as a welcoming gesture. They played Bilma (clap-sticks) and Yidaki (drone-pipe); I still have the original recordings. We heard later that these musicians had toured China.

Work at the Mission

My job at the workshop and around the mission was varied and interesting. Malcolm Bray, the manager, was a short, intense, softly-spoken fundamental Methodist and long-term lay missionary at Yirrkala. Malcolm was firm but fair and ran a tight ship. Then there was Dan Aubrey, also a fairly serious Christian with whom I'd go spear-fishing, just out from Wilama beach. There was Witjiwitji, Marritngu and new recruit, Djinyini, who later became a church minister and community leader, all of whom I was to meet again over 40 years later.

I was part of the weekly roster of basic maintenance of the newly installed electric generator, powered by a Ruston Hornsby single-cylinder diesel engine. The engine had recently been relocated to Yirrkala from its original location, on a Murray River pumping station. I remember a specialist coming from England to assemble and install it to running condition. My roster involved the 6 am start and 10 pm shutdown. The massive flywheel was recessed into the floor and rose about two and a half metres above the floor level. It was about five metres in diameter and had to be rotated by hand, into the position just below top dead centre, using a long steel bar that fitted into holes around the outside of the flywheel.

Once in the correct position, you'd turn on the air from the air compressor tank to turn over the engine and it would fire up. The engine ran all day at very low revs and it was a peaceful sound, not unlike a grandfather clock, but a bit louder.

I also did repairs to equipment, welding gates, checking the water pump down at the creek, and other things that a rural maintenance fitter does. We soon became friends with the Yolngu whom we worked with, and their families, and went hunting with them in the Land Rover, on the weekend. I would sing Yolngu folk songs like Lurd'pur (sulphur-crested cockatoo) and engage in silly antics with Witji and Marritngu as we worked on a trailer or the hygiene tractor at the well-equipped workshop.

There were only two vehicles on the mission at the time and there was a lot of excitement when our Land Rover was unloaded off the barge from Darwin. One of the teachers, Ron Argoon, picked it up from the barge landing at Melville Bay and was most impressed with it. The missionaries and teachers generally didn't have their own transport. Without the Land Rover, we wouldn't have been able to enjoy the weekend trips as far afield as Caledon Bay and Blue Mud Bay to the southeast of Cape Arnhem as well as hunting trips and picnics in the adjacent bush, swimming holes, fishing, and getting crabs at low tide in the mangroves along the coast.

The hygene team Yirrkala, 1968.

The administration of the small mission school had recently been transferred across to the Aboriginal Welfare Dept. The school was staffed by a head teacher, Barry Dufall and his wife Jan, Terry Parry, Ron Argoon, Keith and Nita Hicks, and teacher linguist, Joyce Ross.

Other people we got to know were Jack Maggs from Wallaby Beach camp, Ted Egan – the patrol officer and his wife Rae from the prospecting camp and others from the nearby ELDO tracking station which I'll talk about soon.

Community Gardens

There were two gardens - the old established one opposite the school and a more recent extension, carved out of the monsoon rainforest near Wilama Beach. Jonatani's outstanding rapport with the Yolngu agricultural workers made a lasting impression on me and I had great respect for him and his fluent Yolngu matha. Whenever I saw Jonatani and the workers, they were always laughing and joking together. Whenever I was in the garden, a standard joke was that they'd give me a hand sign meaning buku yaytjgurru or funny or ugly face, and I'd return the compliment. I was highly amused at this and other antics. I earned a reputation as the snake man and they would come for me if there was a death adder in the bananas. Death adders often hid under the leaf litter there. I'd go and collect the offending reptile and relocate it out of harm's way.

This monsoon tropical garden was vibrant and productive with pawpaws, bananas, melons, and a full range of seasonal vegetables which were sold in the shop. There was a bit of a problem, however, with working relations.

Turning the Other Cheek

The shop manager would leave notes for Jonatani rather than speaking face to face regarding the delivery of garden produce and other things. One day, Jonatani confronted the manager and let fly with a quick left hook to his jaw. The manager regained his composure, turned the other cheek, and got another whack for his troubles. I was to relay this story to Jonatani's relatives at Matuku in the Southern Lau Islands in Fiji many years later.

Terry Parry

Terry Parry was a school teacher from the Village Green, Calne, in Wiltshire who had hitch-hiked across Europe and Asia. During his travels, Parry had landed himself in jail in Afghanistan, charged with vagrancy, having run out of money.

His mother sent him enough money for his release and ongoing travel to Australia. On his arrival in Darwin, Parry applied to the Welfare Dept for a teaching job. Parry explained that he was short of a quid and they gave him an advanced payment of salary and sent him on his way to Yirrkala. Parry soon thrived in his new environment – well, apart from being hungry a lot of the time.

Rose and I took a liking to this quirky but likable Pommie bloke from Wiltshire and we spent time together. Parry, a survivor, would turn up for a visit right on meal time, and even more often on a weekend. He relished Rose's specialty of coral reef and surface fish baked whole with black bean sauce. On a balmy evening, after dinner, we'd sit on the floor in sarongs, sometimes with others, to listen to the Beatles, Rolling Stones, Dave Van Ronk, and other blues music.

Parry, an accomplished musician, often strummed his guitar and sang songs. One of those songs remained with me.... *"let me take you by the hand and lead you through the streets of London... I'll show you something to make you change your mind."* Parry was to accompany us on many remote bush hunting and fishing trips with the ten-foot dingy tied to the roof of the Land Rover.

Flying Again

One day we decided to have some fun on the airstrip. We'd start from one end and after building up speed, climb up onto the roof via the forward hatch. We'd stand on the roof, knees slightly bent, legs apart, and lean into the wind with arms outstretched. In this way, we simulated flying, for the remaining length of the airstrip.

ELDO Tracking Station

The European Launch Development Organisation (ELDO) tracking station, (now the site of the Garma festival), 25 kms from the mission was established in 1962 for the purpose of tracking the launching of rockets and other things from the Woomera rocket range in SA. There was a full complement of staff – catering, communications, diesel fitters, and a host of other technical people, from Australia and overseas. Doug Cole, a smoker, and drinker introduced us and we got to know some of the staff on a superficial level – enough to get the odd invitation to their movies and have a beer. The mission authorities took a dim view of their staff fraternising at ELDO, as I was to find out. ELDO seemed to have been very well-resourced and Peter and Roy Linnett, both English chefs, put on sophisticated celebratory banquets at every opportunity, even failed launch attempts. They would break out into song... *"On Ilkley Moor Baht tat, on Ilkley Moor baht tat, on.... Ilkley.... Moor.... baht tat."*

Ted Egan seemed to be always there singing his songs to the savage rhythmic beating of a beer carton... *"and there are some bloody good drinkers..... in the northn teratreeee"* and *"poor bugger black fella dis cuntreee guvment work no wages weeee.... oh poor bugga meeeee."*

One evening we were watching a movie-tone news segment. Elgar's Pomp and Circumstance came on and Parry, overcome with emotion, stood to attention and was soon followed by the other British ex-pats. He never lived it down. In hindsight, poor Parry must have been pretty homesick.

Our evenings were sometimes cut short when I was on the generator roster. Sometimes, we'd join some of the mission teachers and ELDO staff like Bob, the electrical technician, and Ranga, the hairy diesel fitter swimming at a water hole on the Giddy River.

On one occasion when I was on the roster, we were half an hour late getting back. The generator ran until 10.30 pm, before I could shut it down for the night on our way in. I was summoned to the office before morning prayers the following day and reminded of my responsibilities. I was also reminded that partaking in alcohol wasn't appropriate. Anyway, we continued to enjoy our visits to the ELDO tracking station at every opportunity.

A Buffalo on the Ridge

Late one Saturday afternoon, Rose and I were on our way home from a visit at ELDO and Ted Egan had asked us to drop his 10-year-old son, Mark back home at the old prospecting camp near the mission. We'd just left ELDO when we spotted a huge buffalo up on a ridge to the left of the track. I had the shotgun and one solid bullet left.

With a well-placed shot, I could drop him, so decided to have a go. Rose stayed in the Land Rover and Mark came with me. We headed up the slope towards the buffalo. I was a bit nervous and it was the biggest one I'd ever seen. He just stood there facing us with his head down. I got within thirty metres and fired the one shot from the left-hand barrel.

The buffalo slumped to the ground, then got up and, hobbling along on three legs, came straight for us – a lot faster than you'd think! I'd got him in the left knee. We turned and ran down the ridge towards the Land Rover. Rose sat watching. With the buffalo almost on top of us, we had no time to open the door to get inside. We swung around the front to the other side of the vehicle and were saved as the great beast collapsed onto the track, as he attempted to turn after us. We were able to get in and drive off. The buffalo hobbled across the road and into the bush.

When we got back home I told the Yolngu about our close encounter, and Witjiwitji and some others came out the following morning and tracked the buffalo down. They instructed me to climb to safety up a nearby tree, while they dispatched it with a headshot. It took two hours to butcher and two trips to bring all the dark red meat back to the shop. With a muster of the Welfare Department cattle occurring only once or twice a year, fresh beef was a bit of a luxury. Buffalo meat sold at the shop for only 50 cents a kilo. We ate mostly seafood, and Rose corned and roasted the local buffalo meat when it was available.

Me with buffalo horns, Yirrkala 1968.

Bush and Beach

Our Land Rover was always in demand on a weekend and we'd often enjoy the company of Yolngu friends out hunting, fishing, and harvesting bush tucker. Women would collect pandanus fronds for processing and weaving baskets and circular floor mats. Picnics and hunting trips were an important part of life at Yirrkala for Yolngu and missionaries alike.

For Yolngu, regular contact with the homeland country was and still remains critical. I had my old 32.20 saddle carbine and double-barreled shotgun which I shared with the Yolngu who demonstrated their expertise in how to stalk kangaroo, buffalo, emu, and bustard. By using the wind and cover of tree trunks and foliage for concealment in the patches of monsoon jungle and out in the open Stringy Bark forest, you got much closer for a more effective shot. Other food included reef fish, mud crabs, huge mangrove oysters, and flying foxes from the mangroves and creeks at low tide.

Rose and Juwandjika collecting pandanus leaves for weaving, 1968.

Spear-fishing

Dan Aubrey and I often went out spear-fishing between Wilama beach and a small off-shore island. There was a 10-metre channel between the island and the beach with huge bommies of brain coral towering up towards the surface.

Yangurryangurr and his friends offload their catch at Wilama beach, 1968.

There were caves around the base of the bommies that provided cover for big coral trout, cod, and other reef fish and it was here that we focused our efforts. Because of the depth, there wasn't much time to muck around at the bottom. We needed three lead weights to get down there in as short a time as possible to see a fish in a cave, spear it and get back to the surface.

Our gear included flippers, mask and snorkel, weight belt, knife and long spear gun with a wooden stock. Dan would take a small surfboard on which he'd carry his fish. I had a length of fencing wire around my waist to hold my fish so that both of my hands were free. The end of the wire was threaded through the fish's heads, leaving the fish to dangle behind as I swam. Despite talk about the need to stay close to each other for safety, we'd often get carried away chasing fish and pretty well always end up some distance away from each other.

One day, I got a fish and on my way up to the surface, I noticed a dark cloud descending over me. I looked up and was terrified to see a huge Manta ray casually passing overhead. It was like an aeroplane with a white underbelly, flying in slow motion through the water. My fears were unfounded and I relaxed when I saw that this majestic ray was not in the least interested in me and continued on its way.

One day, there was a storm brewing and we thought we'd better shelter in a cave on the beach on the island – we were closer to the island at that stage and as the wind picked up, we swam as fast as we could to the beach. When I waded onto the beach, I was perplexed as to how I ended up with only fish heads on the wire around my waist. Dan and I were amazed that a reef shark had taken all my fish leaving only the heads on the wire, without my feeling the slightest tug or anything else.

Yangurryangurr and his friends also went line fishing off Wilama beach and around the island to return with a full load of reef fish in their dugout canoe. During the day, Yolngu could see fish from the shore and would often spear a mullet to cook with mud crabs, mangrove oysters, and flying fox on the coals on the beach. I often felt inadequate because let alone not being able to spear a fish in the surf from the beach, I couldn't even see them, even with Yolngu pointing "there Wawa (brother)there" They could see through the surface reflections, and then calculate the correct angle to launch the spear.

Jonatani introduced me and Parry to spearing fish by wading in knee-deep water along the beach on moonless nights using a Yolngu four-pronged spear and gas lantern. The advantage of this was that there was limited surface reflection. We got mostly mullet. We'd often get a fright on being suddenly poked behind the knee by a Long Tom fish that had been attracted to the lamplight.

As a practical joke, we'd also frighten the life out of each other by suddenly screaming out "shark" or "croc," sending each other floundering for the beach. We often visited Jonatani and Lossa and they said my laughter echoed all the way to their place and it made them happy too.

King Fish

During the Kingfish season, despite being told that they were too big and strong to manage, I went for them. I'd make my way over the little rise through the rainforest at the back of the gardens and down to Wilama. I'd position myself just under the surface and cling to a rock a few metres out from shore and lie in ambush as the big fish would come around the headland on their way west along the coast. I made just two attempts at this and failed on both occasions.

Spearing a kingfish was easy but then all hell would break loose. With the spear firmly embedded in its flesh, the Kingfish would take off, dragging me underwater along the rocky outcrops after it, bending the spear, and causing severe cuts and bruising to my legs and arms on the rocks. One afternoon on the way back home I saw a small Yolngu boy carrying a kingfish on a line across his shoulder with its tail dragging on the ground.

Strange Phenomena

During the dry season, a blanket of fog would descend on the bush and remain until about ten o'clock in the morning. It was most spectacular over billabongs. In the wet season, you could see rain approaching. Grey-black rain clouds appeared on the horizon out to sea and heavy showers, like a big broom, would sweep over the land.

Seasonal coral spawning caused outbreaks of diarrhea at the beach camp. A reddish brown slime would wash up on the beach at high tide – sometimes you could see long ribbons of it coming in on the tide. If it washed up at night everyone at the bush camp got sick and would have to relocate up to the bush camp and stay there for several days until the threat had dispersed.

Caledon Bay

The longest trip that we attempted during our stay at Yirrkala was to Caledon Bay. We actually made the trip twice. Parry came and so did Yungalama (my adopted uncle) and Witjiwitji, ever keen to visit relatives and do some hunting on the way. Apart from our own supplies we also got kangaroo and emu. We also brought some banana suckers for Djiring and his family who lived at Caledon Bay.

There was a hand-built airstrip there. Bapa Sheppy, the Reverend Harold Shepherdson from Galiwinku, Elcho Island, would make regular flights in his home-built aeroplane to deliver supplies such as tea, sugar, and powdered milk, and pick up croc skins to trade. Sheppy also held church services and conducted medical evacuations among other things.

From left - Djiring, Witjiwitji, Parry and Rose with women and children at Caledon Bay, 1969.

Djiring's family lived just back from the beach in a beautiful traditional village. The village consisted of several small houses of bush timber frame, clad with large sheets of soft bark from the nearby Melaleuca trees – the main house being a two-story structure. There was a tree burial not far from the camp with some bones remaining in the fork of the tree. The whole sandy campsite was raked clean every morning.

There was a long grey sandy beach, on which lay a dugout canoe. The sail, attached to a mast, was stored on the roof of one of the houses. The beach terminated at the mouth of a large mangrove-lined estuary to the north. It was muddy at low tide.
Djiring was most appreciative of the bananas, we helped with the planting and were invited to stay overnight.

Yungalama at the guest house, Caledon Bay, 1969.

The village was a peaceful and harmonious place, run by the women on a hierarchical basis. We camped in the guest house, and on daybreak, the women could be seen quietly going about their daily chores, preparing breakfast for the children, while others got ready for the days' hunting and food gathering. By the time we had eaten, the older women had gone bush for the day. On the return trip to Yirrkala, Witji managed to spear an agile wallaby with his fishing spear.

Near Caledon Bay, 1969.

During another hunting trip with Witji and Yungalama, we were walking along a narrow pad across the neck of a peninsula single file when Yungalama quietly drew our attention to the clear silhouette of a tall man standing out on the rocks at the point. The person seemed to be peering out to sea as though searching for someone or perhaps a canoe. I asked Yungalama, who that might be, and he said that it was a

Birrimbirr or the spirit of a man recently deceased. He was on his way to his spirit land and we should continue on our way.

Not far from that point, we came across the remains of a small campfire on the side of the track. I asked about it and Yungalama explained that it was a bushman's cooking fire – the bushman, in this context, refers to the Birrimbirr. I assumed that it was the same man. Asked why he thought it was a bushman's fire, he demonstrated that there was no evidence to suggest otherwise due to the undisturbed environment around, including the absence of footprints. Grass and other vegetation showed no disturbance such as broken stalks and so on. I was convinced and we quietly moved on. This was not the first experience I had with spirits and will talk more about them later.

A Rich and Complex Culture

My cross-cultural and spiritual experience was limited and to attempt to describe it is beyond the scope of this book. For readers interested in researching the topic, from a mainstream perspective, founding Methodist missionary, Wilbur Chaseling's 1957 publication YULENGOR - Nomads of Arnhem Land and R.M. and C.H. Berndt's 1964 anthropological work – The World of the First Australians, and more recently, Henry Reynold's publications may serve as starting points for further study. However, I can provide some reflections of my own from our time at Yirrkala.

Public mortuary ceremony, Yirrkala, 1968.

Public mortuary ceremony and dance, Yirrkala, 1968.

Yolngu culture dominated everyday life at Yirrkala. It was profoundly spiritual and informed complex relationship structures, standard protocol, and other aspects of life. It was rich and diverse, encompassing relationships and connections with the natural and spiritual world.

Western and Yolngu cultures including values and views of the world were often in contrast and often clashed.

Europeans, for example, were unable or unwilling to observe simple everyday protocols such as avoidance, which, for example, dictated that a man avoided contact with specific relatives such as his mother-in-law. It was not considered appropriate for women to wear short skirts in public and so on. The Yolngu though, were ever tolerant of the complacency and ignorance of outsiders and I will enlarge on this later.

Most mission staff of the day were invited to public events including aspects of initiation, maintenance, and mortuary ceremonies. For example, the European staff, mostly lay missionaries and teachers, would be ushered into their position as spectators, prior to performances. I felt privileged to have permission from Yolngu organisers to record performances on film and audio tape to review later with participating Yolngu. These recordings and images now reside in the Buku-Larrnggay Mulka Centre at Yirrkala. There was another kind of culture operating in the area at the time, that I feel compelled to mention.

Mortuary parade passes the shop, Yirrkala, 1968.

Galarrwuy Yunipingu leads a cross cultural funeral procession along the beach, Yirrkala, 1968.

Ranga at the Water Hole

On one occasion Parry and I met with some of the ELDO staff for an afternoon at the Giddy River water hole, not far from the ELDO tracking station. Ranga – after orang-utan, because of his heavy long arms, and excessive curly body hair, was also there with his flagon of fortified wine. His hanging on to a rope with one hand, flagon in the other, and swinging right out into the deep water was truly remarkable.

I'd been to this spot before with Yungalama in very different circumstances - hunting for freshwater crocs. Yungalama stood on the high bank, very quiet and still for a while. He was looking for movement in the water weed in the shallows, waiting to spear a crocodile.

Goings on at the Mission

At Yirrkala, there were regular mandatory church rituals and other activities. The little tropical church had an energy of its own that I somehow enjoyed.

One of the Yolngu contributions to this special space was the production of two enormous panels depicting their ancestors, creation, and spiritual beliefs. These panels dominated the front of the church which attracted a strong Yolngu congregation. On church days, missionaries were in their Sunday best, me included, with long white socks and shoes. I remember sweating my way through Sunday mornings in the wet season. They sang hymns in Yolngu Matha in beautiful harmony from a Yolngu hymn book, translated by the MOM linguist, Beulah Lowe. It was mandatory to participate in the weekly bible study and fellowship nights held at the respective rostered missionary's house. If it was your turn you had to bake cakes or biscuits and make the tea.

Then there were morning prayers. I lived in fear of being called upon to perform, and then, inevitably the day came. I was to prepare the night before, to lead morning prayers at the church before going to work. It was an anxious time and I got little sleep the night before. I had made notes about what I'd say and the bible reading for the day. I got myself down to the church early for a dry run, and the rest of the missionaries eventually arrived.

I said something about welcoming them to morning prayers today and lead a prayer about someone who was sick in Darwin, and a couple of other things, and did the reading from the bible. It all seemed to have gone reasonably well and there was no feedback. I was quite proud of myself and almost looked forward to my next roster but it never came and I was never asked to lead morning prayers again. Rose and I had a lot of spare time outside mission responsibilities.

On one occasion Parry caught a catfish in a creek and impaled his finger on a venomous spine. He was in agony for hours and eventually lost part of the finger as it rotted away before he got treatment. Another snippet that springs to mind is the huge groper caught by an Eastern European man that worked for the Nabalco mining company. He had played the fish along the beach at Rocky Bay with a heavy hand line for over an hour until it gave up the fight and he was able to beach it. We heard about it and I went down to take a picture.

By the time we got there, he had strung it up on the branch of a tree and he posed next to it. This fish was longer than him. Incidentally, some years later when we were at Lajamanu, we heard that this same man had been involved in the theft of a skull from an Aboriginal burial site in a cave at Pigeonhole or Walangeri on the Wickham River just west of Victoria River Downs cattle station, some 400 kilometres southwest of Katherine. I was keen to get a crocodile.

Aunty's Cat

There were crocs everywhere, and, for the experience, I was keen to get one to skin and taste the meat. So I approached Witji to see if he could give me some guidance. His instructions were to get hold of a large shark hook, a short length of heavy chain, and some steel cable and leave the rest to him to organise.

I asked him about bait, suggesting that we go out and get a wallaby and he said that he could get a cat which was better. So on the following weekend, we headed down to Rocky Creek just upstream from the mouth, equipped with the heavy-duty tackle. Witji brought the cat, explaining that it had to be prepared for bait. He got the black cat out of the bag, and grabbed its hind legs. Witji explained that it's best live but in these circumstances, too hard to thread onto the hook. He deftly swung the cat, dashing it against a tree. It was a humane and painless operation. On my inquiry as to where this cat had come from, Witji explained that it was one of his Aunty's spare ones. We threaded it on the hook, threw the tackle into the creek, secured it to a mangrove tree, and went back home. We returned the following morning only to find that we were too late. A croc had already taken the juicy morsel and it wasn't until the drive out of Arnhem land a year later that I eventually did get a croc which I'll talk about later. Let me now share a story about a surprise visit from Rolf Harris.

Ted Egan was a mate of Rolf Harris and somehow persuaded Rolf to do some concerts through Arnhem Land. Rolf turned up at Yirrkala. He did his famous Jake the Peg song and dance act one night from the back of a truck trailer. Everyone from ELDO and Wallaby Beach camp was invited to the show. Parry's primary class performed the supporting act. Parry was embarrassed because it went on a bit too long. Rolf Harris was well out of his depth in this environment. Without an introduction, Jake the Peg emerged on stage with a long coat and three legs and launched straight into the act. There was absolute mayhem. While some of the older kids were laughing, others, terrified, ran for their lives.

It was at this time that the Gove land rights case exposed what should have been recognised as criminal behaviour on the part of the government and Nabalco mining corporation.

Banjayi watches for mullet at the mouth of Rocky Creek, Yirrkala, 1968.

The Gove Land-rights Case

We knew nothing about land rights until we met Melbourne Barrister, John Little, who was to act as Junior Council for the Yolngu in the Gove Land-Rights Case – Milirrpum and Others Versus Nabalco Pty Ltd and the Commonwealth of Australia. Without consultation with the Yolngu, the Commonwealth granted a bauxite lease to Pechiney in 1963 and in 1968 Nabalco started prospecting in the area around Yirrkala.

So far as the MOM was concerned, John Little wasn't welcome at Yirrkala. Mission staff refused to provide either accommodation or the use of a vehicle. That was when Roy Dadaynga Marika brought him over and introduced him to us. Rose and I immediately offered any resources we had that would be of use, including accommodation, meals, airport drop off and pick up, and use of the Land Rover. John made several visits to the mission from his base in Melbourne, stayed with us and we would take the Yolngu Elders out in the Land Rover, to their traditional homelands, and sacred places which John would document as evidence of their ownership of and ongoing connection to their land.

On one of these places, stood an ancient Banyan tree, in the bush at Melville Bay, the proposed site for the development of a huge harbour facility about 25 miles from the mission. The company cleared the area around the tree with their bulldozers and graders, leaving the tree standing in the middle of the now dusty, desolation prepared for later mining infrastructure. Mungurrawuy and the others viewed this as being disrespectful of a sacred site and objected and the company built a fence around the tree. We heard later that the tree died - probably from being smothered by the red dust.

I arranged with John and Roy Dadaynga, for me to help with correspondence to and from John's Melbourne office. Dadaynga and I would attempt to answer any queries from John and forward them to him. One day, the mission Superintendent called me into the office and told me that our letters should go through the mission office before being forwarded on. I felt that the mission was not supporting the Yolngu and had no right to scrutinise or censor their private communications. We didn't trust them. Our letters went directly into the mailbag and onto the plane.

It wasn't long before the MOM chairman Gordon Symons made another routine visit and as usual, stayed with us for lunch before his afternoon flight back to Darwin. Gordon advised that Rose and I were to be transferred to Croker Island. We didn't want to leave Yirrkala. We wanted to stay and support John and Dadaynga. We were left with no choice but to resign. Nobody said anything apart from a wisecrack from the Superintendent about Rose and I being 'tourists,' with the implication that we were not committed missionaries at all.

We came to understand that we were over our depth and that there was nothing else that we could have done for the Yolngu and their country. We kept in touch with John for the following year or so. Disillusioned and appalled at the injustice that the Yolngu were facing, John wrote of overwhelming corruption and greed on the part of the Government and Mining company. John eventually left to take up legal work in China and we never heard from him again. Isolated and without support the Yolngu lost their case. We visited Yirrkala 35 years on, and I'll talk more about this later.

Out of Arnhem Land

Parry left at the end of the second term in 1969 on his way to Papunya to take up a school principal's position. Rose and I began preparations to drive out of Arnhem Land and for me to begin full-time study in teacher training. We agreed that nursing and teaching were good professions because of the holidays and you could get a job anywhere.

Jack, Rose, and friend, on the track south of ELDO, 1969.

We had already met Jack Maggs, a diesel mechanic from the Wallaby Beach prospecting camp. Jack was from Wangaratta in Victoria. He was quietly spoken with a droll sense of humour and we enjoyed his company.

Along the edge of the escarpment - central east Arnhem Land, 1969.

A camp on the Goyder River, eastern Arnhem Land, 1969.

Sometime before we left, Jack was planning a trip out to pick up a Land Rover and we asked him to bring back a 10-foot dingy and 3-horse power outboard for our trip out, which he did. He brought the dingy back on the roof of his soft top short wheel base series 2. Jack was to leave as well so we teamed up for the trip.

The first leg of the trip took us south from Yirrkala mission through central east Arnhem Land. Government Water Resources people drove through once a year and there was a defined track through to Roper Bar from Minoru Station and Bulman prospecting camp. We carried extra petrol and shared all our gear.

An ancient stand of cycads near Minoru Station, south eastern Arnhem Land, 1969.

Roper River, 1969.

One of Jacks' work mates from Wallaby Beach got wind of the trip and at the eleventh hour, Jack asked if we'd mind if he tagged along. Our guest, about our age, had an enormous nose and was from Switzerland and seemed OK so we welcomed him aboard.

We'd planned thoroughly, had plenty of supplies and the beginning of the trip went well. We had assumed that Hans would be prepared with his own provisions but he wasn't. By the time we reached the Goyder River crossing, a couple of days into the trip, we were down to three eggs and seriously depleted in other areas as well. Jack had his own provisions.

On reaching the Goyder, we loaded our gear into the boat – swags, tarp, rifle, food and fishing gear, and it was approaching dusk by the time we found a good campsite, about a kilometre downstream. We set up camp and decided to finish off the last of the eggs for dinner. We didn't have a spare egg for Hans and he became indignant and lectured us about the importance of sharing. Hans offered no financial contribution to fuel costs, did nothing, and expected to be waited on hand and foot, and it was this egg episode that broke the camels' back, causing a rift between him and the rest of us.

Roper Bar River crossing, 1969.

Rose with her skinny-fish, Cox River, 1969.

To our relief, Hans announced that he wouldn't be accompanying us across to Cairns and we were more than happy to take him to Katherine to drop him off. We made Ngukurr (Roper River) by nightfall the following day. We camped at Roper Bar on the riverbed. We awoke in the morning to find that even at ninety kilometres from the mouth, the river had risen to above the axles of the Land Rovers during the high tide overnight, and we lost a few loose items that floated away.

We had replenished our supplies in Katherine for the rest of the trip back to Ngukurr, through St Vidgeons Station, and across the gulf country to the Tablelands and Cairns. We were relieved to be rid of Hans, but we should have made it clear from the outset that he had to provide food for himself.

We camped near the crossing on the Cox River on St Vidgeon's Station about 50 kilometres from the mouth. The Cox River flowed into the south western corner of the Gulf. The river was shallow and wide, with blue-grey brackish water which rose and fell with the tide. We always used a lure and there was plenty of fish. Rose got a big skinny fish from the boat almost immediately.

We also decided to try for a croc – the skins were quite valuable. Jack shot a wallaby for bait and we rowed across the river to tie the tackle to the trunk of a big melaleuca tree, hanging over the milky water.

That night Jack was bitten. He preferred to sleep on the ground and something got him on the neck. He was in a lot of pain and woke us up. We thought it was a scorpion or spider bite and we were very worried. In the absence of any painkillers, Rose washed the bite area with some perfume, because it had an alcohol base, which gave him some relief from the pain, and we were awake for the rest of the night.

By morning he was OK and we went to check on the bait. We got to the other side and sure enough, there was a big croc mouthing the bait on the hook. I got a close-range headshot from the boat and the croc slowly sank out of sight. With an oar from the boat, we managed to lever the head of the croc to the surface and wrapped some chain around it, tie a rope around the snout, and secure the chain to a tree on the bank.

A Ringer's camp at St. Vidgeons Station, 1969.

Cox River crossing, 1969.

Me with crocodile, Cox River, 1969.

I waited on the bank, while Jack went and got his Land Rover to tow the croc up ready to skin. We towed the croc up the bank and I was poking around, trying to find where the bullet had entered. Then I got an awful shock. I'd only stunned it and it began to thrash and roll around, dislodging the rope around the snout. I had just gotten out of its reach in time. Another shot killed the croc, and then we spent most of the day skinning, preparing, and salting the skin to sell in Cairns. We broke camp the following morning and headed east across the Gulf country. We were still on St Vidgeon's when we hit deep yellow bull dust. At one point, Jack's Land Rover was almost entirely engulfed in the billowing clouds of powdery dust as he drove through with only the roof and part of the windscreen visible.

Jack in the bull dust, St. Vidgeons, 1969.

Reflections

Memories of recent experiences, and First Nations Yolngu people we had the privilege to know, dominated my thoughts as we drove east across the Gulf country. How were the Yolngu going to come to terms with the betrayal of the church and the injustice they faced - the stealth and violent destruction of their country, and their way of life. I wondered how they would cope with the ignorance and racism, drugs and alcohol, and the other ugly and brutish aspects of a mining culture about to be forced on them. During the long drive, I thought about the hunting trips and ceremonies and heard the folk songs around campfires in the cool of the evenings at Yirrkala.

In my mind's eye, I saw Yangurryangurr and his friends at Wilama beach unloading their catch from their dugout canoe. I saw Nalakan in full ceremonial regalia, showing off and standing proud. There was Yungalama and Wulayngpuma. Among Yolngu warrior heroes are Mau, Djiring, Mathaman, Daymbalipu, Narritjin, Wongu, Damputjawa and Wirilma. There were our friends, Witji, Marritngu, Djinyini, Roy Dadaynga, and Yinyindjurr. I was often visited by these thoughts and visions and the frustrations and anger I still feel, and how powerless I was in attempting to change the way things are. I will never forget the Yolngu of North East Arnhem Land and I know that their rich and powerful culture will endure and they will have victory in the end.

Further on Down the Road

For the rest of the trip, the road through to Borroloola, Burketown, Normanton, Croydon, Georgetown and Mt Surprise, was mostly unsealed. We made camp by the side of the road several times along the way, finally reaching the Atherton Tablelands and down the Gillies Range to Cairns. We off-loaded the croc skin to a dealer who offered us a fraction of what we thought the skin would fetch, cut our losses, and divided the $81 between us.

It was late in October 1969 when Jack headed off back to Victoria to join his family. Rose and I got a little flat in Aumuller Street, Cairns, where we made plans for the following year. It turned out that Brisbane was the best option because, to get into Teachers' College, I needed to complete my Senior and that was offered by Kelvin Grove Evening Classes. We got down to Brisbane in early January, in 1970. Rose got a job as a secretary at Stafford Light Leather and we rented a house in Appleby Road Stafford.

Chapter 4
Brisbane - Building Connections

Appleby Road

At 25, my first full-time study was a real challenge and I struggled through the first term. I needed to pass four approved subjects and I chose English, Ancient History, Geography, and Zoology. I enjoyed these subjects and the teachers identified with mature-aged students and were very supportive. For example, there were a lot of hands-on dissections in Zoology, and my work was usually accepted as a model for other students to follow. Perhaps it was partly informed by my early attempts at taxidermy. For Ancient History, I chose to study Ancient Rome. The teacher brought in a silver coin – a hand-struck Roman Denarius from Hadrian's time. It was handed around the class and I found it difficult to come to terms with the fact that I had, for a short time, held this beautiful and ancient coin which long ago was in the pocket of someone's toga, and used the same way that we use money today.

Unlike any past school experience, this teacher had brought the topic to life by presenting the Denarius and letters from Pliny, a governor from Alexandria wanting to know how to deal with the Christians, and that there were just too many to crucify. Hadrian wrote back to say, "Well, you're the governor, keep me posted". Despite the amount of work that I put in, I still only managed passes and failed Ancient History which I had to repeat costing us another year before I qualified for Teachers' College. But there was more to Brisbane than studies, and we made the most of it.

Stafford was a sad lower socio-economic Brisbane suburb, our house was small and unimaginative and in a heavy downpour, the area would flood. I met a couple of preparators at the Queensland Museum through my zoology projects. Tony Hiller, a long-haired London hippy, and his mate, Jim Wertz, a short American with a drawl and a big beard. We'd congregate at Hiller's place in Milton, on a weekend. It was here that I caught up with the psychedelic music of the period – Jethro Tull, Janis Joplin, Jimi Hendrix, Pink Floyd and others.

Wertz and Hiller

Hiller had a big disco ball hanging from the ceiling and they partied well into the night. Wertz was scathing of Aussie culture and one night went down the road to buy some meat pies. The pies ended up smeared on the Genoa lounge, the walls, and the ceiling, and Wertz chased me up the road with a meat pie with sauce.

The morning exposed the extent of the mess. While we were cleaning up Wertz found the missing lens from his glasses under the old Genoa lounge. He wiped the congealed pie fat off it, pressed it back into the frame, and put his glasses back on as though nothing had happened.

Hiller often worked from home and was into reptiles to the extent that one bedroom was full of snakes of various kinds in cages for observation. The stench didn't seem to worry him. Both Hiller and Wertz were preparators or taxidermists by trade. They were employed by the Queensland Museum in Brisbane. Hiller's fridge was stuffed full of road kill and there was even a small bear, that had died at the zoo, waiting to be stuffed and mounted.

Hiller had a Fiat Bambino car. One night, we accompanied Wertz and Hiller up to Mt Glorious for spotlighting in the rainforest. Wertz refused to drink any water, even from the pristine mountain streams, without a purifier capsule. It was interesting, and we also came across an enormous file snake.

Hiller took an interest in my Zoology course – it was very similar to the first-year uni course. I talked him into having a crack at it. He couldn't cope with the coursework and dropped out. We also met Hugh, a second-year medical student at one of Hiller's parties. He'd fried gold top mushrooms on toast, as an experiment, and asked if we'd take him in the Land Rover around the city to see the lights.

Hugh had eaten too many mushrooms and had a bad trip around the city. He got paranoid, convinced that everyone could see him and the police were after him. Hiller and Wertz had befriended a woman - a robust, rustic German wench who told us about how she could extract wooden fence posts, single-handed, by wrapping her massive arms around the post as in a bear hug and wrenching the post out of the ground. She was very dominant with her boyfriend and I think she later married him.

On another occasion, I was showing slides of our experiences in Arnhem Land and a picture of the croc we skinned on the Cox River. Wertz, filled with anger and contempt, attacked me for killing a croc. On the other few visits, I made to the museum, to meet with Wertz and Hiller, Wertz would ridicule me as an ocker wearing thongs and so on. I thought it was all a joke. He was very witty and I enjoyed his sophisticated sense of humour. At first, I thought his behaviour towards me was part of this humour, but it wasn't, and our friendship, if there ever was one, ended. It was 25 years later that by chance we caught up with Wertz and his family in the Daintree on friendlier terms. I'll expand on that later.

Goings on at Appleby Road

As tenants, it was our responsibility to maintain the yard at Appleby Road and I mowed the lawn. There wasn't a tree or shrub or any garden - just a lawn. As a protest, I left a strip between the right-hand side of the house and the fence as a kind of nature strip. The one-metre by ten metre strip of grass grew waist high and the only things that lived in it were cane toads. There was no ambiance at Appleby Road. We only held one party and that went pear-shaped.

Parry had brought a teacher friend, Carol from Papunya in the NT over for the Christmas holidays. The house was tiny with little space for privacy and I could see Carol getting dressed, looking at herself in the mirror, and rehearsing some dance steps. Carol was an impressive woman with long wavy red hair. Once things got underway at the party, she came over and sat on my lap rotating back and forth making me feel awkward and embarrassed. Wertz, Hiller, Vic, Sally, and some others also turned up and someone got drunk and vomited over the front fence.

We lived in a part of Appleby Road that was flood-prone. There was a heavy downpour. Poor Parry had to wade through the muddy floodwaters to get to the front door and back from his Land Rover parked in the drive. The flood, with water over a foot deep flowed through the yard leaving plastic bags and other rubbish caught in the chain mesh fence – nice.

By now, Rose was working for Stafford Light Leather and walked to work. Two old women there gave her a hard time and she didn't stay long. Rather than drive the heavy Land Rover to and from evening classes, I decided to buy a motorbike. It was a little blue 75cc Honda, very reliable and I rode it to evening classes and other places around Brisbane. We enjoyed swimming and camping on the beach.

Thank God for Lifesavers

We were away from the depressing Appleby Road at every opportunity and at weekends went to the Sunshine coast beaches, body surfing. Having come from the freedom of remote northeast Arnhem Land, I was keen to get away from the regimented lifesavers and their rules and would swim and surf away from the flags. One day, a lifesaver came strutting down the beach, waving his arms about, beckoning me to get out, and thrust his finger toward the flags shouting *"get between the flags."* I took offence and shouted from the surf for him to go and get ..... I told him I didn't want to be saved, and that he was a dick head, with a stupid cap. He shouted back about getting the police, and I ignored him and continued surfing. Rose used to get embarrassed when I did these things and pretended that she didn't know me. It wasn't long before we relocated to Fernberg Road, Bardon.

Fernberg Road

We made the shift to a flat on Fernberg Road in Bardon, opposite the Queensland Governor's residence. Rose was working as a secretary for Silovac – a vacuum cleaner distributor and met a sales rep. Ron Glidden and his wife Joan. We also met Sally, their daughter, and her boyfriend, Victor Calthorpe, a Cockney butcher from London. Sally was a voluptuous blond with a quick wit, and Vic was a great entertainer who played on his Cockney accent and took the piss out of our Aussie expressions. We enjoyed their company and spent a lot of time with them. We went to their wedding.

The Governor's place was surrounded by lovely gardens, a high fence of elaborate cast-iron pickets with spearheads on top, and two huge gates with the Queensland State Coat of Arms with "Dieu Et Mon Droit" in the middle.

Fernberg House as it was affectionately known by the tenants was a big old federation house converted into three flats. Rose and I moved into the one-bedroom flat off a hallway at the front. Ross Bonanno, a resident and law student from Innisfail, was out the front when we arrived. We introduced ourselves but Rose and I were a bit perplexed, to see that Ross immediately rushed back inside. He had apparently gone to report to his flatmates that a bushman in a Land Rover had come to live here. *"He's got a Chinese wife, a swag, a knife and a gun with him."* Ross lived in the large five-bedroom flat at the end of the hall. We also met the two French girls, Michelle and Christine, from the flat across the hall.

A Governor's Gardener

I took a job as a governor's gardener across the road while finishing part-time study. Of all the gardeners, I was the most recent arrival and lowest ranking gardener - number ten. I was assigned to a variety of menial tasks, not popular among higher-ranking gardeners. I started raking leaves and lawn clippings and hosing down the Governor's driveway. I was eventually invited to take part in a lawnmowing course.

I soon got bored. During the summer months, I'd get into my togs, hide my towel and clothes down the back behind some bushes and go for a swim in Governor's pool. One of the leading gardeners referred to the pool area as a 'blacks' camp' because that section of the grounds was left as a nature reserve.

I'd carefully ease myself into the water so as not to cause any tell-tale splashing. I would watch for the Governor as he hobbled down towards the pool, chasing a golf ball. I would quickly escape, but not without splashing water on the poolside before he arrived. I often wondered whether or not he'd twigged that something was amiss but nothing was ever said. I continued to enjoy this little diversion from the day's monotony.

I thought that the gardeners were all a bit odd – gnome-like in their routine - especially the English one with the army background. This gardener, a fairly recent arrival, had just bought a tiny square-shaped Honda car and kept it very clean. At smoko time I'd watch, fascinated, as he'd wash his hands very thoroughly and wipe them on a clean little white towel. The fetish extended to folding the towel, corner to corner with military precision, before hanging it on the back of his chair. He then adjusted it so that it was perfectly square. It was said that he was a former mercenary.

I would get through my assigned tasks fairly quickly and often find time to go and visit the Government house laundry man for a chat as he attended to the Governor's clothing and all manner of linen to be washed, starched, ironed, meticulously folded, and sent up to the residence as part of an age-old ritual.

Another ritual that I enjoyed watching, was the chauffeur attending to the two magnificent and immaculate vintage navy blue Bentleys. Once a week, the chauffeur would roll them out of the garage, and go through a rigid maintenance routine including polishing the leather upholstery, mahogany interior woodwork, and the enormous chrome headlamps.

For the end-of-year Christmas celebrations, the Governor made a point of visiting the gardener's shed, with some beer and nibbles and gave us the afternoon off for our annual Gardener's Picnic.

Rose had another job, this time with the Nissan, Datsun distributor for Queensland, Ira Berk. Rose was the private secretary for Ian Selvage, the Managing Director and she enjoyed the work. It was a short bus trip away to Wharf Street in Brisbane.

Michelle and Christine

Meanwhile, across the road at Fernberg House, life seemed to revolve around individual study, parties, banquets, practical jokes, camping and body-surfing at Caloundra. We saw more of Christine and Michelle. Our flat was adorned with the beautiful roses, that I would discretely collect, on my way home from work.

Michelle and Christine seemed to spend more time at our flat than in their own. Christine was a reserved sort of person whereas Michelle was a party animal – a robust woman with a thick French accent, who liked to chase me, out of the flat and onto the street, threatening to grab me - I was never sure where, and wasn't taking any chances.

I had the advantage of speed on foot, thank goodness. In one of these episodes, she caught me off guard and I had to jump over a big stone fence next door and was severely lacerated by the rose thorns in the garden. On another occasion, I was laying on my back on the bed and Michelle jumped on my legs, bending my right knee back beyond its natural position causing long-term recurring pain and discomfort. However, the two girls were a lot of fun and Michelle became a lifelong friend, who I will be talking about more, later on.

Moving in at the end of the Hall

The students in the big five bedroom flat at the end of the hall were John Evans, Mario Barbagallo, and Sam Calabro, all doing their 3rd-year pharmacy. And there was Ross Bonanno (Rosco), who was finishing his law articles, and lastly, Kirk Smith, or Smithy, who was in his first year of Vet Science.

On Sam's departure, Rose and I moved into the big flat at the end of the hall. The common living area was huge and lined with wood panelling with a mantle shelf all the way around which was rapidly filling up with Evan's beer can collection. Someone stood on one of the old wooden chairs which had weak joints, causing it to collapse. This chair was sprayed mat-black, and hung from a corner of the ceiling, as a feature. The small kitchen was separated from the living room by a bench. There was a wide set of windows in the living room with a view overlooking the Brisbane CBD. At night, with the spectacle of the city lights, Fernberg House could have been an up-market restaurant.

Rose organised a cleaning roster, which was established soon after our arrival, and generally, most people were responsible, and cleaned up on time, usually on a Saturday morning. There was the occasional slip-up though, and when this happened, especially in the hot weather, the bin in the kitchen became a seething mass of maggots.

We awoke one balmy morning to find that the maggots had spilled over the edge of the bin and were fanning out in every direction across the floor.

It was cold in winter and we used the oven to heat up the flat until the landlord found out and threatened not to pay the electricity bill. Cooking was an individual arrangement except for banquets when everyone would prepare a separate dish. A banquet involved shifting the large tables and chairs from the other flats, joining them up with ours, to form one long table, and using bed sheets as tablecloths.

Rosco

Rosco had prepared Italian pasta in a huge pot and stored it in the oven. There was a lot of food that night, and the pasta was overlooked. A couple of weeks after that event, someone noticed a vile smell in the kitchen. The now grey-green pasta was found and thrown out. Rosco felt dejected and went into a huff, then after a while, emerged from his room, fully recovered, and back to his usual old self. Rosco was, by nature, a sensitive and vulnerable person.

For instance, on one occasion, after a lot of heavy rain, there was a leak in his bedroom ceiling. The water-logged particle board ceiling had collapsed almost on top of him as he slept. On another occasion, he was polishing his up-market shoes in preparation to meet a new girlfriend. He had carefully placed them on the concrete around the back, to dry, when Evans had a brainwave. We were to hide the shoes on the roof of Evans' car. It went pear-shaped when Evans, forgetting that the shoes were on his roof, drove off up the road. Rosco was in despair. One shoe had remained on the roof and the other flew off 50 metres up the road. Rosco sported a droll sense of humour and a way with words.

For example, one day, I was introducing my sister Elaine to the group. Elaine was on holiday from Victoria. Ross came out with *"ABCDElaine"*. Something similar happened with our friend Parry, when he arrived, on school holidays, from the Northern Territory. Rosco came out with *"good to meet you, Hairy Merry Wary Terry Parry."*

The Rolling Stones

One afternoon in 1971, we could hear the Rolling Stones and it turned out there was a concert at the Milton oval. The sound blasted clear across the city and we opened the windows to the sound of the 60s classics – Honkey Tonk Woman, Ruby Tuesday, Little Red Rooster, Carol, Paint it Black, It's only Rock and Roll and others. In some ways, it was better than actually buying a ticket and being there. The concert cast an unusual atmosphere over a conservative Brisbane that night. I thought that the whole city should have been jumping to the Stones' rhythm and blues. Smith had a lovely little Ford Anglia.

The Demise of Kirwin

Smith had acquired a 1960 blue Ford Anglia. He named it Kirwin. Smith parked his little car on the roadside at the front of the flats. It was lovingly cared for by Smith, and he was very proud of it. Unfortunately, one night, a taxi managed to run head-on into it and wrote it off.

Smith was so upset that we organised a funeral ceremony for Kirwin. Everyone decided to dress up and I wore my black cassock. It was decided that I should take the role of facilitator, in a remarkably well-executed ceremony, which took place at the front of the flats. Smith found closure and made a full recovery from his grief and loss.

A memorial ceremony for Kirwin, Fernberg House, 1971.
From left, Smith Rosco, Bronwin, me and Rose.

Richard and Jill, Maxine and Shane, and Peter Marsh

Maxine and Shane, and Richard and Jill, often turned up at the parties and banquets at Fernberg House. Maxine, Rose's cousin, was going out with Shane Kelly who was working with Richard See. Jill was Richard's partner. We used to play a regular game of squash together. Richard and Jill often accompanied us on other Fernberg outings with Rosco, Smithy, Mario, and his girlfriend, Carmel, and Evans, to Breakfast Creek Hotel for an enormous steak meal and red wine. Then we'd continue on to camp overnight at Caloundra on the beach.

Maxine was impressed by Peter Marsh, my old childhood friend. On one occasion, Peter made a visit from Melbourne in his Red MGB.

I remember one afternoon, on Fernberg Road out the front of the flats, Peter, with a full audience assembled, performed the perfect doughnut, simultaneously sporting a cheeky grin and a wink. During his stay, he told us about his experience with the traffic police when he had his 1950s Bentley. The police pulled him over for speeding. Asking the reason for exceeding the speed limit, Peter explained that he had a bowel problem and they let him go without further delay.

From Fernberg Road to Indooroopilly

Early in 1972, Tom Gough, a friend of Rose's brother Jeff, was selling his Honda 175 and I was upgrading from my little blue Honda 75. Jim Varghese, a divinity student from UQ responded to my advert, and at the time, he was looking for a couple of people to house share with him and his brother Matt at Indooroopilly. Their parents, academics at UQ were on sabbatical leave for 1972. The house that Jim and Matt had rented at 39 Goldieslie Road was ideal, being closer to Rose's workplace, and closer to the Mt Gravatt Teachers College, where I was to start my Grad. Dip. in Teaching.

Jim Varghese

So, by June 1972 Rose and I were house-sharing with Jim and Matt in Indooroopilly. Matt was a young, quiet and reserved pathology student in contrast to his brother Jim, who was competitive, ambitious, and highly articulate. At the time, Jim was busy campaigning against Wayne Swan and David Russell for President of the U.Q. on-campus Community Action Team – CAT. Rose and I were happy to help paint his campaign banner – VARGHESE FOR PRESIDENT – CAT 1972.

I found Jim highly entertaining. He used me as a sort of punching bag for his winning of arguments, or what he referred to, as verbal gymnastics. For Jim, it was about winners and losers. I was happy to be the loser and I was always impressed by Jim's rhetorical talents, meaningless as the content may have been. We agreed that I should have access to debriefing. Jim had a big blue teddy bear, which served as a scapegoat on whom I could take my revenge by hitting it, which I did.

There seemed to be a good cultural mix operating at Goldieslie Road, especially of a culinary nature. One of the dishes Rose would prepare was whole fish baked in black bean sauce. Others were roasts, stir fry, and rice. Jim and Matt's mother had left them some Indian curry recipes. One evening when Rose was working, Jim and Matt made a hot curry - so hot that it left us all gasping for air and came close to burning out our sphincters. We later found out that the spice ingredients should have been halved.

Jim and Matt listened to our stories of adventures with the Yolngu in remote North East Arnhem Land and viewed slide shows of our exotic lifestyle. There were pictures and recorded music of public ceremonies and hunting in the Land Rover. Jim came to refer to me as the 'Great White Hunter.' We had similar tastes in music.

I admired Jim's musical talent as he would play the guitar and sing Cat Stevens songs. Jim enjoyed our Dave Van Ronk and Jethro Tull music. Other student friends, Ted Chicoteau, and Dale Martin often visited. Ted was a sensitive soul, midway through his thesis on Alienation. On one of his visits, Ted walked in and proclaimed, *"You're all mad."* Practical jokes, too, were part of the scene.

Inspector Richard Head (me) from Queensland Special Branch rang Ted regarding their investigation into his involvement in subversive student activities on campus at UQ and wished to interview him. Head, arranged to meet Ted that afternoon and agreed to meet with him halfway down Batty St. where Ted lived, so as to avoid embarrassment to his parents. Ted blabbed on the phone that it was Jim Varghese who was driving the campaign and that they should be talking to him about it. On another occasion, a booby trap was elaborately set for Dale Martin. The trap involved a bucket of porridge suspended from a tree in the backyard.

Anne and Errol Klibbe

I met Errol Klibbe at Mt Gravatt Teachers College - we were doing the same unit. The thing I liked about Errol was his dead-pan face, droll sense of humour, and his appreciation for John Cleese and Monty Python. Anne and Errol invited us for fondue at their place. Errol's wife, Anne was quirky. After graduation, Errol went to Wynnum High and I went to Richlands. By the start of the 1974 school year, Rose and I were back in the NT.

Chapter 5
A Return to the Northern Territory

As a potential new recruit with the Commonwealth Teaching Service, I expressed my concern about my abandonment of the contractual arrangement with the Queensland Education Department, or "bond" as it was referred to. They said that they didn't know about those things, and I became a permanent employee of the Commonwealth Dept. Education.

It was early January in 1974, the year of the big floods when we drove up the Queensland coast, on our way to my first teaching job at Hooker Creek. We stayed with our old friends, Jim and Nora Hull in Townsville and found out that the road was cut west of Charters Towers. After picking up some supplies, we put the Land Rover on the train. We were able to camp on the train, having the entire flat-car to ourselves - the Land Rover for protection against the weather and to sleep in. The lavatory was discretely over the side of the flat car, as the train lurched and rumbled over the western plains.

Rose and I had travelled through this way in the old short wheel-based Land Rover to Alice Springs back in 1967 but weren't expecting this. Most of the way to Mt. Isa, through Hughenden, Richmond, Julia Creek, and Camooweal, was usually the rough, hot, dusty, black soil of the Mitchell grass plains. Now it was transformed into a brown inland sea, all the way to the horizon, in all directions, with only an exposed strip of railway track, a few inches above the water, stretching away to the west.

In Mt Isa, we overnighted with Michelle, who was now married and had come to live there from Fernberg Road in Brisbane with her husband, Anton. We picked up extra fuel and enough supplies to carry on across the border into the NT.

Driving through Camooweal, we crossed into the NT and the Three Ways, Dunmarra, Top Springs, and Wave Hill, before turning south along the 116-kilometre bush track to Hooker Creek. The track was flooded and we walked the Land Rover through low-lying areas. With bare feet, you could feel where the road was. On approach to the settlement, the first thing that came into view was the high water tank on a stand rising out of the vast Tanami Desert. It was a sight for sore eyes, especially when we weren't sure that we were on the right road. We were relieved to have arrived safely before dark. We were allocated the outgoing cattle manager, Stan Andrew's house, which backed onto the community gardens. We wasted no time getting the house keys and settling in for the night.

Lajamanu (Hooker Creek)

For the purpose of this story, Hooker Creek is referred to as Lajamanu (the Warlpiri name for the area) or simply the "settlement". The new teachers were Jim Mathieson, David and Monica Holt, Anne, Sue Simpson, John and Jedda Hingston, and Ludo Kuipers. David was to take up the principal's role while Monica was the home economics teacher. Anne was the teacher-librarian. Lionel James was my teaching assistant, and as part of a non-teaching role, we developed a Manual Arts facility and program for the post-primary boys, over the first semester. Sue took the middle school, while John and Jedda were responsible for the upper primary group. There were other staff on the settlement including Don and Marlene Holiday in the shop, Jonathan Brown, the administrator, Carl Baume, the agriculturalist, Graham, maintenance and works officer, Tony the incoming cattle manager, and his wife, Joanne, Stan the mechanic, Lother Jagst, the resident linguist and Ivan Jordan, the Baptist missionary, his wife Verle and their two boys, John and Jeffrey.

We had a few days before the start of term. On the following morning, Rose organised the house, and I went with some of the other teachers to see Tiu Kroon, the incumbent preschool teacher. The incoming principal, David, hadn't yet arrived and there were some rumours floating around, about the outgoing principal and his running of the school and his departure, and so on. Jim asked Tiu about it and she gave him a severe reprimand for being a busybody. Things were a bit uncomfortable after that and so I withdrew and waited for the arrival of the principal.

On his arrival, David hit the ground running. He was an excellent operator and worked tirelessly to rebuild the school. The staff were enthusiastic and cooperative and we all got on with our programs, rosters, staff meetings, ordering stationery, sports equipment, and other things, and the term got off to a good start.

I was allocated an old wartime Nissen hut just across the road from the community bakery and kitchen. The long steel structure was ideal for my purposes and I immediately got to work on the design of a Manual Arts facility. I'll describe this project later.

A Remote Government Settlement

The Lajamanu settlement is on a mostly dry creek bed on the northern fringe of the Tanami Desert.

Aerial view of Lajamanu settlement, 1974.

The Aboriginal residents were a traditional Warlpiri population of around 800 people. Like most First Nations groups the Warlpiri have their stories of violent dispossession of land and culture, assimilation, displacement, and forced relocation among other things, along with many health issues and other problems common to colonial countries. The Warlpiri people are the custodians of this Gurindji country. Their homeland was part of the southern Tanami and down to Wirliatjarrayi or in English, Willowra Station, which straddled the Lander River, and which would be handed back to the Warlpiri traditional owners in 1976.

Ludo researched and published two books where Warlpiri people describe their lives and those of their families as like being inmates in military-style concentration camps, having been coerced and forced into a life on the settlement from traditional life in the bush in the early times. They made reference to their lives in the post-WW2 period and, among other things, lived under a regimented military-style control of daily life. Further south, dislocations of the Pintupi and other groups occurred on a massive scale in an attempt to clear people from their homelands, which were located in the Commonwealth Government's designated areas of radioactive contamination that occurred during the Maralinga atomic bomb tests.

Reminders of this period were all around. Outside the front of the corrugated iron-clad administration office, was a flag pole surrounded by large rocks arranged in a circle and painted white. There were other rows and circles of white-painted rocks placed within the administration precinct and may have provided a sense of superiority, structure and order amidst an otherwise fearful confusing and hostile cross-cultural environment, way out in the remote desert of northern Central Australia. The emphasis on the colonial/military-style layout of the settlements of the time reflected earlier government policies of smoothing the pillow of the dying race. When they saw that Aboriginal people were, in fact, actually increasing in population, the policy of assimilation was introduced.

Assimilation was dismantled by the Whitlam regime around the time that we arrived during the early 1970s and was replaced by Self-Determination, though there wasn't much evidence of that. The vegetable gardens, cattle project, slaughter yards and meat house, supplied the kitchen. Ablution blocks, rows of one-room "transition" houses, a medical clinic, a bush airstrip, a fuel dump and a generator with Aboriginal workers managed by white expatriates were all functioning as they had done except for the chook house and piggery which had recently been dismantled.

In hindsight, any casual observer could have been forgiven for thinking that in terms of physical health and well-being, under the assimilation policy, people were all better off. The most obvious thing was that the settlement community was almost self-sufficient and sustainable with fresh vegetables and beef produced locally on-site, and there was no police presence. Pretty well everybody was employed.

There were Aboriginal ringers, cooks, bakers, gardeners, shop assistants, office workers, mechanics, and carpenters - and traditional life went on. We were invited to attend public ceremonies. On a weekend, there was an exodus with everyone out hunting and collecting bush food.

A Dependence on Air Services

During the 1960s and 70s remote communities were dependent on the services of Connair, as mentioned earlier, for travel in and out. The mail came once a week with perishable freight from Alice Springs. It was referred to as the milk run.

Connair DC3 arrives at the air strip, 1974.

Thursday mail and perishable food days, were a social event, with everybody waiting at the admin. office for their mail and perishable food orders. The airstrip wasn't fenced and there was always the risk of cattle or horses getting in the way. One day, the DC3 had a flat tyre on landing, causing it to skew violently from left to right down the airstrip and came safely to rest on the apron. After a short delay, the tyre was repaired and the plane continued on.

On another occasion, one of the workers backed his truck into the rear of the plane, while unloading the perishables leaving a severe dent in the fuselage, under the cargo door. Shortly after, a fence was erected around the fuel dump and apron areas with a sign. The DC3s didn't have pressurised cabins and had to go around any storms during the hot season.

I dreaded going through turbulence and getting airsick. There were other regular air services as well.

The flying doctor used the De Havilland Dove which we had to use a couple of times. Building and maintenance contractors, bureaucrats, politicians, and others flew in and out on private flights.

Administration Office Lajamanu, 1974.

The Admin. office was the hub of the Canberra-based day-to-day running of the settlement.

Our outside communication was the radio phone at the Admin. Office, with daily schedules shared by other onsite departments such as the school, medical clinic, Church, and so on. Jonathan was the Aboriginal Affairs Superintendent in charge of the day-to-day running of the settlement. There was a .303 military rifle on a gun rack on the wall behind his desk and leaning against the wall and behind the door were a collection of confiscated spears, boomerangs, and fighting sticks. Maurice Luther Jupurrula and Jerry Jangala were the administration's Liaison officers and there were three office workers. There were no police stationed at Lajamanu.

Life on the Settlement

For us, having the Land Rover was essential, and apart from a lot of school work, Rose and I were able to get out bush with the Yapa (Warlpiri people) and we learned a lot about hunting for bush food, and other things about this beautiful desert country, stretching south to Supplejack cattle station, on the old route to the Tanami gold fields and beyond.

Administration staff (L-R): Jerry Jangala, Jonathan Brown and Maurice Luther Jupurrula, 1974.

According to Warlpiri protocol, as with most of the staff I was allocated a Warlpiri Skin name. It was Jungarrayi. It automatically followed that Rose, being my wife, became Nangala. The Yapa always referred to me as Jungarrayi and Rose as Nangala. In theory, having been given skin names we could then slot into the Traditional Warlpiri kinship structure. I struggled with complex social rules including those of avoidance and other protocols and made many cultural blunders. The Yapa, like the Yolngu of northeast Arnhem Land, were tolerant of my inadequacies. However, I made a genuine effort to learn the Warlpiri language including regular attendance at Lother's language classes and the Yapa appreciated it.

Barney Jangala instructed the post-primary boys in traditional crafts such as the processes involved in making spear shafts, from the long saplings of a particular wattle called Parap, which grew in a small stand, not far from the seven-mile bore.

As well as being a practising traditional healer, Barney was of high status within the Warlpiri hierarchy. Barney became a close friend over the years and I'll have more to say about this friendship later.

Barney Jangala extracts opalite from an ancient quarry, 1974.

Spinifex Japangarti was born in the desert and during the Second World War, walked from the old Tanami gold fields to Darwin. Neither of these men spoke much English, and I learned a lot of Warlpiri idiosyncrasies on our bush trips. Having the Land Rover also provided the opportunity for us to get the class out to remote locations to teach traditional craft skills.

Parents made toys for their children. In the lower school, kids could be seen playing with tin trucks made from used milk powder tins and fencing wire. A tin was filled with sand, a small hole made in the centre of each end, with a long length of fencing wire threaded through the tin, and twisted up into a loop to form a steering wheel. Girls had coolamons and boys also had toy spears and boomerangs, slingshots, and other play weapons.

Business

It was early in the following year when I was advised that about half of my class were to participate in the first series of initiation ceremonies. As novices, between eleven and fifteen years old, the boys were to be escorted out bush and isolated from their families and the rest of the community. From my understanding, these group initiations were an adaptation to life in settlements. The novices were under the care and guidance of the organisers and owners of the ceremonies. This was the initial phase of the Warlpiri lifelong learning program – a traditional education system. I'll expand on this later.

Baptist Church Mission

Ivan Jordan, the Baptist Pastor, lived with his wife Verle and eight-year-old twin boys John and Jeffrey - their nick-name was Langa Wiri Jarra (two with big ears) and sister, Joy. I loved their old mission house surrounded by shady peppercorn trees. The church was a no-frills affair – an old corrugated iron shed- the bell tower having blown away during a recent storm. Ivan also had big ears, and was a singer-songwriter of some note. Later in 1977 he was to write the theme song for the Lajamanu Rodeo.

Aboriginal Welfare

Jonathan was from Canberra. Part of his role was to oversee the Aboriginal Welfare Department's transition to Self Determination. When we first arrived at Lajamanu, the settlement was largely self-sufficient with pretty much, full employment. The various projects I've already mentioned were all staffed and often run by the Yapa. Teachers usually joined the rest of the community for a cooked lunch in the kitchen. Henry Cook Jakamarra dished up tender, tasty beef stews or steak and mashed potato and fresh veggies all produced locally, and dessert of tinned fruit and custard. Henry ran the bakery as well and the fresh bread was a sheer delight.

There seemed to be no place for a sustainability and self-sufficiency model under Self Determination. By 1980 Assimilation was all but phased out and the community was on welfare payments and dependent on imported and expensive food bought in to the new supermarket. Access to healthy fresh vegetables and other food items was limited to what could be afforded on family welfare budgets and almost overnight you could see the impact on health – particularly where the kids were concerned.

The Works Manager

Back in 1974 most of the old system was still operating and Graham was the works manager. Graham saw himself as a no-nonsense ideas man but nonetheless, a clown, sporting high arching eyebrows, and it seemed that everything he touched, went pear-shaped. For example, there was the Kirkalandji incident, the fire at the fuel dump, the pit toilets, and the mud puddle outside the Admin. office, all of which I'll deal with separately.

The Kirkalandji Incident

It was early in the wet season and the road to the north was already becoming impassable in some of the low-lying places. The shop manager had ordered last-minute supplies from Darwin and the new truck, the Kirkalandji, fully laden with supplies had got as far as the Nineteen Mile and was bogged down to the axles in deep mud. The Kirkalandji, (Warlpiri name for a species of hawk), a white Mercedes, was Don's pride and joy and a good truck to drive. After the driver was picked up, there was a meeting that evening, to determine what should be done, and it was agreed that the truck should be unloaded, dug out of the mud, reloaded, and escorted for the rest of the trip to Lajamanu. Graham had other ideas, and later that night, set off towards the 19 Mile, in the D9 bulldozer, with a heavy steel cable. He arrived early in the morning, hooked up the cable to the front cross member of the Kirkalandji onto the D9, and tore the front end out of the truck.

The Mail Plane has Crashed

One afternoon we were finishing off a bough shelter that served as an outdoor classroom. Barney Jangala and Spinifex Japangarti were there to supervise. It was on a small rise a few miles from the settlement, with views of the surrounding country. It was a mail day and the DC3 had made its approach when the boys drew my attention to a mushroom cloud of black smoke in the direction of the airstrip. It was like an atomic bomb. Horrified, we thought that the mail plane had crashed, so we hurriedly packed up and made our way back to investigate. It turned out that Graham was burning off some long grass in the compound around the fuel dump and shed which housed the generator.

Collecting and sorting the mail when it arrived, was also one of Graham's responsibilities. On hearing the plane making its approach, he dropped what he was doing and went up to the Admin. office to attend to the mail.

The fire near the fuel dump Lajamanu, 1974.

The fire got away and into a huge pile of six-inch black poly pipe, stored in the compound, ready for the pensioner's camp water supply. They were saying later that if it had got into the fuel dump, it could have blown the whole settlement sky high.

Gelignite and Pit Toilets

On another occasion, Graham had just returned from an explosives course in Darwin, and was keen to build a series of pit toilets for the pensioner's camp. In theory, the idea was to blow out the top and bottom of a number of 44-gallon drums, rather than cut out the tops and bottoms by hand. He'd then join four together, to form a steel tube for the pit. The procedure was explained in detail to staff waiting for the mail plane at the Admin. office. The staff were duly instructed not to go down to the creek during the rest of the week because of the risks involved with explosives, but not to worry, it was all part of the process. Towards the end of the week, just out of curiosity, I went down to check on Graham's progress. The area was strewn with bulging 44s that had been split down the seam, with the tops and bottoms still partly intact. Things had gone pear-shaped and the project was shelved.

Where's the Camera

This episode focuses on a red mud puddle, out the front of the Administration block. It was a mail day and Graham was in his element with an audience assembled. It was the storm season late in the year and the depression out the front was full of red muddy water. Graham was on his motorbike, heading straight for the mud, and to the amusement of all, toppled off his bike in a spectacular sort of body roll, into the mire. He was covered in the red ochre-like mud. In jest, Sue asked him if he would do it again if she went home to get her camera. He said he would, he did, and she got a great shot of the event, all over again. Our weekends were generally taken up on hunting trips with the Yapa.

We soon became familiar with places like Jilpirli, the Seven Mile, the Jump up, Nineteen Mile, Catfish, and other places along the Victoria River. Other more distant places were Nangurru Lake and the old Tanami gold diggings and the Tanami rock hole. We also spent time at the old gold diggings at the Granites. We learned much from the Yapa and sometimes shared earth oven-baked goanna, blue tongue, bustard, duck, budgie, and kangaroo as well as seasonal berries, yakatjirri, bush beans, and tomatoes.

We kept bush meat in the freezer along with other frozen food. At one stage we were billeting a student teacher from Sydney. Rose asked her to fetch something from the freezer for dinner that evening. When the student lifted the lid and saw a big perentie, (a large desert goanna) coiled up in the freezer, she let out a scream that could be heard up the road, but soon settled after it was explained that the perentie was for another meal.

Rose and I often went to Jilpirli or Frog Valley, about forty kilometres, south of the settlement on the way to the old Tanami gold fields. It was a desert oasis - a beautiful secluded water hole at the end of a stony creek gorge and we spent hours swimming and exploring the surrounding hills. In the hot weather, sometimes straight after school, we'd drive out to the seven-mile to swim in the bore tank and be home before dark.

Out hunting with Rose, Lionel, and students, 1974.

Occasionally we camped at Catfish, a large waterhole on the Victoria River, about fifty kilometres to the northwest of the settlement. The water hole was deep in places and ran through a narrow gorge with steep shiny black rock walls. I'd swim quietly along and sometimes had to climb up out of the water, to avoid running into freshwater crocs, then get back in again at a safe distance from them. They always stayed in one place as I approached. I never swam there at night. I'll talk about another incident at Catfish later.

The Tanami and the Granites

Gold was discovered at the Granites and the Tanami early last century. Tanami is a Warlpiri water hole, deep in a chasm in the ancient red rocky range of hills a few kilometres west of the old gold diggings.

Water was a problem for the diggers. It was said that the goldfields were abandoned by about 1911. However, they must have been operative much later because some of the Warlpiri men told me about the days within living memory when they would casually turn up out of the desert and get employment on the stamper, which was going day and night. They said that they would stay on for a few days, collect their tobacco, tea, and other forms of payment and continue en route to some planned destination.

Badlands topography, Nineteen Mile, 1974.

At Jilpirli rock hole, 1974.

Old Tanami gold diggings and stamper, 1974.

They also recognised old relics such as tin match boxes, tweezers, spent bullet shells, and other stuff I had collected. By the 1930s a series of wells had been sunk along the road south from Lajamanu, out of fears that people would perish through lack of water, on their 400-kilometre trek through the desert to the Tanami Goldfield. The Granites are also an important site about six hundred kilometres to the northwest of Alice Spring. There are ancient rock carvings and paintings in caves, and on the face of the huge granite tors, set on an escarpment rising out of the desert.

It was during the mid-year holidays one year when Parry came down to visit. We had planned a trip to the Tanami gold diggings, and the Granites, about another 80 kilometres south of Rabbit Flat. Jack and Pat Maggs were on a visit as well. We drove south through Jirlpirli, across the spinifex plains, through Supplejack and finally arrived at Tanami. We explored the mine shafts, slag heap and the stamper, remains of an old steam engine boiler and other ruins, all well preserved in the dry desert climate.

Barney Jangala had given me some directions on how to get to the Tanami rock hole, and we walked over to the hills a couple of kilometres away. We also saw what we thought was a grave at the entrance to the small gorge. It was rectangular and bordered by long narrow slabs of rock set into the ground. We followed the narrow pathway with sheer red rock walls on either side of the gorge until we came to the rock hole, hidden around a corner. The rock hole was full of fresh, clear green water, shaped like a caldron, about four metres wide, deep and dark down below.

Back at the diggings, Parry had a hand winch on the front of his Land Rover, we winched him down to the bottom of a shaft. This derelict shaft was about sixteen metres deep. It was originally reinforced with heavy wooden logs. The whole thing was very unstable and there were echoes as loose rocks tumbled down into the darkness below. Parry was a couple of feet from the bottom when he spotted a brown snake in the torchlight.

We heard his muffled cries for help from the darkness to winch him up quickly. He said that there were a lot of animal skeletons down there, where they had fallen and perished.

Camp at the Granites gold field, 1974.

We camped at the Granites in what looked like the ruins of a fortification set on top of a rise. It was a three bed-roomed house with very thick concrete walls and slab floor. There was a fireplace. There was a cold howling wind that night and we were pleased to be able to have the shelter, put on the billy and drink tea by the fire. At daybreak after a good night's sleep, we had breakfast, broke camp, and drove back to Tanami. We camped the night at the bore and prepared for the long return trip north, back home to Lajamanu. I knew there were dingoes in the desert.

Warnabari

During that same year, I had become friends with Lionel James, a student from Kormilda Teacher's College and my teacher assistant. We'd often go hunting in the Land Rover at the weekend.

I had mentioned in conversation with Lionel that I would like to get a dingo for a companion. During the breeding season that year, Lionel mentioned that he knew of a lair, out on the plains, not far from the seven-mile bore, and that it was likely there would be some pups.

Lionel said he would show me and I jumped at the opportunity. We drove out to the lair which was protected by a small stand of wattle. It was just a small hole in the ground, not half a metre wide and Lionel said there would be a tunnel running off the main shaft about a metre deep.

Using a long stick with a hook on the end, Lionel hooked out the pups one by one. It was late afternoon and the mother wasn't there.

We selected the most robust male from the litter, and carefully put the other pups safely back. The pup's little blue-grey eyes had scarcely opened. Lionel named him Warnabari meaning wild dog. Warnabari was red in colour and already displayed the typical white tips on the tail and the feet, with a darker muzzle. Rose was able to get some milk formula from Alice Springs and the little dingo thrived and grew quickly. Warnabari was highly intelligent, and everyone commented on how well-behaved he was. When he was a bit older, I made a leather pad for the top of the fuel tank of my off-road motorbike. Warnabari would jump up and sit on the tank as I rode around the settlement. More about Warnabari later.

Mums Visits to Lajamanu

Mum made a number of trips to visit. She stayed with us at Lajamanu, Numbulwar in North East Arnhem Land and then Papunya.

She loved the desert. It reminded her of her childhood in the Victorian Mallee. Mum was an accomplished landscape artist and used oil on canvas. She was prolific in her work and we often drove out in the Land Rover for picnics and camp overnight at newly discovered places like Winneckie Creek, Train Hill and Jerry Jangala's camp, to the south, on a rise surrounded by spinifex sand plains. Mum gave Jerry a painting of his family's camp. Her representations of the Tanami landscapes reflected a connection that she held for the country.

We cherish the artworks that she kindly gave to us. Mum got on well with the Yapa and their families and would often sit with the women during the afternoon exchanging stories and jokes over a cup of tea by the fire, in the creek bed. Mum also took up the invitation to join them at an initiation ceremony.

Jerry Jangala's camp south of Lajamanu, 1977.

It was late in 1974 when we took Mum for a drive down to Tanami. It was shortly after some rain and the wildflowers were out. The red sand dunes were ablaze with purple, blue, red, yellow, white and orange flowered shrubs and perennials. I recorded these spectacular landscapes on film. We set up camp at the bore.

During breakfast, we could see a black storm building fast, from the south. The Land Rover canopy was at home and I had a makeshift frame over the back. I used an old discarded sheet of corrugated iron as a cover. The storm was angry and powerful and slowly gaining on us as we headed north.

We got past Supplejack and I was concerned about getting through the black soil plains on the southern approach to the settlement. This storm seemed to be intent on pursuing us like a giant savage black beast, trying to devour us, as we drove north. A wild, thundering deluge came within a few minutes of us getting safely back home.

I got up onto the roof of our house with a camera and tripod. As the storm approached that evening you could see fork lightning striking the ground causing spot fires that merged into broad fronts burning across the spinifex plains.

The storm on arrival back home, 1974.

Mum paints Train Hill, 1974.

Death at the Admin. Office

Barney Jangala had chosen an open area out the front of the Admin. office as a stage for a public confrontation with a man from Yuendumu. Earlier that afternoon, Mum had set up nearby and working on a painting of the Admin. block. Suddenly finding the awkward position she was in, and not knowing what to do, she decided that it was better to stay put.

Ignoring Mum's presence, the two men confronted each other and Barney launched a spear at his opponent as a demonstration of the strongest protest against this man who had committed some past offence. It was commonplace to brandish a weapon at the height of a conflict. It was said that Barney had no intention of taking the man's life. However, a freak gust of wind caught the spear in mid-flight, causing a change in direction sufficient to strike the man front on, penetrating his aorta below the ribs. He died of internal bleeding within minutes.

Barney was detained by police, and spent three months in Darwin, while the authorities struggled with how, or whether or not, to apply State law since Barney would have to face Traditional law. It turned out that they chose to recognise Warlpiri law.

Barney returned to face the consequences, and a ritual was organised by the relatives of the dead man. My understanding was that Barney was duly speared in the thigh. Warlpiri people don't have prisons. With a deep wound to the thigh, you couldn't do much until it healed anyway. It was around this time that I was having mechanical problems with the Land Rover.

Singin' like the Andrews Sisters

The community mechanic, Stan had recently arrived. I was having some difficulty tuning the Land Rover. Our trusty Land Rover was often ridiculed and referred to as a "fartbox". Stan knew otherwise. He was brought up with them in the bush and he was familiar with them. He had great respect for Land Rovers as reliable bush vehicles. Within half an hour of my arriving at his workshop, he did some rudimentary adjustments to the carburettor, put in a new set of spark plugs, and fired it up. *"There"* Stan proclaimed... *"She's singin' like the Andrews Sisters"*. After the tune-up, the Land Rover reached 70 miles per hour on the soft sandy roads.

School

There were about a 130 Warlpiri kids attending the school, which offered preschool, primary and post-primary education. There was a teacher allocated to the English as a first language class, set aside for mainstream families. My main task was to develop a Manual Arts program and facilities up to year ten. The Nissen hut was fit for that purpose. It had an angle iron frame, clad with corrugated iron, and concrete floor. The education department provided basic tools and equipment. I made benches and set up three separate areas where the kids could do graphics, theory, woodwork, plastics, and metalwork. I also fenced off an area for a veggie garden. The building was equipped with evaporative air conditioners, power and water.

For woodwork projects, the boys made toys for the preschool and table tennis bats for themselves. The preschool toys included wooden telephones, aeroplanes and trucks. They also made tucker boxes with leather handles. We restored old furniture and cupboards for the toys. Their metalwork projects included billy-cans, dippers, and dustpans among other things. For graphics, they did introductory work on isometrics, mechanical drawing, and perspective. Plastics included designing and building a moulding machine to make sculptures which they hung on the new School library wall. They made laminated pendants of different coloured acrylic plastics.

Extracurricular activity included excursions to a creek, just south of Wave Hill station, where we dug jasper and agates from the creek bank, made pendants, cut and polished stones to sell so that we could buy more tools and equipment. The money went towards paying for trips. Apart from the conventional curricula we had the freedom to develop community-based programs, for example, the sequential maths and English schemes and the bi-lingual program.

Manual Arts class, Lajamanu, 1974.

Cultural Studies

Cultural programs were developed in consultation with parents and community leaders. For cultural extension of Manual Arts, the class went on excursions and hunting trips to places such as Catfish on the Victoria River, south into the desert for kangaroo, emu, plain turkey, and goannas. We also went to Jirlpirli, to swim. A special place we went to was Nangurru Lake, a large salt lake, only a few inches deep. We were accompanied by elders, Barney Jangala, Spinifex Japangardi, and Henry Cook Jakamarra.

Barney took the class to an ancient quarry to demonstrate how ancestors of the Warlpiri Nation produced stone tools such as knives, scrapers, and spearheads from parent pieces of opalite and jasper. The boys spent time with Barney back at school learning traditional skills of percussion and pressure flaking.

Spinifex Japangardi owned the skills of producing handles, for knives and stone axes, and other hand tools, from a particular species of spinifex, found only in certain locations in the desert.

Barney and helpers at the completed school bough shelter, 1974.

Using a shovel, we dug out tufts of spinifex to form a heap about two metres high. This spinifex had dry sap crystals clinging onto the lower stems. The crystals were dislodged from the stems by beating the spinifex over a sheet of corrugated iron, along with some fibre. There was half a billy-can of the precious powder.

The powder was gently heated over a fire and kneaded with the right amount of fibre which served as reinforcement. When heated, the particles melted into the form of a resin with the pleasant aroma of the spinifex. While still hot, it was kneaded with a blunt stick until it had a smooth, plasticine-like consistency. It was shaped into a ball for storage for later reheated for moulding into handles for knives, scrapers and holding stone axe-heads in place, stone tips on spear shafts, and scrapers for spear throwers.

I was impressed by this technology. Spinifex resin could endure many applications. As the stone tips on tools lost their edge and had to be replaced, the spinifex resin would be reheated and a new stone tip installed. The spinifex resin had thermal memory, a property similar to acrylic plastic. It has been known and used for tens of thousands of years in First Nations Central Australia.

Barney demonstrates preparation of a spear shaft as part of the cultural program, Lajamanu School, 1974.

Barney Jangala instructed students on how to produce spear shafts from Parap, wattle saplings. The process involved among other things, selecting potential spear shafts of the right length, stripping the bark, and heating the shaft over a fire so that it could be straightened, ready for the insertion of hardwood mulga tips.

Purlapa - Public ceremony, Lajamanu, 1974.

Lifelong Learning

An initiation program was developed and facilitated by the elders. Most of my class were involved as novices in isolation.

Traditional learning activity was often held through the night, and I was invited to come out several times during the week and teach some mainstream lessons in reading, writing, and craftwork through the day. For example, the boys made leather handles for their tuckerboxes. The program worked well and gained recognition.

The students were enrolled in the school's Cultural Studies program for the duration of the period under the instruction of the elders out bush. Specific ceremonies marked the return of the initiates. The initiates who had left their families eight months earlier were now greeted as young initiated men, who had acquired a new set of responsibilities to their country, families, and the wider community. They were now eligible for participation in future educational advancement when called on. They were now part of a lifelong education system that spanned thousands of years of Warlpiri tradition. I felt privileged to have been asked to be part of the program. It was around this time that a medical emergency was unfolding.

Nurses are Flown out

During the second half of 1974 an incident occurred at the medical clinic, partly as a result of inadequate communication, between the nursing staff and the community. Some relatives of a sick man arrived at the clinic, armed with spears, and were anxious about the welfare of the patient. Nurses were fearful and interpreted the incident as threatening.

They reported the incident to Darwin and were flown out, leaving the community without services. The community were advised that apart from the regular monthly flying doctor visits, there would be no medical services at Lajamanu until police protection could be provided. To my knowledge, there was no attempt by the authorities to investigate the situation before withdrawing the nurses, and leaving the community in such a vulnerable position. Would a mainstream white community have been callously abandoned like this?

It was during this period that several young children presented with life-threatening conditions requiring medical attention. Rose was the only person in the community who had nurse training. While Rose had six months of nurse education to complete for registration, she found herself having to offer emergency assistance.

Rose radioed through to Darwin and was told that there was no protection for her under the circumstances and that any medical treatment would have to be undertaken at her own risk. Only by good fortune were there no reactions to the treatments. It was six months before police officers were deployed there.

Rose remained the only medical support person until the end of the year when they finally installed two policemen and their families. The department transferred the lock-up from Gove into one of the policemen's backyard as a temporary measure. We were on the move again, this time, back to Cairns for Rose to complete her nursing qualifications. We had full intentions of returning to Lajamanu.

Ceremonies merge with the night. Lajamanu, 1974.

A Brief Return to Far North Queensland

Rose had six months left to complete her nurse education and decided to finish the course through the Cairns Base Hospital. I applied for six months' leave without pay and we packed up and drove to Cairns at the end of the school year. We got a flat at Clifton Beach. Anne and Errol Klibbe were planning to move to Cairns from Toowoomba, Errol having scored a teaching job with TAFE. When they arrived, we decided to share a small house in Sydney Street at Bayview Heights.

Anne and Errol's furniture and other belongings had only just arrived when the real estate agent advised that the owner was selling the house and, regardless of a six-month contract, gave us the notice to leave. I was outraged. We refused to leave, and the ensuing battle between us and the owner went on for three months. I was not working and had time to spend with the Ombudsman, who was sympathetic and actively supportive.

The owner lost sales because we refused to allow prospective buyers onto the property. By the end of the three months, the Ombudsman advised that, according to law, the owner could have us evicted. We then packed up and left for a new place to live in Edmonton.

Edmonton just south of Cairns was a peaceful and pleasant experience. We all got on well and had a lot of visitors over the following few months.

Flying Again

It was during this time that I was to advance my flying experience. Errol and I met Laurie Linnewebber and Howard Newell during one of their hang-gliding sessions at Red Hill.

One day Errol and I, while driving past Red Hill into town, saw Laurie landing in the cane field, just off Mulgrave Road. We went to introduce ourselves and told him that we would like to take up hang gliding. Laurie and his mate Howard were pioneers in hang gliding in the far north. They were experimenting with nose angles greater than 90 degrees, which was the traditional angle for Rogallo hang gliders ever since World War two, when they were used by English commandos in Europe.

Laurie and Howard invited us to come up to the top of Red Hill, to participate in launch preparations. We were keen to start. Errol bought a hang glider on Laurie's advice and I helped Laurie build my hang glider, which had a 92-degree nose angle. Howard stitched the fabric. We added bamboo slats and wheels. After some reading and research on how air behaves close to the ground, and other relevant aspects of flight, our first flight was scheduled for the elevated site of Bromfield Swamp, a flooded, extinct volcanic crater, up on the Tablelands.

Errol was heavier than me, and on his way down from the rim of the crater, his knees suffered as he ricocheted off the fallen trees lying on the ground and was badly bruised. After repeated injuries, Errol chose higher wind gusts for more lift in future launches and we progressed quickly. We were soon ready to launch from the top of Red Hill. Anne was often present during our training and would shout encouragement to us as we were poised to launch - *"Commit yourself! Commit yourself!"*

On an early occasion, almost immediately after a launch, a strong gust of wind lifted my right-wing tip, banking the hang glider and I found myself heading at speed, back into the side of the hill. I remember squealing and wetting my pants in fear before regaining my senses. I managed to thrust the A-frame forward, lifting the nose, only moments before impact into the side of the hill. I received some wire burns to my upper arms on impact and bent the high-tensile steel heart bolt. In between hang gliding, we spent time spearfishing on the reef.

Born Free

When we weren't hang-gliding, on a weekend we'd go up to Port Douglas and head to the outer reefs with Lee Earl on his boat, the Born Free. The boat was an old wooden-hulled ex-fishing vessel. It was slow getting out past Low Isles, to the outer reefs, and it was about a four-hour trip. We often went to Opal Reef to anchor there overnight, and fish in the early morning before returning to the mainland. We chose the days when visibility was at its peak and sometimes you could see forty meters or more which was ideal for spotting any approaching reef sharks and moray eels.

We had all our own gear and we had access to the galley. I was the only one spearfishing. Lee would help with cleaning fish and stand on the bow with his .22 rifle, watching out for sharks while I was in the water. Everyone else did line fishing from the boat. One day I had a crack at a Maori Wrasse. It dived suddenly and kept getting deeper and deeper, taking me along for the ride, until I could no longer stay with it. As a result, I had to cut the cord from the spear gun and lost my spear. We would always return home with enough fish including Coral Trout, Sweetlip, Red Emperor, and Cod, to do us for a couple of weeks.

Rose and me, centre, with friends, 1975.

Mount Peter Road

Back at home, maintenance was pretty limited with occasional lawn mowing around the house with an Allen Oxford motor scythe. Visitors that came to stay were Carol Davies, a teacher friend from the territory, her parents, and Terry Parry.

Rose's brother Jeffrey, Kirk and Bronwin Smith from Charters Towers, also turned up. There was a perpetual party atmosphere, in this old wooden tropical house. Rose and I took Parry to the Trade Winds Restaurant on the corner of Lake and Florence Streets in Cairns, and it was there that he met his future wife Sue from Singapore. She was waitressing at the restaurant.

Charlie, our next-door neighbour, did maintenance and servicing of cane harvesters from his big old corrugated iron shed. Charlie had two sons who slept in their swags in the loft.

Jeffrey was an excellent chef and with Rose, prepared banquets of whole baked reef fish, done with black bean sauce, onion, ginger, and other spices. We had veggies and rice on the side, and wine. In the season, we picked mangoes, lychees, and pawpaws from the backyard.

By late June I was advised by the Department in Darwin that my position at Lajamanu had been filled and would I like to go to Numbulwar. We jumped at the opportunity, given that Numbulwar was a very remote Anglican Mission located on the mouth of the Rose River, on the western coast of the Gulf of Carpentaria. A return to Lajamanu would have to wait.

We decided to approach the owner of the property privately, and asked if the property was for sale. He advised that it was and that he would find out how much it was worth on the market and let us know. Within a very short time, he came back to us with the amount and we clinched the deal privately. It was in mid-November 1988 that we secured the property in Atherton.

It was the best position on the street. Two and a half acres, mowed, with a large rose garden at the front, established orchard, well-drained, with a gradual slope, down to the western boundary, along

Mazlin Creek. Being part of the lava flow from Bones Knob, a shield volcano to the northwest, the block had deep fertile red volcanic soil. The creek formed the boundary of the old lava flow.

Our visions of building a vee-shaped brick house overlooking the remnant strip of rainforest and creek were soon dashed when we saw how expensive it would have been. We looked at other options and it wasn't long before an opportunity emerged. We would relocate a Queensland house from Cairns.

Numbulwar

From Roper River to Policeman's Crossing

We packed up supplies, hang glider, motorbike, dinghy and outboard and headed off across the Gulf country via Ravenshoe, Georgetown, Normanton, Croydon, Doomagee, through St. Vidgeons and on to Roper River. At Ngukurr (on the Roper River) we stocked up on some supplies for the 150km drive north to Numbulwar. There was no road between Ngukurr and Numbulwar. We engaged a local ringer, who was happy to guide us up to Policeman's Crossing. He had relatives in Numbulwar. We spent our first night with the ringers, at their stock camp, about twenty kilometres north of Ngukurr.

The Land Rover was fully laden with all our supplies including all the essentials we needed to start on arrival at Numbulwar. Every night, we had to unload in order to set up camp. Warnabari was with us. The following morning we arrived at a very steep creek crossing and unloaded everything and carried it across to the other bank. I was apprehensive about this crossing, for fear of ending up balancing halfway over the bank.

With the Land Rover unloaded, I eased it down the steep bank in low range, and just before the end of the downhill run, hit the accelerator. I came flying up the opposite bank, engine screaming, and jumped over the crest, to land safely on the other side. We lit a fire and put the billy on, hoping there wouldn't be any more serious challenges over the rest of the trip. We headed off in a northerly direction.

For most of the trip, the only indication of a track was a slight discolouration of tall grass where water resources vehicles had been, before the last wet season. Sometimes there was no indication, leaving it down to guesswork. One day we got completely lost. All we knew was that we were travelling in a roughly northerly direction. We came to a creek and unable to cross it, made camp with a view to using the motorbike the next day, to follow the creek through the bush to find a safe crossing. It was only then that our guide told us that he had been to Numbulwar on horseback, leaving us feeling a bit apprehensive about ever getting there. We had a cup of tea and Rose opened the Lion's Christmas cake box, only to find that the cake was green with mould. The following morning, I followed the creek on the bike, to find somewhere to cross.

It took a couple of hours but I found a place where I thought we could cross – a rocky bed that was safe. We continued on, only to find yet another creek, with soft mud and much wider. I wasn't able to find anywhere to cross. It was only by sheer coincidence that there was a group of men from Numbulwar, making their way south to Roper River, hunting along the way. They saw us from a distance and came to investigate. We asked if they were able to help make a bridge. I had an axe and so we set to work cutting trees and positioning the logs, for a makeshift bridge.

We got across the creek and put the billy on, and shared a cup of tea and a chat with the men before parting company. Further north, was a vast spear grass plain so I decided to head straight for a spot on the treeline that we could see, across the other side of the plain.

Herds of buffalo had moved over the plain during the last wet season, leaving deep wallows and large foot-holes in the soft mud which had dried out. It took a whole day to travel five kilometres over this uneven ground. Reaching the tree line, we camped for the night, next to a billabong. Rose caught a good-sized barramundi in a deep water hole, and Warnabari amused himself with a young resident brolga.

The next couple of days were comparatively uneventful. We had run out of food supplies, apart from a potato, some tea, and some cooked barramundi.

Isherwood's Australia

A makeshift bridge, north of Roper River, 1976.

Traversing spear grass plains, north of Roper River, 1976.

Me with Warnabari and Brolga, north of the Roper River, 1976.

We weren't concerned about starving, because I had my shotgun and there were ducks and fish in the billabongs along the way. The camp we made before reaching Policeman's Crossing was a beautiful place, under a stand of shady Melaleuca trees, on the edge of a billabong. I got the shock of my life when we arrived at Policeman's Crossing.

I couldn't believe that this was a crossing, and walked to the east and the west of the crossing, along the river, to see if there was anywhere better to cross. It was at least fifty metres wide at the crossing, varying from one to three feet in depth, on an uneven, jagged, rocky bed. The water was flowing fast. I waded across with great apprehension, thinking about what might happen if the Land Rover stalled, fully laden, mid-stream.

The tide was running out, the water was brackish, and we didn't know if there were crocs about. Having waded across and back, I had some idea of where to go and how fast we could go. In low range, we headed slowly down into the river. I walked the vehicle across with no mishaps. We were so relieved, having gotten to the other side that we had another cup of tea. There were about fifty kilometres to go along a rough two-wheel track, heading in a northerly direction towards Numbulwar.

For the rest of the trip, we had a clearly defined track. It was mostly open savannah country, dominated by grey magnetic termite mounds, and the odd stand of Darwin stringybark, pandanus and cabbage palm. The country was interspersed with large billabongs. It was a six-day trip by the time we arrived at Numbulwar.

Numbulwar, an Anglican Mission

Having met Colin Gilchrist, the Anglican missionary, the school Principal, and some other staff, we were able to shift into our one-bedroom, prefabricated Worldwide Camp, demountable house. It was a small but comfortable house, with cashew apple trees out the back. We unpacked and spent the day settling in. We spent the following morning around the mission, getting oriented. The whole place was built on sand dunes and everywhere you went, you trudged laboriously through soft sand.

The village on the mouth of the Rose River, Numbulwar Mission, 1976.

The Mission farm was about half a kilometre away. It had good soil, and like other church missions and government settlements at the time, was self-sufficient, apart from staples such as sugar, tea, flour, and tinned food. The school was built at the highest point. There was a medical clinic, shop, church, and office. I was most impressed by the architecture of the high-set wooden mission houses and cottages in the Nunggubuyu village along the banks of the river. The architecture of the Anglican church was interesting too. It was typical of the style of early mission churches built elsewhere in the Pacific.

It was all timber with hopper windows held open by props along both sides, under the shade of the almond trees. The pews were rough-hewn slabs from local timber. The short legs, on either end, were rough slabs of timber, morticed into place. There was a rudimentary altar and a sand floor. It was dark, cool, and inviting inside. There was an air vent on the roof that spun on worn bearings. It made a mournful sound, complementing the atmosphere of the building. Further down the shady pathway, towards the beach, there were large, Leichardt and Almond trees, leading to the health clinic. Similarly, the clinic had a romantic atmosphere like something out of a classic movie. It was dark and cool under the trees.

There was a radio hut and aerial located in the middle of the settlement which housed the communication system. Daily radio schedules were organised for mission staff, school, medical, shop, and farm. A dominant feature of this quaint little place was the abundance of billy-goat flowers, which grew in the sand around the buildings.

Our World Wide Camp demountable, Numbulwar, 1976.

It wasn't possible for us to have a garden because it was all sand, but we were fortunate enough to have the cashew apple trees which provided shade and a delicious treat in the wet season. The fruit ripened into yellowish-pink, with a shiny, waxy skin. The cashew nut was suspended from the bottom. We ate the sweet, juicy fruit and discarded the nut. There was no problem getting greens from the shop which was supplied by the farm. Most of our protein was fish, mainly barramundi from the river.

School

My initial task at the Numbulwar school was to develop a Manual Arts facility, from a disused ablution block. The job included a basic Manual Arts program, including a cultural component using the resources available. The boys were happy to participate and we knocked out the toilet pedestals and urinals and cemented up the holes, got the plumbing reconnected, hand basins installed, removed walls, put in fans, and created learning spaces. The department sent chairs, desks, benches, chalkboards, basic tools and other equipment.

Racing the finished canoes, Numbulwar, 1976.

It was a similar situation to Lajamanu where I had to make my own classroom and set up programs. I was most interested in the cultural program, where parents and elders rallied to teach the class the ancient crafts of building miniature dugout canoes with outriggers and sails. Parents participated in local excursions into the nearby monsoon rainforest, where suitable logs were selected from a stand of milkwood trees. The objective was to build scale models of about a metre and a half in length. When the canoes were finished we had races during low tide in the shallows.

With Mum at the airport, Numbulwar, 1976.

We also made multi-pronged fishing spears using steel concrete reinforcement rods, sharpened to a point, set into the end of the shaft, and secured with copper wire. There was a depression in the other end of the shaft to take a woomera. There was very little support from the school administration and I was happy to work independently. While my reports were signed by the Principal, they were actioned by Head Office in Darwin. My support came from Subject Advisor Sam Leigh, in the form of visits at the end of each term. Sam was very experienced in working in isolation on remote mission stations throughout the Pacific and was a great help to me. We became personal friends. Another part of my role at the school was to take the senior class for literacy and numeracy. There was no bilingual program running at the school and according to UNESCO the Nunggubuyu language is endangered.

Henry Gray

Henry Gray, a primary school teacher, was a likable and eccentric character. You could hear him whistling on his way to lesson preparation at school, as early as six o'clock in the morning. He and his wife, Margo, had three kids and he was dedicated, spending most of his waking moments on innovative lesson plans and programming and extracurricular activities for the school. A lot of his family photos and other personal household effects were transferred from his house to his classroom.

Henry's classroom was something very special and I admired his enthusiasm. Even the ceiling was adorned with photos and every square inch of the walls had children's work on display. One day I went to visit Henry after school – he hadn't got back home yet. I heard kids playing inside and water splashing. I opened the front door to be met with a flood of water flowing out the doorway. It turned out that the kids were playing, unsupervised, in the overflowing bathtub.

The Missionary and the Buffalo

The founding Anglican missionary, Colin Gilchrist retired and departed that year, and was replaced by Ron Butler from Adelaide. I attended one of Ron's sermons in English which went completely over the congregation's heads and was completely irrelevant to First Nations Nunggubuyu people and their lives. It was said that during one evening at home, Ron had quietly gone down the stairs into the backyard for some reason or other, when he was surprised by a buffalo that chased him back up the stairs.

Crocodiles

Crocs were a part of life at Numbulwar. As the tide came out, these enormous man-eaters could be seen drifting down the river like logs on the tide. It wasn't uncommon for the crocs to drop in to visit the village on their way past, causing a lot of commotion. It was a mystery to me why the missionaries would have built the village right on the banks of the river. I recall one time, when Mum was with us, camping on the high bank about ten kilometres upstream.

On her return home to Victoria from a visit, Mum told our relatives, that a croc could have come for her as she slept on the river bank. She said that she could easily have been taken while Rose and Alan were safely snuggled in the back of the Land Rover. (We were all actually safe on the high bank) We had our ten-foot dinghy with a three-and-a-half horsepower Seagull outboard. Whilst out fishing, or on other trips on the river, you could see crocs, lazing in the sun on the surface. On approach, as close as a few metres away, a croc would suddenly flick his tail, causing a big splash, and disappear into the depths.

One weekend we were camped with another teacher on the lower bank of the river just downstream from Policeman's Crossing. We assumed that it would be safe enough there because when the tide was fully out the water was fresh enough to drink - the main concern being saltwater crocs. The camp was only inches above high tide. I woke up at daybreak to see a huge croc lazing in the river only metres from the camp.

We never used bait when we were fishing, and learned that a particular variety of wobbler, gold and black, was the best for Barramundi and Mangrove Jack. We used nothing less than a hundred-pound breaking strain line. We trolled close to the mangroves and at Policeman's Crossing, anchored in the middle, and fished from there.

With Warnabari on the Rose River, Numbulwar, 1976.

One day, Rose hooked a 30-pound Barramundi. It was so big that we had trouble landing it. We found a special place a few kilometres up the coast where you could hook big mud crabs from the hollows under the rocks, and cook them in the coals on the beach. Barramundi became our staple and Rose often cooked it whole, with lime, ginger and garlic sauce, to share as a banquet, with other teachers on a weekend. We also used a smoker.

Ancestors

My Nunggubuyu teacher aide invited me to a historic place. There was a wave-cut platform, suspended above the existing shoreline. Embedded in this smooth rock platform were the fossilised impressions of what he described as those of his ancestors - a woman, and beside them, those of a child. The footprints covered a length of about three metres across the smooth flat rock along the direction of the coastline and then disappeared. I had limited resources at school.

Challenges

There was no bilingual program running but I was able to draw on my limited skills and knowledge in teaching English as a second language with the senior class. It was difficult because I had limited resources and I was experiencing some ongoing behaviour management issues. With limited support from the school administration and a lack of resources, there were conflict situations that I had to address in isolation. It was a highly stressful time.

As a recently graduated teacher, I saw Lajamanu as a benchmark against which I could compare professional situations throughout my teaching career in the Northern Territory.

I was happy to receive notice of a transfer by the end of term three. The transfer took me initially to a temporary position at Darwin High School and then Wave Hill Station until the end of the year. Henry became the principal of Numbulwar School the following year. For me, the stress of teaching at Numbulwar had taken its toll. The Department was supportive. They provided extra funding for the removal of a row of seats in the DC3 to accommodate my hang glider. I left for Darwin and Rose went south for a brief holiday to see Mum, Judith, and other friends.

Darwin and Wave Hill

I was in Darwin for only a couple of months and then moved on to Wave Hill. My role at Wave Hill was to help with the development of their language program. My classroom was an ex-army igloo. I lived in a large, off-road caravan, commonly known as a silver bullet, parked adjacent to the school. I found the work interesting and the Gurindji community was accommodating and helpful.

About ten years before, First Nations activist Vincent Lingiari, a Gurindji man, led around 200 of his people in a strike where they walked off Wave Hill station. He had national union support for his demands for better pay and conditions for his people. Rose and I planned a trip to America. I was at Wave Hill until the end of the 1976 school year and then a permanent position became available for me at Lajamanu for 1977.

America

Rose and I travelled around America, visiting Rose's relatives in San Francisco and then Renton in Washington State. I had investigated the opportunity to take up teacher exchange work in British Columbia and we had planned to go and talk to the Education Authorities there. There were blizzards occurring to the north, and through the midlands where some people had frozen to death in their cars. We saw the news on TV where, in Chicago, there were over one metre-long horizontal icicles attached to the corners of the buildings in the CBD. We determined not to go north or to travel east. So we decided to spend the rest of our time in Los Angeles, Arizona, Louisiana, and Mississippi and spent the 1976 New Year's Eve in Basin Street in New Orleans.

Back to Lajamanu School

Back at Lajamanu, I looked forward to getting to work. I became deeply involved with the bilingual education program and was responsible for the upper primary group. David and Monica Holt and Jim Mathieson were still there and the new teachers were Ian Daniels, who inherited my Manual Arts program. There was also Margaret McHugh, middle primary and John and Jedda Hingston, grades two and three. Monica Holt was still the Home Economics teacher. Sue Simpson and I took upper primary and Polly Ploughman, infants. Anne was the teacher-librarian. Working relations were productive due in no small part to David Holt's amazing talent and energy for holding everything together in a remote working environment.

While I felt that I needed more professional experience, David encouraged me to apply for the band two Acting Deputy Principal's position. The pay was encouraging enough, and I accepted the position. Apart from organisational skills, which I felt reasonably comfortable with, I also had many hours of administrative work, which meant completing seemingly endless departmental forms. There was all the school and staff housing maintenance, playground duty, and other staff rosters, chairing committees, travel to Darwin, supervising student teachers, lesson programs, and so on.

I was further encouraged that year, to apply for a permanent band 2 level Deputy position. After months of preparation and compliance with procedures, involving assessment panels among other things, I was unsuccessful and felt betrayed. I resigned from the acting position immediately. Jim Mathieson took the position and I went back to classroom teaching.

Bruce Mercer

Bruce Mercer's role was to develop and facilitate sporting activities for young people. Mercer became a close friend. We shared similar world views and I thought his cross-cultural people skills were outstanding for a nineteen-year-old. He genuinely fitted in with the

Warlpiri young people. The Yapa referred to Mercer as Jakamarra. His knowledge and skills in the different sports were enviable to any PE teacher. For the first time, the Lajamanu football team was well organised. The young Warlpiri men took football very seriously and indeed became a formidable team.

Mercer would turn up right on dinner time and it wasn't just once. We enjoyed his company. Mercer was possessed with black humour and full of cutting-edge remarks based on his observations and his provocative and perceptive mind. For example, after eyeing off our tie-dyed wall hangings and my buffalo horns I got at Yirrkala, and other things hanging on the walls, he'd raise his chin saying " *You and your paraphernalia*". I enjoyed his challenging conversation.

Our exploits together included long hikes in the bush. For example one weekend we went down to Jirlpirli, a favoured haunt which I've already mentioned. We scaled the rugged hill slopes and returned home exhausted. We also spent time hunting in the desert with Yapa. But there's something else that I need to say about this extraordinary man.

Mercer shared a comprehensive repertoire of music that reflected his unique personality and his view of the world. He introduced me to the music of people like Ian Drury, Tom Waits, and Frank Zappa. Mercer will pop up now and then in the stories that follow.

The Flying Doctor

On our return to Lajamanu, we soon met the flying doctor John Humphries. John was from Oxford and had brought his family out to Katherine. Lajamanu was part of his circuit. John and I got on well from the start and a pattern soon emerged whereby once a month John stayed with us on his visits, usually overnight. At the end of a hot day, we'd drive out to the Seven-mile and swim in the bore tank.

John was vulnerable to Aussie practical jokes and bullshit. For example, we stripped off and climbed into the Seven-mile tank to swim, and I explained that it was necessary to keep moving because if you stopped for any length of time, you could be attacked in the groin by enormous water scorpions which I had shown him earlier – a fearsome crustation, over two inches long with a boat shaped body with two enormous clasping front nippers, and a sting in the tail. John was terrified at the spectre of being stung in the groin by one of these things and I never got around to telling him any different.

It was about that time when I was afflicted by a series of boils, and a painful carbuncle developed under my left arm. There were others, like the one on my right thigh and another one on my left wrist. But it was the carbuncle, like a shield volcano, with fissures all around the central core, that was causing the main concern. It was developing into a very painful pressure point. The nurse rejected my application for sick leave from work. It was fortunate that John was due to arrive and after a quick glance at the carbuncle, supported my application for sick leave. He put me on antibiotics and I had a week off work. John and I were to become close friends into the future. By the way, there were ghosts at Lajamanu, that deserve a mention.

Spirits

Ian took up my position after I had moved over to the community-based bi-lingual program. Ian's wife was Margie from the Torres Straits, who had difficulties adjusting to the new cultural environment in the desert. Ian was a sensitive and gentle person. One day, the Home Economics teacher's husband, who had been sick for some time, died very suddenly. I remember seeing him, trying to keep cool with a wet face flannel – wiping his legs and arms with cold water. I was surprised to hear he had died so suddenly and I was quite shocked. Some days after that, Ian was lying on his bed sleeping and was woken suddenly by what he thought was somebody tugging at his big toe. He told me about it and said that it was the ghost of the dead person trying to communicate with him.

A Seance

Another time, Ian, David Holt, and a couple of other teachers had planned to go out to the Seven-mile to hold a séance. I declined the invitation and stayed home. It was Friday night when they set up a table and some camping chairs, out on the plains, not far from the bore. To their horror, they were visited by the spirit of an old Gurindji woman who set about terrorising them, and they panicked. They had no strategy in place to manage the situation. They packed up and fled the scene. They returned to the settlement to tell their story and to make a pact, never to get involved in seances again.

Peter Batty

Peter Batty was a Vietnam Veteran, and worked as a plumber, on the construction of the new School library complex. While suffering a degree of war trauma from Vietnam, he had an interesting personality. We'd have a smoke during the odd evening and listen to John Mayall and other blues. He also helped me make a copper water tank for the Land Rover, which we fitted underneath, in front of the left-hand side rear wheel.

It was a weekend around mid-year when we were camped near the Nineteen-mile bore. Rose was pregnant with Miya. It was freezing cold and Peter was standing with his back to the fire when the back of his jeans suddenly caught fire. It was like spontaneous combustion. In a frenzy of panic, Peter called on Rose for help. In her pregnant state, Rose had switched off, and took the situation calmly and casually, telling him to roll on the ground. He sat himself down in the sand and extinguished the flames and there were no serious injuries.

The Lajamanu Rodeo

It was early in 1977 when the word got around that Dave Jennings was organising a Rodeo. A site near the Seven-mile bore was chosen for the event, where there were rudimentary cattle yards and some other basic infrastructure. It was a massive undertaking, and nobody thought that he'd ever be able to pull it off. Dave worked tirelessly and as the weeks went by, a comprehensive and professional rodeo ground took shape. People rallied and a date was set for June.

Dave arranged the substantial prize money, drawing contestants from far and wide. For example, competing ringers were from all the neighbouring cattle stations including VRD, Wave Hill, Inverway, and Supplejack, and from cattle properties across the Queensland border as far away as Mt Isa and beyond. The school was involved, and we made pots of beef stew, and beef sandwiches - the proceeds going towards excursions and other things. Ivan Jordan, the Baptist missionary, and accomplished country singer-songwriter, composed a theme song for the event. The chorus went: *"Lajaman' rodeo is on today, on the edge of the desert where the Warlpiri kids play. People come from the south, the north and the west, Lajaman' rodeooooh one of the best."* It was a huge success and there was talk of holding a rodeo as an annual event. Miya was born at Katherine Hospital on Saturday 27th August 1977.

Lajamanu Rodeo at the 7 Mile, 1977.

Miya is Born

The normal practice for expectant mothers in remote areas was to move to the closest hospital, a month prior to the expected date of birth. Since Rose was a nurse and familiar with procedures, John advised that it was all right to wait until later. Rose had an early show and they flew her straight into Katherine Hospital during the evening. She had a trouble-free birth and little Miya was born in the early hours of the morning. We named her Alissa and The Yapa named her Murrumiya a local place name and her Warlpiri skin name is Napaltjarri.

Miya and her companion, Warnabari, Lajamanu, 1978.

Rose's Uncle George named her Mee Lei – meaning, Beautiful Girl. She was duly registered as Alissa Murrumiya Isherwood. The Yapa doted on little Murrumiya and watched out for her through her early years in the community. Warnabari was protective and would often be seen sitting next to her, guarding her as she played. Mum came to visit us again just after Miya was born and spent several months helping Rose with the new baby and joining us on excursions out into the desert where she would set up and paint magical landscapes.

Nangurru Lake

Bob Scandrett a new teacher, came to Lajamanu at the beginning of term 3 and lived across the road from us. Bob had a 500cc Yamaha and I still had my 250. I mentioned Nangurru and Bob was keen to ride out there during a weekend. I'd been out to Nangurru earlier with Barney Jangala and I was familiar with the route. All we needed to do was to leave a drum of petrol halfway along the track for a refuel on the return trip and pack some food and swags. It took most of the day to negotiate the rough track. The worst part of the route was over the black soil plains. These plains were dominated by blue gums. There were sand patches, washouts, and loose stones. We arrived late in the afternoon.

There was enough time before dark to set up camp at the edge of the lake and eat dinner. After dinner, right on sunset, armed with my camera, we walked out about two hundred meters in ankle-deep salt water. We stood stock still and waited for the radiating circular waves we'd created, to dissipate. Within a few minutes, the wave circles had gone. I had never experienced anything like this. It was as though we were standing on a vast mirror that reflected a magnificent red and orange sunset.

We returned to camp and put the billy on. By now the sky was clear and the stars were so bright that I set up the camera on the seat of my bike with the shutter fully open to the night sky. The plan was to capture the earth's rotation in relation to the stars using extended time exposure. It worked, but something unexpected was also in the frame. At around midnight, we were awakened by a boom that sounded like a supersonic aircraft breaking the speed of sound. We looked up to witness the white-hot tail of a meteorite on entry into the earth's atmosphere in a most spectacular event. Back at the settlement, the staff wouldn't believe us until I showed them the print. The Yapa calmly accepted our meteorite story and said that it wasn't uncommon to see this phenomenon in the desert sky.

Sydney Excursion

When I told David that I'd chosen Sydney for the excursion he had reservations about approval, especially since it was such a major undertaking. The kids hadn't been further away than Yuendumu - and it was getting later in the year. There were twelve kids, thirteen to fifteen-year-olds. Sue Simpson took charge of the five girls, and I took the boys. The school was to partially fund the excursion and the Commonwealth would match it dollar for dollar.

Students watch a busker in Pitt St. Sydney, Excursion, 1977.

Lajamanu students ride the Sydney ferry, 1977.

During the months prior to departure, we made money by selling beef hamburgers, garden produce and pendants made from laminated acrylic and tumbled agates. The school fete had games like bash the rat, air rifle shoot, and so on. We got on the plane at Alice Springs.

The kids were cooperative and embraced the big city environment with confidence, taking the whole experience in their stride. Their first experience of the sea was during their ferry trip to Manly. They felt the thick wool on a sheep for the first time at a sheep station and walked in the Blue Mountains. They had pizza at a restaurant in the city, ate ice cream in the park, and watched a Salvation Army brass band playing a march. In Pitt Street, they stopped to watch a busker play his violin and strode down to Martin Place. Before returning home, I took the opportunity to go to a blues concert at the Basement while Sue kindly looked after the kids. A few more days of touring Sydney, and we were all back home at Lajamanu.

Catfish

During the winter time of a weekend, we spent time at Catfish on the Victoria River. Some trips involved hunting with Lionel and some of the kids from my class. We got plain turkeys, water monitors and sometimes ducks, among other things, with the shotgun. Rose and I set up camp at the usual spot and just do some fishing, swimming, and exploring the country.

On one occasion, I was walking downstream with Warnabari, looking for ducks. It was late in the afternoon. We had just crossed a shallow part of the river when I spotted two dingoes some distance away and moving down towards us from the high bank. We kept walking and I kept an eye on them. It wasn't long before they broke into a trot and then from about a hundred meters away, started running full pelt towards us. Warnaburi was under attack.

Warnabari saw them now and stayed with me for protection. We stood stock still and when they got within a few metres, I took aim with the shotgun and fired at the one on the left, dropping him instantly. The other dog took fright and fled. I was badly shaken and hadn't expected anything like this. I could only conclude that they were defending their territory against an invading stranger, Warnabari, and hadn't even noticed me.

One day in September I decided to ride my motorbike to Catfish just for the hell of it. I carried some extra fuel and plenty of water. It was really tiring because of the sand patches, loose gravel, wash-outs, fallen tree limbs, and creek crossings. I'd gone about fifty kilometres when I started negotiating a steep creek crossing with large loose river stones in the dry bed. The front wheel slipped from under me and I was thrown over the handlebars, ending up on my knees on the loose stones. The pain was excruciating and I felt sick in the stomach.

I had a drink of water and lay under a shrub to shelter from the hot sun and recover. I had thoughts of dying there. As the pain and nausea eased, I was able to stagger over to the bike and inspect it for any damage. There was only a minor dint in the side of the tank, and the spare can of petrol was still intact. Relieved, I got back on the bike and it started on the first kick. The pain soon returned and I had to stop to rest on several occasions before finally getting back home. I was keen to fly my hang glider.

Hang Gliding

There weren't any launch sites for the hang glider at Numbulwar and I was keen to do some more flying. I'd already begun to explore potential launch sites on the mesas and buttes in the northern Tanami area. John Humphreys was excited by the idea of hang gliding in the desert and was eager to come and be my assistant in carrying the machine up steep scree slopes onto the top of a hill and assembling the kite. I'd stake out strips of cotton fabric on sticks, up the slope, to indicate wind direction and velocity, and we'd wait for a consistent breeze, to launch the kite. We had a few successful trips which John had recorded on film.

Launch

I'd been talking to Pardipardi (Henry Cooke Jakamarra) about my hang gliding exploits and he was also keen to come out to the Nineteen Mile to see how it all worked. We arrived at the mesa and lugged all the gear up the scree slope, around the back, and finally to the top of the cliff facing into the wind. We had placed the usual sticks with a small strip of fabric up the slope.

Gusty conditions are common in the desert, and you have to wait for a consistent rate of knots - around 18 knots being ideal. We assembled the hang glider and I strapped myself into the harness, while Henry patiently held the nose into wind gusts of over thirty knots at times. The gusts were eddying over the top of the cliff and hammering down onto the top of the wing. I wasn't aware that the steel heart bolt had bent under the strain, leaving the right wing tip slightly raised. We waited up there for over two hours, and I was unsure about whether to launch or just pack up and go.

Then the wind indicators up the scree slope showed some brief consistency and I stepped off the cliff top. The hang glider skewed wildly to the left, because of the damaged heart bolt. Fortunately, I had enough height to correct and was able to avoid getting injured. But that wasn't all. The day was very gusty and during the glide down I'd suddenly sink then gain height and so on. After a rough landing on the rocks and spinifex, I was so happy to have escaped unscathed and made a pact that at least when I'm on my own, I will never attempt to fly in such hostile conditions again. But there was another mistake I could have avoided.

Having been out with us on a previous occassion, one of the new teachers, Margaret, wanted to have a go at hang gliding and I gave her one of my books on the study of how air behaves close to the ground. When the day arrived, Margaret was confident and we headed out to the Nineteen Mile. David and a couple of other teachers came as well. Margaret had agreed not to launch from a spot any higher than halfway up the scree slope for her first flight. Everything was set up and she was ready to go.

Wind speed seemed right, I let go of the nose and she was in the air. It looked good initially and Margaret was euphoric as she glided down the scree slope. Then, without any warning, it happened. A violent gust lifted the nose. Margaret froze, unable to get her weight forward. The kite flipped over backward, landing upside down, further up the slope, leaving Margaret suspended like a rag doll, hanging there in the harness. She had broken her arm. Seeing what was happening, David and the others panicked and scrambled up the slope to help. It wasn't at all necessary and Margaret and I were having a joke about it as I held the kite to prevent it from blowing away.

When they got to us David stepped onto the wing and inadvertently ripped a hole in the fabric in his attempt to save Margaret. I released the harness and we helped her get clear. Margaret was diagnosed with a green-stick fracture of the right forearm and recovered quickly and all was well.

Self Government for the NT

The NT gained self-government in 1978, with future local decision-making, resting with the new N.T. Legislative Assembly. One of the first things that happened was that the new N.T. flag was issued to all the remote communities. The new red ochre flag with a desert rose in the middle was duly hoisted up the flag pole in a ceremony outside the front of the Admin. block and flew upside down for weeks until someone from Darwin picked up on it. It was duly hung up the right way. It was now towards the end of 1978 with more changes on the horizon.

Study Leave

I was taking Indigenous education and other issues quite seriously. I applied for a Commonwealth Teaching Service Grant and ended up with full paid study leave for 1979. I enrolled in a radical new Graduate Diploma in Aboriginal Education, offered by James Cook University in Townsville. I took leave and for the second time left Lajamanu and prepared for travel and a year of full-time study.

It had become normal practice for us to have two main stops when we were travelling across from the Territory to North Queensland. The first was with Michelle in Mt. Isa. The second stop was with Kirk and Bronwin Smith in Charters Towers. In Townsville, we always stayed with Jim and Nora Hull. I wrote about Smithy and Michelle earlier when we were students in Brisbane together. While the kids were little, Rose would fly with them to escape the heat, I'd drive the

Land Rover across, and we'd meet up in Townsville or Cairns. We were soon settled in Townsville in the house in Cook Street, North Ward and I was preparing for a trip to China.

A Delegation to China

The Commonwealth Teaching Service Union were calling for participants to form a delegation to China. The delegation would report on education trends and innovations that were implemented in mainstream communes and for ethnic minorities. It was an opportunity not to be missed. I was away for three weeks.

It was winter time in China and in the north, the daytime temperature climbed to minus 15 degrees Celsius. Travelling north from our first port of call in Shanghai, I noticed that the sun scarcely rose above the horizon throughout the day. Travel was by air and rail and the service was second to none.

The country schools were not well-resourced and were to some extent, dependent on the teachers and community. There was an image of Chairman Mao positioned above the chalkboard in all the classrooms. We were invited to give a short lesson on Australia. I did a presentation on Numbulwar and Lajamanu and the kids were spellbound.

On arrival in any new province, the delegation would be formally introduced to a new guide. In Beijing, a couple of us escaped our guide's custody for a couple of hours. We had a great time roaming the back streets, getting a chance to connect with the people in restaurants and other local haunts. I bought a few things at local markets. While in Beijing, we were challenged to a table tennis tournament and a few games of basketball. On both occasions they let us win. I thought it was a bit of a diplomatic overkill, especially since both sports are Chinese in origin. We felt privileged to be shown the restoration work being done on the Great Wall and on the ancient murals in the Forbidden City. We went to a rally in Tiananmen Square. The ancient architecture was on a monumental scale I'd never imagined.

Outside the wall, there was a moat around the Forbidden City crowded with skaters travelling at breakneck speeds from all directions. There was black ice on the streets – ice that had become grimy and remained frozen. It was hard to walk on without slipping over. There were images of Chairman Mao everywhere – in public places and on household crockery, alarm clocks, and a diversity of revolutionary posters, depicting epic victories over the regime, the long walk, and military ballerinas, dancing with assault rifles. I was swept away by the enthusiasm of the time without having much understanding of what it was all about. I purchased a Mao jacket and wore it everywhere. I brought back about twenty political posters, to display in our house in Cook Street in Townsville. China's an exciting and incredibly diverse country and I was bent on returning with my family sometime in the future.

The GDAE Course

It was early in 1979 and I was preparing for the Grad. Dip Aboriginal Ed. Course - a year of full-time study. Miya was still a baby and Rose looked after her full time, taking her to yoga, and visiting Jim and Nora Hull, and other friends around Townsville.

The course was issues-based and heavily influenced by Henry Reynolds and Noel Loos, radical historians, with a fixation on the history of race relations in North Queensland and other groundbreaking research of the time. The majority of participants were teachers employed by the Qld. Education department who had come from or were planning to teach in remote Aboriginal communities. These places were mostly in Cape York - such as Bamaga, Lockhart River, Mapoon, Pormpuraaw, Aurukun and Kowanyama among others.

Our lecturers included Julia Koppi, Noel Loos, Sandra Renue, Barry Osborne and Jeff Coombs. Students included Mark and Rose Hollands, Chris Fry, Sister Carmel from Palm Island, Brett and Michelle, Paul Keenan, and Jenny and Kevin Gates among others. Paul Keenan and his partner, Loisie from the Torres Strait had moved in to share the house in Cook Street with us. I found the course challenging and enjoyed the social life in Townsville and on campus. For me though, the highlight of the year was my fieldwork in Guadalcanal, and it's these experiences which I'd like to share.

Guadalcanal

Having come from traditional First Nations communities here in Australia, I wanted to do something different for my fieldwork and nominated for the Solomon Islands. The Ministry assigned me to Tadhimboko Bay, about fifty kilometres along the coast, west of Honiara on Guadalcanal Island. I was met by my mentor, Mr Mose'. In Honiara.

Chinese traders dominated commerce and the shops stocked everything imaginable. The Solomon Islands had gained independence from the British only the year before I arrived. Evidence of a colonial past was most obvious in the tropical architecture, and the number of Land Rovers around and I felt quite at home. I stayed overnight in Honiara and picked up some supplies before leaving in the morning. The road, originally built by the Japanese during the second world war, had deteriorated to a rough bush track and I arrived at Tadhimboko in the mid-afternoon.

A walk along the beach. Tadhimboko Bay, Guadacanal, 1979.

At picturesque Tadhimboko education centre, the scattered buildings were made of traditional bush materials with bamboo frames and roofs thatched with sago palm fronds. The walls were woven palm fronds. The flooring was split bamboo. The new senior's classroom, however, had a commercial hardwood frame, clad with sheets of galvanized iron with a concrete floor, and by the afternoon, as hot as hell. But they seemed to be very proud of it. They said it was fire-resistant.

Everything was maintained by the parents. There was a beautiful veggie garden with long bamboo bean trellises, chooks, and so on. Staff lived on site and most of their food was supplied by the parents. The kids came from small neighbouring villages and walked to school along jungle pathways. They all carried a machete, to casually cut at stray vines that would otherwise block the pathway. Other kids walked from their villages and waded, waist deep, across the river to get to school.

My house was of traditional thatch, and cool, with a bed with mosquito net and a small bench. The entire interior was covered in thick, accumulated, solidified deposits of white DDT spray.

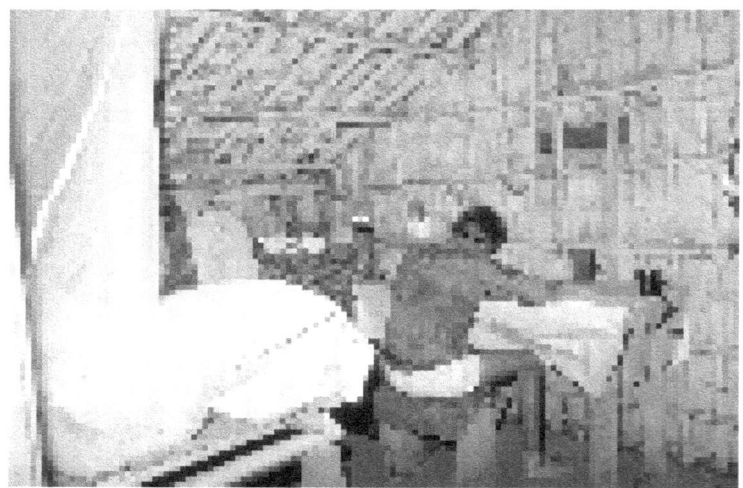

Lesson preparations. Tadhimboko, 1979.

There was no power or lighting and there were no mosquitoes. There was a rudimentary shared ablution block, a kitchen, staff quarters, classrooms and a thatched, open under-cover assembly area. There were remnants of an English as a Foreign Language program, operating, and the school was generally under-resourced with a lot of rote learning happening. Classrooms were busy and productive learning environments.

There were five women on staff, and two of them were single. Mr Mose' sensed that I was under threat and kept a close eye on those two, for the duration of my stay. I prepared a basic lesson plan for my first day.

Breakfast at the mess was rice and tinned fish every day. There was no parade the first day and when I got to the senior's classroom, the teacher stood them all up, and in superb harmony, they sang three wartime folk songs that I recorded. One was about shooting down Japanese fighter planes over the bay. These kids and their teacher were transfixed as they listened to stories of my family, Lajamanu, and the desert. They viewed slides of public ceremonies and listened to recordings of Yolngu folk songs. I enjoyed the school routine. There was a particular aspect of past Australian-Melanesian relations that I should share.

With staff, Tadhimboko, Guadalcanal, 1979.

The Blackbirding days had long gone but they weren't forgotten. Blackbirding is a colonial term that referred to dodgy recruitment, or the kidnapping of labourers for work in the Queensland sugar industry. Consequently, Australians were not held in high regard. I understood this and kept my distance. During the second week, however, Mose' invited me to his home village. I felt very privileged and he was delighted with my offer of a presentation on my life in Northeast Arnhem Land and the Central Desert.

En route through Port Moresby, I was able to pick up a 12-volt slide projector, on loan from the University, and a battery. Fully equipped with a projector, battery, slides, and tape recorder we set off along the jungle path for the isolated village. It must have looked a bit like an episode of The Phantom – the great white hunter among loyal companions travelling in single file along the jungle pathway, hacking at invading vines with machetes – two men with the bamboo pole on their shoulders with a 12-volt battery and other equipment suspended in the middle.

We were formally welcomed by the Headman and invited to take some afternoon tea at the guest house. It was an immaculately laid out village. There was a central courtyard where some men were busy splitting coconuts and laying the copra out to dry in the sun.

Preparing copra for the market. Mr. Mose's village, 1979.

He took us on a tour of his village explaining how it all worked, and we eventually arrived at a stately building. It was their equivalent of a community hall, where rituals were held and important decisions made.

As we entered the building, I was struck by the bright shafts of afternoon sunlight from intricate patterns in the palm-woven walls high above the central fireplace. I was shown ancient clay cooking vessels, a German short sword, a battle axe, and other clan heirlooms. A long time ago, Mose's grandfather had acquired the battle axe from an unwelcome German gold prospector.

Legend has it that the hapless German was cooked. The meat was so tough that it was discarded, and his boots were more tender and eaten instead. Of his food supplies, a tin of fish, (with a label depicting a fish, on the top,) was opened and the insides discarded as entrails and the tin eaten instead. Things went so well here that Mr Mose' asked me to make some further visits to other remote villages and I was more than happy to oblige. During my travels around the district, I noticed relics of the Second World War.

Along a jungle pathway to Mr Mose's village. Guadalcanal, 1979.

Reminders of World War II

One afternoon, after school, the kids offered to take me down the river to the coast. We waded in waist-deep water. It was easy with the sandy bed, and we made good progress with the gentle current. As we waded along, towards the river mouth, one of the boys produced a heavy glass Coke bottle from the river bed exclaiming that it was American, from the wartime. Other reminders of the war were the American oxy-acetylene gas bottles suspended from trees and used very effectively as village bells. Whoever was on the roster, would select a rock or two from a pile on the ground, near the bell, take a couple of steps back and throw it against the steel gas bottle, producing a penetrating ring that could be heard through the valley. The process would be repeated a number of times, depending on the nature of the event.

There were comfortable aircraft pilot seats out on verandas in the villages. Banquets including pork and plantain were cooked in large aluminium aircraft fuel tanks. Fish and beef were barbecued on steel grids used for driving over boggy conditions by the troops during the war.

At a village banquet given in honour of the first birthday of the School Principal's son, there was a lot of singing in beautiful harmony. Some of the songs had been introduced by African-American troops during the war such as "Pistol Packin' Mama" and others of the period. Other songs were descriptive of the battle of Guadalcanal, and more still were ancient folk songs, some of which I recorded on tape. I was able to record some impromptu acoustic guitar instrumentals in a genre peculiar to this rich, and wonderful Melanesian culture.

Parents cut grass on school grounds. Tadhimboko, Guadalcanal. 1979.

Mr. Mose' owned a small copra plantation here on the coast. He told me that there were so many people killed in aeroplanes shot down over the bay, that the sharks developed a liking for human flesh, and it's still dangerous to swim there. I was also told that the reason for the past high incidence of malaria on Guadalcanal is due to the thousands of bomb craters all over the island, filled with stagnant water in which the mosquitoes breed.

Mr. Mose' and his family also told me stories about the occupying Japanese troops. Relations were so bad that many people fled into the hills and to neighbouring islands to escape the Japanese, until the arrival of the Americans. For many of the survivors of the war, all this was still within living memory. The stories were told with such imagery and intensity that to me it seemed as though it all happened only a few years ago.

Football and Beetle Nut

Mr. Mose' and the other teachers invited me to join them on a trip to see a local football match. On arrival at the oval, we settled down at a good vantage point and someone produced the beetle nut. I had no experience in the use of this drug. But I was willing to have a crack at it. It was red and mature and its impact, in my case, was severe. The rest of the afternoon was a complete blur and when I got back to my quarters I couldn't climb the steps.

Building school bean trellises, Tadhimboko, Guadalcanal, 1979.

I must have been laying there for at least half an hour and when I fully regained consciousness, I was nauseous, my head was spinning, and I was flat on my back on the ground, sweating in the hot sun. They were all concerned about me and I learned that when you take beetle-nut, you spit out as you chew, especially with the strong ones. I had another couple of goes under more advanced supervision. I had my green beetle nut and Mr. Mose' showed me where to find the essential vine leaf and the grinding of antler coral.

You begin with dehusking the nut, which is a bit like a miniature coconut and chewing the kernel. When it's pulverised, you then roll up a vine leaf, moisten it with saliva, and dip it into the coral powder. Bite off this powder-coated section of the vine leaf, being careful not to allow it to touch the lips. The lime (powdered coral) will burn the lips. Further chew the mixture, spitting out often. You notice that soon the spit comes out like a scarlet red dye. The minuscule amount of juice ingested will have the desired effect – such that you become numbed and relaxed, yet still alert to what's going on around you.

It was sad to leave but I had study commitments and a report to write back in Townsville. I'd spent my last dollar in Honiara and learned on arrival in Port Moresby, that there was a ten-dollar airport departure tax to pay, and I couldn't leave the country until the payment was made. Fearful of missing the connecting flight, I rushed outside and onto the street, in search of a sympathetic soul who might give me a loan. I was only a few paces away from my suitcase when I looked around to see that a man was making off with it, down the road.

I caught up with him and explained that it was my suitcase, took it back, and went back into the airport lounge looking for the loan. There was an Australian expatriate, from Cairns standing close by, and I asked for a loan for the airport tax, assuring him that I was from Townsville, and would send him a repayment on my return home. He grudgingly gave me his address and the ten dollars, and I was on my way. Shortly after my return to Townsville, we were faced with an unexpected problem with Warnabari.

Back in Townsville

Being a pedigree dingo from the pristine Central Australian desert, Warnabari, was unaccustomed to domestic fleas. We noticed fleas on him and used a fairly standard dog wash from the pet shop, to kill them. Within minutes of this application, poor Warnabari collapsed on the floor and went into uncontrollable spasms and fitting. We rushed him down to the vet. The vet calmly examined him and we immediately washed him down with the hose out the back. There was no charge, no more fleas, and Warnabari made a speedy recovery from his ordeal.

The rest of the year in Townsville went well. I had applied for Lajamanu School and for the second time, told that there was no position for me there for the start of the year. Instead, I was offered Willowra Station and looked forward to new adventures.

Willowra Station

It was early in 1980 and Rose was a few weeks into her pregnancy with Sara. Unlike a lot of other women, Rose never suffered from morning sickness and this second pregnancy was free of problems. Willowra Cattle station, or in Warlpiri, Wirliyatjarrayi, had recently been bought by the Commonwealth government and handed back to the Warlpiri owners of that country. It was a rich and picturesque place, including endless fertile flood plains along the great Lander River.

The small three-teacher school was part of the homestead complex. There was a large water tank fed by a bore, maintenance shed and other outbuildings. The school staff houses were built along the high river bank. Our place was only a few steps away from my classroom. It was comfortable, with a full-length verandah, backing onto the wide sandy river bed.

With staff at Willowra School, 1980.

Many Yapa had recently relocated back to Wirliyatjarrayi and established their humpies along the northern side of the homestead. Yapa visitors usually set up camp along the other side of the river. Jim and Jocelyn were kept on at the homestead, to continue management. Jocelyn managed a shop and stocked essentials such as tea, tobacco, flour, powdered milk, and a variety of tinned food. She was also a nurse. We were missing Warnabari and the opportunity came to raise another dingo. His name was Japalyi, and I'll talk more about them both later. We became friends with community leader, Stumpy Martin.

Stumpy Martin Jampitjinpa was a quiet and gentle soul and often took on the role of spokesperson on behalf of the Warlpiri community. He was heavily involved with Land rights and the handing back of the cattle station. They had many meetings while we were there at Willowra Station. Stumpy was always there to fill the cross-cultural gap, as new teachers arrived. Stumpy told me about his life experiences on cattle stations and the issues facing his people. He invited me to join him, with a small group of men, involved in a maintenance ritual at a special place, not far from the station. They guided me through the process. It was an experience that I'm not at liberty to elaborate on, but will never forget. The Yapa at Willowra suffered unimaginable brutality and trauma at the hands of the police in the not-too-distant past.

School Cultural activities Willowra Station, 1980.

Coniston

On one occasion, I went to Central Mt Stuart, to do a bit of exploring around the main peak, and in the surrounding rocky foothills. There were spectacular caves perched high around the main peak. I set up the camera with wide angle, and composed pictures of the surrounding landscape, framed by the silhouetted outline of the cave entrances. It was when I was sharing these pictures with some of the older men that I became aware of the Coniston Massacre, the last known mass murder of First Nations Australians. We were viewing the slides of the caves on the screen, and there were a lot of hushed murmurings. I was told that they remember hiding there during the "killing time." One day shortly after our slide viewing, George Jungarrayi showed me where his father was killed, just down from our house on the river bank. George told me that he was "wee-high" and hiding up in the foliage of a nearby helicopter tree at the time.

During late October 1928 between 60 and 170 men, women and children were brutally murdered in reprisal for the murder of a dogger near Coniston cattle station. Police Sergeant Murray, in a punitive expedition, including local cattle station owners and others from Alice Springs, rode along the Lander River, shooting people indiscriminately. There must have been inter-generative trauma for the Yapa, who generally kept it to themselves. For some, it was within living memory.

A view from one of the caves, where Warlpiri people were hiding, during the Coniston massacre. Central Mt. Stuart, 1980.

School

At school I was assigned to the upper primary class and Maryanne Gale was the teacher linguist. Geoff Gleave was acting Principal and lower to middle primary teacher and George Jungarrayi was the Janitor. I didn't have a teacher's aide but I wasn't too worried about that. It was a Warlpiri community and I was able to introduce myself as Jungarrayi, Rose as Nangala, and little Miya as Murrumiya or Napaljarri. Having completed the Grad. Dip. course the year before,

I was enthusiastic about getting into some language work. I had prepared some language resources prior to our leaving Townsville and was able to use them effectively. Without going into too much depth, I shall briefly explain the basics of my project.

Upper Primaries

In an environment of scarce resources, my program was tailored to an integrated learning approach. We were fortunate to have advisory expert English as a Second Language Teacher, Carol Davies, able to visit regularly from Alice Springs, to monitor my progress and keep me on cue. I spent a lot of time doing lesson preparations and planning. The classroom resembled a studio with appropriate seating arrangements with individual microphones and earphones, large audio speakers, radio, theme posters, and so on.

As an introduction to listening to the radio, and to start the day's activities, we kicked off with a theme song – Charlie Pride's Sunshiny Day. Before school, I would record a passage from the daily weather report and transcribe the passage on the board. The kids would listen to it, say it, write it, and discuss its meaning, and so on. At the time, the Iran-Iraq war was in its fifth year and became one of the major themes integrated across the areas of maths, science, language, art, geography, and social science.

The kids, previously shy and reserved, took to their listening, speaking, and writing skill development with great enthusiasm. On top of this, there was a lot of land-rights activity with people coming and going, meetings, and so on. I took advantage of this by inviting people from Canberra, Darwin and elsewhere, who were involved in the proceedings, to give a talk to the class and answer any questions about land rights issues. Some changes were afoot at the school too.

It was around this time when Geoff decided to go for a band two promotion. He had been in the position of acting band two now for some months and it made sense to him to have his position substantiated. Geoff was confident and asked me for my support. I spent time and energy promoting Geoff and his professional attributes, meeting with the Schools Inspector, and so on. It all paid off for Geoff and we celebrated his promotion. There were often whole school excursions to spots along the river. In the absence of a school vehicle, my class squeezed into the back of my Land Rover, and off we'd go.

Boomerang and Kunajarrayi

At Boomerang waterhole, some parents brought along a hind quarter of beef which was hung up on a tree. It was an efficient way of organising lunch. All you had to do was grab the knife, carve off a lump of meat from the bone and roast it on the coals on the river bank, and enjoy with a cup of tea. It was all so easy. No fuss at all. Parents supervised the kids while teachers had a break. The kids played in the river and went hunting along the lower bank. There were other favourite haunts too.

A bit further downstream, there were black bream, catfish, and barramundi at Kunatjarrayi, where, a small distance to the north there was extensive longitudinal sand ridge country. The kids would dig into the top of the dunes for little water frogs, bloated with reserves of fresh water for dry times. Along the top of one of the dunes you could see where, on the smooth windswept surface, a hawk had ambushed a marsupial mouse. There were also clear dingo prints along the red ridge tops and evidence of diggings for water frogs. On one occasion there was a shower – only a few drops of rain fell. Yet the little frogs responded, digging their way out, perhaps from a metre or deeper. There was a rainbow over our camp in the desert - I recorded it on film.

Another rather spectacular place was Windtijangu. It had a typical badland topography with a small, isolated cluster of buttes with steep scree slopes. We'd set up camp there for the weekend and go exploring and collect perfumed sandalwood to burn on the fire.

Miya and Japalyi at Windtjangu, 1980.

Willowra was about an hour's drive from the Ti Tree turnoff, about three hours north of Alice Springs. As usual, we had a standing perishables order from Woolworths. There were times when we would drive into Alice Springs to replenish supplies of food and other items. We'd drive past central Mt Stuart which could be seen some distance towards the north.

Rose and baby Sara Kuliliya, Willowra, 1980.

Sara is Born

We were at the Alice Springs hospital when Sara was born on the afternoon of 1st August 1980. Rose's brother Jeffrey came from Santa Teresa to help with little Miya. Rose and the new baby remained in the hospital for a few days before the flight back home. Once Rose and Sara had settled, Jeffrey, Miya, and I drove back to Willowra, stopping halfway to put the billy on, as the sun sank over the spinifex plains in a big red ball.

Miya and Sara were usually referred to as Napaljarri jarra. (the two Napaljarri's) Sara was also given the name of Kuliliya (Budgerigar).

Jeffrey stayed on for a few days after Rose and baby Sara returned and then went back to work at Santa Teresa. I was back teaching and things had settled down to a routine again. The build-up was approaching.

Build up

It was getting hot in mid-November and the storms were building. One late afternoon, we noticed a large electrical storm on the eastern horizon. About a couple of hours later as it got dark, there was a long glowing strip on the horizon. Lightning had set fire to the spinifex plains and it looked quite close. Geoff and I went to investigate. We guessed the flames would be a couple of kilometres away – four or five at the most. We kept heading eastward towards the firefront.

The speedo showed that we'd travelled twelve kilometres before we reached the front. From this experience, we came to the conclusion that out there on the flat spinifex plains, it was twelve kilometres from where you were standing, to the horizon. In other words, given that you're standing on the ground, twelve kilometres is as far as you can see to the curvature of the earth.

Green time

The kids called it Green time – the dramatic changes of the Lander River flood plains as they were transformed from bare red earth to an endless carpet of emerald green. It's only then that you understand why the invading cattlemen were so intent on settling the region. It was bright green as far as you could see along the river.

One afternoon, a group of kids came up the stairs onto the verandah shouting something about the water coming down the river. We went out to the verandah to hear a faint rustling sound. Within minutes, the wide, dry sandy river bed was as if metamorphosed into a moving tide of red-brown muddy water that gently rose to more than a metre within a couple of hours. The Warlpiri kids had seen all this before.

A Nasty Gash

The river settled into an easy flow and was deep enough to take the dingy out with the kids. It was late one afternoon, close to dark when I was on the way home, pulling the dingy back upstream. My left leg caught on something below the surface of the red silt-laden river, like the jagged end of a star picket. It started to sting but I ignored it in my effort to get back before dark.

It was just dark when I pulled the boat up the bank and it was then that I saw the cut. The outside of my left calf was torn open in a five-inch-long flesh wound. I went across to the homestead for help. Jim and Jocelyn were both concerned and without anaesthetic, Jocelyn attempted to scrub the mud out of the wound and stitched it up. I was watching the procedure and went into shock, saying I felt nauseous.

Jim ran for a bucket. Jocelyn put fourteen stitches in, pulling the gaping wound together, all the while complaining about how hard it was to get the needle through the tough skin. Within three days or so, the wound began to get hot and swollen, and I found that I had to raise my leg to ease the pain. I drove into Alice Springs with my leg up on the dash, using the hand throttle to drive. When the nurse lanced the wound, about a cup full of yellow-green puss spurted out, easing the pressure. They cleaned and re-stitched the wound, and within a few days, I was back at work. Food gathering excursions were the order of the day during the green time.

School picnic - Kids cooking bush beans. Willowra, 1980.

Kids and their parents directed me to where the bush beans and bush bananas were growing, and we roasted them in the coals. Later in the season, there were round, olive-green bush oranges that hung from a long stalk high up in the trees. The fruit was a bit like passion fruit inside, only sweeter. Small sweet watermelons and Yakatjirri, small black, grape-like berries were also in season, and we'd have a break from the confines of the classroom to go down to the river to play and pick fresh bush food.

The boys made sand castles. They built sculptures about a foot high by scooping up a handful of water and fine sand from the river and pouring it into one place. They would repeat this process about ten times. Each time the water would run off, leaving the deposition of fine sand into free-form sculptures. In some places, erosion of the banks formed sand cliffs and the kids jumped and slid down into the water. I thought that these kids had a good lifestyle. And they had unusual pets.

Roy and Bus

One morning as I approached the school, Roy, a young bull, was casually emerging from the door of my classroom, chewing on one of the kid's workbooks. The door had somehow been left open overnight. Roy was often teased by the kids. Roy grew bigger and soon became a threat to everybody's safety. He became increasingly irritable. One day while Pat and Jack Maggs were visiting, their four-year-old son, Darren, wandered under the fence and into the schoolyard - Roy's territory. We heard yelling and crying and rushed out to see Roy rolling Darren back under the fence. There weren't any injuries but it was bound to happen sooner or later. Roy began chasing the kids and ended up in the meat house. There were donkeys too.

Bus, Willowra, 1980.

There were a lot of feral donkeys on the station and sometimes young ones were reared by hand to become pets. Bus was deformed and a bit longer than normal. He was quiet enough, and it wasn't unusual to see four or five kids on his back, repeatedly digging their heels into his ribs to get him to move.

Japalyi

The school Janitor, Jungarrayi, told me about a lair in a creek bed not far from the station and I went out with a couple of men to collect the pup that they had already chosen. They showed me the lair which was well concealed under the exposed roots of a river gum, not far from a water soak.

This pup was a few weeks older than Warnabari had been, and I called him Japalyi – short for Japaltjarri (my son). As a half-grown pup, Japalyi had persistently worried Roy the bull, by nipping at his heels, every time he put his head down to graze or drink. I have heard stories about dingoes worrying cows.

The hapless cow eventually succumbs to exhaustion, starvation, and thirst. I remember being out at the Seven Mile near Lajamanu, when Warnabari would disappear for half an hour and bring a small mob back to us just for the hell of it. Unlike Warnabari, Japalyi was prone to wander and on several occasions, stole food from the Yapa. One afternoon he bought home a bag of flour and it took me ages to find the owner, return the flour and apologise. Japalyi was eventually to come with us to Papunya.

A Productive Garden

I made a chook pen underneath the water tank and we filled it with chooks. I also fenced off sufficient space for a garden in the beautiful red alluvial soil. During the winter, we grew peas, tomatoes, silver beet, carrots and lettuce. In the summer, we had sweet corn, beans, zucchini, and other veggies. The chooks ended up with a lot of greens and in return, we always managed to get enough fresh eggs for the family. That was until a little truant sussed them out and stole three good laying hens from under our noses in as many days. The truant was seen cooking one of the chooks down in the riverbed.

Bogged at Ingallan Creek

It was in late January 1981 when we were driving back from Townsville. We picked up some perishables and other supplies in Alice Springs and I paid them a visit at the Regional Office for work-related business and to send the principal at Willowra, an ETA, (Expected Time of Arrival), a standard safety procedure for providing advanced notice that we planned to be at Willowra that evening. It hadn't been raining for some days, and the road was reported to be passable. It was approaching dusk when we arrived at Ingallan Creek, half an hour away from the station.

There were two approaches to the crossing. I made the wrong one, taking the left-hand fork. The Land Rover sank to the axles. The left side wheels had broken through the dry crust, leaving the vehicle on a list such that you couldn't open the left side door. Dark clouds were gathering and we strung the tarp up and waited for someone to arrive to tow us out. No-one came. We set up camp for the night. It hadn't rained overnight and Geoff in his Land Rover and a Toyota turned up in the mid-morning.

Bogged. We spent the night at Ingallan Creek, 1981.

With the two vehicles hitched up, our Land Rover popped out of the bog and we were soon back home at Willowra. It was a Monday, my first day back at school and Geoff requested that I come immediately to take my class and attend a staff meeting. I refused on the grounds that my family was in need of urgent help to unpack and settle in. I advised that I'd be in to start work the following day. Geoff radioed Regional Office and they demanded an immediate return to work or drive back into Alice Springs to answer for my actions. If I wasn't so exhausted I would have contacted the Union and taken a stand but instead, complied with their demands and just moved on. Working relations remained at a functional level and I was determined to get through the year as best I could and go for a transfer.

Sara is sick

It was the Easter holidays and John Humphreys, his wife Lenore, and children, Thomas and Nina, were visiting. Sara was nine months old. One morning Sara developed a high temperature and began fitting. Jocelyn was away for the weekend and, as usual, had passed on the key to the clinic to Rose, in case of emergency. Rose and John were able to find medication and call for the flying doctor from Alice Springs.

Sara's little veins were on the verge of collapse. John assumed that Sara had contracted bacterial meningitis. He was able to find a vein on the back of her hand and gave her an injection of antibiotics, followed by valium to bring the fitting under control. Sara was still being breastfed but was now in a coma. John monitored Sara as we waited the three hours in the shade of the bough shelter at the airstrip for the arrival of Air Med.
Rose and Sara were attended to by the pediatrician at the Alice Springs Hospital and transferred to Adelaide via St Johns Air Ambulance. Sara was three weeks in intensive care and Rose was accommodated at the hospital. I was assigned to Sadadeen primary school but had no teaching responsibilities. Miya and I stayed with Margaret McHugh and Vicki Shardlow in Alice Springs to wait for news of Sara's progress.

We were advised that if Sara was to survive meningitis, there was a chance that she would be severely afflicted by blindness, deafness or, some other impediment. These were anxious days and I remember whittling away at a repaired rifle butt as a diversion. Sara made a quick recovery without any problems and I attributed it to John's decisive action and treatment in a critical situation out there in the bush. If John and his family had not been there at the time I hate to contemplate what would have become of us. Sara's illness marked the end of our time at Willowra and I was transferred to Papunya as a permanent band two Out Stations Coordinator.

With Japalyi, en route to Papunya, 1981.

Chapter 6
Papunya & Beyond

Considering the gravity of her illness, little Sara made a rapid and full recovery and we were all at Papunya for the start of term three in 1981. Before leaving Alice Springs I had the opportunity to meet some of the staff.

Aerial view of Papunya – rows of transitional houses, foreground, 1981.

Like Lajamanu, Papunya wasn't the most popular destination and someone from the Alice Springs regional office said that Papunya meant "Poop on you". I looked forward to my new challenge. Our allocated house was just down from the old health clinic where little Miya thought there were ghosts, and possibly for good reason.

British nuclear weapons testing, with the full support of the Australian government, was carried out on Maralinga lands at Emu Field in South Australia and elsewhere during the 1950s. The presence of First Nations people on the test site at the time is well documented. Survivors were forced to leave their homelands. Papunya was one of the purpose-built settlements to which hundreds of surviving families were forced to relocate.

Atomic Bombs

An extract from the Royal Commission report:

Permission was not sought for the tests from affected Aboriginal groups such as the Pitjantjatjara, Tjarutja and Kokatha. The use of atomic weapons contaminated great tracts of traditional land, and transformed an independent and physically wide-ranging people into a semi-static and dependent group - forced relocation was one of the traumas they suffered. The damage was radiological, psycho-social, and cultural.

Studies of the health impacts of the weapons tests have excluded non-urban Aboriginal people (e.g. the study by Wise and Moroney, first presented to the Royal Commission, which states: "Two population groups are excluded from the calculations. They are the Aboriginals living away from population centres and personnel involved directly in nuclear test activities ..." (Keith N. Wise and John R. Moroney, Australian Radiation Laboratory, May 1992, "Public Health Impact of Fallout from British Nuclear Weapons Tests in Australia, 1952 – 1957", Dept. of Health, Housing and Community Services, ARL/TRI05 ISSN 0157-1400, p.2.)
From Jim Green, Friends of the Earth campaigner.

10 years after the Australian Government declared the clean-up of Maralinga as completed (in 2001) erosion continues to expose radioactive waste repositories.

Working at Papunya

My band 2 position of Outstations Coordinator was one of the highest-paid, easiest, jobs I think I've ever had. There wasn't much in the way of long-term satisfaction in it though. I never really got to know the school staff, kids and wider community as I had done in previous teacher roles.

An outstation was an early form of homeland centre established at the request of local Aboriginal groups. Teachers volunteered to teach in outstations. It wasn't for the faint-hearted, because they were often required to camp out with minimal amenities. For example, there were no buildings apart from the traditional humpies, a meter or so high.

They were built from whatever materials were available, usually sheets of corrugated iron, star pickets, fencing wire, chook wire, spinifex and any available bush materials.

Food was stored in the fork of a tree if there was a tree close by, or on the roof of the humpy away from the dogs. Mt. Liebig or Watiyawanu was settled by former residents of Papunya and Haasts Bluff. They were multi-lingual with Luritja as a first language. Later there were Pintupi, Warlpiri, and Arrente people. Teachers were paid a camping allowance, had a department four-wheel drive, supplies for the week, and camped in their swag.

Kids at school, Kintore, 1982.

My responsibilities involved visits to outstations, providing professional support to teachers and keeping their bilingual teaching/learning materials up to speed. For example, one of the earliest four-wheel drive bush trips I made was to the recently established Mt Liebig – a sort of semi-permanent camp near the foothills of Mt Liebig about eighty kilometres west of Papunya settlement. They had radio communications with Papunya and the nurse visited once a week.

The teacher, Jeff Hulcombe was sitting out there, in the Central Desert, with a small group of scruffy little kids, teaching them to read and write in Luritja. The make-shift classroom included a little chalkboard on an easel. The kids had workbooks to write in and the only protection they had from the elements was a corrugated iron wind-break and that was about it. These rudimentary working conditions were offset to some extent by the spectacular view of the highest Mountain in the Territory – Mt Liebig. New Bore was another outstation. Jeff and I became friends and he spent time with us when he was back in the settlement. One of the other teachers was Alistair.

Alistair Burns

Our house was previously allocated to Alistair Burns, who was taking the infants class at the time. Alistair always reminded me of the day we first met when I introduced myself saying "....and you must be the pastor".

He had recently separated from his wife, Kerry, who had returned to Adelaide with the children. Alistair, from Nimbin, grew vegies and shared beautiful silver beet with us. He came to Australia from a family from Christchurch, New Zealand, a private school, and so on. He told me about his mother coming to visit him at Papunya.

Alistair's Mum was appalled at his domestic state of affairs and having to drink tea from a grimy pannikin, among other things. We became friends and spent time together. Alistair and I went out bush of a weekend, listened to Chad Morgan, Jethro Tull, John Mayal and other classics of the sixties, and exchanged ideas and experiences. We played regular tennis with Jeff and Adrian, the resident doctor. As dilapidated as it was, full of pot-holes, gaping holes in the fence and an uneven surface, it was a tennis court and we appreciated being able to play a game. It was around this time that the petrol sniffers were causing havoc around the place - this is worth a mention.

Petrol Sniffing

It wasn't long after we'd arrived that, like any other petrol vehicle, our Land Rover become a target for petrol sniffers. We'd never heard of petrol sniffing before. The sniffers were mostly teenagers who ran rampant through the night sniffing petrol. They sniffed usually from half a soft drink can and slept during the day. On several occasions, we were awoken at 2 or 3 o'clock in the morning by sniffers levering and banging at the Land Rover cap or the 44-gallon drum with a star picket or anything else they could find, in their attempts to get at the petrol. Sometimes I'd chase them away through the darkness of the night but they were back in no time and we were beginning to suffer from sleep deprivation. If we were to stay at Papunya the only solution to the problem was to get rid of the petrol Land Rover and go with diesel.

The grey series 2A that we had since the days in North East Arnhem Land in the sixties was well maintained and looked good. I sold it to Scobie for $3,000 and we bought a new 1981 Long Wheel-based hard top 2 ¼ litre series 3 diesel Land Rover for $11,000 from Sutton Motors in Alice Springs. The sniffing community soon learned that there wasn't any petrol around our place and there were no more disturbances.

TAFE

I was offered a band two Adult Educator position by the end of September. I had the opportunity to expand and develop programs and courses for Papunya and neighbouring Haast's Bluff. I was also responsible for the Yuendumu programs. I took community development seriously and soon had Health Worker training, Bookkeeping, Numeracy and Literacy, Driver Education, and courses for the YMCA and the women's centre up and running.

I developed my own resources for occupational Numeracy and Literacy and facilitated the Papunya and Haast's Bluff Health Worker Training program, using existing resources. I employed and assisted part-time instructors locally and from Alice Springs to teach other courses. I made monthly visits to Yuendumu and Haast's Bluff to monitor programs.

I also developed a reporting template and wrote monthly reports to TAFE manager, Tom Marling at the Alice Springs office. Tom was very supportive and helpful and approved just about anything I put up. Peter Toyne, the Adult Educator at Yuendumu was already running a comprehensive TAFE program and my visits were purely a formality. Peter's project was working with the Yapa on the development of a local radio station. Brilliant!

As part of my role as Adult Educator, I was the editor, reporter, and photographer of the school and community monthly newspaper – Tjakulpa. The production team included Thomas Stevens, artwork, Kevin McAuley, printing, and Charlotte Phillipus Napurrula and John Heffernan, translations. I put a lot of effort into this publication and it was distributed as far afield as Alice Springs, Yuendumu, and elsewhere. It was part of the bilingual program and I was passionate about achieving a professional standard for the community. We had a fully equipped print shop and a full-time printer, who produced all materials associated with a thriving bilingual program. Part of my role was to encourage meaningful school and wider community contributions.

I received many positive reports on Tjakulpa from the Alice Springs Regional Office and other schools, and I was quite proud of my achievement. However, due to the development of toxic work relations, this was not to last. My TAFE work went on as usual. Community Adult Education notices and reports as contributions to Tjakulpa continued and I was relieved that I was out of a stressful situation. I had plenty of free time.

Life Outside Work at Papunya

My sister Elaine and her family were at Wave Hill and Mum came up from Melbourne to stay with us in October 1982. We shared Christmas with Elaine, John and their kids, Dan and Rachel at home in Papunya. Mum stayed on through January 1983.

We spent many happy times together, often on trips out in the desert, where Miya and I'd go exploring, and Rose would look after baby Sara, while Mum set up her easel, and painted. We were always so impressed by the enormous skill Mum had in capturing the very essence of the desert landscapes.

We took trips to Mt Liebig, Waru Wiya, Wimparrku, Ulampara, Yalkipi, Ilpili and Yayiyayi, Haast's Bluff, and the Derwent River. The Central Desert landscapes were breathtaking and we often made trips out camping in the pristine, sandy river beds, under ancient ghost gums.

During our time at Papunya, friends, Mark and Rose Hollands, Chris Fry and Terry Parry came to stay. We also billeted student teachers and others from the department.

It was during the Easter holidays, that we were camping on the bank of a river bed near Mt Liebig. We had ordered some Easter eggs for the girls. I was out of the swag before dawn, on that freezing cold Easter morning, lit the fire, and put the billy on. I made rabbit tracks from the camp, around a couple of spinifex clumps to where the Easter eggs were hidden. We'd reminded the girls about the Easter rabbit the night before. They were out of bed at the crack of dawn, followed the tracks, and found the eggs in no time at all. It was shared experiences like this that made life in the bush something special.

Grandpa has Passed Away

Mum was with us at Papunya when Grandpa died on 15 August 1982. Grandpa was 92 – born in Hawthorn, Victoria on 6th April 1890. Mum got the news that Grandpa had suffered a major heart attack at Apollo Bay, and a few days after that, suffered a fatal one. It was sudden. On the morning after Grandpa died, Mum told us of a dream she had the night of his death. She said that it was vivid. She was holding her dad in her arms attempting to save him from being sucked down into a whirlpool.

Mum was very close to her dad and although he was ninety-two, they still wrote to each other regularly. It was a huge loss to her and I'm glad that she had the support of family at this sad time. We recalled the days back in the 1950s and 60s on holidays we shared with Grandpa and Ella at their beautiful home, his English garden, and his music, from the rise near the Otway Ranges down at the Bay.

Standing Orders

We had the usual weekly standing order of perishables from Alice Springs which arrived on Connair on a Thursday morning. About every three months or so, we'd make the trip to Alice Springs to pick up extra supplies. We would pack everything we needed for the trip the night before. We would be up and gone by three o'clock in the morning, to be in town by nine, for shopping. The kids slept in the back of the Land Rover and when they woke up at daybreak, Rose would give them a prepared breakfast as we trundled along the sandy corrugations.

One morning we were about five kilometres out from Papunya. From the rearview mirror, I noticed a lot of sparks and flames shooting out from behind the car. I thought the worst. We pulled up and I ran to investigate what was going on under the bonnet. I found the remnants of a smouldering rag still there on the hot manifold. I had inadvertently left an oily rag there while checking the water and engine oil levels the night before, and it had caught fire. There was no damage and we continued on. Miya was nearly five and proud of her sight reading. On another Alice Springs shopping trip, Miya read the word... "stop". It was the stop sign at the T junction as we turned south onto the Stuart Highway.

The Derwent is up

During the wet season of February 1982, the Derwent River was in flood and the community was cut off. The supply truck was loaded with flour and other items for the shop. The white fellas were concerned about running out of food and a working party was pulled together to ferry the supplies across the river.

Staff ferry bags of flour across the Derwent River. February, 1982.

There were teachers, police, the shop manager, the mechanic, and others – seven of them. They formed a human chain across the waist deep water and were shouldering flour bags up the steep and muddy bank when someone had an idea. The bonnet of a car wreck would be used. They tied the bonnet on a long tow rope to the ute, stacked flour bags onto the car bonnet, and towed this makeshift sled, up the muddy river bank where the flour could be stacked into the tray of the truck and ferried back to the settlement.

While all this was going on, a group of Yapa men arrived at the scene in their Holden sedan. They were on their way to Alice Springs. They simply manhandled the car, pushing it across the river and up the bank on the other side, piled in, and off they went. "No worries" the caption read. I did a full-blown report on the proceedings as a feature for the news publication.

The rain soon transformed this dry landscape. The whole place was awash and the muddy red torrent flowed down the road, through our yard, and under the house. Yapa kids played on the road in the mud. It was great to be around for the storms and floods. Soon after the water began to recede, we were out for a drive to Ulumpara Range.

Kids playing in flood water at Papunya. February, 1982.

Neanderthals in the Mist

Under normal clear conditions, from our kitchen window, you could view the western face of Ulumpara Range as it glowed red in the late afternoon sun. This time, the mountain was obscured in a low cloud. We walked the Land Rover along the road where the water was up to a couple of feet deep. We picked a full bucket of mushrooms from under the mulga trees along the way. These mushrooms were quite strong in flavour.

Miya requested some clouds in a jar. The views from the top of the foothills were spectacular with the roar of crystal clear water cascading down the gorges and over the dam wall. One afternoon, Jeff, Adrian, and I had stripped off, had a swim and decided to climb to higher ground to see the cloud over the range. I brought Miya's jar to fill with some clouds to take back home. We spent some time up there, like a small Neanderthal hunting party moving from place to place to take in spectacular views of this ancient place with its dramatic exposed rocky ridges and steep gorges now heavily shrouded in gentle swirling mist.

South of Papunya - background, Mt Liebig, 1981.

I already knew the place, having on several occasions climbed to the top of the range. You could see the Papunya airstrip in the distance, to the west, and Haast's Bluff over to the east.

One afternoon when Mum was painting on the creek bank I took little Miya up through the main gorge. There was a breeze there and she got frightened of the Pangka Langka and we had to go back. The Pangka Langka is a giant mythical creature with one short leg and a big foot that stole unsupervised children who wandered into his range. Sometimes on a dark night, you could see his campfire burning near the top. There were interesting personalities at Papunya at the time.

Local Characters

John Thomas

John was a fair cop. A recently recruited constable. John enjoyed fraternising with the teachers, and would often just turn up out of the blue on a casual visit. One evening, John came to visit to show us his gun. He invited me to come with him for shooting practice at the firing range the following weekend. The handgun was a .32 calibre or something similar and had a vicious recoil that just about knocked you over backward if you weren't properly braced against it. That was its only virtue – even at a ridiculously close range, it was sheer luck if you hit the target.

John showed particular interest in our new Land Rover and had a drive in it. He decided that he wanted to buy one, but mine was far too slow on the highway for his liking, and he asked me about the new series 3 with the big Isuzu engine. I advised against it but he bought one anyway and was initially very proud. " Nice motor car," he said, as we drove out on the road for a spin.

It was fast and powerful. After a couple of months, John came back to me, bitterly disappointed in his new car, saying that the body was falling to pieces. For example, among other things, the rivets were popping out of the roof gutter and other parts of the bodywork, the roof was leaking, and the galvanised steel windscreen frame had developed fractures. John had driven his Land Rover hard - over miles of severe sand corrugations, and rough bush tracks at high speed, giving the bodywork a real hammering on over-inflated tyres.

Leon and Julie

There were also Leon and Julie. Leon was the policeman in charge and Julie was a teacher at the Papunya School. Miya was five and she was in Julie's English as a First Language class. Leon organised once-a-week film nights for settlement staff, held at the police station, and I shared responsibility for ordering 16-millimetre films. Leon was about seven feet high and slim with it, while Julie was a petite five feet something. Whenever I saw them together I thought they looked a bit incompatible.

Others were Papunya Community Government Councillor, Alison and partner Steve. I met Alison during my office training and book-keeping course. Alison was a dominant person in the community and everyone seemed to bow to her command. I liked Alison and we got on well. Alison became an MP along with Peter Toyne from Yuendumu in the N.T. Labor Government.

It was around this time too, that it was felt that the Health Department wasn't providing adequate services to Papunya. There was a flash new health centre, complete with an operating theatre, but no resident doctor to deal with the widespread chronic illnesses. So an independent health service was formed. The service was staffed by doctors, Adrian Sleigh and Jenny King, Elizabeth, and Yapa health workers. It all seemed to be progressing well, and I got involved in Health Worker Training. I ran weekly classes using the Health Department's programs.

Adrian knew what was required from a trained practitioner's perspective and Alison wanted more communication – more meaningful consultation with Yapa. Adrian argued that the service didn't have budgetary provisions for the resources or staff and so on. It didn't work out and was reverted back to N.T. Health.

Alison's partner, Steve, was employed to monitor the Papunya Power Plant. This meant that he had to read and interpret the dial gauges, indicators, and instruments in the power plant and make daily entries in a log book, among other things. My task was to develop a one-off training program for Steve. Steve became a part-time TAFE student, and I worked with him on occupational numeracy. We worked well together and Steve made good progress.

Steve was also an enthusiastic gun collector, and had a formidable arsenal of weaponry, from sophisticated high-powered rifles, to elaborate limited-edition handguns. Regular shopping trips to Alice Springs continued and sometimes when in Alice Springs, we stayed at the Pines Resort.

Erik and Henry

At the Pines resort in Alice Springs, proprietors Erik and Henry were always friendly and would treat us to a fancy, full English breakfast for the road. They took us up on our invitation to visit us at Papunya. They were to visit on a couple of occasions. On the second occasion, they arrived with an old car. I was amused at Henry hoisting a jerry can of petrol out of the boot and talking to himself, saying aloud, "Now deep breath in". They explained that the old car was in exchange for a traditional painting of the mythical Pangka Langka of Ulumpara.

When we eventually saw the painting I was amazed at its size and complexity. It represented months of work, and potentially worth thousands of dollars. This leads me to another emerging issue.

A Used Car Industry

Around that time, there weren't many cars in settlements. I had concerns about a burgeoning, dodgy used car industry. This was based in Adelaide, where second-hand cars such as Fords and Holdens, were shipped to Alice Springs specifically for the local First Nations market. We'd heard that if you expressed an interest in a particular car, in some used car yard in Alice, the dealer might advise that the car is earmarked for Aborigines and direct you to something else. My observations over time were that a group of Yapa would pool their money, make a trip to Alice Springs, and buy a used car, only to find that it had mechanical issues. They'd be lucky to make it back home.

More Land Rovers

It had been about six months after I'd sold the grey series 2 and noticed it, whilst out on a drive. Scobie had abandoned it, leaving it quietly resting out on the spinifex plains. One day we stopped to have a look at the wreck. The bonnet was lying some ten meters away. It was flattened, and most of the rivets were popped out, but the frame was intact, and it was recoverable. I inspected the rest of the vehicle and found that all the lights, windscreen, windows, and instruments had been broken.

The body was still straight with no dints. The tyres were still intact and inflated. The wiring was in knots after many attempts at makeshift repairs. The engine bay was pretty well complete, but there was sand inside the rocker cover. There was still oil in the engine and it still had compression, the radiator was still full and there was no apparent damage underneath. I reckoned that our old Landy was salvageable and I went to see what Scobie wanted to do with it.

Scobie said it was finished, and that he was intending to put a match to it. He said that nothing worked after the kids had been at it and the gearbox was blown. Apart from hunting trips, Scobie had used low range for pushing large dead trees for firewood. I bought the wreck back for $200, and it lay in our yard for six months until I finally committed to repairing it, registering it, and using it as a bush vehicle. Terry Sutton sold me a complete working series 2 gearbox – transfer box and all for $100. During a trip to Darwin, I bought new windows, windscreens, instruments, lights, and everything I needed as replacement parts, from the army Land Rover wreckers. John helped me with the wiring and the resident mechanic gave me advice on the mechanical aspects. John organised registration. In an initial test run, it travelled at 70 miles per hour along the dirt road out to Ulumpara.

Another project involved making a trailer. I heard of an abandoned wreck of a long wheel-based six-cylinder Land Rover at rest, just this side of Yuendumu.

I towed it back to Papunya to make a trailer out of the back. Towing 1.7 tonnes, over soft sandy roads was a challenge. I cut through the chassis at the back of the cab, leaving the back tray, with tailgate, and all the fittings intact. I retained the axle, complete with spare diff, wheels, and brakes.

The two sides of the box section chassis extended forwards. I then cut, folded, and welded these inwards, to form an A-frame, on which I bolted a trailer hitch. At around this time, two German backpackers turned up from Kirk and Bronwin Smith's place at Charters Towers. They stayed with us for a couple of weeks and helped with the painting. We painted the chassis black and the bodywork was Bahama Gold – the same as the new Land Rover. The trailer, being of the same wheel width, tracked perfectly behind, even in soft sand, and corrugations. It was a ripper, and the Germans officially named it, "Unzerverslik" (indestructible.) We used Unzerverslik for many years.

Japalyi and Twinkle Toes

I've already mentioned Japalyi and his antics back at Willowra Station. Now he was here at Papunya with us. It wasn't long after we settled in, that he placed a dead duck on our back doorstep. It belonged to the Pastor, and I just wasn't game enough to return it. Then there was the cat. Somehow, we'd acquired a cat - a half-grown skinny black cat that the girls called Twinkle Toes. The two played together. Japalyi would grasp Twinkle Toes by the loose skin around its neck and drag it around. Twinkle Toes would object loudly but never struggled. He probably knew instinctively that to struggle whilst in the grip of a dingo would be fatal. To outsiders, it must have looked as though the dingo was playing with a dead cat.

One afternoon, in the heat of the day, Japalyi was asleep in the shade under Jeff's ute. Jeff drove off, running over him. Japalyi was dragging his back legs along the ground. Jeff was upset and brought Japalyi home, where we did what we could, to make him comfortable. There was a scheduled visit the next morning, by the vet from Alice Springs and I was able to get him to examine the dog. The vet advised that Japalyi had suffered a crushed pelvis and surgery would be prohibitive.

Rather than prolong his agony I put him as gently as I could beside me on the front seat and drove across to Ulumpara. I carried him a little way up from the creek, ended his suffering, wrapped him in a blanket, and gave him a proper burial. I gave him protection under a pile of carefully placed, heavy stones. The grave site was on the hill slope, overlooking the gorge. I must have been a couple of hours there. It was an emotional time for me.

Tom Marling had approved my leave without pay for study leave in Adelaide in 1984. Keith Thiele, the Director of TAFE offered us his house in Balhannah, in the Adelaide hills for rent.

South Australia

I was on leave without pay and enrolled as a full-time student in the Grad Dip Further Education course, at the Underdale campus at the University of South Australia. Miya was seven and enrolled in the year two class at Oakbank State Primary School. Her teachers were Vera Mignone and Rhonda Haldane. Sara was only four and recovering from open heart surgery. We became recipients of welfare payments for the year. We bought a sporty little light green Renault to get around. Keith had a chook pen out the back, and we bought some Sussex hens.

As new arrivals, we soon found that the rural community of Balhannah was insular, and we became the target of exclusion and racism. For example one afternoon, Rose was taunted by a busload of school kids while waiting for Miya. I met several of Keith's friends and acquaintances, who played tennis and was keen to join them for a game. They never got back to me. On a superficial level, people were friendly enough and Miya's school and her teachers were progressive and supportive and she enjoyed her experience there.

I drove down to the Underdale Campus several times a week to attend lectures and tutorials. The course was interesting and challenging and as I sit here at the computer I recall cutting and pasting the old way. Essays were handwritten on foolscap sheets, which were then cut and stapled, with a few lines added in between, making a train of paper, from the ceiling down to the floor and beyond. I couldn't type and Rose would key it in on her portable Olivetti.

Church

Among the Balhannah locals we got to meet, was the Reverend Adcock, an articulate person, and close friend of Keith Thiele. They were Lutherans and everybody seemed to be involved with the church. As temporary visitors, we went along occasionally and were welcomed there. The Reverend Adcock paid us frequent visits and always seemed interested in how we were faring. He seemed particularly interested in my views on indigenous issues, environmental concerns, political leanings, and values and attitudes that we would discuss over a cup of tea.

The Reverend was friendly and seemed genuinely interested in what I had to say. There were a couple of occasions when Keith came back to Balhannah and I saw him in the church. Keith was active in the church, and one of his rituals was to slowly and deliberately, slide his hand deep into his trouser pocket, and produce a lolly for each kid who was participating that day.

The Fox and the Chooks

The Sussex chooks were doing well and we had plenty of eggs. There were eight in all. One night we were awoken by a commotion down at the chook pen, and I realised that I'd forgotten to shut the gate. A fox had systematically taken one hen at a time, from the perch, outside the pen to bite the neck and suck its blood out. We got down there in time to save the last hen. The fox had fled into the night, leaving our prized chooks dead, with their necks chewed, and scattered around the pen. The locals explained that when this happens to livestock, it's usually a pregnant vixen that prefers blood, over anything else and they will keep going until they clean up the whole pen. I felt very sad and Miya and I wrote a book about it, entitled 'The Fox and the Chooks' Miya wrote the story, and I did the illustrations.

Uwe and Cathy

We'd met Uwe and his partner, Cathy, back at Papunya when they'd arrived for semester two in 1983 to take up teaching positions at the school. Uwe was an intelligent, friendly and charming person. Uwe was recently separated from his wife and had two small children in Adelaide. Uwe and Cathy came down to Adelaide to see the children. They were appreciative of our friendship and support and would bring the children up to Balhannah to visit. I shared various issues that emerged from my studies, and we had some quality time together. I'll talk more about our friend Uwe later. There was an interesting student in my group, Joe Lane.

Joe Lane

Joe Lane and I had one important thing in common and that was, to some extent, an understanding of First Nations Rights. Joe was originally from NZ and married to Maria, an academic in Indigenous Further Education at the University. Joe was a satirist and a lot of his conversation took the form of challenging questions. Some years later, Joe and Maria made a couple of visits to Atherton. Maria was originally from a mission near Murray Bridge and they both spent a lot of time there. Joe was an academic and always seemed to be researching issues surrounding Indigenous Education.

Flying Again

It was in September that I decided to bite the bullet and purchase an ultralight aircraft. I'd done some research and decided to settle for the Tyro, from Geoff Eastwood of East Coast Air at Aldinga. The Tyro came with all materials and plans for construction. It was of all aluminium construction, with flying surfaces covered with fabric. It had full 3-axis controls with a high wing configuration, a wing span of 29 feet 2 inches, a wing area of 113 square feet, and a total length of 14ft 6in. It was powered by a 44.7 hp Rotax aero-engine. The cruise speed was 55mph, stall speed 19 mph, with a maximum speed of 70mph. I put the building of the Tyro on hold and between assignments on weekends went to flying lessons at Aldinga Airstrip. My plane was a sporty aerobatic low-wing trainer with a Rolls Royce engine. The instructor sat at his controls in the rear.

I started with the basics of take-off, straight and level, stalls, and approaches. On my first powered stall at the top of a steep climb, the nose dropped and we were no longer flying. We went into a dive and I was enjoying the thrill of it until the instructor, with some anxiety, began pointing out the windscreen towards the ground. The ground was coming up fast. The instructor took the controls for recovery with not much altitude left to play with.

On another occasion, I cut the engine and raised the nose, deliberately causing a stall. You could feel the controls go limp as the nose dropped and we went into a spin. The spin continued until, on further instruction, I kicked the rudder and made a full recovery with plenty of altitude to spare. I was quite proud of this achievement. I would have happily done training every day but study got in the way and I was forced to reduce my hours in favour of getting assignments in on time.

Holidays

We went on a holiday in the mid-year break and drove the little Renault to Victoria. The trip provided an opportunity to visit a site that Mum had spoken of, near the old farm in the Victorian Mallee.

Mum described her discovery during the late 1920s, of bleached human skulls and other bones exposed on the sandy surface, from a shallow mass grave surrounded by white lilies. There were ghost gums along the banks of the Murray, near where Mum's family went on regular picnics in the horse-drawn cart, by the river, on a Sunday afternoon. There were holes in the skulls and some children's skulls were exposed on the sandy surface.

Mum never accepted the explanation of neighbouring farmers, that the site was a gazetted cemetery. My investigations at the SA University confirmed that this site was one of several massacre sites, strung along the Murray River valley. My Aunt Lil gave us accurate directions of where to find the site. By 1984 all that was left were skull fragments and other small bones which had, over the decades, been pulverized by the hooves of sheep and other animals. The site was as Mum had described, all those years ago, and was still surrounded by white lilies. There was a strange energy there, and it wasn't a pleasant place to be. We left to continue our trip.

We drove down and along the Victorian coast, through Port Fairy, the Twelve Apostles, and visited Darby and Lyn, Peter Marsh, Mum, sisters Elaine and Judith, and other relatives and friends. I remember thinking how different our lives had become. It was good to catch up with everyone but we were also happy to be leaving to return to Adelaide to finish my course and get back to a challenging, and meaningful life at Papunya.

We returned from our holiday to Balhannah, time went by quickly and at the end of the year, we sold everything up, including our trusty little Renault. We got the same amount that we paid for it. I couldn't get out of the place quick enough and it was good to get back to Central Australia.

We picked up some food, fuel, spare parts, and other supplies and stopped at the Regional office. Uwe Kiebat was there. Noel Coutts had moved on, leaving the Principal's position at Papunya school up for grabs. Uwe put his hand up for the job and was now the Acting Principal of Papunya school. I had some misgivings when Tom Marling said, in my presence, to Uwe "So you'll be looking after my Adult Educator"

I was confused. Did this mean that Adult Educators in remote areas answered to Acting Primary School Principals? It didn't make sense. Adult Education, I thought, had nothing to do with primary school. It must be purely an administrative convenience. We exchanged our farewells and I drove with the family back out to Papunya to basically pick up where I'd left off the year before. Armed with new qualifications, new understandings, and fresh ideas, I was enthusiastic about a future in Adult Education in the NT.

Back at Papunya

However, back at Papunya things were going pear-shaped. It was the start of the year in 1985 and I was alarmed to learn that in my absence whilst on study leave, the department had revised its administrative structure, placing Adult Educators directly under the control of School Principals. So far as I understood, I still held a substantive band two position, responsible for the development and implementation of TAFE Adult Education programs at Papunya, Haast's Bluff and Yuendumu. I was reporting to Tom Marling at Regional Office in Alice Springs. I was also answerable to a primary school teacher. The new arrangement didn't work well.

For example, I had to submit detailed documentation, to get approval, in advance, for access to the new photocopier. It was crippling and I spent a lot of time at the expense of the programs, raising my concerns about the new administrative arrangements, and applying for a position within the new structure that was appropriate to my experience and qualifications – to my knowledge, I was the only fully qualified Adult Educator in the NT.

Keith Thiele wrote a letter to the director addressing my concerns. The letter explained in part, that I felt that I was entitled to advancement through the system commensurate with my experience and qualifications and so on. There were no words of support or encouragement to apply for a more suitable position for me within the TAFE system. Despite all the discouraging things that were now happening with work at Papunya, we enjoyed our family life and the time we had left in the bush.

Rose, Mya and Sara at Yalkipi, 1981.

Relief From Work

I got away most weekends with the family to enjoy the desert. We camped out west of the settlement and I continued to pursue my long-term interest in landscape photography. For example, when we were camped near Wimparrku (Mt Blanche) I was out of the swag before daybreak to clamber to the peak, armed with a camera and tripod, to capture the sunrise over a glowing Mt Liebig, and the rolling red sand dune country, spread out in the distance. Parry made another visit and we camped at the remote and isolated sites of Tarn of Auber and Muruntji Rock Hole – tiny dots on the map, way out across the vast red sand dune country. I also had the Land Rover project that I was working on at home.

By now Adult Education in the Territory, like Bilingual Education was in decline, nobody seemed to be taking any interest in what was happening at Papunya, and I was feeling professionally alienated. Our time in the bush was drawing to a close.

Leaving the Bush

It was the 19th of August 1985 when Sara became ill and there was no medical staff at Papunya. We took Sara to the doctor in Alice Springs, and it was then that we decided to pack up and leave for Darwin. We drove out of Papunya, the back way, through Mt Wedge and Yuendumu, The Granites, Rabbit Flat, and the Tanami. We arrived at Lajamanu late the following afternoon, only to find that everyone was in mourning. It was then that Joe James Japanangka whispered to me that Maurice Luther Jupurrula had passed away. It was a sad time. We stayed overnight at Lajamanu and continued on to arrive in Darwin on 9th September.

Darwin

We were allocated a house at Glencoe Crescent, Tiwi, and I went into the Adult Education and Training Branch, Curricula Development unit. They gave me a desk and my job was to rewrite the content of course material as a second language for remote area TAFE courses. Miya and Sara were enrolled at Leanyer Primary School. We bought a Mini Moke to get around in, and often spent time with Jack and Pat Maggs at their property at Humpty Doo. I bought a canopy frame and army canvas cover for our trailer from the wrecking yard. Elaine and John came to visit and I saw a lot of Parry as well.

I found my work and the staff at head office to be deadly dull and the days dragged on. I found myself constantly checking the clock and praying that the time would go faster so I could get out of there.

There was no air conditioning in the house at Glencoe Crescent. It was stifling and stayed hot until late into the night. While Miya and Sara were at school, Rose had to spend most of the day in the airconditioned Casuarina shopping centre, to escape the oppressive heat. The schools and head office were air-conditioned.

Since self-government in the NT general support for Indigenous education had begun to wane. There was no future for us in Darwin. It was time to leave and I applied for a teaching job, back in North Queensland.

I began my job applications for Queensland in early December. The general tone of work relations at the head office was punctuated by the daily queue at the photocopier. No one said anything but it was obvious that I wasn't alone. It was as though everyone was clambering over each other in their efforts to leave the sinking ship. I wondered how things could have got so bad. So much for my newly acquired qualifications and visions of a career in TAFE in the NT. I resigned from TAFE while we were in Ingham. It was an emotional time for me to cut the long-term ties with the Northern Territory. I rang the TAFE Director advising him of my letter of resignation and other details, and his response was simply .... *"another one."*

I was offered a teaching position at Ingham Special School with a year's paid study leave in Brisbane. Townsville Regional Office seemed to have the view that there was some kind of link between Indigenous Education and Special Education. For example, with a background in Indigenous Education, I would be suited for Special Education. Regional Office had advised that I could take my pick of a range of areas in Special Education for study in Brisbane.

Chapter 7
North Queensland

Ingham Special School

Our personal effects were delivered to our rental house in Ingham in early February 1986, only days after cyclone Winifred and the subsequent floods. I was given the senior class and commenced duties on 10th February, with a view to making a choice of study options, should I want to pursue a career in Special Education. Miya and Sara were enrolled in the Plantation School and, as usual, with Rose's support, were settling in well.

I was never able to settle into the special school and like most of the staff, I was on edge most of the time. There was limited opportunity for staff to relax, socialise, plan ahead and exchange ideas and strategies, as you would normally expect in any other staff room. Instead, everyone seemed to be out on playground duty to prevent the kids from injuring themselves and others. It was like a war zone. For example, one day whilst on duty, I had to intervene to stop a boy from breaking his knuckles from punching a brick wall. I was badly shaken by the experience. I felt a lot of sympathy for the dedicated staff whose only opportunity for relaxation and social interaction, was the "happy hour" of a Friday afternoon down at the local pub.

My class of 18 students ranging in age from thirteen to eighteen and in disability, from passive resistance to violence. I had limited access to teaching and learning resources – you had to book everything in advance from the resource room. The only permanent AV equipment I had was a little cassette tape recorder. I used it until a student, while I was out of the withdrawal room, flung it against the wall smashing it to pieces and leaving me wondering what in the hell I was going to do next.

I was soon consumed with despair and, as an escape, attempted a cooking session with the kids in the Home Economics Room. We'd only just got into the lesson when someone threw the cake mixture onto the walls and ceiling. I rang Rose and she came and saved the day.

Just to top it all off on the last day of term, we had a near fatality on an excursion at Jourama Falls when an overzealous student, slipped from a rock ledge into deep water and had to be rescued. It was a case of the student having absolutely no idea of their own physical limits.

By the last week of term, I was at my wit's end. I'd had enough. Special Ed. wasn't my cup of tea. I rang Regional Office about a transfer. They were as understanding as could be expected and offered me a position in Manual Arts at Kirwan High in Townsville, for the second term.

On a positive note, during our short stay in Ingham, I bought my Norton 750 Commando from Mark Holland's cousin in Cairns. Ross had won a local government promotion to Boulia, out west, and couldn't justify keeping the bike. It was sensational – a decommissioned 1970 Interpol - a police pursuit bike with all the extras and spare parts for $3000. It went like the clappers. The purchase of the bike was a windfall that overshadowed all the pain and suffering I had to endure at the Ingham Special School.

Early in April, shortly before leaving Ingham, we drove down to Townsville to a Dire Straits concert at the Showgrounds. It was a fabulous event. Mark Knopfler and the band performed Money for Nothing, Sultans of Swing, and Walk of Life among other great songs. Miya and Sara were peeved at not being allowed to come because it was on a weeknight. We talked often to friends about how good it was and the kids never really forgave us. Our short stay in Ingham had come to an end.

Townsville

With regard to the family, as usual, Rose quietly managed yet another upheaval while I made preparations for the transfer to Kirwan High. We were determined to achieve a measure of stability and bought our first house, a lovely Queenslander, complete with bay windows, in Hooper Street, Belgian Gardens. Miya and Sara started at, yet another new school - Belgian Gardens State School, just a short walk from home.

Belgian Gardens

We bought the Hooper Street place in a shabby and run-down state - and there was a stench of cat urine. One of the bedrooms, for instance, had a sheet of galvanised mesh for a door to keep the cats in. We moved in and arranged for the house to be cleaned and painted. We chose a period colour scheme and had the floors polished.

While the block was very small, the previous owners had planted a rainforest around the house and hauled huge weathered granite stones there as garden features. It was a unique and beautiful place to live. The downside was that the rainforest was unsustainable and required $800 a year in water bills to keep it alive. There was an important project that I was keen to start.

The Tyro

I started work on the construction of my Tyro ultra-light aeroplane under the house. While I had a set of detailed plans to work from, I found it a real challenge. I wanted to get the most difficult components out of the way. I started with the wings, based on the Cessna wing– a rigid construction using stressed aircraft aluminium, bolts, and monel rivets for the ribbed and tubular frame, and leading edges. I had to make a jig from heavy craft wood, to ensure that when it was all finally riveted together, the wing was straight. The floor was uneven. There were a lot of phone calls to Geoff Eastwood, in South Australia, who patiently gave me ongoing advice, at every stage of construction.

Rose was a staff development officer at the Mater Hospital and since we were both working full time, we placed the girls with a family daycare mum. We soon found that things weren't suitable. Miya was appalled at being put in front of a TV to watch Rambo and other dubious American shows and reported it to Rose. Miya was eavesdropping when Rose very diplomatically gave the daycarer the flick. The new daycare Mum was better.

We saw a lot of our old friends Jim and Nora Hull, frequently had meals, and went out together on walks to Shelly Beach and other local haunts. Often on a weekend, we'd enjoy a 'rough red' out on their balcony overlooking Magnetic Island. On one occasion Jim and

I decided to go to the Townsville Yacht Club for a game of snooker. It was a seriously dedicated snooker room. The massive table was lit by an elaborate overhead lamp, and you paid two dollars for the half hour. Further, into the game, we got a bit sloshed and it took hours for us to get all the balls in and we spent a small fortune.

The Shade House

The Shade house attached to the back of the house was a large structure of hardwood timber slats that ran alongside and under the casement windows of one of the bedrooms. We placed an outdoor furniture setting on top of the shade house with access through the casement window. The girls would climb out onto the shade house run along the slats to the end and jump down into the compost heap below. At the weekend, we'd have afternoon tea there, during the hot weather, under the shade of the rainforest trees.

Other Goings On

Miya made friends with the kids across the road. They had pet flying foxes that would fly to her and cling to her blouse. One afternoon I saw one of the flying foxes crawling across the road and rescued it. Another time a baby brush-tailed possum came into the house and Miya remembered it swinging precariously by one claw from my left nostril. We made several weekend trips up to the Tablelands. Miya was hit on the arm by a stinging tree.

Stingers

On one occasion while we were staying at the motel in the Tolga Scrub, Miya accidentally brushed against a stinging tree on the edge of the rainforest. She suffered a prolonged burning sting to the forearm and we took her to the hospital. It was very distressing for the family, especially when we were told that there wasn't anything that could be done and we would just have to let it run its course. When you brush up against the stinging tree leaf, the hairs or fine silica fibres break off in the skin causing irritation. We later heard stories from descendants of pioneers, where fully laden pack-horses on the way up from Gordonvale, went mad after contact with stingers, growing along the Gillies Highway (then only a dirt track) and tumbling to their death, over the edge. It took weeks for the stinging to subside. I clamped a large leaf between two sheets of clear acrylic and back at school in grade five, Miya did a show-and-tell presentation of her

Kirwan High

It was the 14th April 1986 when I transferred to Kirwan State High School – The school seemed to mirror this new Townsville suburb – a featureless, uninspiring and soulless place. However, the staff seemed to make the most of it, there was a congenial work environment and the kids weren't too bad. I had Manual Arts, Maths and Graphics classes in years 8 to 10. The Kirwan routine soon became an overall uneventful and boring experience compared to that of the remote bush communities. Nevertheless, I did meet a couple of interesting people in Alan Churchill and Edwin Roelink at Kirwan.

Alan Churchill

I had a reasonable timetable and made friends at Kirwan High. I had always enjoyed the Townsville social scene and in many ways, we were able to pick up where we left off so many years previously. I took a liking to the subject master, Alan Churchill and we became friends with two important things in common. The first was motorcycles, and he was excited about my new Norton. Alan was a skinny long haired hippyish pommie from Hammersmith and shared his personal dilemmas of fear and admiration for the sound of approaching Police Nortons of 1960s London. We also had a mutual hero in John Mayal, the iconic father of British blues. I also became friends with Edwin.

Edwin

Edwin had come to the north from his family home in Adelaide. He was an innovative Art teacher, always willing to stretch the boundaries. He was also a motorcycle man, some years younger than me, very relaxed with an almost demure disposition. Yet on the Kawasaki 900, it was another story, bringing his rebellious nature to light. Edwin had recently bought an original Queensland house and was doing it up. We also shared a passion for Queensland houses, Australian period furniture and Australian pottery.

Edwin was an impressionist and took to the tropics like a duck to water. I enjoyed and admired his talent and his brilliant and colourful stylised interpretations of tropical landscapes – coconut palms and Queenslanders and so on. We also shared blues music and spent a fair bit of time discussing aspects of restoration on our houses.

On one occasion we took the bikes to Charters Towers for a run. It was the first serious trip I'd made. We didn't make it. The Commando couldn't sustain 100 miles per hour, and the big end failed on our approach to Mingela. What a bugger. While I stayed with the bike under a tree, Edwin rode all the way back to Townsville to pick up the Land Rover and trailer, to transport the bike back home for repairs. It took the whole day. I began to dread returning to school after the weekends.

Comparisons

The days at Kirwan dragged on. On an afternoon I found myself starting to nod off, or checking the clock on the wall out of sheer boredom. There was the marking, endless detentions, playground duty, bus duty, committee meetings, staff meetings, reporting and so on.

My preferred areas of teaching were Adult Education and Indigenous Education with experience in Bilingual Education and I held appropriate qualifications. I really had no enthusiasm for mainstream classroom teaching. Career opportunities for my preferred discipline, were limited or non-existent in Queensland, despite a high population of Islanders and Aborigines. The cultural difference wasn't taken seriously. My diploma in Aboriginal Education and Bilingual Education wasn't valued, and, as in the NT, TAFE services, especially for disadvantaged First Nations people were in decline. The only advantage I gained from my Graduate Diplomas in Queensland was a higher rate of pay. All this was unsustainable, and something had to give. It was well into term three in 1987 when it all came to a head.

Physical Education

I was taking a year nine PE class out on the oval. After a warm-up, I made a start on organising a game of softball. One of the kids decided to make life as difficult as possible for me, by jumping up and down and waving his arms about in front of me, physically obstructing my lesson. I grasped him by the shirt and told him to wait on the side until I could attend to him, and that I would be escorting him to the Admin. office. The student took it upon himself to leave.

Immediately after the lesson, we packed up and I went up to Admin. The offending student was there, and had apparently briefed them on what happened out on the oval, and that he had recently undergone surgery on his neck and so on. My behavioural management strategies were called into question. I was almost speechless at having to defend myself in such circumstances. However, I received a phone call from the student's father during recess time the following day. I explained the circumstances and he apologised and gave Michael a dressing down and that was that.

Enough

I'd had enough and submitted an application for extended stress leave. They seemed sympathetic and I was encouraged to *"get in there and fight it."* I got approval for leave without pay until the end of the term. It was the 19th of January 1988 when I approached Regional Office about a transfer to the Tablelands. I was advised that there were transfer applications for the Tableland schools from teachers who had been in Cape York for many years, and I would need to join the queue.

I resigned on the spot. We had planned some time ago, to build our home base in the Tablelands. Leaving permanent employment in Townsville wasn't an issue. I was ready and it was entirely on my terms. We decided to sell up and leave for the Tablelands. We weren't in any way phased over relocating with no employment. I was confident about getting casual and supply work at schools when we were ready.

Goodbye Hooper Street

We managed the sale of the house at Hooper Street, excluding real estate agents. There was nothing much to do except some research on how to sell real estate and hold an open house. The house was freshly painted and decorated inside and out and presented well. Indeed, it presented so well, that two prospective buyers began bidding for it over the phone. We knew that our only option was to put an end to the situation for fear of losing the sale and accept either one or the other's offer before things got out of hand. We took a punt, and the transaction was successful. We packed up, putting our stuff into storage until we found a place to rent on the Tablelands.

Atherton Tablelands

We stayed for a few days at the Woodlands caravan park while we looked around for something to rent. The old farmhouse on East Barron Road between Atherton and Malanda had a pleasant feel to it and we rented it for $60 a week, from the dairy farmer just up the road. From their bedroom window, Miya and Sara had a commanding view of the Herberton Range and Barron River valley looking down towards Atherton. The living room had tongue and groove natural silky oak walls and ceiling and we were instructed not to paint it.

The girls caught the school bus out the front gate to go to Atherton primary school. They were enrolled in the family group. Their teachers, Grace Chapman and Geoff Schultz had embraced the open-plan classroom model and were a dedicated and progressive team. Miya was ten years old and at year five level, and Sara, seven, at year two. Rose got an office job with Bob Prince, an Atherton-based accountant. She drove the Moke to work. I put my name down for casual contract and supply teaching in Tablelands High Schools but was in no hurry to start work. My priority was to buy a property.

New Territory

We soon learned that the Tablelands was a region of diversity in altitude, microclimate, soil, rainforest, open forest, and small and larger acreages. We looked at Tolga, Yungaburra, Malanda, Atherton, Herberton, Tumoulin, Ravenshoe, and everything in between. Given our limited experience, we weren't entirely sure of what we wanted in a property, only that we didn't want to live in a town.

Influencing Factors

It was amazing that here, in this picturesque, isolated little place tucked away in the Atherton Tablelands in Far North Queensland, Atherton High was enjoying a reputation of being the second best in the state – second only to Brisbane High, according to OP (university entrance) scores. I thought that this was in part due to the Atherton

Shire being a National Party stronghold (Premier Joh would overnight with friends in Atherton whenever he was up in the north). Other services in Atherton were second to none.

For example, services including the schools were so well-resourced, that there seemed to be a disproportionate number of private doctors, dentists and other professionals, set up on the Tablelands. In view of our priority for the best education services on offer for our kids, we began to focus on the Atherton Shire as a place to build our home base. We soon realised though, that it was going to take some time to buy what we wanted, and soon established a routine at East Barron Road. An old hang gliding friend Howard Newell was living with his mother in Atherton and we saw a fair bit of each other.

Howard and Laurie

After we left Cairns in mid 1975 to return to the NT, Howard and Laurie continued tinkering with the original Rogallo wing design and flying their new versions. They were real pioneers and were prepared to take risks. It was by no coincidence that Laurie became known among the fraternity as 'The Red Baron.' It was some time after we'd arrived in the Tablelands that Howard shared some of his more recent life experiences with us.

They were at the new site on the top of the Gillies Range at the end of Boar Pocket Road and had cleared some of the tall trees just below to get a clear run on takeoff. On that particular day, Howard had launched his machine, ran out of lift, and crashed landed on the rainforest canopy further down the slope. It was a soft landing onto the crown of an emergent tree and he wasn't injured. Howard was quite secure hanging from the harness until he decided to attempt to climb down. He unhitched the harness and clambered for a hold onto a branch. Howard slipped and fell some 20 meters onto the slope below, landing upright, and damaging vertebrae in his spine.

During his years in recovery, he lived with his Mum in Atherton and took up the flute. He was most fortunate that he didn't end up a paraplegic, but the bouts of pain continued to haunt him.

He became a talented self-taught musician and taught Miya to play the flute. After his Mum passed away, Howard and his partner Helen bought a house on a block of land up on Rolley Road, near

Wondecla, in the tall sclerophyll forest. Helen worked for the Qld. DPI and Howard grew bean sprouts and sold them locally. They were concerned about bushfires. During the dry season, they had to pack up and vacate the place because of the thick smoke that hung in the atmosphere. The atmosphere around was polluted for days on end. They'd then return to a parched and blackened landscape. We were never concerned about bushfires at East Barron Road. Only white tail rats.

White Tails in the Sunset

Our landlord hadn't mentioned anything about white-tailed rats in the farmhouse ceiling. He probably didn't know. But soon after we had moved in, we were disturbed in the middle of the night, by some heavy animals, romping and galloping around, up in the ceiling. At first, we thought it was possums. You could see these animals making their way to the roof of the house along the electricity cable after dark – real acrobats. I acquired a trap with some bananas as bait and caught one in the roof cavity.

It was a big white-tailed rat. I brought it down through the manhole in the ceiling to show the kids. It was our first experience with these large, smelly creatures. We sat there on the floor, watching it run around in the trap, and Miya gave it a bit of a poke with a stick, to see what might happen. The whitetail grunted and squealed in protest - just like a piglet. We recorded it and let it go down at the river. The whitetails were established in the roof cavity of the farmhouse, long before we arrived, and they plagued us until we eventually left. They're probably still there.

It is said that whitetails are literate. They will read the label on a food tin before biting into the metal to get to the desired contents. Indeed, with their formidable set of teeth, they grind through the hard kernels of macadamia nuts, to scoop out the flesh. White tails aren't particularly endearing. Chooks and ducks don't like them either, and I'll talk about another whitetail encounter later. Sara had a nasty fall from her bike.

A Nasty Gravel Rash

One afternoon Miya, Sara and I went on the bikes for a ride up the road towards Schaeffer's dairy farm. It was mostly downhill on the way back and Sara's bike developed a speed wobble. I was behind her and watched helplessly as the wobble intensified until poor little Sara lost control and went flying over the handlebars. She ended up with a severe gravel rash with small stone fragments embedded in the wounds on her elbow, chin and hip, where she slid along the road. We got her into a warm bath with Dettol and Rose picked out the bits of gravel from her stinging wounds. We were most fortunate that there wasn't

Friends and Neighbours

Alistair Burns made a visit with Ada, his new partner from Papunya during the school holidays. It was cold and rather than sit in the farmhouse, which had no fireplace, Ada preferred to stay out by the fire she had lit, in the open part of the shed, and do traditional painting. The old shed had a dirt floor. There was a superb view across the hills from there too. The landlord discreetly came down one day on his tractor to investigate. We wondered what went through his mind as he discovered this black woman from the desert sitting cross-legged by her fire in the shed.

The landlord had a neighbour diagonally across the road from his dairy. The neighbour's place was completely obscured by woody weed – a thick, well-established, and widespread cover of tobacco bushes. Keen to meet Bill, I walked up the road to introduce myself. I couldn't raise him and there, under the shade of the tobacco bush, were a couple of full-grown bulls, resting at his back doorstep.

I never did meet him. Bill's brother, Frank, was there at one stage too. According to the landlord, Frank turned up one day in his old Chev truck. He parked the truck just inside the gate down from the dairy and took up lodgings in the tin shed nearby. He would help bring the cows in for milking in the afternoon. Frank had passed away, long before we arrived and as a kind of memorial, the truck is still resting there by the gate.

Paul and Margaret

During warmer weather, we'd often go down across the paddock from the farmhouse, down past Briggs and the Peever's place to the water hole, at the old bridge on the Barron River, for a swim. One day we noticed a sign out on the roadside advertising custard apples for sale and made a detour into the Brigg's orchard to investigate. Paul and Margaret and their teenage children, Mitchell and Nicole lived there. Paul and Margaret were teachers and worked producing custard apples, avocados, and stone fruit in their spare time. We had a fair bit in common.

Apart from teaching, they spent time in New Guinea where Paul was a Patrol Officer, in remote tribal areas. Margaret was teaching full-time at Malanda High, and Paul worked at Atherton High and later did supply teaching around the Tablelands. They both enjoyed baiting me about my left-wing views. I think that Paul may have felt a twinge of regret about his use of conventional farming methods with insecticides and so on. They produced enormous Pinks Mammoth custard apples, nectarines, and peaches.

Anne and Errol

Anne and Errol made frequent trips from Cairns to visit us, and enjoyed the peace and quiet of the country farmhouse. Anne would point out the blue silos to their children Henry and Ellen, as they turned left into East Barron Road. During their first visit, Rose and Anne were in the kitchen with the kids. Errol and I were out in the back chatting. There was an easy, peaceful silence, as we watched the Friesian milking cows quietly grazing, knee-deep in an emerald green pasture in the house paddock.

In Search of a Property

Our search for a property wasn't progressing very well due to the incompetence of the local real estate agents. For example, one agent became exasperated at not being able to sell us anything. One of the properties he showed us, was strewn with old refrigerators, other discarded white goods, car bodies, and other junk. The agent commented on how useful the stuff would be to us.

Despite our detailed descriptions of our requirements, another agent insisted on taking us to see everything that we weren't interested in. During the last trip coming back into Atherton, I asked about the fluid compass thing that he had attached to the dash of his car. He explained that it was in fact an indicator that showed whether or not the customers were on the level.

The last agent proved to be very productive. He took us to Glenwood Close where he showed us a place down the end of the road.

Glenwood Close

We decided to approach the owner of the property privately, and asked if the property was for sale. He advised that it was and that he would find out how much it was worth on the market and let us know. Within a very short time, he came back to us with the amount and we clinched the deal privately. It was in mid-November 1988 that we secured the property in Atherton.

It was the best position on the street. Two and a half acres, mowed, with a large rose garden at the front, established orchard, well-drained, with a gradual slope, down to the western boundary, along Mazlin Creek. Being part of the lava flow from Bones Knob, a shield volcano to the northwest, the block had deep fertile red volcanic soil. The creek formed the boundary of the old lava flow.

Our visions of building a vee-shaped brick house overlooking the remnant strip of rainforest and creek were soon dashed when we saw how expensive it would have been. We looked at other options and it wasn't long before an opportunity emerged. We would relocate a Queensland house from Cairns.

A Queenslander

I contacted the Cairns House Relocators and was inspired by the manager. He invited us down to Cairns to view some of the work he had completed. We were most impressed by the professionalism, and quality of the restorative work done with the Queenslanders, that they had moved to the various new locations around town.

We were offered a choice of five excellent houses for removal and it was the Lake Street one that we finally chose. We checked over the house with a friend, a well-qualified carpentry and joinery teacher at the local TAFE campus. Wayne was impressed by the high quality of the house, in particular, the high ceilings of fibrous plasterwork, with ornate art deco mouldings, quality of the timber, quality fittings throughout, long casements windows, and french doors leading out to the verandah.

I spoke to the long-term resident next door, who shared his first-hand knowledge of the history of this house. Among other things, it was built in 1940 by Master Builder, T.B. O'Meara and Sons, Spence St., Cairns, who also built the Mt St Bernards Convent at Herberton and the Cairns Ambulance 1921, the Tramway, Crown and Commercial Hotels, and other residences in Cairns. The O'Meara family is related to the Lennon family who lived in the Lake Street house.

The Atherton Shire Council Building inspector commented on the roof cavity, observing that there was "a forest of bull oak up in the roof cavity". Having secured approval of the building for relocation, the next step was to make an application for its relocation to Atherton. I pegged out the position that we wanted for the house on the block. I met with the shire council representatives on our proposed site on the block and withdrew down to the shed, leaving them some space to discuss the matter. They were apprehensive and we were convinced that they would reject our proposal.

Anxious Times

We were in touch with other local councillors about our concerns regarding approval for the relocation. We had already met three local councillors. They were most interested to hear that the house in question was built by Tommy O'Meara. Most councillors knew of O'Meara and had great admiration for him and his outstanding work. They told us about the scheduled town planning meeting the following day. We were advised to attend this meeting and have a few notes ready if needed to argue a case.

The agenda item was opened and in no time at all, there was a unanimous vote in support of our application. I rang the house relocators that afternoon and set the wheels in motion for the relocation. The contract was signed in early February 1989.

I was most impressed by the level of efficiency of the relocator team. The house was cut in two and the roof was removed for transport. There were two loads in the space of three days. The house in transit was uninsurable. For technical reasons, the two braced halves of the house were not secured onto the tray of the truck. Each morning they left Cairns around 2.30 am with a police escort travelling up the Kuranda Range and across to Mareeba at speeds of up to 90 kilometres per hour.

I met the first half at 6 am on the 9th and the second half at 5 am on the 11th of February. I used my Norton motorcycle to escort the truck on the final leg from the Golf Links Road turnoff. There had been an early shower and the site was slippery. Maurice, the farmer from across the creek, bought his tractor around and towed the truck with the second half, the final couple of metres into position.

Preparing the left side of the house in Cairns for transit to Atherton, 1989.

The rest of the relocation progressed smoothly and payment of a total of $55,000 was made in stages of work completed and approved by the Shire Building Inspector. A plumber from Cairns replaced the tin on the roof, installed the septic system, and did other new work. The electric wiring was upgraded and the house was painted. We acknowledged Shire Councillors and others who had given us their support for our application with an invitation to afternoon tea and a tour of the house. We gained final approval and moved in on 7th April 1989.

Over the years I restored the house in consultation with the Lennon family, members of whom took an active interest in the restoration and made a special trip to view the progress.

The first thing I did after moving in was building a chook pen from the original cypress stumps and tin from the roof of the house. By early December, an extension was in place on the existing shed for cover for the vehicles. We started a veggie patch. Then there was the longer-term tree planting program, under the guidance of a friend, Geoff Tracey, and local tree planting organisations, TREAT (Trees for the Evelyn and Atherton Tablelands) and WTTPS (Wet Tropics Tree Planting Scheme). I'll expand on this project later.

The first half of the house arrives on site on 9th February, 1989.

Neighbours

It was said that Glenwood Close was the dress circle of Atherton. It was well established and our block was the last one to be built on. There were seven other acreages and it was a peaceful and secluded setting on Mazlin Creek. Soon after moving in, as a gesture of goodwill, we invited the neighbours to a party as a way of introducing ourselves as new arrivals at Glenwood Close.

I made personal visits to the neighbours, inviting them to join us. Only a couple of neighbours responded. The kids from across the road threw rocks on the roof of our house soon after it was set in place. Perhaps they knew something about the ghost.

A Ghostly Presence

We had engaged a plasterer from Tolga, who was particularly interested in the house, and when he came over to view the task, explained that he and his family of ten, rented the place when it was in Lake Street in Cairns. He brought his wife over to see the house. They pointed out that when they lived in the house in Cairns, there was a resident ghost. At night, you could hear disturbances, like crockery and cutlery rattling around in the kitchen. John went ahead and did a great restoration job on the fibrous plaster ceilings and art deco mouldings in the living room. We assumed that the ghost, if there was one, surely wouldn't have come up to the Tablelands with the house, and the subject wasn't mentioned again – that was until she re-appeared within weeks of our occupancy.

Sara was home from University and it was late in the afternoon. While cooking in the kitchen she became aware of the subtle presence of a young woman. The woman had a dark blue dress on and her hair was pinned up. Sara described an unusual quality of light and distinct feminine energy, which lasted for no more than a few moments or so before disappearing. Later, in 2004 Shannon Smith experienced a sombre momentary spiritual presence in the form of a smoky grey silhouette that she interpreted as a young woman, moving from Sara's room into the living room. During the following years, when the girls were away at university, in the dead of the night, you would hear floorboards creaking and occasionally, books being re-arranged in the bookcase in Sara's room.

There were also times at night when Rose would catch a whiff of old-fashioned perfume. She asked, *"Can you smell that perfume, Isha?"* On another night, Rose picked up the strong odour of aromatic pipe tobacco smoke. It was our policy to turn the light off once you'd finished in a room. Yet, on some nights, some lights were left on.

We never asked the Lennons if anyone had died in the house and there was no mention of any deaths during the time the family lived there. We could only guess that the ghost may have been present at Glenwood Close before the house was in place and thought the house was the ideal place to take up residence. We never felt threatened or uncomfortable with this gentle spirit and soon came to accept her presence in the house. After about fifteen years with us, she quietly left and we haven't seen her since.

A Return to the Whiteboard

By early April I'd signed up for casual tutoring at Woodleigh, a residential college in Herberton. I worked there from half past six to half past eight in the evenings, Monday to Friday. The college catered for kids from Cape York and Torres Strait, who attended the local high school and Mt Saint Bernard Catholic school during the school term. Most of them would always attempt to get out of doing their homework, saying that they'd not been given any, and would prefer to do nothing during the two hours allotted for help with homework. The kids often felt bored and homesick and it was a battle to get them to do anything other than watch a video. While the money was good, I felt that it was a waste of time.

I registered at Regional Office for casual teaching and contacted Atherton, Malanda, Herberton, Mareeba, and Ravenshoe State High Schools, advising them of my availability as a secondary supply teacher. Often, I found myself having to decline a day or a week here and there due to heavy demand. I'd usually get an early morning phone call with enough notice for travel and preparation. It paid over $200 per day but sometimes there were issues. For example, some administrations and staff were not supportive of supply teachers and I felt that my work wasn't valued.

I downsized to Atherton and Mareeba. Atherton later adopted, what I felt was an inappropriate and cumbersome behaviour management model. I preferred Mareeba High's approach to relations with the kids and more active support for supply and contract teachers.

Visitors

It wasn't long after moving in that we had a number of visits from long-term friends. Our very old friends Jim and Nora Hull came up from Townsville early in 1990 and were most impressed with the house and what we'd achieved. The verandah reminded them of their life in Colonial Borneo, Darussalam, Nairobi, Mombasa, and Entebbe in Kenya. A world of white dinner suits, khakis, pith helmets and mosquito nets in the African savannah.

Our friend, John Humphreys visited in June and was amazed at the progress we'd made since his last visit. The place was still in disarray. *"Impeccable timing,"* said John.

Joe and Maria Lane came early in July and we took them on small excursions through the Tablelands. Maria was so excited at her first sight of tropical landscapes and animals and plants. She'd call out to Joe, *"Joey Joey Joey, look at this.........."* But she was astonished when she saw the sign 'Nigger Creek' on the little bridge near Wondecla. The sign was replaced some years later.

Miya's teacher from Oakbank primary school, Vera Mignone came up from the Adelaide Hills later in the year and we went on excursions including Lake Eacham. Imagine this - Vera is in the lead, Michael behind her, and me at the rear walking along the track around Lake Eacham, a crater lake. We were negotiating a narrow part of the track which was cut into the steep, almost vertical side of the crater. Vera was fascinated by the maidenhair ferns and other exotic vegetation along the sides of the pathway.

Suddenly I heard a shriek from up the front. It was Vera. A little tree snake had taken fright, as we were approaching, and in the confusion, poked his head out from the maiden hair ferns in the rock along the side of the pathway, right in front of the oncoming Vera. She panicked, lost her balance and toppled over the side of the track, and just saved herself from plummeting down into the water below, by grasping hold of some vines as she slid down. Luckily Michael was able to pull her up by the arms and back onto the track. Vera was shaken by the ordeal, saying that we lived in a wild and dangerous place. She enjoyed the rest of her stay with us and we have kept in contact with her.

Incidentally, it was early in 1990 that a Lear jet, on its approach to the Mareeba airstrip, crashed into Mt Emerald killing 11 people including the Cairns Mayor, an Atherton Shire Councillor, Ivan Wilkinson, and Sister Nadia, among others. Sister Nadia, a member of the Sisters of Mercy, was to set up a respite care centre on Cook Street in Atherton.

Having been a past student at Townsville's St. Patricks College, Rose wrote to the Sisters of Mercy with an expression of interest to assist the Order in establishing the respite care centre. Rose got the position. Bethany Respite Care Centre was in a new purpose-built facility in Cook Street with eight support staff. Rose coordinated the centre until 1994. It was around this time that our family went on a trip to Fiji.

Fiji

We landed at Nandi, spent some time at Lautoka, and hired a taxi to get to Suva via Sigatoka. We spent most of our time in Suva where we had a comfortable room and shared facilities at the Fijian-run South Pacific Hostel. The food was so good at the Hare Krishna Indian restaurants that we repeatedly went for wonderful spicy multi-course meals, before wandering the Suva streets and markets. We were also invited for dinner with a local Indian family.

The museum was dominated by exhibits of the cannibal culture and I had a macabre fascination with it all. On display were the accessories of serious cannibalism, complete with beautifully carved cutlery, a range of herbs and spices, and vegetable side dishes. There was a large wooden block with a groove in the top and an elaborate hook and other instruments for brain extraction. Fiji wasn't known as the Cannibal Isles for nothing, I thought. We also travelled around Viti Levu stopping at rural villages set in old cane fields and other deforested landscapes. Miya met some schoolchildren in one of the villages and they became pen pals.

I had spoken to Jonatani Rika, still at Yirrkala, and we were invited to stay with his relatives at the remote village of Makadru on Matuku Island in the southern Lau archipelago. We decided earlier that the conditions were a bit too risky for the kids. For example, some of these old vessels' steel hulls are so thin, after years of chipping of surface rust, that occasionally during bad weather they would break in half. Rose, Miya, and Sara returned home from Suva leaving me to extend my time and make the journey down to Matuku.

I'd met the Fijian skipper of a trading vessel, berthed at the Suva wharf. He explained that he was operating through the Lau archipelago and that the time of departure was dependent on the weather and the tides and that I should be ready to come on board early the next morning. I had to re-book my accommodation in the South Pacific three times because of bad weather. One night there was a big Tongan man in the spare bed in the shared room who kept me awake for the entire night with his explosive snoring. I had plenty of spare time and spent days wandering around. I set myself a challenge – getting access to the old British colonial Fiji Club.

I put on my best clothes and gave them a sophisticated spin about having been a missionary with the Methodist Overseas Missions and succeeded in procuring a nice meal. The club fraternity was, without exception, pompous elitists, maintaining the old exclusive, colonial rituals. And the irony of it was that there wasn't a Brit to be seen – they had long gone, leaving the higher-ranking Fijians to carry on the tradition. They left it to their Indian subordinates to turf me out. I was relieved to finally be on board the ship on the fourth day and set up my little camp space on the open deck in preparation for the voyage south.

Into the Unknown

On the way south, the ship anchored off remote Islands to drop off supplies to communities. I often had enough time to dive overboard for a swim and be back on board before departure. I was warned by the skipper that if I wasn't on board when they were ready to go, I'd have to swim ashore and wait for the ship's return trip. On the return trips, they picked up pigs, chooks, and other livestock, cassava, taro, kava, and other produce for the Suva markets.

I was invited to join the crew for kava during the night. They said that the ship was on auto-pilot. I relished the thought of my immersion in true Fiji culture. On deck, outside the wheelhouse, there were cannibal jokes for my benefit and many interesting stories told over bowls of kava through the night. For example, during his stint as captain of a tourist cruise boat, the skipper and his crew would sing certain Fijian songs for the American tourists, en route to their resorts. If the Americans knew what it was about, they would have been offended at the ridicule and obscene lyrics and the entire crew would have been sacked. Instead, the crew was given standing ovations. During my trip south to Matuku, there was an emergency that deserves some mention.

Blood on the High Seas

One afternoon one of the crew called me to come quickly – there had been an accident. I arrived at the scene on deck. A man had cut his foot – there was blood. I found the young Englishman sitting on the deck, holding his injured foot up. He was in some distress and explained that he had stood on a razor blade. Someone had apparently had a shave, folded the razor blade, and it ended up on the deck where the now vee-shaped blade came to rest standing on its edge.

John, unfortunately, stood on the blade in bare feet, with the blade embedding itself deep into his left heel. The skipper said that we would soon be anchoring off an island where there was a health clinic and John should get some treatment there. We were also told that they were on a tight schedule and couldn't afford to miss the tide. I made a bandage from a t-shirt to stem the flow of blood and within half an hour we were struggling and sweating on the climb up a steep jungle pathway from the beach toward the clinic.

The blade had left a deep and painful wound and John was terrified that he might contract aids. The health worker cleaned and dressed the wound and we got down the hill in time to catch the last dinghy back to the ship.

I could have done without all this. I had no idea that this bloke was on board – hitherto he'd maintained a low profile. All I wanted was an uninterrupted cultural experience. I found it irritating that because I was white, the skipper determined that John was somehow my responsibility – all they did was wash the blood off the deck. I was the mug that had to lug an injured man up a mountain in the tropical heat to get medical help. Anyway, I thought I did pretty well, satisfied that I'd done my duty in the eyes of the Fijians. I looked in on John's progress a couple of times during the rest of the voyage south. I was excited at the prospect of my arrival in Matuku and meeting Jonatani's family.

Matuku

I got a warm welcome on arrival at Makadru village. Jonatani must have given me a good wrap - they couldn't do enough for me. It was getting late in the afternoon when the organisers wasted no time in getting everyone together in the courtyard and directed me to the rostrum. I wasn't good at impromptu presentations. As the courtyard began to fill, I went into a panic calling on my unconscious mind for advice. *"You can do this Isherwood, just describe Yirrkala, how you met Jonatani and Lossa, and build on it as you go."*

I was very nervous as I began to tell them about Yirrkala Mission, spear-fishing with a lamp along the beach with Jonatani and Parry, and the problem with the shop manager. I told in detail about the manager leaving written notes to Jonatani, in his attempt to avoid contact, regarding the delivery of garden produce and other things. I described Jonatani's, response to what he must have viewed as offensive and insulting in the manager's notes. Jonatani confronted him and let fly with a left hook and so on. I obviously got away with it and there was a request for a repeat the following day before my departure back to Suva.

Kava and Cannibals

I was honoured to have been invited to a traditional Kava welcoming ceremony that night in the village hall. There were about fifteen men present. We sat in a circle around the ornately carved Kava or Yaqona bowl on the floor with legs crossed. A gift or Sevusevu was presented by one of the men. The Kava drink was passed around in a carved coconut cup.

Jonatani's brother sat next to me and walked me through the procedure, including when to clap, where to relieve myself out in the bush, and so on. Drinking kava has a sedative effect and makes your mouth feel numb. It also produces mild euphoria and is good for inspiration. There was a lot of storytelling and jokes and laughter through to about three o'clock in the morning.

Until that special night, I was harbouring a morbid fascination with cannibalism until it was explained in a matter-of-fact way in response to my rather philosophical questions about people eating each other. For example, cannibalism was part of the rich and vibrant culture of the Polynesians. As opposing ranks of warriors confronted each other on the battlefield during an impending conflict, they would hurl fearful threats across to each other, like, ….. *"we're going to have you for our lunch tomorrow"* – and indeed, would carry it out in style with elaborate victory celebratory feasts. Meat from slain warriors was very much a part of the Fijian cuisine, witnessed by horrified early missionaries. The next morning, more villagers gathered to hear my stories about their beloved Jonatani, a fellow Fijian and missionary at remote Yirrkala, so far away, in the Australian Northern Territory over twenty years before. It wasn't long before I was on teaching contracts back up in Cape York.

Up the Cape, Torres Strait, and Across the Gulf

By 1992 there was lots of funding for the Priority Educational Country Area Program (PECAP), for Cape York and Torres Strait schools. Teaching staff would be offered in-service courses in Cairns or Townsville. I missed teaching in the remote Territory and welcomed the opportunity to work in remote communities again. Soon after commencing duties at Normanton, I learned that there were behavioural management problems there. A teacher I was replacing, had recently been thrown over the balcony by the students. The kids seemed well behaved and I took great interest in the old town. Mounted in front of the Shire Council Office was a life-sized model of the 28-foot croc, shot in the Norman River by an Eastern European woman croc shooter during the 1950s.

At Kowanyama I was advised not to go into the water in the nearby creek because of the crocs, and a young boy had recently tipped a drum of dieldrin in there to stun the fish so that they could be easily caught. Ray Armitt was the Principal – Mark Hollands re-named him

Armpit. Armpit and I shared a dark sense of humour. For example, he had a barbeque at his place for the staff and he broke into laughter when I came down the stairs with my pannikin of tea, wearing a heavy leather gauntlet to protect my hand against the hot handle.

Mr Bean, Turkey Roast, and a Pantomime

By 1993 I'd apparently earned a bit of a reputation up in the Cape. I was very much at ease in the remote environment. I didn't really care much about whether or not the outgoing teacher had left work for me, now I was armed and prepared with my own resources, of which the most important was a videotape of six episodes of Mr Bean. Without exception, Mr Bean had the kids rolling on the floor in stitches – I'd won their hearts and earned the nickname of Mr Bean. This Mr Bean thing was deeply entrenched.

I recently bumped into Bruce at the Yungaburra markets. Bruce was teaching at Kowanyama when I was there, 30 years ago. I was with a small group of people when he told them a story of my getting off the plane with a bag full of Mr Bean tapes, and that I was known universally, across Cape York, and Torres Strait as 'Mr Bean.'

At Kowanyama at the time, the teaching staff were friendly and accommodating, and I felt the need to contribute to their communal dinners. I would bring a turkey hind quarter, potatoes, plenty of garlic, rosemary, and other ingredients to put on a roast to share.

They couldn't have been more helpful and Kowanyama became one of my favoured destinations in the Cape. My turkey roasts had earned institutional status, to the extent that word got back to Atherton about Alan Isherwood's fabulous roasts. Another time, again at the markets, Rose and the girls were approached by a couple of teachers, who also knew me from Kowanyama. Rose was surprised to hear how good Alan's roasts were as the family had never experienced a roast cooked by Alan.

The principal arranged for a Christmas school pantomime, to be held at the local canteen before the close of the school year. There was a surprise visit by a Carlton United Brewery representative as the focus for the evening. It was late in the afternoon when the plane touched down. They soon got the pantomime and hot dogs out of the way and quickly lined up the kids. The beer rep made his entrance, resplendent with a big cloth bag full of Christmas knick-knacks slung over his shoulder.

Full of sugar from their soft drinks, the kids ran amok, and it took a lot of work to contain them and get them ready to receive their Carlton United Christmas presents. Then the beer man announced drinks on the house, and within a short time, most of the Kowanyama community seemed to be at the canteen. I was perplexed as to why alcohol should be promoted in such a way, given the reputation of these communities being hot spots for complex social problems and alcohol-fueled violence.

Doomadgee and Mornington to Bamaga

October of that year was a particularly busy month for me. I spent time at Doomadgee, or Doom City as Mark called it, and on Mornington. Mornington Island, in the Gulf of Carpentaria, was Gulf Savannah country, broken only by the isolated rocky outcrop, and surrounded by a turquoise sea, the homeland of author and artist Dick Roughsey or Goobalathaldin. Dick Roughsey had recently passed away and I made a point of visiting his grave. When they were little, Miya and Sara enjoyed his stories such as the Giant Devil Dingo, Quincans, Rainbow Serpent, and others.

Early September and late October found me at Bamaga State High School. I knew Neil from Malanda and always got on well with him. Neil offered me accommodation in his house and took me fishing in the estuaries for mangrove jack and bream. I was at that point applying for a contract back in the NT and he wrote me a glowing reference. We joked over his use of the term nuances. Neil would cook up a heavy steak meal for dinner, with ice cream for dessert. On the first night, I declined the ice cream on the grounds that I was full of steak and he polished off the entire 2-litre tub in one sitting. I was also offered sweets at any time. The crisper in his fridge was full of Cherry Ripe chocolate bars.

Lockhart River, Pormpuraaw and Coconut Island

I always demanded a limit of two weeks on contracts in the Cape Schools based on the grounds that I had family commitments at home.

The Department never had a problem with this. And so, supply and short contracts continued on the Tablelands and I still had work in the Cape during 1994.

It was most unusual for contract teachers to be placed in Torres Strait schools but nevertheless, I was invited by the Acting Principal of Coconut Island School to fill in for a week. I met some of the Islanders who told me about the bad old days before the Coming of the Light. Their ancestors lived their lives in fear of headhunters from the North. One story was about the terror and panic the ancestors experienced at the sight of a flotilla of war canoes on the horizon heading straight toward them. There was nowhere to go. Another story was about a boy who, while out on an early morning walk along the beach, found the headless body of his uncle lying on the sand. The uncle had got up in the night and gone for a pee on the beach and was ambushed by the headhunters. During walks along the beach, I thought of Murray Island and the achievements of a true hero, Eddie Mabo.

Lockhart River is one of the most beautiful natural locations I've seen. The most prominent landforms are the massive granite tors, scattered along the tropical beach, and the rainforests of the adjacent Iron Range on the eastern side of Cape York. The most outstanding thing about my teaching experience there was that the outgoing teacher hadn't left any work for me, and I was told to get f.. kd by a year one pupil. It was Mister Bean that saved the day.

Pormpuraaw, halfway up the western side of Cape York, lies adjacent to the most desolate coastal country I've ever seen. The endless salt pans, dotted with stunted vegetation extend for miles north and south and there's no fresh water anywhere. At daybreak the silence is broken by the raucous call of the blue-winged kookaburra echoing over a parched landscape, heralding yet another hot and oppressive day. The mournful cry of crows is all that you hear during the relentless, shimmering heat of the day. I imagined that the wet season storms would bring a welcome but only short reprieve for Pormpuraaw.

I would drag myself through the heat, up the beach to the Chapman River mouth, and attempt to do some late afternoon fishing from the top of the steep bank. One afternoon on the way up, as I waded through the shallows I spotted a huge croc a hundred metres offshore. I used a hand reel and wobblers but never caught a fish. There wasn't as much as a nibble there, and I had to get out well before dark and before the tide started coming in. At my fishing spot, I thought that there were more crocs on the opposite bank than there were on the croc farm.

Acres of stinking grey mud, sweating in the hot sun, seething with angry crocs behind the six-foot mesh fence was someone's idea for a community enterprise – a croc farm. These crocs at the farm were fed on cartons of cubed portions of feral pig – big, half-frozen lumps of stinking, half-rotten meat, with black hair and skin, attached. They were also given half-frozen lumps of dead cage chickens probably complete with lashings of antibiotics and steroids. It was about this time that crocodile meat was being promoted in trendy restaurants in Cairns. Such was the cabaret of the early nineties, and I'd had enough of life up on the Cape.

Back on the Tablelands

I was spending a fair amount of time at Atherton High, mainly to support Miya. I became involved in the school community, attending staff meetings, replacing the tennis court fencing, and other extracurricular activities. Miya was a model student and was awarded Junior Dux in 1993. Sara joined Miya at the high school as a new year 8 student.

Miya was in year 11 starting her senior. For year nine, Sara chose to enrol in Distance Education. She was already familiar with the use of the radio and we found that the learning resources were excellent and up-to-date. We made a trip down to South Brisbane to meet with the Distance Education teachers and pick up some learning resources. Miya did senior geography through distance education as well. She went to Japan on a school excursion and addressed a Japanese school parade in Japanese.

Cockatoos, Bettongs, and Feather-tails

The previous owners of our block had built a fancy aviary down the back and left some cockatiels in a couple of the bays. I had offered to look after them until he could find a place to house them.

Miya and Sara ready for school, 1990.

Within a couple of weeks, a python polished them all off in one sitting. The owner had also left a sulphur-crested cockatoo and offered it to us as a pet. Cocky had been left in a cage down on the creek bank, at the mercy of the whitetails. I shifted him up closer to the house and built a summer house for him.

When we were home, he spent most of his time on the clothesline, just as Moe had done in Ringwood a generation before. Cocky had also been injured earlier in his life, whereby his right wing had been partially severed, leaving him flightless. There was also a claw missing from his left foot making climbing more difficult. Cocky was well adapted to a restricted lifestyle and wild cockatoos would be attracted by his squawking and were sometimes invited to share food and perch with him on the line.

Occasionally we'd let him climb up into the trees along the creek. He had difficulty getting down again and would stay way up in the tree top for days, with nothing to eat or drink. We were having a picnic down at the creek one afternoon and heard a thud nearby. It was poor cocky who, out of desperate hunger and thirst, attempted to climb down to us, lost his grip, and fell heavily on the sloping creek bank. Miraculously, he wasn't hurt.

On another occasion, he was out on a limb and was chewing his way through. Cocky was on the wrong side of the limb when it snapped off! He fell, hurtling, spinning, out of control and we heard the sickening thud as he hit the ground. In no time at all, he came into view strutting up to us looking for a feed. How he survived that one without injury I would never know.

We were out the back having pizzas for dinner by the fire with friends one evening. Cocky enjoyed the company. Rose had put a hot pizza on a chair and Cocky was perched on the top of the back of the chair. On several occasions, he attempted to get down to investigate the pizza but was foiled each time as I would threaten to take him back to the summer house if he touched the pizza. He couldn't help himself and climbed down onto the hot pizza. It was like a slow version of an Irish jig, as he would put one foot down onto the hot and sticky molten cheese, lifting it with attached threads of the cheese, then the other, and so on. I rescued him as soon as I could from his unfortunate situation. Cocky didn't seem to have suffered from any burns to his feet.

Cocky would strut around the line yelling and shouting about things in general. His cage hung on the line, door open and supplied with seed and water. He'd hook seed out of the little dish in the cage and broadcast it around the lawn, drawing in the little Northern Bettongs who would congregate underneath the line for the discarded mixture of seed.

Resident Northern Bettongs

Phil and Muriel, our neighbours on the northern side, were both from dairy families around the Milla Milla district. While reluctantly tolerant of our efforts to regenerate the rainforest on our property, they drew the line when it came to protecting rare and endangered species. Before I put up the dog fence, the little Bettongs would wander onto Phil's place during the night, only to fall victim to his traps. Phil referred to the Bettongs as kangaroo rats and believed that they lived in the long grass, and came out at night to dig up his lawn.

Our neighbour on the other side, had been given a black and white cat that would sleep a lot and often come across to our place to stalk and kill honey eaters, doves, and other native birds and mammals throughout the night. One morning, I spotted the cat playing on the neighbour's lounge-room floor with what was left of a rare and endangered feather-tailed glider, that it had caught down at the creek. The neighbour maintained that her cat was harmless. One of our neighbourly duties was to feed this destructive predator when she was away. Thankfully, it eventually died of old age, and she didn't bother getting another one.

Erik the Expert

Erik was a pedigree miniature fox terrier. His show name was Beaukita Startrek. His father sold for $11,000 but we bought Erik for $100 because his tail wasn't right during the show stance. He was highly intelligent and full of mischief. Erik was highly strung and energetic, black and white, and easily noticed. Let me describe a few incidents involving Erik.

Erik the expert.

I was taking him for a walk up into the hills behind our place early one morning and as usual, he ran in 50-metre circles around me as I would climb up the slopes. As we got halfway up, there were two dingoes heading straight for Erik and they meant business. He ran towards me with the dingoes in hot pursuit. I was alarmed and it wasn't until he jumped into my arms that the dingoes gave up the chase. The dingoes were defending their territory, as they did during a similar incident with Warnabari at Lajamanu in the NT. I didn't bring Erik with me on those walks again.

There were five grey-hounds living up on Golf Links road and could be seen in the morning walking on the golf course with their owner. They were firmly tethered on short leashes and muzzled. On one occasion, Erik teased them by running right up to the group and suddenly turning away at the last moment. This was repeated time and time again until there was absolute mayhem. Erik then ran away, leaving the owner cursing and swearing. One morning they were on their way back home when Erik appeared out of nowhere and began taunting them by dashing in and out of the throng, entangling the big dogs up in their leashes and tangling up their owner by the legs. As I watched on, embarrassed and helpless, Erik had left them as quickly as he had come.

He ran down the road towards me and from the safety of a clump of guinea grass, peered out to watch the noisy confusion. The owner was enraged. Fist clenched and arms waving as he attempted to find his balance, he shouted down the road to me. " If I see that f..ng dog here again I'll kill the f…ing thing" and that was that. From then on we never took him out of the yard without a leash.

Erik was good with the chooks and ducks and never attempted to harm them. With the ducks he would nuzzle in between the feathers and you could see him quivering all over as if he would just love to sink his teeth into that sweet-smelling and juicy meat that ducks are known for, but he never did. Erik was a finicky eater.

Erik turned up his nose at the perfectly good family leftovers until I trialled an experiment. I put him into the chook pen with his bowl of food, and the chooks went for it. While not harming any chooks, Erik savagely defended the bowl, chasing off the chooks, and bolted down every last morsel and I never had to worry about him not eating his meals again.

Erik developed a serious relationship with a neighbouring Chihuahua, who lived down the road. Erik would discard the little coat that Miya had made for him, every time he went down to visit her. Miya insisted that he saw the coat as an embarrassment and an affront to his masculinity. Marnane's red cattle dog across the creek was another story.

Erik was easily led astray by this cattle dog, who would make his way across the creek from the farm to visit Erik, and together, they'd go on their wanderings around the area. Erik would be gone for long periods causing some concern and, sure enough, late one afternoon, a tragedy was unfolding. Erik had gone with the cattle dog down to another neighbour's place. They had a lot of chooks free ranging and the two culprits were getting into them.

Muriel, from next door, came to tell me that she had spotted Erik and the cattle dog down at the Cotic's place. She reported that Erik had hold of the neck of a chook, and the cattle dog had hold of the other end, and they were tearing it apart. The hillsides were strewn with dead chooks and there were dead chooks floating down the creek. It was a complete disaster!

The Cotics took it well, but Erik was now a full-blown killer of livestock, and we had no choice but to give him back to Edna, his original owner and breeder. Edna took Erik back, shampooed him, clipped his nails, and immediately put him out to pasture with the other foxies to breed. Edna eventually found another home for Erik down at Mackay, and we made a visit to see him one year on our way through. We had Erik for about three years and it was another three years until we saw him for the last time.

He was busy chasing kids around the house when we arrived. He recognised us immediately, and it was a moving little reunion, albeit, tainted by a dead duck on the back doorstep. Erik had a girlfriend on the cane farm down the road. She was a friendly border collie. He seemed very happy in his new home. It was around this time that I caught up with Jim Wertz.

Wertzy

Jim Wertz had separated from his wife, remarried, and settled in the Daintree. Late in September of 1992, we overnighted with Jim and Jenny – his new wife, and kids Jessica and Rubin. It was a pleasant reunion of sorts and I had determined to let bad memories pass. He had a few acres at the bottom of Devil's Thumb range. It was a bit unusual in that it was mostly cool, due to a cold air flow into the valley from the rainforest high above.

Wertzy took us on a tour of his place, explaining that, among other things, he felt that it was too late to save the rainforest and that it was inevitable that it would be transformed from its current status to something else. He had no qualms about its demise. Over time, Wertzy went about establishing a bamboo farm and introduced all manner of exotic species.

We kept in contact and visited a few times over the following years. Jenny was teaching music at the time and had developed a relationship with one of her students, a house painter. Eventually, their lives became more and more complex and confused. A couple of years later, during a visit, it was uncomfortable and there was an open conflict so we made it the last.

Later on, Jenny started another relationship with a builder, and she bought him up to the Tablelands for a visit. We never heard from her after that. We also heard that Wertz had married a woman from the Philippines, and in 2009, died of cancer. By contrast, we were enjoying a stable family life in our new home. Miya and Sara were doing well at school and had made new friends. Rose and I continued working. Rose had set up and was managing the respite care centre in Cook Street, in the early 1990s. I was still doing local supply teaching and Mum was relocating to Far North Queensland.

Mum Comes to Atherton

Some years prior to her move to Launching Place in Eastern Victoria, Mum had suffered a nasty fall as a result of a rail on her back porch breaking away. We reckoned that the fall triggered her late-onset diabetes. She was diagnosed as "brittle" and her blood sugar levels were difficult to stabilise. She had suffered "hypos" where she would momentarily lose consciousness. She was becoming increasingly dependent on Judith and Elaine.

It was after we'd moved to Atherton, that we became concerned about Mum's ability to manage on her own and we had a meeting with her and the family about the possibility of her selling up and moving to Atherton, closer to family, with a view to my relocating a timber cottage for her onto our block. Mum's difficulty in making a decision and her hesitance in agreeing to the plan was not taken very seriously. No one understood the symptoms of early dementia or could have foreseen the drama that was about to unfold over the following months.

Mum stayed with Judith and Elaine while I spent a week or so, packing up Mum's household effects for removal to Atherton and preparing her property at Launching Place for sale. While I was there, an old family friend, Charlie Martin from the Ringwood days, got wind of Mum's situation and came to visit. He was sad to hear about Mum and had some misgivings. I explained that given Mum's difficulty managing alone, there wasn't much choice. I was saddened by Charlie's news of Moe, our family cockatoo. When she left the family home in Ringwood, Mum had reluctantly passed Moe on to Charlie and his family. Moe was to die tragically in Charlie's house fire some years later. After I'd finished at Mum's place, and on my way back to Atherton with Mum, I spent some time with Mum's sister, Auntie Lil and that was the last time I saw her. Auntie Lil died from Parkinson's disease soon after.

To help Mum settle in at Atherton, Sara gave up her bedroom for her and we put all her household effects into temporary storage. It soon became apparent that Mum was suffering from more than Diabetes. There is no point in my describing Mum's symptoms of depression, confusion, and paranoia. It was a tough time for everyone. After several weeks, it was obvious that Mum couldn't stay with us and we arranged a rental property for her in Canopus Circuit, close by.

It was a pleasant place with views across farmland to the hills behind our place. Mum would often drive down to our place to visit and seemed to be better in herself, but it wasn't to last. If it wasn't for Rose I don't know what I would have done. I was always impressed by Rose's diverse skills. Rose organised an assessment for Mum for aged care services including Meals on Wheels, respite, and daycare. Then one day, Judith turned up out of the blue.

Judith packed up Mum's stuff put it in storage, and shipped Mum back to Victoria. Had she talked about it with us, she would have perhaps done things differently, because Mum had been diagnosed with early dementia and finally Alzheimer's disease. By now, Mum was in her late seventies.

A couple of years later we visited Mum at the aged care hostel at Cobram in Victoria. Judith had moved to Leongatha. Rose was appalled at the conditions Mum had to endure at the hostel. Rose immediately arranged Mum's relocation to the more professional Leongatha Aged Care home close to Judith. Mum was a lot happier there in the pleasant environment and Judith was able to visit her more often and spend quality time with her. In hindsight, I thought that the biggest mistake that Mum ever made was to leave her long-established friends and the old family home in Ireland Street, Ringwood, to attempt to build a new lifestyle at Woori Yallock and later at Launching Place. Mum's condition gradually deteriorated, and my phone calls to her became scarcely more than an ongoing and painful chore.

Chapter 8
Politics

A full account of events during my experience in politics through the 1990s would be well beyond my purpose here. Instead, I'll attempt to limit this section to a brief history and, share a few of the more poignant events that spring to mind.

I was 50 when I became involved in party politics. It was altogether a vibrant and colourful time and it felt right. I was consumed by the plethora of local, regional, state, federal, and global issues during the 1990s. I was going to make a difference.

Concerns about sustainability, protection of the natural environment, and social justice issues had come to me early in life. As mentioned earlier, Mum and Dad played an important part in the development of my consciousness, for which I remain eternally grateful. I was five when we moved to Ringwood Victoria. At the time I had developed a connection with, and respect for, the natural environment.

We'd lived there happily for ten years before the bulldozers arrived. My first conscious action against environmental destruction was to hurl mud on the walls of buildings under construction.

It seemed that in this scheme of things, nothing was sacred. I gradually became aware of a pattern developing in my life, where environmental destruction seemed to follow me. One of the most disturbing trends was mega-scale mining, which was wreaking havoc, socially and environmentally, in the remote pristine places we got to know and respect. I became part of a vibrant environmental movement on the Atherton Tablelands.

Raising Awareness on the Atherton Tablelands

By the late 1980s, significant parts of Queensland's Wet Tropics were inscribed on the World Heritage list. For me, there was no option but to become actively involved in the face of powerful state and local opposition to the listings of what was left of the Tableland's rare and endangered rainforest ecosystems. For example, Federal Minister for the Environment, Graham Richardson, was jostled and threatened by crowds of timber workers during his visit, as part of the nomination of remnant rainforest around Ravenshoe in 1987, for World Heritage status.

I first became involved with a number of environmental organisations on the Tablelands at the time. It was all about awareness raising and the Yungaburra market stall was the place to be. There was solidarity among the different environmental groups and we held permanent monthly community information stalls. We rostered ourselves on the market stalls complete with banners and provided current information in the form of posters, brochures, and flyers. There was a lot of interest and membership grew.

For example, there was the Atherton Greenhouse Information Network or AGRIN. There was the Australian Conservation Foundation or the ACF. There was Greenpeace Australia. There was the Cairns and Far North Environment Center or CAFNEC and there were the local Landcare and the Upper Barron River Catchment groups. I was also curious about party politics.

Party Politics

My earliest diary entry on 17th Feb 1992 was a request for policy information kits for our Market stall at Yungaburra. Another entry on 1st October 1993 mentions a contribution and in December of that year, I was on the Environment Committee. For my purpose, here, I will refer to the Australian Democrats as "the party".

By 1995, we came to the decision to rent out our property in Atherton, and move to Brisbane for that year, to support Miya in her first year of university.

Brisbane

Miya and I were day students at the Mount Gravatt Griffiths University Campus. Miya was doing her first year in the double degree in Environmental Science and Law while I started full-time coursework for the Master's in Environmental Education at the same campus.

Sara was a year ten, day student at Stuartholme. Rose worked with Catholic Social Response, as a case manager at Ipswich Road, Chardon's Corner, to provide financial support for the family for the year. Initially, we rented at Verny Road East, Graceville. We saw a lot of our old friends, Jim Varghese and Ted Chicoteau, and caught up with others from the Fernberg Road era. We relocated to Dunella Street, Sherwood later in the year. While at Graceville, Jeff Hulcome, Jim Varghese and I played tennis on the courts on the Uniting Church precinct across the road.

A Bad Witness to the Community

I booked a court according to how we were situated for time. During my initial inquiries about access to the tennis court, I was surprised to meet again with the Reverend Trevor Foote. Trevor's wife, Dawn, usually attended to my bookings for the court. It was Reverend Foote who, nearly thirty years before, in 1968 had billeted us as lay missionaries at his home in Broome when we were en route from Perth to Darwin to take up our jobs at Yirrkala Mission in North East Arnhem Land.

It was a Sunday morning when Jeff and I were having a rather spirited hit of tennis. I was calling out the scores in my usual way when the Reverend Foote came striding out from the Church towards us. He appeared upset. Apparently, we were disrupting the morning service and the Reverend accused me of being *"a bad witness to the community."*

The Party

I wasted no time in contacting people in the Australian Democrats and soon became involved with branch meetings. I felt very welcome and was involved with the Environment Committee, campaign meetings, information booths, and the dining club. On the 16th of June, I was participating in the demonstration against the French nuclear tests in the Pacific. I was able to participate in campaign and media workshops prior to the elections and on polling day, the 15th of July I was handing out how-to-vote cards in the State Elections.

They were very supportive of me. Being in Brisbane was a great opportunity to get involved and learn more about party politics. As the year progressed I met the Rural Spokesperson. I also met with many others and become familiar with the workings of the Queensland home office. I was comfortable with the party structure and was impressed by the democratic processes.

The family was well organised and by mid-February, Rose was providing our income, Sara was at Stuartholme, Miya and I were full-time students on campus at Mt. Gravatt. My year was full-on with family, academia, tennis, party politics, and social activity.

On campus, by mid-March, I was formulating a research problem, and there emerged an area of interest at this point. A diary entry for March 18 read, *"(given that) schooling is a social control mechanism to perpetuate the status quo, should EE (Environment Education) research efforts focus on schools?"*

Other things were happening on the political front too. On the same day, there was a media workshop. And there was an incident at the home office where a representative of the Shooters Party had somehow infiltrated the meeting. It was agreed that we would need to be more vigilant in the future. Sara and I went on a trip down to Melbourne.

Gemini

Early in July, Sara and I had the opportunity to drive down to Melbourne. We drove Jim Varghese's Gemini car down to his brother in Brunswick. Before delivering the car, we stayed overnight with my nephew Victor and his family at Bayswater. The Gemini driver's seat was so bad that I had severely injured my lower back and hadn't realised until we arrived at Vic's. I was in agony and unable to climb out of the car. I slowly and painfully eased myself down onto the ground from the driver's seat and crawled to Victor's front door. I spent the night in agonising pain. On the following morning, I went to a chiropractor who immediately diagnosed the problem, strapped me onto a sort of rack, and turned me upside down. The relief was instantaneous and we were able to carry on with our itinerary.

I showed Sara where I had attended school at the Ringwood State Primary and High Schools. We visited my old high school friend Hoyte, my sister Judith and others, and Mum at the aged care home, before returning to Brisbane.

Environmental Politics

Some of the students that year were school teachers. Course Convenor, John Fien, was a clever and polished presenter and facilitator. John was an award finalist in the Social Science category in 2002.

My course wasn't issues based and I was concerned about John's approach to environmental issues. He was happy to endorse research, seminar, and assignment proposals relating directly to environmental jobs in the mining and eco-tourism industries. Schools-based proposals were also encouraged. Other academics shared John's views. I was vocal about my position on these issues.

There was no doubt in my mind that the idea of private, profit-driven mining and tourism, and having an authentic concern for the welfare of the natural environment was a contradiction. The idea that mining and concern for the natural environment could coexist didn't make any sense.

In class, I would argue that, among other things, children and adolescents had enough on their plates, such as personal development, and that they didn't need the added burden, of having to deal with complex environmental issues. While I felt that children shouldn't be entirely sheltered from environmental issues, going home from school to influence or instruct their parents on how to behave responsibly, was an unreasonable expectation of them.

I had other views on that topic as well, and by late March I had formulated a research problem. Given that schooling is a social control mechanism serving to perpetuate the status quo among other things, should Environment Education research efforts focus on schools? I was discouraged from going there, on the grounds that the topic was beyond the scope of a 40CP research project, and reluctantly proposed something more manageable and still within my chosen area of Adult Education.

The research project I settled on was "Vegetation and Biodiversity Management: A Course for Shire Councillors". Helen Spork, a faculty staff member and one of my lecturers supervised my project. If it wasn't for Helen's support and encouragement, I may not have completed it the following year. After my return to the Far North, it was completed and assessed. I was enthusiastic about its potential and presented it to the Regional group of Councils at their general meeting. It was met with silence. One councillor took a hard copy and lost it.

In mid-September, we met with visiting Danish academic, Bjorne Jensen to plan a three-month study trip to Copenhagen for the following year. We were to look at pharmaceutical toxins in the environment – a significant environmental issue for Europeans. We were back in Atherton when another issue emerged.

A Party Response to the National Competition Policy

The National Competition Policy (NCP) Reform Act, was passed by parliament under the Keating Government in 1995. They endorsed the Hilmer report of 1993. The report recommended far-reaching major economic reforms, including a review of the constitutional limits, regulations, and other impediments to competition. There was also structural reform of "public monopolies" or publicly owned assets such as essential services, other public services, and utilities.

The NCP was pushed through on the back of the budget by senior bureaucrats leaving the public in the dark as to the fact that it was based on support for corporate market dominance.

The Hilmer Report offered limited public consultation. The rapidity of implementation of the report's recommendations enabled few opportunities for public education and debate. There was a hostile public response, which was evidenced in the rise in support of Pauline Hanson's One Nation party. The report was endorsed in its entirety, opposed only by the progressives.

I clearly recall my thinking at the time – the NCP was uncivilised and grossly unfair. It set the scene for privatisation, at both the Federal and State level. It institutionalised competition at its worst, like unrestricted corporate greed and aggression. And there were tricky aspects to the policy implementation, such as the demonising of unions, protection, and regulation. For example, the deregulation of the dairy industry placed farmers at the mercy of the global corporate market.

Free Trade was underpinned by the freedom to exploit.

The NCP set the scene for the privatisation of public assets, by setting in place all the necessary mechanisms for the sale of publicly owned assets – our assets - such as railways, electricity supply, and telecommunications. Such assets were demonised as "public monopolies." It was outrageous, but with the backing of the mainstream media, would become a normalised and acceptable policy.

Deregulation

For me, deregulation held a special interest. It was Senator Woodley, who chaired the Inquiry into the Deregulation of the Dairy industry. Deregulation was an important item on the Senator's agenda. As a community liaison staffer, part of my role was to accompany John at the Malanda Milk Co-operative's meetings where he would provide first-hand updates on the progress of the Senate Inquiry. While the writing was on the wall, it became incomprehensible to the local dairy farmers, who had plodded along for generations, under the protection of price regulation, subsidies, and other sustainable policies.

Ultimately, the farmers thought they'd be better off under deregulation. For example, according to sophisticated corporate spin, presented to farmers by representatives of powerful transnational companies, dairy farmers could name their own price for their milk. The Malanda Milk Museum stands testament to the destruction of a once secure, independent, and sustainable local dairy industry. Some years later, the local member observed that the dairymen of the Tablelands didn't know much, but soon after they'd signed off on the deregulation they knew that they were out of business.

The family left Brisbane on 14th December 1995. We went to the Democrat's 18th anniversary and Christmas party which seemed to serve as a closure to a very satisfying year. Among other things, I'd established a rock-solid network, got most of the Master's coursework, endorsement of my research proposal, and preparations for Copenhagen out of the way.

Miya had done well in her first year and was comfortable with the prospect of life on campus in 1996. Sara completed her year 10 at Stuartholme with good results and made some good friends during the year. It would have been a real struggle without the tireless and steadfast support, financial and family-wise, from Rose.

Back Home to the Tablelands

Not long after our return from Brisbane, Rose and I, Miya and Sara became active members of the Cairns branch of the party and I travelled down to meetings in Cairns to represent members here on the Tablelands. Activities on the Tablelands continued and it was essentially promotion and awareness raising, including the information stall at the Yungaburra markets that dominated our activities in those early days. It was all about building a party presence in the north.

Sara's Return to Stuartholme

We all agreed that it might be beneficial for Sara to spend the year back at Stuartholme as a year 11 boarder. We got Sara on the train at Gordonvale. No one was happy as we were left standing there at the station waving goodbye, as the train slowly pulled away. We regularly spoke on the phone. Sara always shared her experiences with the family and seemed to be doing well until a few weeks passed when everything changed. Some of the other boarders had invited Sara out to the pictures one night during a weekend. They ended up at a bar at one of the nightclubs in Fortitude Valley. We suggested that Sara come back home and complete her senior high school certificate at Mt Saint Bernard's or externally, or a combination of the two. It was a relief for everybody when Sara was home within a couple of days.

The year 1996 was an enjoyable and productive time for the family and our involvement with the local membership, and party politics. I put a lot of enthusiasm and energy into what I felt was a genuinely worthy cause and that I was able to make a difference. I believed, that we were offering a decent alternative, to the incumbent Neoliberal conservatives. We had comprehensive policies that made sense. I believed that the public was listening. The federal elections were set for early March.

The whole family were very much involved with the organisation of polling booths and rostering how-to-vote card distribution. There were regular phone hookups and so on. Our Cairns-based candidate did pretty well with over 5%. Senator Woodley was the Rural Spokesperson for the party. I organised itineraries for his visits to the Far North. We flew all over the electorate, meeting with local government and the media.

The Senator would time his visits to coincide with our meetings and the local markets information stall, where he would engage the public on relevant local issues. For one of the visits, Rose and I organised a garden party at home here, featuring the Mareeba Line Dancers, and the Senator gave an update on what was happening in Canberra. For me, the highlight of 1996 was the three-month study trip to Denmark under the auspices of Danish academic Bjorn Jensen from the University of Copenhagen.

Copenhagen

I arrived in Copenhagen early on 30th June and stayed in a student unit on campus. The Danes seemed to share much in common with us. They spoke fluent English and enjoyed Monty Python and other English black humour and had an excellent Blues bar in old Copenhagen. But I found Denmark a bit difficult to navigate – signage and labels were in Danish. At the shop, for instance, you were hard-pressed to determine whether you were buying shampoo or detergent and I found myself dependent on the locals for help. Learning Danish was a real struggle for me.

Danish is one of those ancient Nordic languages with a really tricky sound system and basic rules didn't seem to have much in common with English. All the road maps were in Danish as well. You just had to ask for all information. The Danes were a bit quirky too, but I understood that their social, environmental, and public policies were progressive and more advanced than ours.

They were happy paying taxes and they had excellent public services. The Danes seemed altogether a more sophisticated and civilised society than Australia and America. Everybody rode push-bikes, with road rules to match, ensuring their safety. I bought a pushbike from one of the Danish students. I used it for transport and rode around the countryside on the weekend.

I enjoyed a refreshing social interaction with international participants - Danes, Australians, Americans, Indonesians, and Hungarians. I met with local students at Monk's Cellar- an ancient wine cellar in the heart of old Copenhagen and a favourite student haunt.

There were dinner parties as well. I celebrated Mum's 81st birthday on 16th July in Copenhagen. I participated in excursions around research topics, including ozone water treatment, lead contamination, and pharmaceuticals in the environment. Cultural exchange presentations were a lot of fun. Assessment items included assignments and a challenging group seminar presentation.

A Hungarian

Students were left to organise their own groups for seminar presentations. The dominant Danish and English speakers rushed to form their groups. I was a bit slow and was left with the Hungarian. He lacked basic research and other academic skills and had limited competency in English. He was obstructive and belligerent, and argued the point over the most basic academic protocols and so on. How this person came to be a participant in a Master's level education course was a mystery to me. There were also two Indonesians, and a Danish student in my study group.

I was annoyed and disappointed with the course coordinator and registered an objection to the ad-hoc way in which the groups were formed and the potential impact this might have on my overall assessment. The Coordinator assured me that, under the circumstances, I would gain a satisfactory assessment outcome. It was by now the end of August. Group presentation aside, I enjoyed my time in Denmark and on the return trip home, took advantage of the opportunity to visit my ancestral homeland in Derbyshire.

England - A Sense of Place

I had already been in touch with John Humphreys in Oxford and planned to stay with him. It was my first time in England. I planned to stay the first night in a cheap hostel in London and catch a bus to Stockport and on to Marple in Derbyshire. The cheapest place was about $250 per night, so I decided to get a bus straight to Marple.

I arrived at Marple late that afternoon. It was getting cold and I couldn't find anywhere affordable to stay. I resolved to spend the night on the street when a taxi turned up at the hotel, and the driver took me to a B and B that he knew in Stockport. The following morning, I found a place on the outskirts of Marple and stayed a couple of nights. Everything was within walking distance.

I spent time wandering around Marple, and along the canal. I met some local men who told me about what was happening during the immediate post-war period. Gordon and his friends played around Marple Hall during their childhood. Gordon also knew the caretakers of the Hall. The Crosbys sold apples, plums, and pears from the orchard, under a copper beech tree.

Wybersley Hall, Derbyshire, 1996.

He mentioned Basil Townsend, Mrs Isherwood, and Richard Isherwood who later relocated from Marple to nearby Wybersley Hall which was also part of the original Isherwood estate.

I was told of people clambering over the rooftops of Marple Hall on moonlit nights, pilfering the lead flashing from the roof. By the late 1950s, the Hall had fallen into neglect. Its last owner, Christopher Isherwood, Author of Goodbye to Berlin, Mr Norris Changes Trains, My Guru and his Disciples and others, seemed nonchalant about the role Marple Hall played in hundreds of years of tradition and the English revolution.

Interior fittings, furnishings, tapestries, carved stone features and anything that was movable was either stolen, sold, auctioned off, or dispersed. The Hall descended into ruin, was passed on to the local authorities, and demolished in 1959. The site was turned into a recreational park. The rest of the estate was sold off for housing development, complete with a street named Isherwood Street and a school called Marple Hall School. One day while I was at the site, I met Steve, the school's history teacher, on an excursion with his class. He was a sensitive man and most humbled to have met an Isherwood right there at Marple Hall.

I may have imagined it, but during my visit to the site of Marple Hall, a feeling of belonging came over me. I sat there on the edge of the original foundation next to the massive red sandstone lintel with a brass plaque - all that was left of a place that had played such a pivotal role in the revolution. The ruins of the clock tower and stables amidst the tangle of blackberries were still there and the ancient copper beech trees stood testimony to a once great and powerful institution.

I explored the grounds and climbed down to the Goyte River, which flowed through the valley below and tried to imagine the drama of life in those distant days. I didn't want to leave. I was drawn back to this place, time and again, before I finally left for Oxford and my friend John Humphreys.

John's life had changed dramatically since we'd seen him last, some 20 years before. He had returned from Australia with his family to Oxford to set up his own practice. I stayed with John and he shared his experiences with me and insisted that I use his BMW motorbike to explore the south. I inadvertently collected a parking ticket at a car park at the Salisbury Cathedral, and John insisted on paying the fine. Having spent a night in Bath, I promised myself I'd return. I left Oxford and England feeling so indebted to John, and he made a pledge to come and stay with us in Atherton. I was looking forward to the challenges that lay ahead in the local politics at home.

Facing Reality on the Tablelands

By late October 1997, our party leader was replaced by Meg Lees, for whom I held great respect and admiration.

Initially, my working relations with the new State Secretary and other Qld. staff were positive and I was endorsed as a Candidate for the lower house in the upcoming Federal elections.

Candidate for Kennedy, Federal Elections, 1998.

As a candidate for the 1998 federal elections, it was necessary to be seen to be exercising some solidarity with the Cairns-based candidate.

In 1998 I continued to build a party presence in FNQ and separated from Cairns to establish a robust and active Tablelands Branch in the face of opposition from the state executive. I didn't fully understand why this was. An expansion in the north was consistent with party policy, and I ran with it, happy to face the consequences later on.

Yungaburra markets information stall, 1998.

With the support of the Senator, during the post-election period, we continued to build a presence in the Far North. Things were going pretty well, as reflected in my early 1999 diary entry:

Monday 11th January
- Register Land Rover
- Home brew
- Contact Senator - has applied to Minister for senate office for FNQ
- Pick up kids
- Rose request position description for Vanuatu
- Spread chook shit/replenish
- Secure passion fruit/grapes
- Weed trees
- Email copy of branch news from local electorate to Nat Journal and Qad.

Further Progress

Late in June of the same year saw me in Canberra, learning the ropes under the guidance of a staff member. I was also preparing for my new position as Senate Liaison Officer for North Queensland. As part of the process, I developed a set of working guidelines that were approved for use by all liaison staff. The new North Queensland Senate Office was located in Atherton.

With Senator Woodley on a tour of Kennedy Electorate, 1998.

I organised a tour of the electorate for the Senator in early August. A Gulf tour was also scheduled for October. John was invited to a monthly slot with Mt Isa's local radio on What's Happening in the Federal Parliament. John was later to have the slot transferred to me, and I was to be briefed on regular progress – it never eventuated. I was advised that under the new policy of targeting seats, our electorate wasn't a priority. Despite the leader's support for the regions, the FNQ office was still viewed by the Home Office as the Senator's 'quirky thing.' On one occasion whilst in Canberra, I was referred to as the "Minister for the North" I had been nominated for an ordinary member position on the management committee and advised that there was no actual position. This was also the time when the issue of my approach to press releases had first emerged.

Press Releases

The Queensland media advisor had convinced me to save time by using already researched materials, in this instance, the new Senator's press releases, and simply top and tail, adding a local comment.

It was highly effective in getting the party message across in FNQ because I was known to the local media. The Senator and I saw no problem with this.

Line dancing - a fundraising event at our place, 1997.

There were objections and demands that I should do my own press releases. I was too naïve to see what was happening at the time, but in hindsight, it was all related to the undermining of our efforts to progress the regional party profile.

I was confused. What was I to do? Who do I go to for clearance of press releases? I had no choice but to continue down the same path. The researcher had taken over the responsibility for the clearance of my press releases and nothing more was said.

In late September the press release issue resurfaced. We did not know that they were plotting against us – subtly at first, but increasingly undermining everything we were doing for the regions. People from the home office were by now familiar with my convictions, having taken up my offer to accompany the Senator on one of his official visits, overnighting with us and taking in the Tablelands.

By early October, our branch began work on the development of a website. We were to be the first branch in Qld, to have our own website. The website would raise the party's regional profile and increase membership. And to top it off, our branch newsletter, was to be circulated with the National Campaign Newsletter.

Under Attack

At every opportunity, they went on the attack. They had taken to calling repeatedly on my private phone which was in breach of protocol, creating ongoing communication problems between the Atherton and Brisbane offices.

During a period of the Senator's absence, one of my antagonists was appointed to the position of temporary office manager. Now unchecked phone harassment and bullying intensified, leaving me with no alternative but to make myself unavailable to them. They then resorted to bullying emails and so on. The phone calls and emails went unanswered until the Senator's return from overseas.

In early May of the same year, I'd been invited to join a Native Title Coordinator and his Aboriginal delegation to Canberra to meet with Ministers and other MPs to discuss Federal ATSIC funding for the organisation. Members of the delegation included the Cultural Heritage Coordinator and members of the Governing Council, who were scheduled to meet a number of MPs.

Interference and Undermining

Back home, the bullying and harassment were replaced by manipulative interference and undermining by home office staff. During the wet season, early in 2000, a woman contacted our Brisbane office about concerns regarding an electricity power lines issue. The power line company had proposed to relocate their power lines from a World Heritage Area to private farmlands.

Rather than refer the woman to my Atherton office, they chose to take on the issue, prioritised it, imposed directives on me, and sent the Senator up north to deal with it. It was a highly inappropriate action to take, a waste of funding and inconsistent with both Liaison Office Guidelines and Environmental Policy. Due to poor and insufficient preparation, discussions with the local Government went nowhere, and the Senator and I ended up stranded by flood waters at Silkwood.

During the period leading up to the 2001 Federal Elections, a particular campaign issue had been gaining momentum. The issue in question involved the economic use of resources by targeting voters.

Targeting to Harvest Votes

There had been a recent visit by a representative of the English Liberal Democrats, who gave a talk to the State Council about their successes in targeting votes in the leafy suburbs. State Council embraced the model without question. Our local branch felt betrayed and we conveyed our sentiments regarding the issue, via our Branch Convenor's Report in December 2000 in response to an article in the party newsletter. I'll share this extract from our Branch Convenor's Report:

...The party has never exercised a narrow focus on votes and cannot afford to adopt the LDs strategy of concentrating resources in urban ...electorates. In the Australian context, ...embracing such a strategy risks the alienation of rural and regional Australians from the political process. Such a strategy is contrary to party principles...

At best, the article sends a message of confusion as to how resources may be allocated to regional seats and are counter-productive in providing encouragement to members and branches to contribute, at any level, in the lead-up to and during elections.

At worst, it alienates branches and members outside the South East Corner. It conveys the message that, if you're not in the South East corner (Qld) forget it - you don't have the support of the Campaign Committee or the Division. It may also be construed as a reflection of a 'keep out of the bush' mentality with narrow economic fundamentalism applied to campaign management.

One way to rectify this might be to encourage regional members by sending the message that even though we have to target seats we will still support your efforts in whatever way we can. This message of support and encouragement needs to be clarified at both the National and State level and it needs to be done soon.

Visit to Lajamanu

The family had planned a trip for August/September 2000 to visit some Warlpiri friends at Lajamanu and reconnect with the desert country. We took the Tanami Road, just north of Tennant Creek, which was open for only a short time. It took three days. It was overgrown. We followed this rough track driving west/northwest through the Tamami via Mirirrinyunga (Duck Ponds) north of the Buchanan Hills, across Winnecke Creek, and northwest to Lajamanu, where we lived and worked in the 1970s and where Miya was born.

Miya on the Land Rover - enroute to Lajamanu, September 2000.

It was, as usual, good to catch up with the Warlpiri people we had known in the past. An old friend, Jerry Jangala made a point of expressing his deep concern about the Tamami open-cut gold mine and water contamination. We also met with some teachers who had been to Kalkarindji (Wave Hill) to the north, and Daguragu to celebrate the Gurindji Freedom Day. They gave us a video of the event. We stayed at Ludo Kuiper's old house alongside the airstrip.

The trip coincided with recent issues regarding Indigenous Health. Whilst in Lajamanu, we conducted an unofficial survey of local community access to fresh food. The community gardens had long gone, replaced by a supermarket. Given the high level of unemployment and low income, among other things, it was found to be very expensive to access healthy fresh food. It was getting hot by the time we departed for the return trip back home to Atherton via Kalkarindji, Mt Isa, and across the Gulf of Carpentaria. We were home by the 9th of September.

Branch Website Up and Running

On the 15th December 2000, our branch website was up and running. Here's my diary entry:

Friday 15 December
Email: network recipients re RR policy/cover letter; with details of the meeting for inclusion in the National Conference program;

Branch Website
9am FNQ Computers $100 quote
Contact PTG for website procedures
Email ... RE: website details for inclusion in Nat Conference program for RR meeting at lunchtime Sunday 21 Jan. 2001

11.30am Website up and running.

Treat - Lake Barrine cruise
SES - sausage sizzle at HQ 7pm family

We hit the ground running in 2001 with the official opening of the Far North Queensland Senate Office on 2nd January. But I knew that our days with the party were numbered as reflected in a diary entry.

Monday 15th January
- Attend campaign committee requests and candidates meeting – request phone hookup contact ... via party office re issue of press releases;
- Contact Qld electoral commission re guidelines for independent candidates

- Procedure for resignation as branch convenor/spokesperson from political party;
- Rose prep letters of resignation from branch for me, Rose, Miya, Sara;
- Party leader to launch me either 17,18th March 3rd April.
- Pre conference RR policy photocopy agenda x 30
- Email copies of com development reply to …

National Conference

I was transfixed by the high standard of our leader's PowerPoint presentation. It was up-market. I wasn't impressed by the fact that rank-and-file members and people of my level, for the first time, were refused face-to-face access to our Senators. The Senators were booked out for sessions with corporate CEOs and other representatives from the corporate sector. Nobody else seemed perturbed by it. For me, it was highly offensive. But there was more to come. Firstly, they cancelled the RR meeting downstairs in the board room.

They set me up, demanding my attendance at a dodgy meeting - I was effectively on trial and I played right into their hands, despite a warning not to attend.

Diary entry, Sunday 21st
- don't resign from the party
- register a vote of no confidence in the campaign director
- resign positions of NQ spokesperson, branch convenor, secretary and treasurer
- run as an independent, and maintain FNQ office as a party member
- Need to act soon.

I had unanswered questions regarding the website and media statement. If they were to run a plastic candidate for my electorate I'd have to respond, with the risk of damaging the party profile. Could they withdraw my membership effectively closing down the FNQ office anyway? The timing was also important. But there wasn't enough time to think about it or seek further advice.

While the outcome of the meeting was a forgone conclusion, I have to say that I wasn't prepared for the humiliation, and vicious personal attacks regarding my approach to press releases. There was no opportunity given for me to defend my position, leaving me with no alternative but to interject, and strongly object to the bullying, and Rose and I walked away from the meeting and the conference. Back at the Division office, the following day, I submitted our letters of resignation from the party.

There was a lot to do back home in Atherton, with only 3 weeks before the Qld. State elections. I ran as an independent, knowing full well it would be a disaster. There was an urgency to tie up the loose ends and get closure. We all felt a deep sense of anger and betrayal.

Friday 26th January
Mass membership resignation with vote of no confidence in Division Exec.
Closure of FNQ Senate office.
Shutdown of branch website.
Eight years down the tube –

Nine years had passed since our resignation, when, out of the blue, the Qld. State Secretary rang to ask me if I would like to come on board and help rebuild the party. I said I'd think about it and did some basic research and declined.

Extract from a letter emailed in reply to QLD State Secretary 15 June 2009:

Thanks for your email and Link to the party website. It was refreshing to talk with you on the phone the other day. Please accept my heartfelt appreciation for your interest and the implicit acknowledgment of the work that my family and I put into the party.

Looking at the website, the party seems, with minor exceptions, much the same. There are a few things that I need to say…
I've come to the understanding that, like any other organisation, as a general reflection of the society from which it is born, (how can it be otherwise) the party can be no less vulnerable now, to domination by seriously wounded personalities than it ever was.

I take your point about not giving up, however, I see an attempt at a comeback for the party could be seen to be akin to trying to resuscitate something that has self-destructed and dead in the water.

Without being too severe, a party rebuild is perhaps a bit like governments or societies attempting to artificially inject new life into the corporate monsters that they've created.

Rather than rebuilding and seeking the middle ground within a system in decline, perhaps we should be focusing our resources on the inevitable challenges of the transformation of modern society involving paradigm shifts - revisiting world views and developing a vision for a sustainable future.
Again, to think that any organisation, our party included, can do more than reflect the society of which it is inextricably a part, is a delusion.

I'm confident about the future. Things can only get better and as the transition to a sane and peaceful world gathers pace, society will come to value our contribution.

As for me, I have to say that I've moved on from party politics and you'll be comforted to know that far from giving up, I'm committed to working towards a sustainable future. I'm working in collaboration with other colleagues on the development of course materials for our online education project called 'Learning for Sustainable Living' L.F.S.L. is a 12-unit course and at the professional development level, addresses the psychological underpinnings of our current crises. Most units are still under preparation, but you're more than welcome to check out our home page…

Should you like to look at some of the units in more detail please let me know and I can arrange access for you. Any comments would be most valued.

Thanks again for your interest.
Regards
Alan

Chapter 9
Beyond the Party

Restoration

I could now see my way clear to start on the long-awaited finer details of the restoration of the house.

Our living room post-restoration in 2002.

It was Gill McIntyre who provided the expertise on the structural work. Gill was a local retired builder who had done his apprenticeship on pre-war Queenslander houses. He also did the major restoration of the heritage Catholic Church at Yungaburra. Gill knew of the master builder Tommy O'Meara who built our house for his daughter in 1940. Gill was happy to take on our project with me off-siding. Gill and his wife Shirley became close friends of the family over the years.

Our Queenslander home in Atherton. Restored in Burgandy trim, 2007.

We restored the kitchen, back and front landings, by using mostly recycled timber, matching the original sections. Some moulded pieces such as architraves, window sills, and skirting boards had to be made up, using original pieces as patterns. The kitchen and front landing were completed in 2002.

Once the preparation was complete, we were able to move on to the interior colour scheme. The Lennon family, the first owners of the house, had taken a great interest in its restoration. John, one of the children, retired in his 70s, was the former Monseigneur Lennon of Edmonton Parish.

The Lennons helped choose the colour scheme during a visit to see the house. The period colours were already there, you just had to choose a patch of the wall to scrape the later layers away to discover the original paint. For example, the walls of the kitchen were Olive Green and Eau-de-nil. We chose the latter. The living room was in Sea Coral and the rest of the house was in Manilla. We chose off-white semi-gloss for the ceilings, to highlight the elaborate Art Deco moulded plasterwork. There was an interlude and we all went on a trip to China.

Sar Chung

Rose's cousins Selwyn and Ian Mar took our family from Hong Kong to Quandong province on a ferry trip to see Rose's Uncle Mar Lok Shan in the village of Sar Chung in China in April 2001. Mar Lok Shan's small factory produced the series of Snoopy characters. He was a personal friend of Charles Schulz the author of the Charlie Brown series.

We went to the family house where Rose's father, Ian Mar Fan (Mar Yin Cheung) spent his early childhood. The two-story house had suffered neglect and even a fire, over the years of vacancy. For example, there were only traces of the hand-painted murals left on the walls of the mezzanine floor. But otherwise, the house was intact with an ancient kitchen downstairs and remnants of the garden still in place. Ian was instrumental in having the house restored in later years. Back home in Atherton, our restoration work continued.

Lajamanu and Nhulunbuy

By early June, the restoration work was coming to a close and we had begun planning temporary work back in the NT, for 2002. I would apply for a teaching position at Lajamanu and Rose, for the position of Regional Alcohol and Drug Nurse based in Nhulunbuy. We agreed that whoever got a job, we'd both relocate to that job location for the duration. I was also looking at a teaching job with the Catholics at Port Keats and in Manual Arts in Kent UK. Rose got an offer for Nhulunbuy. Meanwhile, at home, other things were happening.

Sara was home for the Uni break and was keen to accompany us to Nhulunbuy.

We picked up our Swiss friend Pia Rast from the Cairns airport early in November and spent the following days swimming at Etty Bay and visiting. Rose had received confirmation for Nhulunbuy and preparations for travel were already underway. We took Pia to Dreghorn Station to see the Smiths. I finished preparing the Land Rover, trailer and dinghy for drop off to Gulf Transport in Cairns en route to Nhulunbuy on the 21st November. Pia was back home by

Friday 23rd. Rose and I were at Nhulunbuy setting up our house at Hussnes Avenue by the following Friday.

Nhulunbuy

By early December 2001, I made contact with our old Fijian Missionary friends, Jonatani Rika and his wife Lossa and shared some crayfish, the first since 1968 – over 30 years ago. They had recently returned from a trip back to Fiji and Jonatani was working on a history of their time in North East Arnhem Land. They had raised 4 kids – Jonatani number 2, Moses, Aquilla and Lendua.

I lost no time in making contact with Mandawuy Yunipingu, , Yangurryangurr, Marritngu, Banampi at Lhanapuy, Djiniyini Gondarra, David Wirilma, Witjiwitji, Birrpunu, Gatjil, Galarrwuy Yunipingu, Guayguay, Elizabeth Bangil, Yinyindjurr, Djalinda from Bremer Island, and others we'd known in the days of the Methodist Overseas Missions.

While Rose was settling into her new nursing role, I started looking for supply and contract teaching in the region. Given my professional profile, I was confident enough to secure some supply work. My first port of call was the Yirrkala Community Education Centre. There was no work there. I applied for Numbulwar, Galiwinku and Maningrida with similar outcomes. I concluded that this was due to my declining the Lajamanu position. The school year closed and we all flew back home for Christmas and returned to Arnhem Land in mid-January 2002.

Yirrkala Revisited

I was able to introduce Miya and Sara to Marritngu of the Gumatj clan and Guayguay at the Buku Larangay Cultural Centre at Yirrkala. We saw photos of Marritngu's father, taken at Caledon Bay. It was at the Yirrkala Buku Larrangay Centre that I saw my first viewings of the Ian Dunlop documentaries, produced during the 1970s. In particular, the funeral of Narritjan. I scanned my early 35-millimetre slides of Yolngu public ceremonies along with sound tape recordings onto a disc and presented them to Larrangay to be included in their collection.

I met Wanampi, Yangurryangurr and Marritngu sharing kava at Wilama beach. We drove to Rocky Bay and along the northern beach. We spent time at the art and craft centre and went out fishing in Daliwuy Bay.

Miya and Sara turtle spotting on Daliwuy Bay, 2002.

Out in the community, the environment was very different from what I had experienced all those years ago. There was an air of disempowerment and hopelessness about the place. Employment opportunities for the Yolngu were limited or non-existent. On my first visit to the community, I noticed a white man doing the whipper-snipping. Everything else around the place seemed to be done, or run by white people from the nearby mining town of Nhulunbuy or elsewhere – a dramatic contrast to 40 years ago when all jobs, from administration to farming to maintenance, church, and so on, were held by Yolngu. For instance, back in 1968 when Rose worked in the mission office, seventeen-year-old Yinyindjurr showed Rose how to record and send the daily weather reports to the Darwin Met. office.

David Wirilma, now suffering from emphysema, was the overseer of the construction of the substantial and tropical-designed Yirrkala Mission church. It was the Yolngu who dictated the cross-cultural or two-way approach to learning, strongly reflected in the famous floor-to-ceiling painted panels of the church (now removed). The church has long been abandoned to the more recent Tongan community. Yolngu people had been betrayed by the church. It was obvious that the MOM had abandoned the Yolngu people in favour of mining interests with tragic social and environmental consequences. I have dealt with this topic in more detail in earlier sections.

My visits enabled me to mourn the loss of quality of life and freedoms that we all had, prior to the invasion of the miners. I was able to spend time at the graveside and memorials of Dadaynga Marika, Daympalipu, Millirpum, and other heroes who fought in vain for justice in Australia's first Indigenous Land Rights case, which I mentioned earlier. It was at about this time that I began to renew old Yolngu friendships and acquaintances and revisit my Gumatj and Gupapuyngu language skills.

ARDS and Richard Trudgen

The Aboriginal Resource Development Services (ARDS) was funded by the Uniting Church. I met Richard Trudgen in early January. Richard was in charge of ARDS' Nhulunbuy regional programs. Richards' book 'Why Warriors lie down and Die' 2000, attempted to lay the foundations of understanding why the Aboriginal people of Arnhem Land, faced the greatest crisis in health and education since European contact. Richard, from Milingimbi, was working for ARDS which had its HQ based in Darwin. His main focus was on facilitating cultural awareness seminars for incoming Health professionals and other staff. The emphasis was on cross-cultural communication. I participated in one of his workshops and he offered me a part-time job in language development. His suggestion was that I eventually take over the workshops, freeing him to pursue his passion for indigenous radio work.

For the time being, my role was to pursue language studies which took me to Darwin to attend workshops. As part of my language studies, I had the opportunity to clarify my skin name which is Gamarrang (a shark that protects fish breeding sites) My relationship with Yolngu was slowly re-established.

For instance, Marritngu is my father. Yungalama, now a very old man but still smoking his traditional Macassan pipe and living at Dhalinbuy Girralk (homeland) is my Ngapipi (uncle). I had many other relations at Yirrkala and at the homeland centre of Dhalingbuy.

Rose's work colleague, Yinyindjurr, also from Dhalingbuy, is yirralk rirrikthun. (Very sick at Yirrkala). My old work colleague, Witjiwitji, was now living at Gumurru outstation. (Formerly Gapuwiyak or Lake Evella)

I met with Heather Birrpunu, my yukuyuku (sister) who was a health worker at Yirrkala. I was describing the times when working with Witjiwitji at the workshop and I would sing folk songs to his great amusement. One of the songs was called Lurrpur (sulphur-crested cockatoo). I told Birrpunu that the pet cockatoo we had at home in Atherton could talk - to which she replied *"And does he speak Gupapuyngu?"*

My Yirrkala fieldwork also took me to Yolngu homeland centres. Early in February 2002, Sara and I left Yirrkala to travel to Birany Birany outstation with Marritngu's sister, and Marritngu's sons, daughter, and granddaughter).

We met Marritngu there and we walked along the beach. Marritngu told me about Dakwa, a mutual work colleague at the Yirrkala workshop during the olden days. Dakwa passed away some time ago and is now in the Birany Birany graveyard. I also met Wirilma at Birany Birany and our conversation included problems the Yolngu faced in the future.

We set up camp in the sunset under the Yinyindjurr trees on the beach to spend the night, before returning to Nhulunbuy.

A diary entry made on 4th April:
Call from Wirilma re djorra after 15th.
A key role for me is to "tell Yolngu about Ngapaki rom"(white man's law) Wirilma sees my connection with Miya and my background as crucial to addressing problems and protecting homelands from further encroachments – also talked about proactive planning.
Wirilma also expressed concern over Gurrutu – the challenge for current generations and how to convince youth that their rebellion against the authority of Yolngu leaders may destroy their identity.

Courthouse Observations and Other Things

Courthouse observations were another of my roles with ARDS – the purpose being to record standard court protocols and the associated language, with a view to developing a set of guidelines for Yolngu interpreters. Yolngu were disadvantaged under the court system.

The practice of the day was to recruit anyone from the community to act as an interpreter. This casual approach often put the accused person at a disadvantage. For example, the interpreter may be a woman with an avoidance relationship with the accused, and so on.

Nationally, First Nations people are disproportionately represented in the prison system and it's getting worse. My observations are that people are severely disadvantaged by inadequate court procedures, in breach of International Human Rights laws. I'll be describing more of my experiences at the Nhulunbuy courthouse later in this section.

At Richard's request, I also attempted to provide a Teaching English as a Second Language (TESL) course for interested Yolngu. This meant developing my own programs and resources and securing a venue. I had to go begging for the most basic of teaching resources and the woman at the Nhulunbuy library treated me with suspicion. All I wanted was a small space to work twice a week. Richard even suggested that I should somehow work with Yolngu elders on 'intellectual concepts' I made the following diary entry - a progress report:

Monday 11th February
Feeling marginalised/not valued as though none of my professional knowledge and experience is relevant to the cause except my connections with Yirrkala from the distant past.
No structure to ARDS organisation, no orientation or guidelines except 'learning the language.' All entirely self-directed.
Absence of staff meetings/opportunities for communication except on an ad hoc basis.
Continuing catching up at Yirrkala and homelands/language studies.

Without entering into detail, the report, which I discussed with Richard at the time, reflected a deepening dissatisfaction with my work environment. At least I was being paid a meagre amount by ARDS (Uniting Church) and had the freedom to catch up with the Yolngu and the country. For me, that was of great personal value and despite the church and ARDS, I was content to persevere, at least for a while longer.

Rose had just returned from Galiwinku to find out from her Yapa (sister) Yikarawuy that Yinyindjurr had passed away at the Nhulunbuy hospital.

Galkila

It was the 2nd of March when Reverend Djiniyini Gondarra OAM, invited us to his homeland (Galkila) house overlooking Daliwuy Bay.

We talked about a lot of things. Djiniyini worked with me for a short time during the old mission days. He was now interested in Ngapaki rom (white man's law) and possible overlaps between western and Yolngu governance and gave insights into how a cooperative society might work. We also made a basic interpretation and translation of my English family coat of arms into Gumatj.

We stayed with Djiniyini and his family at their home and I helped with some of his maintenance issues. The house was high set overlooking Daliwuy Bay. It was constructed of a bolted galvanized steel frame, clad with colour-bond material with large verandas to the front and one side. He asked that I take a series of photos of the corrosion that had set in, due to the salt air.

Rose and I were invited to participate in Yinyindjurr's funeral to be held at Dhalinybuy. Several trips were made out to Dhalinybuy, relatives came from as far away as Elcho Island and Milingimbi. There were cement, tools, food and other supplies to carry.

Yinyindjurr's sister, Janet Guypungurra stayed with us for the week in preparation for the funeral on the 30th of March. I rang Mum and sister Judith and wrote to Mum the morning before we left and included photos of our travels in North East Arnhem Land with the Yolngu.

From right - Yinyindjurr and friends, 1968.

Farewell to an Old Friend - A Homeland Funeral

Dhalinybuy is the homeland of the Wangurri clan, about 90 kilometres to the south, southwest of Yirrkala, on the Cato River. We arrived there several days prior to the burial ceremony and camped with Bronwyn Yikarriwuy and her husband, Gurrumin Marika, and their 3 children.

It was determined that the Land Rover should be used as the hearse. It was painted with red ochre. Yinyindjurr arrived by plane. There was great drama and elaborate ceremony that took place during and after the arrival of the body. As the driver of the hearse, I followed instructions during the transfer of the body from the plane and the short trip from the airstrip, and the arrival procedure.

Several days followed prior to the burial with the arrival of more people and organisations . On the day of the funeral, in line with tradition, the ceremony was dominated by choreographed dance and music which ran on through the day, interspersed with tea breaks. Yinyindjurr's funeral, as with others that we had attended in the past, was a fusion of both Yolngu and Macassan cultures. it was a moving experience for us. Here's an extract from Sara's notes.

February 2002:

Yininydjurr (Marilyn), left a daughter, Vietta, and son, John Ryan. She passed away on Friday 15th February 2002 at midnight, aged 48 years. Born 1951. Her homeland is Djarrakpi. Her family surname is Maymurru. Her clan is Wangurri. She married Billy Ryan who worked for Legal Aid in Darwin, an older man who was her second husband. They lived at Giddy Rd, Yangunbi. Her sister Janet Guypungurra is also Rose's sister. Yinyindjurr and Janet worked at the famous Bangara dance company in Sydney. They worked and travelled overseas in the performing arts.

I first met Yininydjurr when we arrived at Yirrkala to work as lay missionaries in 1967. At 17 years of age, Yininydjurr was already working in the mission administration office. Yininydjurr taught me how to read the weather, record it and pass the information via radio, to the Darwin Met. office. I taught Yinyindjurr office procedures.

Witjiwitji is at Gapuwiyak

As already mentioned, Witjiwitji and I worked closely together at the Yirrkala workshop. We did maintenance on the tractor and other vehicles, maintained the power generator, repaired cattle gates and other equipment. Witjiwitji now lived with his family at Gapuwiyak or Lake Evella. I drove out to see him.

I arrived at Gapuwiyak in time for morning tea with Witji's new wife and grandchildren and I gave him a shirt as a gift. I was surprised that he hadn't changed much at all – tall and lanky, still humming familiar folk songs. He said that there was no work available for Yolngu and that he wasn't doing much. Witji was delighted to drive around the community in our Land Rover which reminded him of the old grey series 2 during the mission days.

We drove to the lake (Lake Evella). You couldn't fish there anymore because it was infested with cane toads. Over the years the cane toads had made their way across the Queensland NT border and spread like wildfire across Arnhem Land. Even in broad daylight, the shores of the lake were seething with little grey juvenile cane toads. We did some more development work on Yolngu interpretation and translation of the Isherwood coat of arms.

I arranged to send some early photos to Witji and we had a couple taken of us two. I took more pictures of him and his family which I was told included the descendants of Mau – a warrior hero of the pre-war days. We really enjoyed seeing each other again after all that time. It was Djutjutna (farewell) and back to Nhulunbuy.

Daliwuy Bay

Sara came to North East Arnhem Land on Wednesday 24th April and we went to Daliwuy Bay fishing the following day. We travelled with Garr and Mirriku, Marritngu, Yangurryangurr and Waku ngarraku. It was our third language immersion trip. Mirriku took Sara maypal (oyster) and buma lili (out to get rock oysters) over the other side of the bay near Djiniyin's place.

We were at Dhaliwuy Bay again in late May. We went down to the big granite tors for mud crabs, stingrays, mullet, and other fish and across to the other side for mangrove oysters until the late afternoon, when the sand flies drove us away. Back at Nhulunbuy, we prepared for another trip out to Birany Birany with Marritngu.

Helping Out

We went back to Birany Birany on Saturday 27th April to help Marritngu and his family. Marritngu was to take up his responsibilities regarding a funeral for a young relative – a boy who had recently hanged himself at Yirrkala. The group included Marritngu, Birrpunu, and Yangurryangurr. We camped on the beach near Wirilma's family. We met Minyapa Mununggurr (my poison cousin who calls me maralkur). His wife works at Laynhapuy. He is also Rose's ngapipi (he calls her waku) and he is Sara's mari (he calls Sara, Gutharra).

We also met Dhungala who invited us out to Garrthalala (his homeland at Caledon Bay). Braywa (one of Terry Parry's old students) and Lulpangi, (my wawa, brother,) was also there.

This tragedy was one of many at Yirrkala since the arrival of the miners. I made some diary entries on some Yolngu comments on social issues at Yirrkala.

Tuesday 30th April 2002:
Yikarriwuy - Dhalinybuy
"Yolngu do understand the impacts of alcohol on health but they don't like living".

Minajapa – Birany Birany
"we blame sickness and death on Galka – We call ngapaki ,(white people) galka too"

Wirilma - Yirrkala
"middle aged people won't listen"…. "the ngapaki are getting stronger now……. Yolngu people have no power to fight back"

Garr at workshop
"all that dhawu (stories) is making me sleepy".

Garr's wife at Yirrkala
"old people are jealous"

Marritngu at Yirrkala
"so you're surprised to see we are still alive" "you can come to my funeral too."

Crocodiles and Birany Birany

There's an island just off the coast at Birany Birany and according to local lore, it is the home of the baru or saltwater crocodile. Crocs were created there and the local Gumatj clan are their custodians and look out for them.

The Yolngu have a special relationship with crocs and they know how they think and know where they are in the water at any given time. The crocodiles watch what's happening all the time and don't miss anything. They seldom attack Yolngu people. If they are grabbed by a croc, they just relax and he will loosen his grip and leave them alone.

Something similar happened to a young Yolngu man from Yirrkala. Back in 1968, when he was in a big lagoon getting rakay (water lily roots), just down from the prospecting camp where Ted Egan and his family lived. The story is that the croc had a hold of him around his waist. He knew exactly what to do. He was able to reach down and poke the croc's anus. The croc let him go and he was able to get back to the mission. I remember seeing his wounds at the health clinic. For Ngapaki, however, it's another story. The Ngapaki has a different smell and is more likely to come under attack if unaccompanied. The Ngapaki also has a tendency to panic and attempt to struggle which can prove fatal.

We were back at Dhalinybuy on the following Sunday and camped with Yikarriwuy and Gurrumin (Yukuyuku) and their family. Yikarriwuy was making woven mats and collected pandanus leaves and split them. She added yellow dye that she'd collected from roots, boiled the pandanus leaves in it, and hung the leaves up to dry. We saw a few barramundis and Gurrumin caught one. He pointed out a crocodile nest where the Yolngu collect eggs on a regular basis. Gurrumin and I discussed limited similarities between the Ngapaki and Yolngu rom (law) structures. We also talked about the idea of a radio station for Dhalinybuy and how that might work. Monday was a public holiday and I caught a barramundi downstream, for Yikarriwuy. I was back on Nhulunbuy courthouse observations the following Tuesday.

Back in Court

Court observations provided an insight into the kind of culture, and level of idiocy that the government and the mining corporation so callously imposed on a peaceful, civilised, First Nations community.

By the time we had returned to North East Arnhem Land in 2002, there was a population of about 3000 in and around the Nhulunbuy mining town. There were white people born and raised in Nhulunbuy and identified with the mining town as their home. Many remained irritated by the presence of the Yolngu from the nearby Yirrkala community.

It wasn't always the Yolngu ending up in court for committing offences. I was able to observe two cases involving Nhulunbuy residents, in court. One on traffic offences and the other, assault on a twelve-year-old girl.

The circuit Judge was presiding over the day's proceedings. A repeat offender charged with driving without a licence, unlawful

A hamburger with the lot.

possession of an unregistered and unroadworthy motor vehicle, drunk driving, no helmet, speeding and evading police and resisting arrest.

On handing down the sentence, Judge Leeman gave an example of the effects of too much alcohol – in this case, where a 'bantam rooster became an eagle' - who took on the police at his own peril and whose repeated offences had attracted a 'hamburger with the lot.' The policeman had thrown the book at him. The defendant's comment on sentencing was *"No worries."*

The following case on the list that day was even more bizarre. Another local resident, living on a boat moored at the Nhulunbuy Yacht club received a sentence of three months, suspended for two years for throwing a twelve-year-old girl overboard while drunk and stoned.

There was a pattern emerging from my observations. There were the locals from town, from boats moored at the yacht club, Tongans who dominated the kava trade, and Yolngu. It became apparent that Yolngu were a disadvantaged group and disproportionately ended up in prison, while other offenders got suspended sentences.

I heard of other cases involving police apprehensions of Tongan kava traffickers arriving at the Nhulunbuy airport. Tongan arrivals loaded to the hilt with suitcases full of kava adulterated with flour, would be arrested and their cargo confiscated and used as evidence in court.

A resident of the Nhulunbuy Yacht Club.

By late May there was still a lot going on with ATSIC and ARDS workshops, staff meetings and more homeland trips, another three-day workshop on the failure of bilingual education, and so on. By mid-June, I'd had enough of the confused inconsistency, increasing expectations, and low salary. There had been a great personal achievement for me with regard to the renewal of our Yolngu friendships, and many insights into the destructive impacts of the miners. It was time to go.

I rang Mum fairly regularly, to touch base and say hello. I found calling Mum quite traumatic now, and, I began to dread having to call her. At nearly 87, she'd lost her ability to communicate apart from the odd words due to her Alzheimer's condition. The very last time I spoke to Mum was just before we left Nhulunbuy to drive home. She was crying and in between her sobbing, repeatedly said *"I can't....... I can't."* She had no support staff to help her with the phone and all I could do was reluctantly hang up on her. I felt powerless and devastated.

From Nhulunbuy to Roper River

Sara was still with us and Miya came with Parry, Sue and Richard on their drive out from Darwin to meet us at Nhulunbuy, ready for the drive south along the coast through Blue Mud Bay and on to Numbulwar. The drive out from Nhulunbuy was a very different story, compared to that of the late 1960s when there were no roads.

The plan was to drive to Numbulwar, along the western coast of Arnhem Land, camping along the way. We drove to Policeman's Crossing on the upper reaches of the Rose River, and south through to Roper River. We would then drive east through the Gulf country, to Borroloola, and on to Lawn Hill in Queensland, where we would go our separate ways. The Parrys were returning to Darwin. Rose, Miya, Sara and I, continued driving back home through Porcupine Gorge, north to Ravenshoe and finally Atherton on the Tablelands.

On leaving Nhulunbuy, the road soon narrowed into a winding track through Darwin Stringy barks, Dalpi palms and large Pandanus stands interspersed, with spear grass plains where buffaloes grazed.

Out of fuel and sailing back to camp, Koolatong River, 2002.

It was Tuesday 18th June when we set up camp on the Koolatong River crossing, where we stayed a couple of nights fishing and swimming. It was a magical place on the edge of this large peaceful, waterhole lined with shady pandanus palms. It was in the late afternoon that Rose noticed that Parry had slight tremors.

Rose drew his attention to her observations, advising him that he should get a medical check-up. We were to learn six months later that he was suffering from early-onset Parkinson's disease and had already started on medications.

We drove on to Walker River and along the winding track through the dry open forest country and then to Numbulwar on the mouth of the Rose River. We met one convoy of three new four-wheel drive Toyotas from Sydney, bristling with radio aerials, and expensive recovery equipment hanging off the front. They were top-heavy with roof racks bulging with goodness knows what. And they wanted to talk. We didn't see them again. When we were living in Numbulwar during the mid-seventies, there were no roads and we enjoyed the challenges that remoteness presented.

On arrival at Numbulwar there was nowhere to stay in the community so we set up camp for the night in the bush. On the following day, we wandered around the community. Much like the Yirrkala community, Numbulwar was in a state of decline, socially and economically. We did meet up with some of my old students and others we had known. I showed Miya and Sara around. I showed them where Mum had spent time painting at various spots along the banks of creeks and at the enormous mouth of the Rose River, during her stays with us in the mid-seventies.

The old Anglican mission church under the shade of the Indian Almond trees was now in ruins. The rotating ventilator, on the roof, was still turning on worn-out bearings and was the only sound that broke the silence. There were still a lot of familiar places like the little Worldwide Camp cottage where Rose and I had lived, the old mission house, the radio shack, and the school. I did a service on the Land Rover, on the remnants of the cement slab of the now overgrown basketball court. There was no petrol and Parry had to buy some litres of avgas for the rest of the trip down to the Roper. Parry's spare tyre was punctured. On his vehicle, the tyres are tubeless and there wasn't anyone there who could fix it.

Just south of Numbulwar he momentarily lost control as the car suddenly lurched sideways out of the sand ruts and stopped just short of a big tree at the side of the track. He was concerned about getting another flat tyre with no spare, and it was a bit of an anxious time for him during the rest of the drive to the Roper.

We camped a couple of days, well away from crocs on the high banks of a waterhole, just downstream from Policeman's Crossing.

We caught enough fish to eat. Parry and Richard caught barramundis on lures. On our way out across the river, I noticed a big reduction in the volume of water at the crossing compared to the seventies, during our first trip to Numbulwar.

We camped the next night at Spinifex camp, a road workers' campsite and gravel pit before arriving at Lawn Hill on the 25th of June. Parry had arranged to meet some friends there - a Townsville couple. We parted company the next morning and spent that night at the Croydon Pub. We arrived home on the 28th. Miya and Sara returned to University in Brisbane the following day. Miya rang early that night with sad news.

Mum has Passed Away

Mum passed away at 12 midday while we were camped at the Koolatong River on 18th June. Sisters Judith and Elaine arranged the funeral which was held on 25th June while we were still in transit. Judith's daughter, Gabriel wrote Mum's Eulogy, and I was denied the opportunity to be part of Mum's farewell.

We arranged a memorial service for Mum at home and dedicated a little rose garden to her. My attempt at closure is reflected in the letter I wrote to Mum.

1st July 2002
Dear Mum,
I'm sad I couldn't be with you in your passing. We were all out fishing on the Koolatong when you died. When we got to Numbulwar, I was pointing out to Miya and Sara the places where you did those paintings of the beach and the little creek. Your paintings of Numbulwar, Hooker Creek, and other earlier works are hanging on our living room walls. They remind us of you.

I'll always be proud of your work. I'm also proud that you're my Mum because it was you who gave me the foundations of the values and beliefs I've nurtured and built on, in my ongoing commitment to making the world a better place.

Rose has supported me, Miya and Sara in carrying on the tradition. So, Mum, you are always with us and I'm now thinking about where I can place a little memorial to you – a special place here amongst the trees to make you welcome any time. Where would you like me to place it?

And now at this time of writing, 14 years on, there's scarcely a day that goes by without my thinking of my Mum who would have been one hundred years old last July. Dad would be one hundred and ten. I still often talk to her and ask for advice. So Mum, don't forget I'll always be in debt to you and what you've given me in love and compassion and the cherished times you spent with us.

By mid-July through the rest of the year, there were several challenges on the boil. Firstly, there was the organisation of Mum's estate. The 16th of July 1915 was Mum's birthday. Eighty-seven years on, found myself checking Elaine's list of Mum's chattels. We had agreed that Elaine becomes the power of attorney. Elaine generously gave me my childhood tinplate toys that Mum had preserved for me.

Me and Mum. Cobram, Victoria, 1998.

Environmentalism in Practice

After engaging a rainforest ecologist and developing a comprehensive management plan, I made an application for Nature Refuge status for our property and it was rejected. The property is now listed as Land for Wildlife through Greening Australia. The trees remain unprotected until some alternative form of protection can be found. The issue is yet to be resolved.

I was encouraged to submit an expression of interest for an Environmental Educator's position at Djarragun College. My proposal included a six-month non-teaching role, for the purpose of community liaison and consultation as part of the process of the formulation of a comprehensive program. However, there was an expectation that I would have a full teaching timetable, and develop an Environmental Education program simultaneously. It wasn't to be.

I had finished some basic research on changing over to a domestic solar power system and was ready to make the commitment. However, we failed to get the Qld. Government to agree to buy our excess power to the grid and had to wait another five years before they implemented the appropriate policy in the far north.

As a member of the National Trust, with the support of others, I attempted to save the fragile Atherton Chinatown archaeological site from the state tourism development project called the Heritage Trails Network.

The Atherton Shire Council were given over a million dollars in taxpayers' money to develop the site. For the National Trust and Local Government, this apparently meant bulldozing one of the world's most valued archaeological sites outside of China for development as a profit-driven tourist venue.

While we were at Yirrkala, David Wirilma and I had spent time together in deep discussion about big-picture issues like the unacceptable state of affairs brought about by mining. Wirilma was on the board at Laynhapuy and talked about a future position for me as a personal advisor and on his request, I gave him a copy of my professional profile.

My friend Jonatani was employed at Laynhapuy and had an advisory role. It all ended up with a call to me from Gatjil Yunipingu in early February, requesting that I write an expression of interest to Banampi for a position he described as "Personal Advisor to Wirilma". I felt honoured. I held great admiration and respect for Wirilma, but declined. I didn't want to take Jonatani's job. I also thought I may have ended up in a vulnerable, if not impossible position with regard to Laynhapuy's relations with the government and mining interests.

If my friend and barrister John Little wasn't able to stem the tide of destruction by the miners back in the late 1960s, what on earth would I be able to achieve? Politics was in limbo and there was still some fire left in me and I considered running in the coming local government elections. After considering the incumbent councillors, state bureaucrats and the lineup of candidates, I'd never have been able to work with them. I gave it a wide birth.

Cairns House

Our house hunting during early 2003 culminated in the purchase of a house in Edge Hill, Cairns. Much of my time was committed to repairs and maintenance of the house and yard and the completion of the restoration of the Atherton house. So this meant many trips down to Cairns. Sara and her friend Dom were staying with us. Dom was working at CSIRO in Atherton and Sara was involved with theatre in Cairns and Atherton. Rose was working in Drug and Alcohol counselling and I was considering my options for the longer term.

Back to England, via Sursee

It was Thursday 21st August 2003 that Rose and I were buying some duty-free wine and whiskey at Hong Kong airport, en route to Zurich to see our Swiss friends Pia and Franz Rast and their daughters, Franca and Carla. We were swimming at the local lake at Sursee the next day. Franz and Pia took us to Riggi peak. We went by steam train up the mountain to meet with Franz's sister, Elizabeth, and Remy, at their weekend home, flew to the Matterhorn with Pia and Franz and visited the glacial museum in Lucerne.

I cooked something special for Carla one morning. It was porridge, and she enjoyed it. That evening we attended a concert – the Evita Peron musical on the lake at Thun. Pia took us to Willisau to visit her parents, Sep and Anna Schumacher, view the family coat of arms, and see Pia's childhood haunts around the little town. That night we had dinner with Pia's brother Seppi and his wife Pia and Max and Seppi junior. There was a party at Urchi and George's (Franz's sister and her husband's) place. Friends Esthi and Hubi, Inge and Fritz, and Seppi and Robi were also there.

On Sunday, Franz took us for a drive in his vintage black Mercedes, and in the evening, we were at a winery for dinner with more friends, Suzi and Thomas and Maurice and Tina. Pia and I drove to Lucerne the following day – she had a dental appointment and I relaxed in the waiting room. We visited the transport museum and there was a Classic Norton Commando there on display. We went to the planetarium and drove back home to Sursee through the hills. The next day it was Nebikon Village and Egli Kurt's milling enterprise, where he prepared stock feed under sterile conditions.

That night we dined with Kurt. Kurt showed a lot of interest in my progressive Australian politics and offered to sponsor any future campaign initiatives. Rose had a surprise meeting with Aggie Inderbitzen from Atherton, on top of the mountain - Kriens, Brunier. At Lucerne Kugeeli – we ate pastetli (pronounced pashtetli) Grappa and coffee. The pastetli was very rich - a cheesy comestible that sat for days in my stomach. We climbed up Franz's favourite hill after lunch on the final day of our visit. I congratulated Franz on his excellent hosting. He was a good Gruppenfuher und Berater (group leader and someone who gives good counsel).

England

John Humphreys picked us up from Heathrow in the morning on Friday the 5th of September and after lunch, took us for a walk through Iffley Lock, along the Thames, and into Oxford. John was living in Turner Close, in Cowley. Rose and I based ourselves with Lenore in Headington for the two weeks in England. We stayed with John's Aunt Sheila at Ascot. Sheila took us around inner London and as a friend of Windsor Castle, took us in to view the fire damage and other nooks and crannies not usually reserved for tourists.

With John Humphreys and his BMW.

We visited Jim Purdey, a classic motorcycle enthusiast who owned an AJS at Rugely and caught the train north to the National Motorcycle Museum in Birmingham. We went on to Stockport and Marple, Marple and Wybersley Halls, and back to Oxford to spend time with Lenore. A few days after our visit to Birmingham, we heard that the bike museum had burned down with the loss of two-thirds of the classic bike exhibits – many of them privately owned. Iconic machines on display like Brough Superior, Vincent, and Norton Internationals were damaged beyond recovery. We caught the bus down to Exeter, hired a car, and drove around, visiting a friend's mother at a retirement home in Torquay. On our return home, we overnighted with Miya in Cairns.

The old stables at Wybersley Hall, 2003.

Back on the Tablelands

At home, Lance Johnson, a timber getter from Tarzali was able to fell the last stand of large tallow trees along the southern boundary of the block before the wet season. My job was to cut them up to dry as firewood.

Sara at the pile of Tallow blocks for fire-wood, 2003.

These large exotic eucalypts, some with a girth of nearly a metre across had been planted by the previous owners, some years before our arrival. They grew too fast, too high, and were given to twisting and breaking in stormy weather.

I was able to get into domestic and community activities. For instance, house and yard maintenance, and annual volunteering behind the bar at the Community Hall during the Yungaburra Folk Festival. It included getting a massage or acupuncture, repairs to the lavatory, mowing the lawns, and mucking out the chook pen. There were the Tablelands Motorcycle Restorers' Club rallies, tree plantings, and weekends at Etty Bay. There was supply work, tutoring at Woodleigh College at Herberton, attending committee meetings, hosting visitors and barbeques and New Year's Eve, and so on.

Sara was working as a house parent at Woodleigh College in Herberton. Miya was still finishing her articles in Cairns and Rose had resumed Counselling at Lifeline in Atherton. Mum visited me in a dream on the 26th of November. I asked her if there was a rose that she particularly liked that I could remember her by and she replied *"Elenore Rose."*

I was 59, and the year was dominated by the return to stressful supply and contract work at Atherton and Mareeba high schools, accompanied by visits to the chiropractor for sore neck and spinal adjustments. It was also a year of visitors. Parry and Sue came across from Darwin in January, The Swiss family – Pia and Franz, Carla and Franca in July, Kirk and Erin Smith from Charters Towers, and Anne and Errol Klibbe from Toowoomba.

We went to Melbourne in March to catch up with Darby and Lyn, and Hoyte, sister Judith and nephews, Victor and Tim. Hoyte went to Moscow in May for stem cell treatment. He was suffering from asbestosis. I was still regularly in touch with David and Monica Holt who were here on holiday from Tasmania in September. We maintained contact with Wirilma, Yikarriwuy, Gurrumin, and the Dhalinybuy people from North East Arnhem Land.

Miya flew up to Thursday Island for her job interview with the Torres Strait Regional Authority in March. She was later to set up and maintain the Land and Sea Management Unit based there. She often came home to spend the weekend with the family and we all went down to Cairns to celebrate her admission to the Bar on the 27th of April.

It was early in November 2004 when Cocky passed away. He was interred with great ceremony in the wire enclosure next to one of the raised beds. Sara, Dom, Rose, and I attended the funeral. A little shrine, with a candle, was set up at the cockatoo summer house in his honour. A memorial service was held for Cocky when Miya came home from Thursday Island.

This was the cockatoo that I talked about with Birrpunu at Yirrkala a couple of years earlier. And by the way, Cocky was unpredictable, very noisy, destructive and an irritating bird, and in many ways, his demise was a blessing. But we loved him just the same.

On another note, a rather special motorbike is worth a mention.

An Easy Two

I had done some restoration work during the year on my 1949 Norton ES2 500 single motorcycle which I bought in Innisfail. I had to restore the magneto and dynamo and got a rebuild done on the chronometric speedo. Overall, including a new piston, I reckon I spent about $2000 to bring the bike up to scratch. A local member of the bike club timed the engine to ½" below the top dead centre.

The iconic ES2 or Easy Two, was essentially hand built in the Birmingham Norton factory, a handsome machine to boot, a fashionable luxury item, and very sort after during the post-second World War period. It is, as I write, even to the untrained eye, a joy to behold.

The black frame dictates the elegant lines from the big headlamp to the rear hub and sprung heel. It has the beautifully sculptured saddle tank, chromed, with sweeping silver panels to the sides and top, bordered by the familiar Norton racing signature - 1/8th inch thick red and ½" thick black line-work.

Out and about on an easy two - The 1949 Norton 500 ES2, 2015.

The massive engine was first developed in 1928. It is impressively tall, with a long stroke. It is a thumping 500cc single. The black cast iron cylinder is punctuated by two thick chromed push rod tubes set at a slight inwards angle from the polished aluminium crankcase, all the way up to the rocker box. With a comfortable sprung saddle, the Easy Two is a pleasure to ride, reaching a respectable cruising speed of 60 to 70 mph. This Norton was similar to the motorcycle used by the Cuban revolutionary, Che Guevara.

By August of that year, I was making raised garden beds and an incident occurred that I thought I should mention.

I was preparing to bring a couple of loads of railway sleepers up from Innisfail, to make raised garden beds early in August. I was in thongs and as I started removing the side panels from the tray of Miya's ute, one of them fell across the toes of my left foot breaking two of the smaller ones. It hurt, but there wasn't much pain and it seemed to be only superficial surface damage to the skin, so I kept on working. I continued working through the afternoon and was unaware of the broken toes and the sharp ends of the bones machette-ing their way through the nerve endings.

That night the pain was excruciating and I got no sleep and no relief. The doctor advised that there was nothing that could be done except strap the toes up with the big toe for support. I was in the middle of a contract at Atherton State High School, as reflected in diary entries from the time.

6th September
Derek S. to take my year 8 Graphics and I'll take his plastics (peanut dish) bloody nightmare. Staff photo shot
11.15 hospital for x-ray interpretation
9 graphics – those completing 4.43 start on another drawing of their own choice from section 4.
Computer EQ 0260 in room D10 malfunctioning also EQ 238. Alison Finch.

13th October
see HOD re both 10 shop b classes, concerns relating to:
refusal to follow teacher instructions;
disinterest, refusal to focus on set task;
clarification of theory test requirements;

list of students at risk from each 10 shop B class.
P7,8, 9 shop A, RTC people 1 lesson after intervention by Deputy.

14th October
see deputy re RTC people from yesterday's 9 shop A, the same group visited last week.

18th October
contact union re accusation of sexual harassment during period 5 last Friday.
Peter – left class early last week see notes and grab him.

While I continued supply and contract teaching, 2005 was a year of reflection, consolidation and progress towards sustainable living. A pattern emerged early in my life where I developed the urge to embrace further study in areas of personal interest. For example, I started my working life with an apprenticeship in Fitting and Turning. I soon found that a trade was inadequate in terms of personal challenges. When I met Parry who was teaching at Yirrkala back in the 1960s, I decided then that teaching was the way forward for me. Though I have to say that at the time, the attraction to teaching was more about 3 months of paid annual leave than any philanthropic calling.

I revisited my Master's degree with a view to either broadening and advancing Environmental Education by way of independent research or committing to a PhD. I examined the membership list of the Australian Association for Environmental Education (AAEE) and found a very interesting person by the name of Werner Sattmann - Frese. Werner was writing up his PhD on the topic of Living Sustainably. In his doctorate, Werner established the links between the personal, psychosocial, institutional, and environmental aspects of the modern crises. Werner had a background in psychotherapy and psychosomatic medicine. New discoveries stemming from Werner's work deserve some further deliberation.

Chapter 10
Consolidation and Progress

Werner Sattmann - Frese

I worked with Werner on his Learning for Sustainable Living online course, contributing to the review of the literature on Education for Transformational Change in preparation for the development of unit 7 of Werner's series.

It was the beginning of a long-term friendship between me and Werner as we planned the workshops. There were two separate one-day workshops introducing Ecopsychology and Environmental Education. The course included aspects of Eco-psychotherapy as ways of enabling people to further progress towards personally sustainable lives for a sustainable future.

The workshops targeted Environmental Educators, Psychologists, Psychotherapists, Health Workers and Counsellors, as well as anyone committed to a sustainable future. The inaugural sessions were held on the Tablelands and then in Cairns. I did the promotion and setting up of the venues and Werner flew up from Sydney to facilitate. As part of the course, participants were invited to tours demonstrating aspects of sustainable living such as rainforest restoration, biodynamic gardening, house relocation and restoration and solar energy. I ran the tours at our property in Atherton.

By 2004 Miya and Sara had graduated from university. Our purchase of the house in Cairns, served as accommodation for Miya to complete her Articles in Cairns. We stayed there with Miya often during frequent trips to Cairns. I was still doing supply and contract teaching, often at Atherton, mainly for convenience – it was only a couple of kilometres walk from home.

The RTP and RTC

As mentioned earlier, a bizarre feature of Atherton State High School was its newly adopted behavioural management regime. Here's the theory and how it worked:

The Responsible Thinking Process or RTP came into effect in the classroom, at the teacher's discretion. The RTP was activated, and the targeted student was formally questioned thus:
What are you doing?
What are the rules?
What happens when you break the rules?
What do you want to happen?
Where do you want to be?
What do you want to do?
What will happen if you disrupt again?

When the student disrupts again, the teacher then discretely says to the student - *"I see that you have chosen to leave."*

The offending student is forthwith sent to the Responsible Thinking Center, a spare classroom set aside for the purpose and referred to as the RTC.

There, the student is expected to reflect on their behaviour, contemplate their predicament, take notes on the circumstances and negotiate with the teacher, a return to class, during the student's own time. In other words, in the teacher's spare time such as recess or lunch break.

It was also about this time that I committed to writing this book. Sara was staying at home with her friend Dom in Atherton after completing her Drama degree. Sara contributed much to the Cairns Theatre Company – Jute, writing and directing one of several plays – 'Death Trap' and later went Woofing (Willing Workers on Organic Farms) in Japan for three months. Self-sufficiency was also an important development on the home front.

Other Goings On

Rose was working as the Alcohol and Drugs Counsellor for the Rural Division of GPs. She worked out of the Weipa and Cooktown local Doctor's surgery. She travelled to these communities on a fortnightly basis. My old High School friend, Hoyte, turned up in late December 2005. Hoyte always had a keen interest in pop music and became an amateur DJ with his kit packed neatly in a side compartment in his motor home. We spent New Years' Eve down at Etty Bay, and Hoyte shared his music with everyone. It was mostly rock and roll. Werner's work led me to investigate the topic of psychopathy and its possible relevance to the modern crises.

Psychopathy

I looked at the 20-point Hare PCL-R Checklist – a list of character traits of recognised psychopaths in institutions and the prison system in the USA and Canada.

My first reaction to the list was to compare Hare's list with my own personal character traits and, on reflection, I did indeed share some of these traits at different stages of my personal growth. For example, I remember that I used to get bored pretty easily, was even a bit narcissistic, and occasionally irresponsible and impulsive during adolescence. But according to the research, that doesn't make someone a psychopath. We all share some of the character traits at different stages of life.

In my fascination with the topic, I investigated the work of authors including Leon Gettler, Robert Hare, Scott Peck, and Jon Ronson. The revelations were profound. For example, according to the literature, behaviour patterns are destructive. And one in every one hundred of us is said to be a full-blown psychopath. And the frightening thing is that there was a much higher concentration of them in corporate boardrooms, political Party rooms, the workplace, and even within environmental activist groups and other volunteer community groups. I was finally beginning to make some sense of my experience during the days I was involved in Party politics.

I was further driven to reflect on life's experiences, particularly on my professional career in teaching and politics – the environment of the staff room, the home office, and the national conference. Were psychopaths capable of holding power? Could psychopaths control governments and societies?

Home life progressed, and there was plenty of supply and contract work. Sara and her friend Chris had returned from NZ and with their help and expertise, there was further development in Biodynamics. They were to develop a veggie box scheme that reached all the way to Cairns. Miya's friends Jess and Danny were overnighting with us when an unwanted visitor arrived on the Tablelands – a category five cyclone.

Cyclone Larry

Larry formed off Cairns in the Coral Sea and made landfall near Innisfail, sweeping across the coast at daybreak on the morning of 20th March 2006. While quickly losing strength on his way west from the coast, wind gusts were still recorded at 180 kilometres per hour over the Tablelands. We stayed in the house and watched the drama unfolding from the front veranda and from the kitchen to see what was happening out the back. The scene was the most dramatic from the front veranda. Amidst the chaos of this howling, swirling wind and rain and sounding like grinding, heavy machinery, I spotted an agile wallaby peacefully grazing in a clear patch of grass near the house, fully protected by the rainforest on either side.

As we watched from the front veranda, the row of tall tallowwoods along the roadside, twisted and broke up in the swirling wind after the eye had passed over us. By midday, Larry had gone west, tearing across the hills of the Great Divide and beyond.

Towards the end of the blow, I ventured out for a walk. I couldn't get to the chook pen through tree limbs piled up on top of each other. I went up into the hills at the back. I saw that the damage wasn't evenly spread. The trees on the exposed ridges were stripped of their foliage and many of them snapped off at the trunk like match sticks, or uprooted.

At home, we were protected from the worst of the storm by the position of our property at a lower level between the township and the dividing range to the west. Still, trees at the front were blown over and the creek was a raging torrent, loaded with silt and other debris from upstream. There had been widespread superficial damage to peoples' rooves, farm sheds blown away and crops laid flat.

It was common practice on the Tablelands to replace endemic native rainforests with exotic species. The previous owners of our property had planted exotic tallowwood and cadaghi trees along the boundaries and it was these trees that did the damage. Along the front boundary, most of the tallows came down on the road and demolished the electric power lines. We were without power for ten days.

At the time, the local State Emergency Service or SES, in collaboration with the local government, was responsible for mopping up. We were all under the command of General Cosgrove. The General was in charge of the post-cyclone relief effort.

Rose and I took leave of absence from paid work to volunteer with the SES. Another teacher and SES member, Margaret, and I were allocated the job of manning the phone, and referring the public to the various sections of the SES and local Council for help with cyclone damage. This also involved liaison with the volunteer SES crews out in the field. Rose had a community liaison role. Towards the end of the two-week stint, General Cosgrove returned and offered a photo opportunity. It was now time for their moment of glory, their reward for giving their all to the cause. The volunteers gathered around him for the ritual. I declined. General Cosgrove went on to be the Queen's Australian representative – the Governor General of Australia.

Law 6 - Control of Nuisances

In September of that year, yet another challenge presented itself in the form of a Local Govt. By-Law 6 – Control of nuisances compliance notice in the letterbox.

Essentially, I was given two weeks to comply with their notice or they would have a contractor come onto our property, do the work required and bill me. Miya's advice was to comply. In the event that they didn't accept my response, commence legal action.

Our property, according to the letter was among other things, unsightly and likely to harbour vermin (rare and endangered species?). Instructions were to 'destroy biomass' and remove all 'ground covering vegetation.' I called the council for clarification of the requirements which applied to 'every square metre' of our three-acre property. Thank goodness Sara and Chris were able to help with this meaningless task. We laboured away – chopping, chain sawing, chipping, digging and raking for the two weeks.

Sara and Chris had volunteered their time. The cost of equipment was $1,500. I didn't put a figure on fuel, our labour and other costs. I advised Council formally by post that the job had been completed and received no acknowledgement. I heard nothing and later found out, by accident, that they only drive past the property. The experience came as a shock and changed the way we felt about our relations with local government on the Tablelands.

Reactions to Injustice

Rose and I were shocked by this experience and we built a dog fence along the eastern boundary on the road side with a 14' gate into the driveway. While we were at it, we put up a bird wire fence along the northern and southern boundaries where there were neighbours on both sides. The chooks were getting into the neighbour's garden on the southern side. The ducks were wandering onto the pavement on the northern side, to squirt their droppings onto the pavement there. Marnane's farm was across the creek. Saeed De Ridder, a friend and local environmentalist helped us with a Greening Australia sign on the new fence. 'Land for Wildlife.' For all intents and purposes, the fencing was to protect our livestock from dogs invading our property. Bella, our first grandchild was born on Thursday Island.

Bella is Born

Bella, was born at Thursday Island hospital at 6.40 pm on Saturday 19th January 2008. Both Miya and baby Bella were well. Rose had flown up earlier for the birth and returned home on 21st February for a celebratory dinner with Sara and Chris. Miya had been working for the Torres Strait Regional Authority on Thursday Island for the past five years and planned to return home when little Bella was strong enough to make the flight safely. We missed life back in the Northern Territory and made return trips every few years to catch up with Yapa and Yolngu friends and colleagues there, since our departure in the mid-1980s. The last trip back to Lajamanu is especially worthy of mention.

A Contract at Lajamanu

It was a one-off semester contract until the end of the year. It coincided with Rose's commitment to doing the marriage ceremony for Parry's daughter, Lian. I bought a Hilux 4WD ute and had it shipped to Darwin by the Dept. They flew us to Darwin and I spent a week on orientation. The Orientation seemed balanced enough with some substantial presentations of cross-cultural issues and the Federal government initiative, 'Close the Gap.' One of the presenters was Henry Gray from Numbulwar days.

The wedding was scheduled for Friday 18th July. We left for Lajamanu the same day and stayed with Jim Mathieson at Katherine overnight.

I was allocated a group of senior boys aged thirteen to eighteen. The classroom was a Worldwide Camps demountable with cupboards and shelves stacked with old student work, old department documentation and a range of inappropriate teaching resources suited mainly to mainstream early childhood and mid-primary levels.

I started school on July 21st. It seemed a bit strange that the principal had got the new teachers to paint the staff room during the last week of the school holidays in time for the start of the semester. Otherwise, things seemed normal enough with the introduction of the School Operational Plan, School Policy Procedures, Behavioural Management manuals, and Teacher Probation Handbook.

Other mandatory tasks included delivering outcomes, observing NTCF protocols and collecting evidence of learning to include in reporting structures and moderation, and ensuring that attendance levels remained over 60% where possible.

The first week was spent dumping loads of unwanted materials and searching for anything around the school that was remotely useful as teaching/learning resources for my senior class.

I found a set of scales, a couple of old wall clocks, pens, pencils, three exercise books, and a metre measuring wheel, whiteboard markers, a few textas, some junior dictionaries. I got some emergency consumer maths and ESL materials posted down from Darwin to assist in the resumption of the NTOEL online IDL courses. The outgoing teacher was unavailable to assist in a handover.

The students had a history of attendance problems and with the odd exception, didn't turn up until week five after the promise of an excursion to Alice Springs. Students would turn up at 10.30 am and just before lunch at 11.30 am to pick up their lunch voucher, or perhaps sometime after 2.30 pm. I saw some students for as little as ten minutes over the whole term where they would come in the door, walk around the room and disappear, never to be seen again. There were 25 students enrolled according to the Roll book. Six students began to turn up regularly to earn their excursion to Alice Springs.

Of those students, the literacy levels ranged from almost nil to year four with enormous gaps in reading and writing skills. For example, no one knew their residential address. One student was of year eight standard and able to write in both English and Warlpiri. My diary entries for the period between Tuesday 29th July to Monday 4th August reflect the situation.

29th July
Eleven students turned up at about 11 am today. They were huge. It was like a room full of Brahman bulls. I thought the classroom floor was going to cave in. Jeff came as part of the Release Scheme to talk about music. Students were intent on basketball and when exhausted, came back into the classroom, panting and thirsty and headed straight to the smoko corner to demolish 6 cartons of juice. Then there was the music and introductions. Some said they were from Africa. We got some work done on signatures and an agreement on classroom ground rules.

Extra School Interests

Diary Entry, 31st July
Went to see Pardi Pardi (Henry Cook) and his son Neil Jupurrula to arrange a Bush trip and decided on Winnecke creek. Joe James was there, we did some reminiscing and I invited him for a meal.
Walked with Pardi Pardi back to his house and he talked about King George and the wartime and his early days as a ringer. Also saw his son, Adam again, and discussed how my slide shows could be managed in the community. Agnes Luther and her daughter, Alison came to visit.

Joe James later told me that Jupurrula and Jangala are my skin group and will support me.
Steve Patrick Jampitjinpa, became the author of the book 'Desert Knowledge – A way of working with Warlpiri People.'

Past students, Douglas Tasman and his wife Pansy Rose also visited. Pansy was a primary teacher at Lajamanu some years ago when there were more kids attending school.

Winnecke Creek

I went south to Winnecke Creek with Neil and his Dad. Jeremiah Japaltjarri now a patrol officer, told me that Neil's older brother, Albert Cook Jupurrula now known as "Strike Me Pink", was in Berrimah prison and due for release soon. Henry shared stories about his uncle Deadwood Laurlpa and his country around Winnecke Creek. The boundaries lay to the east (Kakarrara), North (Karlarru) and south (Kurlarra) of Winnecke Creek.

This homeland is divided between two groups – Wanmanpa and Mulpurru and connected by the Katjarri ceremony. Winnecke Creek is the Jukurrpa dreaming place of the Marlu (kangaroo) totem for Henry and his father. We collected some curved wood from Watiyija or Pangkuna trees, (bush beans) to take back to make Karli (boomerang). Also saw some Yala or bush potato and Miyaka (karajong), and bush peanut.

Brumbies and Rottweilers

Diary Entry, 4th August
Observations. The number of brumbies has increased - drawn in at night to water in the creek and green pickings around the settlement. Jerry Jangala said they can do a lot of damage.
Dog breeds have changed from the old skinny, small, camp dogs and leather dogs.
Disturbing – nurses' descriptions of large aggressive alpha male dogs that dominate. They command packs that run riot throughout the night to around 6 am when all return to quiet. The dogs harass the brumbies and last night rounded them up at around 3 am and corralled them into the school compound with a great amount of disturbance.

The assumption is that these more recent arrivals are derived from large dogs such as rottweilers, ridgebacks, and pit bulls - dangerous breeds bought in or abandoned by mining contractors and others. These breeds have featured in fatal dog attacks in Australian suburbs. There seems to be no control over them here and I fear that someone, an old person or a child may be attacked.

Out in the Tanami

I made sure that my weekends were free so Rose and I went out bush as often as we could with Yapa. The bush roads had changed a lot since the Tanami mining invasion. The main north and south roads were used and maintained by giant corporate mining companies. These roads were enormous. They were built to cover long distances in a short time. They obliterated the fragile and beautiful vegetation along the verges with fine red dust. I thought that the people responsible for the building of these roads must have viewed the Yapa and their desert environment with callous contempt. We stayed away from these roads as much as possible, using what bush tracks we could find.

It was such a pleasure returning to the bush, simply to have a leisurely stroll amongst the pristine spinifex on undisturbed red sand, return to camp to light the fire, sit in the sunset, sleep under a desert sky and wake up to the quiet sunrise. One morning near Winnecke Creek, a small group of rare Major Mitchell cockatoos arrived, landing in the small trees around the camp.

We drove to the old seven-mile bore. A storm had demolished it years ago. We were able to get to Jirlpirli, the 19-mile, 28-mile, and Nangurru, but Catfish on the Victoria River was no longer accessible. Most of the tracks were washed out and overgrown. The Commonwealth-funded cattle project with its service tracks, fencing, windmills, yards and other infrastructure had long been abandoned. Sunday 3rd August found me in bed, delirious, with gastro.

Here's my diary entry:
In bed - Gastro Enteritis. A chance to reflect and ponder. Confused state with only a few emaciated and hungry kids back at school.

They should be back from Yuendumu Sports soon. Dogs on the desks. Eleven senior footballers turned up in my classroom last Tuesday I haven't seen them since.

These seniors really needed more than a prefab. classroom with a whiteboard. The group had well-developed music, football and computer skills. Living with poverty, a lifestyle including football and traditional social commitments, the idea of frequent and regular attendance in class was simply not on their agenda. My program focused on integrated and online Maths and ESL and students enjoyed these activities on the odd occasion when the primary school computers were free.

The rest of the program was taken up with bush trips to make boomerangs and spears under the guidance of Henry, who had participated in cultural activities with my classes thirty years before. As well as that, there was a music program, basketball and pottery. The music program culminated in the Alice Springs excursion where students participated in the Bush Bands Bash.

In the interest of attracting and retaining the senior group at school, I tried to expand facilities and programs consistent with the needs of these students. For example, I requested that a sink be plumbed into the classroom which would have basically been an extension of already existing plumbing to the whole building. Neil Cook, a former student of mine, was a qualified plumber and offered to do the job. I also requested that a phone line be extended from the adjoining room, used by Batchelor College. I requested that a computer be installed in the classroom. The classroom was isolated from the other school facilities. I also offered to investigate the feasibility of restoring the Manual Arts facility and developing a technical studies program.

All my offers and requests to improve facilities and programs for senior students were rejected and I was doubtful that these students would remain at school for very long.

Any Lajamanu Community Education Center (CEC) initiative was compromised by DEET reporting, testing and recording requirements. For example, there was in place, mandatory compliance with the NT Curriculum Framework, Federal Government 'Closing the Gap' along with National Benchmarks. Provision of evidence of learning and complex prescribed reporting protocols was the order of the day. The impact of all this was to stifle teacher enthusiasm and attempts to work collaboratively with the Yapa community. Staff were exhausted, often sick and lacking in energy, with limited opportunity to learn basic Warlpiri culture and language. Yapa assistant teacher contributions were not valued beyond basic behaviour management. First Nations People of high status in the community were employed to round up the children in a bus and 4WD to get them to school. When I invited them to join us at a staff meeting, they declined because they felt excluded from the decision-making and running of the school.

The school cultural program in which elders were meant to participate was ad hoc. Children were crammed into a Troop Carrier and taken out bush as part of the 'Country Visit program.'

Around the perimeter of the school, there are signs on the fence saying that anyone found on the CEC property or the school grounds after 7 pm may attract a $2,000 fine. These and a range of other more subtle deterrents are completely at odds with the orientation I attended in Darwin and the references at school staff meetings promoting equity in the 'Two Way' policy.

By comparison, the student population is less than half of what it was in the 1970s, yet the overall population remains similar. Lajamanu, along with other schools in remote NT had its status expanded to that of CEC encompassing all levels of education, from Pre-School to TAFE and Higher Adult Education. Yet for Lajamanu, the reality is that the CEC effectively offers a basic Pre-School and primary school with a Batchelor College presence. Literacy levels remain low. I saw no choice but to resign with two weeks' notice at the end of the third term.

Observations and Reflections

There were no cleaners employed at Lajamanu School. Teachers were expected to clean their own classrooms. Teachers were allocated one new vacuum cleaner each. Finally, one day the General Manager of DEET came to the school. I saw a professional opportunity. For me, it was standard practice to share my classroom with other staff and people from a range of appropriate professions, inviting them to give a talk to the kids about their roles and what kind of work they did. For example, a lawyer researching the impacts of state law on First Nations People came at my invitation to give a talk about her work and Aboriginal people's rights. The DEET Manager agreed to visit my class and give a brief talk about her work. The Manager never showed up and there was no explanation offered.

Thirty years before, the school was referred to as Lajamanu School, which ran a well-resourced preschool, primary school and post-primary school, complete with Home Economics and Manual Arts, with the priority of genuine community engagement.

We drove out of Lajamanu and camped for the first night at Wattie Creek. We drove through Cape Crawford, Burketown, and Georgetown to arrive home by the following Wednesday afternoon.

Sara and Chris had kept the home fires burning during our absence. There was a lot to do and I worked with Sara and Chris at home while Rose worked in Alcohol and Drug counselling. Among the first things was to shift my office to Sara's old bedroom up in the house and put a back doorway into the shed. I was going to resume supply and contract teaching but decided that I'd had enough.

Poultry

Sara and Chris were developing a biodynamic veggie box scheme and I brought an Allen Oxford scythe from Melbourne for the purpose of cutting lab lab and millet crops for compost. We also installed a cold room for produce. The chooks were doing well, but the ducks were another story.

We had fenced an area for them under the rainforest canopy but they were difficult to manage without an actual pen for protection against the resident goannas. One day a goanna swiped a duck off her eggs causing injuries and gulped down all the eggs in one sitting. This was repeated and the project was abandoned. The turkeys were too difficult to manage without expensive infrastructure.

There was a bantam on 14 guinea fowl eggs that our friend Laurie had collected from a wild nest on his property. Laurie's advice was that you need to spray the eggs with a fine mist of water to weaken the shell close to hatching for a higher survival rate of chicks. It worked. Eight chicks survived. We found later though, as they matured, they bullied the chooks and we had to get rid of them.

Rose and I made another trip to Darwin early in December 2008 – it was Parry and Sue's 33rd wedding anniversary. Parry's Parkinson's condition was beginning to show physically now, five years since his diagnosis. We did go out and visited the Air Force museum with the new Super Marine Spitfire exhibit now on display and a new cinema showing restored film footage of when the 2nd World War came to Darwin. The Japanese had come from Pearl Harbour to launch a formidable attack on Darwin and there were no fewer than 63 bombing raids.

Parry took us fishing in Darwin Harbour against the backdrop of a spectacular top-end wet season build-up. Back at home, we soon heard the sad news that my sister Judith's oldest daughter, Andrea was in palliative care with cancer. She passed away on the morning of 2nd June the following year. It was a tragedy. Andrea was an accomplished writer and only 49 years. She left behind two daughters, Dommi and Lily and her husband Brett. Early in 2009 Rose and I flew to New Zealand for the first time, to attend a Classic Motorcycle festival.

Classic Motorcyles

This iconic racing circuit is in a pleasant rural setting surrounded by undulating hill country on the outskirts of Pukekohe, just south of Auckland. We were struck by the friendly atmosphere and the casual nature of this festival and to the credit of the NZ Classic Motorcycling Register Inc., it ran like clockwork. The absence of police and security guards and the friendliness of competitors and spectators alike, was refreshing. There was free parking and camping under big shady trees overlooking the track and free access to the pits. On day one, we caught up with Jim, Mike and Liz from the Tablelands, and later, with Sue and her Kiwi mates.

There was an interesting mix among riders – young and old, men and women – from NZ, Japan, Australia, USA and the UK. Racing bikes included Vincent black lightning, Brough Superior, Ducati, Gilera, BMW, Gold Star, Matchless, Velos, AJS, Indian and Harley and Norton, among others. There was a series of practice runs and demonstrations on the day.

On day two, Saturday, races kicked off at 10am. At the start, the crackling roar of big singles and twins, clouds of smoke and a waft of burnt methanol were sensational. Events progressed through the day. Bikes tore down the straight, with the sound of ripping canvas - and rolling thunder in their wake. What a treat!

An important highlight of the festival was the opportunity to see these magnificent machines firsthand and have the occasional chat with owners and riders in the pits as they prepared their bikes. You could appreciate the quality of craftsmanship at close quarters.

Champion rider, Kevin Schwantz has been described as the most spectacular rider to ever race in the motorcycle Grand Prix with 25 Premier class wins and 21 lap records. Apart from being a thoroughly decent sort of bloke, his performance on that 1962 Manx 500 was extraordinary. While most riders would throttle off on the approach to the bends, he was able to maintain phenomenal speeds, flinging the bike in and out and tearing down the straight to win every feature race.

On day three we arrived to the sound of bagpipes on the ridge in the morning mist. The highlight of the day was the Manx 500, exclusive all Norton race – there were thirteen of them. I've always found classic motorcycling appealing and I've talked about my bikes in an earlier section of this book. I feel compelled to share yet another event – A surprise visit.

About 18 classic motorbikes turned up on a sunny winter's morning in June. We arranged earlier for the local, and Cairns club members to meet at our place for coffee during a run. Just before 10 o'clock that morning, Charles rang from Yungaburra to say that the Mackay mob had turned up as well – there were about ten of them and asked if it would it be OK for them to come to our place for coffee too. Everyone was welcome. It wasn't long before that distinctive bark of British classics gradually grew louder, the bikes finally making the spectacular entry, down the drive, to park in the backyard, have a coffee and talk motorbikes.

It was an honour to host kindred spirits and their machinery including handsome BSA Gold Stars, Triumphs, Matchless, Norton, Vincent Rapide, BMW, Honda 4, and Scott motorcycles.

Just before we got home from NZ, we heard the news of the 181 people confirmed dead in the Victorian bushfires. Hoyte and his sister Monica had survived and were sheltering at the Marysville Fire Refuge centre. Monica lost everything in the fire except her handbag. Hoyte had his belongings at his home in Buxton and had narrowly escaped the fire.

Sara and Chris' wedding was the 2nd of August 2009. Rose conducted the ceremony as the marriage celebrant, set in the rainforest at home and Mingus played his guitar. Among the guests were Sara's friends, Chris' parents from England and the Smiths from Dreghorn station. Hoyte had been with us for over 10 weeks, living in his motor home in the backyard with Biscuit the cat. Hoyte was suffering from the early effects of asbestosis, but he was still able to set up and act as DJ for the wedding.

There were a lot of requests for high-volume 1950s blues and rock and roll classics. It was cool and we had a warm fire with all the food and drinks set up in the carport. Lindsay Cook from up the road had strung up party lights in the rainforest trees and it was the best wedding. I need to mention another Land Rover that became available.

Land Rover

Having sold our 1981 long wheel-based hard top to Veronica and David up at Bamaga a few years ago, and still suffering from grief and loss, I had an opportunity to get another Land Rover. I bought a 1975 Series 3 ute in mid-September 2009 in original condition with only 62189 kms. on the clock. It was now over 30 years old and I put it on club registration. The Land Rover had been resting in a yard at the Atherton industrial estate. Its previous owner, a local farmer, bought it new and had recently passed away. When I acquired it, it still had the farm registration sticker on the windscreen and it is said to have only been driven on the farm in second gear.

With the help of a friend and mechanic, I completed the restoration in time for another trip to central Australia in June of the following year. I also entered the Land Rover in vintage car shows but never won a prize. One year at the Charters Towers swap meet and car show a small group of young locals walked by my Land Rover exhibit, saying that it was *"a heap of shit."* I could only conclude from this, that the Toyota company had done a good job on the locals over the last three decades with aggressive advertising campaigns. I'm pleased to say that there are other series 3s in Far North Queensland and they are appreciated. It was towards the end of the year that we visited my sister Judith in Bingginwarri in southern Gippsland in Victoria.

Bingginwarri to Launceston

Rose and I flew to Melbourne in mid-November and made a three-hour bus trip to Toora, where Judith picked us up and we stayed a couple of nights at her small property at Bingginwarri. We also visited my nephew Victor at his place east of Lilydale. We flew from Melbourne to Launceston and hired a car to go and see David and Monica Holt at their property north of St Helens. The oysters there were superb and we swam at a beach near St Helens. The water was crystal clear, bright blue, and freezing. As a personal challenge, I swam underwater, being able to manage only a few seconds before being overcome by the cold. Our last night in Tassie was at a B&B Georgian cottage in Richmond just north of Hobart. It was like the Cotswolds in England and I'd like to return one day and spend more time around Hobart. Our friend Lindsay Cook died in tragic circumstances in April 2010 and I feel I should share a bit about this remarkable man.

Death of a Friend

Lindsay Cook died on 29th April of head injuries when he was riding his bike along the Kennedy Highway just north of Tolga early in the morning. He was left lying there on the side of the road until a passer-by raised the alarm. Nobody knew what actually happened to Lindsay that morning, or the reason he made that fateful decision to change his cycling route. There were no witnesses. It was generally thought that he was hit by a northbound truck. Rose conducted Lindsay's funeral ceremony and we hosted a wake for him here at home for his family and friends. Lindsay was a good friend and an exceptionally good man. The Eulogy I wrote for him explains a bit more.

29/4/2010
Lindsay had set out on a ride on his push bike early that morning and was struck by a vehicle at Rocky Creek in a hit-run accident. Miya, me and Bella were walking past Sharen and Lindsay's on the way back home from walking with Rose on her way to work. In her distress, Sharen said Lindsay had suffered severe head trauma in this accident – (she had already seen him) and that it wasn't good. Lindsay died in Cairns base hospital at midday.

There are things that I admired in Lindsay – his focus was on the family he loved. Whenever we saw him he was doing things with the kids – he had his family in mind in everything he did. He often brought Molly and Manu down on their bikes for a cup of tea and a chat or to give us some bananas. Only a few days ago they came down to deliver an invitation to Sarah's 21st birthday party and he and I talked about his dad and the copra industry back home when he was a kid.

From my perspective, an outstanding quality in Lindsay was his connectedness with nature – you knew this from his conversations or if you went with him on a cruise around Lake Barrine. Lindsay had a close relationship with the natural world, as he did with his family and this was apparent as he would introduce visitors to his beloved environment.
Lindsay was thoughtful and sensitive toward others and he had a gentle and generous nature – softly spoken and accepting of even the most offensive behaviour. Perhaps I'm wrong but I'm pretty sure that Lindsay would also accept that the driver of the car was not to blame and that if blame should be attributed, it should be placed squarely on a disturbed and unsustainable society that has created these circumstances that put our everyday lives at risk.

I know that in a sense we've lost a friend and yet we'll still see Lindsay riding in through the gate as he always did and we'll talk with him again, often. He's just too important a person in our lives for it to be any other way.

Lindsay's wife Sharen erected a memorial to him of his bike painted white and set in concrete at the site of the accident. It remains there today. I recall that in our grief, we went out to where Lindsay was hit soon after he passed away. We saw a rainbow shining over the hills to the west. It was the 13th of June 2010 when Rose and I left for Central Australia.

Back to the Northern Territory

This was an important trip. We'd arranged to catch up with teachers from our Papunya and Lajamanu days, Carolyn and David Cann, Margaret McHugh, Jerry and Clare Flattum from Yuendumu, Jeff Hulcome and linguist, Ken Hanson. Parry and Sue were driving down from Darwin. We were to meet in Alice Springs and drive through to Kintore and Papunya and return to Alice springs. The Land Rover was going well. Rose and I got to Smith's cattle station for the first night and the following day we overnighted with their recently married daughter Shannon and Paul in Charters Towers. We arrived at our friend Michelle's place in Mt Isa not long after dark.

Our travel kit included a digital device loaded with music and you listen to it via a set of little earphones. It didn't work because of the whining of the gearbox and the deafening rattle of the diesel engine. I decided to upgrade to bigger earphones, thinking that would drown out the mechanical noise. It was still too noisy and I just gave up and determined to interpret the sound of the engine and gearbox as a musical genre. It worked. We left Michelle and Mt Isa at 6 am a couple of days later, the plan being to make Tennant Creek that night.

We were ten kilometres out of Camooweal and 190 kilometres west of Mt Isa when all of a sudden there was an explosive, terrifying, high-pitched roar, like a barking sound coming from the engine. It was very disturbing. I pulled into a truck parking bay, stopped the engine and anxiously lifted the bonnet, expecting the very worst. I was so relieved to discover that it was only the exhaust pipe separated from the engine manifold and was hanging by a bracket attached to the chassis. The exhaust manifold had broken off at the neck.

No problem I thought. I found a discarded tin – the label said beef and vegetable stew. I had some fencing wire, pliers, and tin snips in the toolbox and got to work on the repairs as soon as the engine had cooled.

I cut the top and bottom off and cut a straight line along the length of the stew tin, opened it up and fitted it around the neck of the manifold. I wired the whole lot up by wrapping wire around wherever I could get it. We started off with black soot and unburnt fuel fumes belching into the cabin. The odour of the remnant hot beef stew from inside the tin was pleasant enough and it eventually burned away.

We continued on to Soudan station a few kilometres further on for help. The mechanic welded the cast iron neck, but it broke again soon after we got back onto the highway. There just wasn't enough metal there to weld. I patched it up as best I could and headed back to Camooweal.

Nobody there, even at the garage was interested, so we parked near the police station to have a cup of tea and ponder our circumstances. I rang Chris Snelling, who had worked on the car, to let him know how the trip was progressing. I also collected a couple of lengths of heavy soft copper wire that had been used to patch the fence, to replace the fencing wire that I had wrapped around the manifold.

On this occasion, using the stew tin and copper wire, I was able to make an effective sling to hold the exhaust pipe up in place. The copper was soft and easier to wrap around the tin providing a better seal. We had another cup of tea and drove out of Camooweal at midday with the view to making the 400 or so kilometres to Tennant Creek that night. The makeshift repairs had reduced the noise level and the amount of soot and fumes coming into the cabin but we were slowed down because of the loss of power.

With Neil (left) and Albert Cook. Tennant Creek, 2010.

We were in Tennant Creek by 8.30pm, tired and a bit black in the face from the soot. We got on to a mechanic the following morning. Clinton found a replacement series three manifold lying in the long grass behind the mechanic's workshop. Apart from some surface rust, and a stud adjustment, it was in perfect condition and within two hours the job was done. Clinton only charged me $100 for the manifold and $70 for labour.

We had previously arranged to meet up with Neil and Albert Cook whom I've already mentioned. Strike me Pink had recently acquired a partner, Diane Kitson whom we met for the first time. They came down to the mechanic's workshop where we had some morning tea and a chat, and Rose passed on some second-hand clothes and curtains they had requested for the family. We left Tennant Creek early the following morning. Apart from the slow puncture, the rest of the trip was smooth and luxurious and we arrived at Jerry and Clare's place in Alice Springs at 9.30 pm that evening.

We stocked up with supplies and I repaired the punctured tyre and replaced the rivets in the bonnet wheel clamp. Jerry took me for a ride around his block on the dirt bikes. We camped with Parry and Sue in a creek west of Glen Helen Gorge and arrived in Papunya at midday on the 25th June to see the house we occupied in the 1980s, the school, health clinic, church, and Arts Centre. Sammy Butcher from the Warampi Band came to see Parry with the news that frontman, George Rurrambu had passed away some years ago.

When we got to Ilpirli rock hole both Parry and I discovered we sustained some damage to our Land Rovers caused by vibrations on the corrugated road. We met up with David and Carolyn at Yayiyayi. David and Carolyn were teachers at Papunya during my time there, back in the 1980s. Parry took up a teaching job at Yayiyayi shortly after leaving Yirrkala in 1971.

At Lampara Bore, 40 years on from when Parry was a single teacher, there wasn't a trace of the two little round schoolhouses that he and the Yapa had built – the make-shift classrooms were eaten away by termites. The ghostly Southern Cross wind pump creaked as the blades rotated in the gentle desert breeze. There was no water, the bore pump mechanism having collapsed long ago. Kids had recorded their names and hand prints on the blades and the evidence was still sharply defined in black paint indelibly etched on the huge galvanised blades. Rose found a 1975 five-cent piece in the sand.

Sandy Blight junction was our last stop before Kintore. Len Bedell's old original aluminium sign that we had seen many years ago had been stolen and replaced by a replica at Sandy Blight.

David and Carolyn had arranged accommodation for us at the Yirara College Campus at Kintore and we spread our swags on the classroom desks. I took the opportunity to perform the daily ritual of checking gearbox oil levels and topping up the engine oil. Since leaving Atherton 16 days ago we had travelled 3,637 kilometres.

The following morning, David and Carolyn went to Sorry camp to catch up with Pintupi people they knew from Yirara – they had a three-year teaching contract there from 2007. Despite over 30 years of experience in Indigenous Education, they weren't able to deliver the departments' stated outcomes – the NT curriculum framework, Federal Government Initiative - 'Closing the Gap,' along with national benchmarks. We also discussed the impact of the Howard Government's Intervention' on the lives of remote First Nations people.

Carolyn brought a leg of lamb from Alice Springs and, with Rose and Sue, cooked a big roast meal in the domestic science kitchen for lunch that day and we were joined by linguist Ken Hanson. There are two sacred places at Kintore. The men's place is called Yunyitju – in English Mt Liesla. The women's place is called Walungurru – and in English, Mt Strickland. These two places combined are known as Purli Kutjarra. David and Carolyn sought permission for us to walk up into Yunyitju. The view from the summit looked out across the sandridge country towards our planned destination of Docker River. You could see the narrow sand track to Docker, but not the corrugations. We left David and Carolyn to continue on to Docker River in the Peterman Ranges close to the Western Australian border.

Rose, Sue, Farry and me, Kintore, 2010.

The corrugations were about 15cm high and about half a metre apart. It may be all right for NT Government Department and Mining Corporation new Toyota Land Cruisers but it was a very different story for us. We'd only driven 30 kilometres along the track before turning back and abandoning the Docker River leg of the trip, to return to Papunya and Alice Springs.

Ilpirli

After setting up camp on the sand plains south of Ilpirli Rock Hole, I discovered that not only was the bonnet catch damaged earlier but the two front shock absorbers had failed. Not to worry – the weight of the wheel on the bonnet kept it from bouncing up and down and the front leaf springs are pretty rigid at the best of times. The following morning was fresh and fragrant. There had recently been enough rain to penetrate an inch of sand and there were a lot of dusky wood swallows and budgies on the wing, against a cloudy dawn sky. It wasn't far to the north of Ilpirli that we set up camp again to the east of the road under the shade of some desert oaks in the beautiful sand dunes. More rain had brought the wildflowers out. It was a relaxing day wandering with Parry through the spectacular, colourful landscape, along the tops of spinifex studded dunes and narrow winding valleys in between until it was time for another cup of tea back at camp. We relaxed around the flickering fire in the quiet starlit night.

The plan was to have one more night with Parry and Sue before parting company to return to Alice Springs and home. It was raining and difficult driving on muddy corrugations. It was cold and wet that night at our last camp on the bank of a creek east of Gosse' bluff. It was the sort of night when five minutes seemed like an hour and you spend the night praying for first light. The light showers persisted and I was up before dawn in search of dry firewood under the roots of the ghost gums along the banks of the creek and managed to get a fire going and put the billy on. The rain persisted all the way through to Alice Springs.

Margaret and I taught together during the 1970s at Lajamanu. Margaret's home is a rambling old original concrete house on the eastern bank of the Todd River, built in the 1940s. It reminded me of the Superintendent's house at Lajamanu during 1970s. The place was rich in ambience and patina. It had large rooms - dark and cool, with white-washed walls and high ceilings, a lovely veranda, a beautiful roofline with wide eaves and an attic with views over the Todd River. In fact, from Margaret's place, you could walk across the Todd River straight into the Alice Springs Mall. The house yard had a huge peppercorn tree against a big old corrugated iron shed. Rose and I stayed there with Margaret for the next few days before heading back home.

We enjoyed a dinner with Margaret and Jeff Hulcome, discussing current trends and politics of Central Australia. There was the threat of uranium mining and radioactive waste dumps. There were threats to water supplies and First Nations Homelands. There were the impacts of Howard's Intervention in remote Yapa communities and the 'Close the Gap' initiative.

Jeff was an outstations teacher at Mt Liebig and New Bore when I was the outstations coordinator at Papunya during the early 1980s. On the 3rd of July, we drove Jeff to the airport on his way home to Brisbane for the holidays, had lunch at the Botanical Gardens and explored the town. In black spray paint, with letters half a meter high, on the white outside wall of the public toilet block, a message read *"Do the cops a favour. Bash yourself up."*

I adjusted my oil levels at Tennant Creek and we stayed with Michelle at Mt Isa the following day. We camped on the Flinders and Norman Rivers on the way home to the Tablelands.

This was a period of a lot of visits and our catching up with relations and friends in Queensland, NSW and Victoria. My sister, Judith would be 69 at the end of the year and there was a lot going on. One of the outings took us to Victoria to visit childhood friends Darby and Sandy, sister Judith and her family in early April 2011. Rose and I went on to Brisbane to see relatives and friends including Rose's Uncle George, cousins Maxine and Leon, Uncle Norman and Anne and Errol at Toowoomba. We were on our way north to visit John and Marie Woodley at Caboolture. We caught the train from Bowen Hills. I was moved to write about the train trip. There was a serious breakdown. Rather than just sitting and complaining, I chose to write about what was happening - a blow-by-blow description as it unfolded.

On a Queensland Railway

Here is my account of our train trip from Bowen Hills on 16th April 2011 It remains in draft form:

The Caboolture train leaves from Bowen Hills at 7.12 am and breaks down at 8.10 am just outside of Petrie en route to Caboolture. The disabled train is suddenly very quiet, lights go off, and seems to start coasting.

Rose says *"We've run out of power."* No, I don't think that's right as the train brakes are finally applied and it stops.

After about 15 mins power seems to be restored as lights come back on, various buzzing noises, air brakes, and so on. But we are not moving and everything shuts down again. A train worker opens the front door of our carriage to tell us that radio communication is down as well and almost straight after that the communication comes back on. The bloke says that we've lost overhead power and that the circuit breakers are cutting out.

While sitting in silence a group of people behind us start chewing loudly on some sort of biscuits, gulping down milk loudly, belching and regurgitating.

After some time the train bloke says that they are going to try and start the train from the rear and this fails too. More time passes before the bloke opens the front door again to tell us that this train has failed. *"This train is a failure."* He starts opening fanlights.

By now an hour has passed and there's a further announcement that another train is on its way to tow us back to Petrie.

Rose rings John and Marie on their mobile phone keeping them informed.

It's 9.17am - bloke walks past announcing that when the train gets back to Petrie — We'll get you out the front door. 9.27 - We hear repeated air related noises and I start thinking about the sale of Qld rail.

10.05am One passenger climbs out via the front door. Other passengers begin to complain. Asian passengers behind us say *"too long, no good."* Others consider climbing down and walking back to Petrie.

10.10 Silence. Can hear sirens. A passenger tries to communicate by pressing the emergency intercom button. Red light goes on but no success. Kids begin to joke into the intercom. *"Hello, how are you today. I wish they'd tell us something."* And *"Nobody told us anything."*

10.20 John calls to find out what's wrong and we notice now that the front door is shut and locked. Rose sees a railway worker with grease all over his hands down on the track.

10.25 We find out from another passenger that the rescue train has also broken down.

10.30 I walk up towards the rear to be intercepted by train workers and told *"Go back that way, we are moving finally."* Train starts to move backwards to the exclamation of a passenger *"We're moving"* - after 2 ½ hours!!

It's very slow. Rose told John that we are locked in here and can't get out and John explained that these are electric trains and all controls are locked.

I'm thinking about a re-draft and offering a copy of this account to the media.

Stopped again and dying for a pee. 10.40 moving slowly again. An explosion from the rear of towing train.

Other passengers want to go to the toilet.

Screaming was heard from outside.

The brakes, like the doors and other controls, are locked on. Noises continue and we no longer hear radio conversations. Now we can hear some muted radio conversations including phrases involving numbers like Number 1107 is disabled, and other numbers, and *"OK mate no worries. Over and out, and the rescue unit will be approaching the rear."* OK thank you, driver.

10.40 The air/clicking noises are less frequent. something or other *"hasn't sealed properly"*, and *"OK so ahhhhh"*.

10.45 It is starting to rain. John is waiting back at Petrie and tells Rose on the mobile that they are going to tow us back to Petrie. The attendant/driver comes by, unlocks and opens the manual fan lights above the windows explaining that they are old and have not been opened for a long time.

More radio conversations - I wonder if, 0700 OK will give it a burl, We've got about 80 people on the train.

10.54 Attendant/driver walks by saying - Finding it hard to get this train going.

11 0clock I am beginning to think that this has something to do with a petition I signed a couple of weeks ago against selling QR.

We finally arrive back at Petrie where John and Marie kindly met us. John then drove us to a student reunion at Maleny. Later, we stayed with Rose's nursing friend Cheryl down at Tweed Heads on the way to the Byron Bay Bluesfest. I found this little diary entry of when we were in the Mojo tent jostling for a decent vantage point to see Bob Dylan.

Byron Bay Bluesfest

Tuesday 26th April 2011. Mud and heavy rains. The whole ground turned into churned stinking mud as in cattle yards.

Up near the stage in Mojo venue, there's me and Rose in front of a woman. Beside me is a bloke jostling to get further forward in anticipation of the big event.

Bloke says to the woman – *"Would you please let me stand there in front of you? I have only 6 months to live."* She ignores him and a couple of minutes later, he says, *"Can I just get past you I have to get something for me little sister."* She tells him. *"No, you can't, Go and get past someone else – Grow up."*

Home Again

Intensive small-scale agricultural projects were progressing well and expanding under Sara and Chris' biodynamic experimental plot using the newly fenced paddock adjacent to the house. Everything that they put in seemed to thrive and I enjoyed being a part of it. In hindsight, it was the envy of a number of people and possibly the reason for the undermining and eventual hijacking of the cooperative that Sara and Chris had set up. They also set up an independent veggie box scheme. One of the first for the Tablelands.

I was 66 and an important thing to note was that by then people we knew were starting to die, leaving me with only four childhood friends left – Darby, Hoyte, Sandy Allen and Peter Marsh. I lost contact with Peter ages ago and Hoyte wasn't well. Over the 20-odd years since we established our family base here in Atherton, we'd lost other friends, neighbours and acquaintances. Attending funerals had become more frequent and reminded me of my own mortality.

One day I noticed an article in the local newspaper – Murdoch's front page headlines read 'Big W comes to look us over.' And within a couple of years, completely unopposed, and with the blessing of the local council, developers gutted the residential heart of the town – Atherton's heritage precinct – to make way for their obscene concrete department store that took up a whole block.

Big W and the state, forced long-term residents to relocate and some Queenslander homes were uplifted and removed. I was alone in my decision to boycott the Big W. A precedent had been set. This development was followed by a further invasion of fast food giants, McDonalds and KFC, closely followed by Harvey Norman, Super Cheap Auto, Bunnings, and so on. Some years on, there was scarcely a family business left in town and many vacant shops along the main street.

Atherton was becoming a corporate town. A sort of FIFO/commuter centre. A diary entry reflects the way I felt about Atherton at the time.

15th April 2012

Walked into town with Rose to pick up some paw-paws at Robert Street. Rose wanted to sit for a while on the bench on the main street near the BV (Barron Valley Hotel) and said she'd meet me on my return. Atherton is a sad place now. The Grand (Hotel) is not so grand, with peeling paint and mould. There's vomit on the footpath outside the Black Stump Hotel – it had spaghetti in it. There are sad people shuffling along the pavement in the drizzle.

Hoyte had left to return to Melbourne. His departure wasn't on ideal terms. He was sick and I was deeply troubled by it. However, it wasn't long after he'd returned to Melbourne that I gave him a friendly call and all was well again. It was in February 2011 when Hoyte's sister, Monica rang to tell me that he had collapsed on the street in Frankston and was now in the Alfred hospital for a couple of weeks and would then be transferred to an aged care facility at Windsor in the Elsternwick area.

Hoyte was making regular trips to Moscow for stem-cell treatment for his lung condition. It was in Moscow that he met his future wife Irina who migrated to Australia and later supported him during his illness. I was never to see him again. Before Hoyte left the north for the last time, he shared his life story about his relationships - a cake metaphor.

Life is a Piece of Cake

Life at the start is a nice big cake. You get married and in a few years, it doesn't work out and after the settlement, you end up with half of your cake. You remarry. This also ends in divorce and you then have a quarter of your cake. You are determined not to get involved with women again. You meet a woman with a drug addiction and you commit to working through it with her and you become embroiled in a drama-filled relationship. She tragically dies and again, you're crippled with grief and loss. The story goes on to end with having to sell your house and business, leaving you with only a sliver of cake or a biscuit, as in Hoyte's case, destined for a life on the road in a motor home with a cat called Biscuit.

It's the 1st of February in 2017 as I write, turning to peer out the window at the gentle tropical rain. There are more showers developing and a string of tropical cyclones predicted for the season, eight in all.

And this takes me back to sharing a recent experience with a record-breaking event – cyclone Yasi.

Cyclone Yasi

Cyclone Yasi was monstrous - consuming much of the Pacific Ocean. She was born in a tropical low near Fiji in late January 2011 and developed very rapidly. She soon intensified into a category 5 storm, rather akin to what happens when stirring biodynamic soil preparations. If you stir vigorously and consistently enough, the eye of the vortex becomes deeper, exposing the bottom of the container. As it is stirred the liquid often develops a lumpiness – where hundreds of little vortices become part of the overall system. The eye of the cyclone was 50 kilometres wide.

Yasi headed in a west-south westerly direction, barreling into the coast near Mission Beach at around Midnight on the 3rd.of February. There were wind gusts of 290 km/h and a 7-metre storm surge. The storm spanned the area between Ingham and Cairns.

It was a highly destructive, dramatic and unusual event where Yasi's intensity penetrated far inland, being downgraded to a tropical low near Mt Isa by 10 o'clock that night. Ex-Yasi continued on her rampage over the landscape. On the following day, the Met. Bureau reported that ex–Yasi was located 85 Kilometers from Yulara in Central Australia. By the 5th of February, she had dumped over five and a half inches of rain as far away as Renmark and Mildura on the River Murray and Lyndhurst, a Melbourne suburb. I'll just share a snippet of our personal experience during this storm on the Tablelands.

As Yasi approached the Queensland coast we started getting emails and phone calls from concerned friends and family down south. We were shutting up the house when Miya decided to bring little Bella and shelter here with us down in the shed along with Rose and me, Sara and Chris for the night. After the cyclone crossed the coast we were soon without power and communications. Before settling in for the night, there was a lot of last-minute movement between the shed and the house.

We chose to remain vigilant through the night, drinking tea and coffee and peering out into the turmoil outside. The sky was white with electrical charge. There were tree branches flying around and there was that constant deep roar. There wasn't any structural damage. We'd lost tallows and cadaghi trees at the front, but very little damage was done to our rainforest – a few limbs were broken, and that was all. It took a few days to clean up.

Other Goings On

In late June that year, Sara and Chris moved into their new house at Beecroft where they were establishing their farm. The arrangement was with Tony whom the family had known for many years. Tony offered Chris and Sara accommodation and a fenced paddock with available water for irrigation just up from the creek. This was in return for looking after the property in his absence and Chris doing paid maintenance work. It was in September 2011, things were heating up on the political front, and I was contemplating the idea of making a return to campaign work. Fracking was one of several issues that could be tackled at the local level. I first became aware of the insidious Coal Seam Gas industry (CSG), when I saw an SBS Insights program on the topic. There was no reference to toxic chemicals injection into the ground, or the impacts of fracking on farmers, communities or the environment. There were 30-40 gas wells planned for the area of Chinchilla and Tara where there was the risk of toxins finding their way underground into the Great Artesian Basin. The Minister didn't know much about it. It was my first contact with Drew Hutton's LOCKTHEGATE alliance. I'll return to fracking later. It was also at around this time that I put a proposal to the family and here's how it went:

A Family Proposal - Working Towards a Sustainable Future
A Draft Proposal – Alan Isherwood, September 2011
Preamble
The world is now experiencing a time of rapid and dramatic changes demanding that we profoundly alter deep-seated perceptions, behaviours, social practices and institutions. We have the opportunity to reconsider the unsustainable approaches to environmental and social change that still widely rely on crisis management, new and damaging technologies, risk assessments and so on. I'm convinced that we should be taking up the challenge to broaden

and deepen our understanding of sustainability and change.

This draft proposal is concerned with the protection and survival of our immediate family into the future. The following proposal sets out some guidelines for further development in the form of practical ideas for dealing with change and possible options available to us.

Possible Future Scenarios

While there is a dearth of literature on the impacts of a modern collapse, a reasonable assumption is that current trends will continue to cause increasing anxiety related to instability and vulnerability in our lives. As part of the development of a vision for sustainable living on the Atherton Tablelands, options for the future may include:

Our family group, (immediate family and partners) pool financial and other resources and purchase sufficient land – say 10 to 50 acres – within an estimated safe distance from urban growth areas. The property should be suitable for the establishment and maintenance of small scale organic/biodynamic farming.

Development of basic infrastructure would include three self contained cottages, a tool and implements shed and other common areas, access to uncontaminated water – creek etc.

Some family members would develop and practice biodynamic mixed farming to a level of self sufficiency and beyond. Others may concern themselves with maintenance and generation of external off-farm income. It would be imperative that the family group negotiate and work cooperatively to create conditions consistent with healthy and sustainable life. To this end, sharing resources, among other things will become a necessary step towards a place over which we may retain a greater degree of ownership and control.

Resources Available to Family Group:
Financial – possible sale of existing assets such as 3 Glenwood Close and 28 Winfield Rd. leaving 184 Greenslopes St as security, and/or combined funding available as payment for rural land/property and infrastructure.

Skills and Knowledge
Among other things, Law, Environmental Science, Education, politics,

nursing, counselling, book-keeping, psychology, mechanics and engineering, water reticulation, coordination, farming and biodynamic practice and value-adding, music and the arts, home-making and parenting, cooking, local knowledge, and local connections.

Other important resources must include – maturity, tacit knowledge and intuitive confidence, trust and responsibility towards self, others and the natural environment, sustainable world views including attitudes, values and sense of place enabling the family group to creatively and fully engage in pursuits necessary for a safe, healthy and sustainable future.

Action Plan
Form organising/management committee for the negotiated development of overall aims/objectives and enabling objectives/outcomes. The committee to meet, communicate regularly, members to keep records. Connect with people with relevant experience and of similar persuasion.

Research – relevant legislation and it's limitations; look at potential models for sustainable living, family trusts, national and global. Future involvement with regional local govt. as it develops with specific regards to location, tenure, exit, multi-title, multiple dwellings etc. Other important aspects to explore may be security of access to uncontaminated water, alternative/renewable power, formation of a company and so on.

All other things being equal, in this way we may be able to work towards avoiding the most damaging impacts of social and environmental collapse. I'm happy to initially take a leading role if preferred."

Your comments?
I really thought I was onto something. I held a Master's degree in Environmental Education and had done literature reviews on Sustainable Living. I never gave up on the idea and still dream about it. Some recent thoughts included the idea of buying next-door's property – the current owners are in their 90s. The idea would be for a family partnership. The sale of Cairns house would enable us to pay our share. The house next door to be fenced off from the rest of the property and rented out in the short term or Sara and her partner could live there and farm the rich red volcanic soil out the back. Miya and her family were by now settled at their acreage at Lake Eacham.

Silas is Born

Our Grandson, Silas, was born at Mareeba hospital at 3.30 pm on Friday the 13th July 2012. Miya chose Mareeba for its family birthing program. Once again it was a quick delivery with Dugan present and Bella arriving just after 3.30 to be with her newborn brother in the Family room. In the interests of perpetuity, Silas's registered name became Silas Isherwood Crothers.

Bella with baby brother, Silas Isherwood Crothers. July 2012.

I spent a lot of time later that month designing and installing shade mesh screens on the shed and the house so it would be cooler in the summer months. I also extended the stingless bee hive. We had a breakdown on the Palmerston.

Rats

Rose, Miya, Bella and I, were returning from a day at Etty Bay one afternoon when the Peugeot suddenly lost power and ground to a halt not far from the top of the Palmerston Highway. Rats had chewed up the insulation on the wiring in the engine bay. It is said that rats are drawn to Peugeots because the company use vegetable oil in the manufacture of the plastics used on the wiring. It cost over $700 for a second-hand engine loom. It was around this time that an old friend passed away.

Hoyte has Died

My high school friend Hoyte died on 21st of August 2012. His sister Monica rang with the sad news. Hoyte had pulled out his oxygen – he'd had enough. I wasn't able to get down to Melbourne for the funeral and so, wrote the following Eulogy:

Eulogy - 29 August 2012
For Klaus, read by Monica, his sister, on behalf of Richard Darby and Alan Isherwood.

Klaus, fondly known to us as Hoyte, has died and we've lost a friend. There was this trio operating in eastern Victoria during the sixties. It developed in Ringwood and reached its fruition during our lives together in the flat in Balwyn. Over the years that followed, there were gaps of many years as we lived our separate and very different lives spread far and wide. For example, during the late sixties, Darby would be gold mining in Victoria, I'd be a missionary in North East Arnhem Land and Hoyte would be doing renovations in WA. But we'd always pick up where we left off as though it all happened yesterday rather than perhaps 15 or 20 years apart.

Hoyte was a Bavarian and there are many things about his life that we've all shared. A few bits and pieces spring to mind as I write, that Darby and I'd like to share with you here today.

Hoyte's exceptional skills and natural flair for design especially in working with wood emerged early. At high school, Hoyte went way above the expectations of teachers and peers, producing a sophisticated hi-fi stereo system, often working over his lunch hour. My project that year, by comparison, was a possum club fashioned out of a discarded Queen-Anne chair-leg from the wood pile down the backyard.

He was a bit odd though - Hoyte - no doubt about it. Half of the time he seemed to be a step ahead of himself and at other times a step behind and rarely on cue and it sometimes got him into difficulty - all in good humour though.

For example, Hoyte was in the Navy during the time we were living in the flat in Balwyn. Sometimes in the morning, he'd jump out of bed suddenly in complete panic and fear of being late getting to the ship on time. He'd hit the floor still asleep, collapse momentarily, find his feet and in utter confusion, do a couple of revolutions — like a roulette wheel, with one finger serving as a pointer. Where he stopped, was the direction he would head, usually to the bathroom or the kitchen. He would be so late that Darby would drive him all the way to Williamstown to get him safely onboard ship in the nick of time to avoid severe penalties.

Hoyte was an electrical engineer on the front turret gun on the HMAS Derwent when he finally left the Navy. But there were limited career pathways for such a specialised gunner and Hoyte returned to his former skills in woodworking with a great deal of success.

During the early sixties Hoyte was on leave and with Alan, decided to go to Sydney and purchase an Austin of England — an Austin A40, with a view to driving it from Bankstown, west to the Darling River and down to Melbourne. It cost 29 pounds ten shillings. It was matte black. Way out west on the black soil plains near Wilcannia, an unusual vibration developed in the engine and we pulled off the road to investigate. We opened the bonnet, peering down through the darkness of the hot, oily, soot-laden, black and smoky pit that was the engine bay. Hoyte, with one foot on the front bumper, forearms resting on his thigh, slowly and deliberately shook his head and exclaimed emphatically — "However did they win the war." It turned out that there was a loose spark plug lead. Darby reminded me of a similar situation at the flat in Balwyn with reference to another Austin of England that Hoyte had purchased - that's another story.

Hoyte was intensely serious about his music. We'd wag school and head directly for his place. The route took us across the railway line, through the park at Ringwood Lake, and up through town to Munroe Street. There was nobody home and we'd have percolated coffee with rye bread and Swiss cheese with the music of Johnny Cash, Kenny Ball, Buddy Holly, and others at high volume. Hoyte became an accomplished part-time DJ and only recently provided the New Years Eve entertainment at Etty bay, a secluded beach in Far North Queensland and for Alan's daughter Sara's wedding. Since then, thanks entirely to Hoyte, I've been able to re-discover the rock and roll classics of those fun days of long ago.

A lot of stories about our exploits with Hoyte are bound to live on. Hoyte got married 3 times —with Darby as best man for the last two weddings - and to Irina, thanks so much for looking after Hoyte as you have through the last part of his life. So now we say farewell to an enduring friend. Hoyte, you are loved and remembered.

Alan Isherwood.
28 August 2012.

It was in late February 2013 that Rose and I were to make another trip back to England and Switzerland to visit our friends John Humphries in Oxford and Pia and Franz Rast in Sursee. With about three months to spare, it was the first time that we really felt that we weren't rushed and had plenty of quality time, since we were both retired from paid work.

England with John Humphreys

John worked alternate weeks in Oxford and London and so kindly offered his flat in Cowley for our use while in England. Walking in the Cotswolds with John and friend Stewart took us to an ancient archaeological site in the form of a national trust property in Gloucestershire. The Roman country house had large areas of colourful mosaics in the ancient flooring, painstakingly excavated from under the ground.

At Chedworth, we went to see the Norman church of St. Andrews and at Wilmington, St Michaels, and All Angels where in 1063 they gained their first Minister. Further out in the countryside was a World War two airstrip still with the hangers that once housed the formidable Super-Marine Spitfires.

Later, back in Oxford, James Johnstone played Bach in an organ recital at Queens College and we ate pork pie and lentil soup at the covered markets. We took an easy jet from Luton to Zurich, and on to Pia and Franz at their place at Sursee in central Switzerland.

With Pia and Franz

During the next day, we were walking in the snow along the side of a ridge on Mt Niedenburg. The air was thin and it was hard to breathe. We could see the glacial lake - Lake Sempach below. We drove with Pia and Franz to Indemini, an ancient smuggling town, two and a half hours from Sursee, on the Swiss Italian border. We stayed with Franz's sister Moni and her husband Werni. The township was entirely of small, 3-story stone houses perched on a steep rocky hill slope with narrow walkways and dry stone walls, overlooking snow-capped mountains and valleys. Pia said Indemini was a sad place. We climbed the 500 meters up to an old church above the town. Franz's driving, along narrow roads and hairpin bends, was terrifying as we slewed across the border. Bitte Zeigen Sie Mir den Pass. (please show me your passport) and down to Luino on the shores of Lago Maggiore. Rose had her first Gelato for the season and we sipped on Italian espresso in the soft warmth of a sunny Northern Italian afternoon.

With Rose and Pia, Zurich, 2013.

Pia's mum made us welcome on our return to Willisau. It was snowing back in Sursee and Pia took us shopping for an Alessi pepper grinder in Lucerne. Daniella, a friend of Pia's invited us to her farm and showed us around and we spent our last night with friends, Hubi and Esther for dinner at their apartment. It was an hour's train trip from Sursee to Basel and 3 hours from Basel to Paris on the fast train.

Paris

The hotel St. Charles at Rue de Esperance, recommended to us by Pia and Franz was set in the old part of Paris. As part of our wanderings around Paris, Rose attended a mass at Notre Dame. We caught the Red Bus and went to the Louvre and other sites. A diary entry provides a few reactions at the time:

March 17th 2013

Seems that most of the dominant architecture celebrates French aggression and violence against themselves and others. For example the Eiffel Tower – French Revolution, Arch de Triumph – Bonaparte's victories, and 37 celebrated bridges.

Despite the purpose of the monumental architecture, Paris remains an elegant and beautiful city. French cuisine, including escargot, Cassoulet and onion soup at local restaurants is superb.

In no time we were through the tunnel and back in England to spend our last days there with John and Pat.

English Idiosyncrasies

An item on a French menu read 'Lamb and Forgotten vegetables.' While travelling through the tunnel back to London, a man was coming back to the bus. He wore a bright teeshirt that read 'Nobody knows I'm a Lesbian.' In Addiscombe visiting Rose's niece and family, I spotted a sign outside a fish shop reading 'Prawnbroker.' On a Tesco delivery van, an advert read 'Freshly Clicked' and 'The Green Man' was the name of a pub at Putney Heath. A pub in Soho was called 'The Slug and Lettuce' at Shrewsbury is a pub called 'The Bricklayer's Arms.'

A tabloid headline read 'Kensington digs in with ban on mega basements.' A sign on a Shrewsbury collectables shop read 'Drunk and Disorderly.' Shrewsbury street signs include 'Butchers Lane', 'Baker's Lane' and 'Grope Lane.' A Cornish Road sign read 'Slow Down for Fox Sake.'

On a previous trip with Rose, Miya and Sara, we made a visit to Adrian and Marie Parry in a motorhome. Marie insisted that we park the motor home right out the front so that the neighbours would see they had 'expensive friends.'

A sign at Bodmin Moor read 'Clean up after your dog. We know who you are.'

And finally, Pat sent an email to her daughter by mistake. It read 'Do you remember the name of the book about an Australian Bushfire?' The daughter replied, *"Wasn't it called, shit my bush is on fire?"* Our travels took us from Addiscomb and back to Oxford by train via East Croydon, Clapham Junction, and London, and bus via Gloucester

Green in Oxford and finally a taxi out to John's flat in Turner Close.

It was freezing cold back in Oxford with rain, sleet and snow over much of the UK. There were large snow drifts causing road and school closures. It was the 25th of March when Rose and I drove North with John and Pat through to Marple to show them my ancestral roots in Marple and Wybersley Halls. Marple Hall was demolished in 1959 as a result of neglect. All that remained was the site, a public space dedicated to the hall. Wybersley was another story.

Wybersley Hall

It was during our last visit to Marple that we met the current owners of Wybersley Hall and its remaining estate. The picturesque landscape to the front of the hall had been obliterated by a low-cost housing estate with houses built right up to within metres of the 12th-century sandstone facade of the hall, leaving no access to and obliterating any view of the front of the ancient hall. And there was more. Within the old courtyard at the back, which was flanked by stables, the owners had, with the blessing of the heritage trust, extended the main wing of the original building by adding a new section that served as a modern house, done, of course, to the required standards for a grade two heritage building-site. Essentially they had been given approval for the destruction of Wybersley Hall. I've already mentioned the fate of Marple Hall. So, both of these significant heritage sites are obliterated. I thought that they would have had value as icons of the parliamentarians during the civil war. Was this a final triumph for the royalists?

On the way back to London, we dropped in to see Parry's brother Adrian and his wife Marie in Ilkley and had lunch at their favourite pub. We climbed up to Ilkley Moor. We travelled on through Chester to visit Parry's older brother David and his wife, Hazel. After lunch, they took us to see the Roman Wall and Amphitheatre. Our last stop before heading back to London and Oxford was in Ludlow where we had morning tea at the medieval Feathers Hotel. It was the 29th March when we walked into Oxford with John to do some shopping and pick up train tickets to Penzance. John and Pat returned to London for work, leaving us to spend some time with John's family, Rosie, Nina and Dom and Ella and John's former partner, Lenore. Dom recommended Rick

Stein's restaurant for it's famous seafood cuisine.

It's Cold in Penzance

The next day, Rose and I caught a train at Reading for Penzance, via Bristol, Exeter, and Plymouth. It was freezing cold. Here's my diary entry:

Tuesday 2nd April
It's bitterly cold and by the time we arrived at Penzance, despite the heating in the train, I was numb and essentially brain dead and remained so for the next few days until Friday at the beach. Rose was fine, leading me around like a carer with her client.

A couple of days later we picked up a hire car and drove to Mousehole and on to Padstow before returning to our little cabin out in the country near Carnarvon, from which we walked across the fields and down into a little rocky bay and beach. People were there in gumboots and rugged up against the bitter North-easterlies. I was able to find some shelter from the biting wind, behind some rocks at the other end of the beach where I stripped down to my tracksuit pants to soak up some sun for the first time since leaving home. On our return to Padstow and Rick Stein's restaurant that evening, a diary entry reads:

5th April, Rick Stein's restaurant
Wine list *"I picked out these wines because I think they are so very good"* Rick Stein. Wines were up to 100 pounds per bottle and 45 pounds per glass! We had mussels, limpets, little crabs, and oysters at 3 pounds and 50 p each! Scallops are served in the shell at five pounds each coming to a total of 95 pounds.

Frosty night. John says it snowed again back in Oxford. I took pictures inside the Smugglers Inn on Bodmin Moor. I got hypothermia and slept for 15 hours after walking the coastal track from the cabin. We spent more time around the ancient and lonely stone circles in Bodmin Moor. We went to Port Isaac, the site for the TV series, Doc Martin, which was called Port Wenn.

A further diary entry read:
Monday 8th April, Margaret Thatcher Dead
The tabloids were full of the pros and cons of the expensive state funeral that Thatcher demanded, at great cost to the public. Maggie's taxpayer-funded state funeral with full military honours was set for Wednesday the 17th of April at an estimated cost of 12 million pounds. A couple of days later found us browsing in a curiosity shop back in Penzance. In the shop, there was a picture of Thatcher spewing into a plate of food. It was pinned onto the edge of a shelf and the caption read 'Margaret Thatcher meets poor people.'

I had a dream that night:
Tuesday 9th April
Dream last night – Rose was in hospital for surgery and somehow I ended up under the knife. The doctor covers my big toes with a sheet folding it in two cones that fitted over the toes, and then explained that he needed to check my blood. The doctor produced a scalpel while I was still lying on the bench. He slowly drove the scalpel into the back of my leg, through my trousers, and slowly drew the scalpel downward opening up my calf and I then woke up.

  We went back to Bodmin Moor the same day to spend time at the neolithic stones at Minions, including the Hurlers – three stone circles, the two circles of the Pipers, isolated vertical stones and an old engine house and Trethevy Quoit - a 3500 BC neolithic tomb. The tomb was originally the inner part of an earthen mound which eventually eroded away, exposing the massive stone structure within. We headed for Bath the following day.
  We spent the whole morning at the Roman Bath complex and then went to Bath Abbey to check on organ recital times. After that, we went to the Circus and Royal Crescent. By 10 O'clock the following morning, we were settled in for the organ recital practice run before lunch at Sally Lunn's restaurant, museum, and Victoria Art Gallery. By 5 pm we were back at the magnificent Bath Abbey for the organ recital by the brilliant organist, Simon Bell, a graduate of Shrewsbury Abbey. Rose and I had dinner at one of Jamie Oliver's teaching restaurants. There were four brides' parties running simultaneously there that night. We caught the train for our return trip to Oxford.

From Oxford to Hong Kong

It was an unusual flight from Heathrow with hardly any people on the plane, enabling us to use rows of seats to sleep and had access to the galley for tea through the night. It was approaching the wet season in humid Hong Kong and we ended up dodging heavy showers to spend time at Rose's mother's graveside at the Happy Valley cemetery. Rose's cousin Alison, gave us lunch and a tour of her new apartment in the Serenade building in Tai Hang. We had dinner with cousins, Alison, Selwyn and Emmi, Lucy and Jimmy, Kim See and Jacki at the Hong Kong Jockey Club. It was more relaxed for me during this trip. Perhaps I had proven that I was a responsible husband to Rose, having been married to her for over 45 years. There were many stories and jokes. Selwyn claimed to be a victim of human rights because he was unable to smoke in public places. It was the 18th April when we spent some time at the markets and had lunch at the Hong Kong Yacht Club. We arrived in Sydney, caught our connecting flight to Cairns, and drove home to the Tablelands the next day.

Back to Atherton

There was a lot of looking after the grandchildren, and routine maintenance work going on at home and at Greenslopes Street in Cairns. It was also time to stock up on fuel and other supplies ready for the cyclone season. The nut grass was out of control. I was planting corn and mulching citrus. We were juicing carrots, parsnips, celery, ginger, and beetroot. It was election time too.

It was Saturday 7th September 2013 when the Federal elections were called. Under the threat of a right-wing Liberal National Party victory, I volunteered my services to the progressive left-wing national online activist group, Getup, organising polling booths, and getting an alternative view out to the Tablelands electorate. Key information handed out was in the form of a scorecard. At a glance, on entry to the booth, you could see where the main parties stood on the progressive issues of the day. The results were a disaster and I felt compelled to get back into political campaigning again.

Sara was home again and the Smiths from Charters Towers had come and gone. My sister Judith also made a visit from her home in Gippsland. Miya had won a prize in the Acacia awards and came with me, Rose, Bella and Silas, to Melbourne for a trip. Channel Billed Cuckoos, Rollers, Spangled Drongoes, Pheasant Coucals, (Rose's father called them Ang Gung), Kowels and Catbirds had arrived for the season. It was only just into October when I was struck down by dehydration. I'll recount two separate episodes.

Dehydrated

In the first instance, I had been mowing the lawn with the walk-behind mower. It was midday, getting hot and I felt a bit strange but there was only a bit left to do so I kept going. I'd only done one row and was overcome with dizziness and the need for a lie-down. I left the mower under the tree at the back corner of the shed and collapsed. Rose and Sara came home to find me in a delirious state lying flat on my back on the grass. My pupils were rolling back. Sara called the ambulance and I recall the medics saying *"We're on our way to the hospital, stay with us."* In the emergency room, I felt freezing cold and nauseous. They gave me two bags of saline intravenously in the hospital. I stayed there overnight for tests and an ECG in the morning before going home. The following day I went for a swim at Lake Eacham. I usually did a 40-minute swim, but on this occasion, I soon found that I had no energy and couldn't swim. It took a few days to fully recover.

The following episode occurred a year later, on a normal early October morning. Having got up at daybreak, fed and watered the chooks, and done an hour's weeding, I was up at the house for breakfast. Part of our discussion over breakfast was my maintenance jobs and a mountain bike ride up through the valley in the hills at the back of our place. Rose was to pack for a trip to Melbourne with Miya and the two grandchildren the next day. It was about half past eight and you could feel the air starting to warm up.

At sixty-eight, I was a minimalist with no water, wearing shorts, and thongs. I was feeling pretty fit and had covered a couple of kilometres when I did something I didn't normally do – rather than getting off to wheel the bike along the dirt track, I cycled the 300 meters from the dry creek bed to the top of the small hill. I did find it tough going and thought I'd recovered fairly quickly as I reached the top and rolled on over the crest and down the other side. The following kilometre or so was mostly flat and I took it easy as I rode towards the jump-up.

I approached the crest and rode over the top when it happened. Without any warning, I felt lightheaded and was overcome by a sort of neutral feeling, oblivious to my surroundings, headache, and nausea. I got off the bike and laid down on my back on the stony track and passed out. It seemed to be no time when I came to, vaguely aware of what was happening. The first thing I noticed was that my right arm was shiny with vomit and there was vomit all over my face and neck. In a delirious state, I struggled to a wobbly upright sitting position and vomited again.

Everything else seemed a bit blurry and I reached for my glasses which had come to rest in the dust and rocks about a metre away. Fumbling, in my delirious state, I put them on and thought that I was going blind. To my relief, I felt the encrusted remains of vomit on my glasses. I was able to clean them enough to see again and sat there to think for a few minutes about my predicament.

The sun was getting hotter and the ants closing in. Well, I'm not going to die lying here under my bike in my own vomit I thought. I managed to get back on the bike to head back home. It was only about four kilometres back but I really didn't know if I would make it but had no choice but to give it a go. Thankfully, most of the way back was downhill, I had two rest stops on the way and was so happy to have reached the safety of the front gate. In a weakened state, I got straight into the shower and drank some water before weaving my way up to the house to finally collapse onto the bed. It took a couple of days to make a full recovery. We hosted a New Year's Eve celebration at home.

A New Year's Eve

We had a fire, dinner and classic African-American 1950s swing, blues, and rock and roll in high volume, all inspired by Hoyte. Rose and I were joined by friends Jill and Richard, Grant and Lesley, Mark and Sally and sister Elaine and John. By this time, I had accumulated a number of compilations reflecting the state of my mind at the time of recording. Like Hoyte, I enjoyed my self-appointed role of DJ, using a turntable donated to me by the neighbours, a cassette tape deck given to me by Paul Brigg, two big heavy speakers bought from Mareeba and a cheap DVD player, all attached to an amplifier.

All this gear was set up in the separate part of the shed referred to as the Cultural Precinct. The precinct also housed memorabilia, sculptures, photos, Norton motorcycles and other blokey bits and pieces, all with a story for anyone interested. I have always held a preference for the use of cassette tapes for recording my compilations. My musician heroes included Chuck Berry, Slim Harpo, Little Richard, Jimmy Reed, Sonny Boy Williamson, Muddy Waters, John Lee Hooker, Bonnie Raitt, Dinah Washington, Brook Benton, Howling Wolf, T Bone Walker, Marvin Johnson and Joe Jones, Manhattan Transfer, Frank Sinatra, and Bobby Darin. At the time I was also rediscovering English musicians of the 1960s like Jethro Tull, Procol Harum, Small Faces, Rodrigues, Peter Sarstedt, Ralf McTell, Donovan, Mary Hopkins and Melanie. There was a 2.30 am finish and bacon and eggs for breakfast. It wasn't long before we were on our way to the Classic Motorcycle Festival at Hampton Downs in NZ.

Classic Racing at Hampton Downs

Rose and I were joined by friends Anne and Errol from Toowoomba. Tablelands bike club members, Mike Jeremy and Chris Wood were there as well. The racing circuit was set in a pleasant rural landscape surrounded by cows peacefully grazing on undulating hill country on the outskirts of Hampton Downs with easy parking and camping sites. There was public access to the pits. We were struck by the friendly atmosphere and the casual nature of this festival and to the credit of the organisers, it ran like clockwork. The absence of police and security guards and the friendliness of competitors and spectators alike were refreshing.

We took in many of the events from the balcony of our unit at Hampton Downs Motor-lodge directly overlooking the track. There was a good mix among riders – young and old, men and women. Fabulous racing machines included Vincent Comet, Brough Superior, Ducati, Gilera, BMW, Gold Star, Matchless, Velos, AJS, Indian, Harley and Norton, among others. The post-classic events were new to us. We were able to keep close tabs on the activities with the comprehensive souvenir program.

For example, the wonderful display of machines in the pavilion – they were like fine sculptures but even better – you can race them!

Indeed, they made the hair stand up at the back of my neck and brought tears to my eyes. The track is another story.

Friday was a practice day and on Saturday, the races kicked off a bit late as the track needed to dry out from some light early morning rain. At the start, the crackling roar of big British singles and twins, puffs of smoke and the tantalising whiff of burnt methanol are enough to drive you bonkers. Events progressed through the day – one sensational delight after another. The big singles and other bikes tore down the straight. You have to hear it to believe it!

Another important highlight of the festival was the opportunity to see the magnificent machines first-hand and have the occasional chat with owners and riders in the pits as they prepared for their particular race and checked their machines. You can appreciate the style and craftsmanship at close quarters. Race entries included Vintage and Pre War, Classic 500cc and 350cc, post Classic Junior and Senior, Classic Sidecars, Regularity parade and so on.

Guest Rider, Cameron Donald was a delight to see in action aboard his McIntosh Norton Manx 500 and 1000cc Suzuki. His performance on that 1962 Manx 500 was extraordinary. We were occasionally guilty of making comparisons with the old Pukekohe days. Sadly, those days aren't likely to return. We would have to say though, that this festival went far beyond our expectations

Home to the Neoliberals

We returned home from New Zealand to the news of, the new right-wing Liberal-National coalition (LNP) government's defunding of Environmental Defenders Offices, over 7 billion dollars of cuts to Health and Education services, subsidies and tax cuts for the high-end corporate sector and so on. It was grand theft, and most disturbing was the exposure of ongoing atrocities against innocent refugees and asylum seekers and in particular, those unfortunate enough to have arrived by boat. Families were being held in Australia's hostile offshore detention centres in Nauru and men were detained indefinitely on Manus Island at the hands of the Australian Government.

I became conscious of social decline and was deeply concerned about the direction in which society was heading. I put this down to an insidious undermining of public services and institutions. The decline in public services had gained momentum over the last three decades. It was as though we had been asleep at the wheel. Participatory democracy was under threat. We were now living under the increasing domination of transnational corporations and their representatives in the Australian parliament.

I was angry too, at the prospect of having to compromise the normal quality of life, to work unpaid, to do the job that elected representatives in government were paid to do. For example, the Prime Minister was being paid over $500k of tax payer's money to privatise our public services, give cuts and subsidies to the rich and powerful at our expense, and undermine our welfare system and everything we stood for.

My immediate response was to plan and prepare for participation in the National March in March protest, organised by March Australia, against the recently elected Neoliberal LNP government and its policies. The protest was to be held at Fogarty Park in Cairns on 15th March. So, out of anger and fear for the future of our grandchildren and the planet, I was inexorably drawn again into political activity.

Chapter 11
A Return to Politics

One thing became clear. I was committed to making a contribution to working for a just and decent society and a better world - a sustainable future. I had been struggling for some time with the idea of joining a progressive political Party and, mindful of past experience, resolved that it wasn't going to be Party politics. There were other ways of working for a better future.

It was on the 15th March in 2014 when Rose and I drove down to Cairns to take part in the March in March – the focus being - no confidence in the Abbott LNP Government. Thousands of people, nationwide, hit the streets in protest against Abbott and the Liberal National Party government's antisocial and destructive policies. Chants included – "We will we will sack ya…." and "Shame Abbott shame, not in our name…." and "1234 who's he really working for….."

No, this wasn't Party politics, and yet I felt at home and among friends in solidarity against a common foe. Yes, it was this event that confirmed the nature of my place in future political activity and we went along to a March Australia debriefing and planning meeting.

I wasn't satisfied with procedures, direction, or the progress made following the protest, or for that matter, the whole idea of being beholden to another organisation and resolved to go it alone – for now.

While I really had no idea at the time, where I was heading. A friend, Saeed de Ridder, encouraged me to subscribe to the progressive socialist Green Left Weekly and this was the catalyst for a new approach to politics. A grassroots approach

Grassroots Politics

The plan was to start with community information stalls, as a way of introduction to the public. The initial one was in Main Street in Atherton – a simple set-up with a folding table with a sign on the front reading - *"A new community group for the Tablelands - have your say on government policy"*

First public event - an information stall, Main Steet, Atherton. May, 2014.

Saeed insisted on accompanying me in case I came under attack from rednecks. Then I set up at the Tolga markets. I designed corflutes - Unite for Government that respects Human Rights; Unite for a Government that respects Natural Heritage; and so on, including Future Generations, and Fairness. We booked sites for information stalls at Tolga, Malanda and Yungaburra markets. The market stall coordinators were supportive, giving us permanent status. Rose and I would arrive at the site at 6 am on a Saturday or Sunday morning and set up our signs, information brochures, and other information and we'd hand out printed materials. I fielded questions from interested people - locals, and tourists. Some signed up as supporters. It was all about engaging the public.

Birth of a Community Group

I drafted a letter, tailored to Far North Queensland, to the editor of the local newspapers on 20th May 2014 which was published in the local Tablelander, Advertiser and Express.

TO THE EDITOR
Who do they work for?

HAVING *seen the Federal Budget, it's looking more as if nobody will benefit apart from big business.*
The new budget looks more like a continuing assault on the young, the unemployed, pensioners, and Australian families.

Since the last elections, our Federal Government doesn't seem to be on the right track with its policies. What's more, they don't seem to be listening to us. For instance, funding cuts to health and education services and selling our public utilities and other public assets to private companies doesn't sound like a good idea.

Neither does the illegal and brutal treatment of refugees, contempt for our natural heritage by dredging and dumping toxic dredge spoils onto Great Barrier Reef World Heritage property, withdrawal of funding for our Environmental Defender's Offices, attempts to delist Tasmania's World Heritage forests, ignoring the reality of climate change by supporting the massive expansion of corporate coal mining and dangerous CSG fracking and so on.

Is it our responsibility and our duty as Australian citizens, to keep tabs on our elected representatives? Is it our responsibility to remind them they are, above all else, public servants? Is it right to say our representatives in Parliament are actually employed by us, the taxpayers, to act on our behalf rather than big foreign corporations?

It may be our responsibility to inform our representatives of our concerns with issues that affect all ordinary Australians. Our representatives are among the highest paid in the world and an important part of their job is to listen and genuinely take our concerns on board.

Again, it seems our politicians aren't listening.
Only a couple of months ago, public concern about inappropriate and unfair government policy led to the March in March which was a declaration of no confidence in the Federal Government. Some 800 people turned out in Cairns.

About 100,000 people marched in all capital cities and regions across Australia with 30-50,000 people on the streets of Melbourne alone.
Our representatives in Parliament pretended that it didn't happen. Surely, it's

our job as Australian citizens to hold them accountable.
If you're concerned about expectations of government and how we can improve on the situation, to ensure our voices are heard and what we stand for is respected by our elected leaders, please contact Alan Isherwood.

It was this letter that served as the catalyst to form an alliance of people who shared similar progressive values, world views, and genuine concerns about the way things were going with regard to government policy.

The Tablelands Action Alliance (TAA)

The TAA Brochure served as a charter. The group was formed on 20th June 2014. We were a non-politically aligned, not-for-profit community group, sharing a common vision for better government policies regarding human rights, natural heritage, social justice, fairness, and a sustainable future. We worked from a grassroots perspective, complementing online campaigns.

Our communication with the wider community included community information stalls, other information events, and working with the local media. Our mission was to ensure Government policy respects, in its broadest sense - social justice, natural heritage, a sustainable future for our children, and a planet we all share.

To undertake meaningful, local actions (as individuals or collectively) that are agreed upon by participants in the group, to achieve overall objectives;

To share information and ideas with the broader community about issues associated with government policy, its impacts, alternatives, and actions that can be taken to express our concern as citizens;

To develop creative strategies for engaging with the regional community and key stakeholder groups in relation to political issues of concern to the group.

Our first initiative was a series of public information evenings on the topic of unconventional coal seam gas (CSG) extraction or fracking in the far north and its potential impacts on land and water supplies.

These sessions were held at Atherton, Yungaburra, Herberton, and Malanda.

Another initiative was to support the NOT4SALE campaign, driven by the Qld. Electrical Trades Union (ETU), against the sale of public assets, which ultimately brought down the Newman Government in the Qld. State Elections of 2015. More on that later.

The TAA was an active supporter of the Refugee Council of Australia and other national Asylum Seeker and Refugee advocacies. Then there was the ongoing national LOCKTHEGATE campaign against fracking.

All this was achieved on a shoestring budget. Our decision to support a campaign depended on among other things, access to resources like posters and other printed materials, placards, and documentaries produced or recommended by key organisations. In the absence of a keynote speaker, I'd build on our TAA brochure. We lacked the resources to mass produce anything. We got our printing of brochures, flyers and posters for public information events done by the local MP's office. I already had a screen, made an A-frame, and bought a data projector from eBay. We bought a gazebo for the market community information stalls. A banner was donated by a canvas shop in Cairns. Venues were paid for out of donations, or funded out of my personal budget.

Of the community information nights we organised, the biggest one was on the issue of fracking, at the Herberton Town Hall. About 50 people turned up for the LOCKTHEGATE documentary "Fractured Country" and a talk by the local MP. We made over $70 in donations that night. People signed up as supporters of the TAA. By 2016 there were about 60 supporters on the TAA emailing list.

Active Support - Thin on the Ground

The initial formation meetings of five or six people were critical to the development of the TAA charter in the form of a brochure. It was agreed that the TAA would not become incorporated and we didn't have a website. The TAA would fly under the radar - close to the ground. A fundamental grassroots outfit.

Attendance at meetings soon dropped away, despite our efforts to entice people along, and eventually, with the odd exception, nobody turned up at all. It wasn't difficult to make decisions, there was no conflict, and we had the support of the local media. It was all too easy. Supporters just turned up at events.

At the time, all we saw emerging from Canberra was one measure after another in the LNP Coalition's relentless drive, to transfer wealth and power from the public to the corporate sector in the form of defunding, deregulation, corporatisation, privatisation, division, diversion, scape-goating and so on.

An early TAA market stall, Malanda. July, 2014.

The TAA was essentially a family affair, where I would determine what issue to run with, on the basis of access to resources and so on, pass it by Rose, Miya and Sara, and it would go on the agenda. Updates would be emailed to local supporters who, generally, didn't respond until the day of the event. It's an appropriate time to reflect on TAAs' efforts regarding the ongoing issue of refugees and asylum seekers.

Mindful of Australia's colonial history, the legacy of our White Australia policy and current mainstream attitudes, I was never confident that campaigning for Refugee and Asylum Seeker Rights would be easy. We couldn't take on a broader global approach – it was just too big. Instead, we focused on Australia's offshore Immigration Detention Centres on Manus and Nauru Island, supporting the Refugee Council Of Australia, the Kaldor Centre for Refugee Law and the Australian Human Rights Commission.

There wouldn't be any reinventing the wheel – we already had all the resources we needed to kick off. In contrast to other issues such as fossil fuel and asset sales and so on, the Refugee issue was highly divisive. For instance, when we took on the refugee crisis we lost our only volunteer who would pick up his kit from our place and set it up at the Malanda markets and we would be along later in the morning to relieve him. His behaviour seemed strange and he was hesitant to set up the TAA stall. Our conversation that day revealed a conflict of interest. The NOT4SALE campaign had been ongoing in preparation for the Queensland State Elections called for 31st January 2015.

The TAA now concentrated its efforts in support of the Electrical Trades Union (ETU)'s formidable NOT4SALE campaign against the LNP's unpopular agenda including the sale of public assets. Our local incumbent MP enthusiastically addressed the meetings and there was plenty of media coverage. People sounded their horns in support of us at the rallies. I didn't mind clambering up roadside embankments and climbing trees along the road to nail up the NOT4SALE signs. Family members helped place brochures on windscreens. And the LNP was on the nose.

On election day, there was conflict over the legitimacy of my handing out Union brochures to voters at polling booths until union backup arrived providing proof that all our printed materials had been cleared by the Qld. Electoral Commission prior to the announcement of elections.

It was on the 31st of January and we held an election night special here at home. It was a very close contest with Labor scraping in to form a minority government with the support of an independent. The TAA was also invited to attend ALP victory celebrations in Cairns in appreciation of our support during the campaign.

As things returned to normal, I began to tire of the lack of support in preparations and setting up at markets and information nights and we revised our basic approach. The plan was to close the market information stalls and our last community information evening was in late September 2015. A long-term resident with good solid rapport with the community and local media lead me to believe that life on the campaign trail was about to get a bit easier.

A New Approach

I promoted the TAA and its services targeting community groups and organisations offering screenings of film documentaries, keynote speakers, and question and answer sessions on controversial human rights issues like the refugee crisis, and so on. Half the battle was to have a captive audience and venue rather than having to do all the organising like phone calls, promotion, hiring a venue, and doing all the associated leg work involving posting notices and flyers along the main streets in the towns and so on.

So it was on the 5th of October that I confidently and enthusiastically set to and drafted a generic letter to 17 different Tablelands organisations. These groups included churches, CWAs, Lions, Rotary clubs etc. Letters were individually emailed and hand-delivered. Here's the letter:

Tablelands Action Alliance
5th October 2015

We are planning a series of community information evenings within the Tablelands region and would like to provide a brief introductory session about our new Community Group, the Tablelands Action Alliance (TAA) and other important current issues which may be of interest to members of your organisation and the wider community.
We are a non-politically aligned, not-for-profit community group that shares

a common vision for better government policies regarding human rights, natural heritage, social justice, fairness and a sustainable future. We work from a grassroots perspective, complementing online campaigns. We meet on a bi-monthly basis. Our communication with the wider community includes community information stalls, other information events and working with the local media. For further information, please refer to our brochure enclosed.

One of the issues we are currently addressing and advocating for, is compassionate treatment of asylum seekers and refugees.
We would be willing to arrange a screening of a 52-minute documentary for your members and other interested guests, should you be supportive of this. The documentary, "Between the Devil and the Deep Blue Sea" is recommended by the Refugee Council of Australia. The film looks at the circumstances and decisions that lead someone to become a "boat person". We will be also engaging a guest speaker where possible.

The overall purpose of this information session is to provide members/residents with a better understanding of the impacts of inappropriate policy with regard to asylum seekers and refugees in light of our international human rights obligations. The session would include time for relevant questions, answers and discussion. We would also provide brochures and other information for people to follow up on relevant topics of further interest.

We would be grateful if you could nominate some possible dates and times when it would be suitable for us to attend and deliver this presentation to your members/residents. We are willing to come to your meeting venue and would need access to a power point for our data projector. The duration of the session would not exceed two hours. Entry fees are not required, however, a gold coin donation to cover costs will be most appreciated.

We look forward to hearing from you and would be pleased to provide further information and details if required.

There was no response.

This was followed by a few months' break from campaigning so that I could get back to normal life including progressing this autobiography.

We were later invited through word of mouth to present at the Mareeba Mosque and the Atherton-based Bahai group. Our presentations were well received.

On the 10th of August 2016, the Nauru Files exposed the

atrocities being committed against women and children being held in Australia's Immigration Detention Centre in Nauru at the hands of the Federal LNP government. On the 11th of August, ABC reporter Fran Kelly exposed the failure of the Australian Census after the Treasurer and the Prime minister of the day had defunded the Australian Bureau of Statistics and gave the private company IBM $9.6 million in taxpayers money to conduct the census.

On the 16th of August the same year, ABC 's Q and A program ran a screening of the film documentary, Leaky Boat, exposing more government atrocities against Refugees and Asylum seekers attempting to seek refuge here in Australia. These reports were met with denial, and aggressive attacks, by the government, against the Australian Human Rights Commissioner.

The refugee crisis suddenly escalated late in November of the following year with the closure of the Manus Detention Centre. Activists were encouraged to call the PM's office asking him to intervene to ensure the safety of the hundreds of men in the centre, fearful of attack by locals. Like many others, horrified at these reports, I called the PM's office saying:

"I understand that the crisis on Manus Island has escalated with the Detention Centre being stormed by PNG police with injuries and arrests of refugees and asylum seekers, forcing them to relocate to unsafe accommodation. These human rights abuses have to stop now. Please bring the refugees and asylum seekers here to safety now."

This call was met with hostility. The staffer answering the phone said that she was "not prepared to be talked at" and put the phone down. There were many others who had a similar experience. Refugees and Asylum seekers trapped in the Island prison camps of Manus and Nauru continue to suffer under the brutality of the Australian Government.

I first wrote to Kyihan Abdi on Manus Island in 2014, through the office of Julian Burnside QC, a Refugee and Asylum Seeker Advocate. Here is a second letter I wrote on 30th November 2015:

Mr. Kyihan Abdi
Lorrengau 541 Manus Island, PNG
GRL-32, Manus Island Detention Centre.

Dear Kyihan,
It's now over 18 months since we last wrote to you and we're sorry that this letter has taken so long.
It seems that little has changed regarding the plight of asylum seekers and refugees on Manus Island, Christmas Island and Nauru and circumstances have probably worsened.
We remain ashamed and sickened by the continued atrocities being committed against refugees and asylum seekers in Australian offshore detention camps.
We are continuing our campaign work in support of Australian asylum seekers and refugee advocacies, with plans to run public information nights starting in January 2016. Our offer to community organisations such as churches, charities and clubs, includes a brief introduction, screening of the documentary film "Between the Devil and the Deep Blue Sea", (recommended by the Australian Refugee Council), keynote speaker (where possible) and questions and answers session.
We are also running ongoing public information displays at local markets, most weekends.

Again, we want you to know that our hearts and our thoughts go out to you. We encourage you to stay strong and hopeful for the future. There is more information coming to the mainstream media about Australia's inhumane treatment of refugees and asylum seekers in offshore detention camps. So more people will become aware and there will be a change for the better. If you get this letter, please write to us so that we can maintain contact with you. Stay strong.

There was no reply and we lost contact. The refugee crisis has been going on for so long that it could be that brutality towards others has become normalised in Australian society. There has to be a better way of addressing it. It was way back in 2001 under the Howard Government that current policies were introduced and over the decades, become more oppressive and brutal. TAA supported the protracted Refugee and Asylum Seeker Rights campaign.

We held a vigil in memory of Hamid Kehazaei and his fellow refugees and asylum seekers murdered in Australian offshore Immigration Detention Centres on Manus Island and Nauru. They had fallen victim to the continuing atrocities committed against innocent refugees and asylum seekers.

There was a poor local response to our campaign in support of the Refugee Council of Australia.

There were other issues on the boil as well, for example, government support for powerful fossil fuel interests at the expense of renewable energy and at the risk of large-scale environmental damage among other things. The TAA had supported the National LOCKTHEGATE movement against unconventional coal seam gas extraction (CSG) since its formation in 2014.

An Invitation

As part of our change in strategy, we had written to the new Tablelands Regional Council regarding an invitation to the TAA to provide an information session on the topic of CSG. The purpose of the information session was to encourage the council to follow the lead of other progressive local governments to declare the Tablelands region CSG-free.

It was a year later, in early June 2017 that we were invited to present. In all, there were nine participants. The presentation included a screening of the LOCKTHEGATE film documentary Fractured Country, a question and answer session and the provision of printed materials. The session seemed to go well. The Mayor ended the session by declaring that it was a learning experience and spoke of supporting the TAA in this instance. Late in December, there hadn't been a response. But these things take time and there were other issues to deal with, like the #STOPADANI campaign.

The #STOPADANI Campaign

We started work on the #STOPADANI campaign back in July. Similar in structure to NOT4SALE in the leadup to the previous Qld. State election. It was a powerful campaign. The Qld Government were forced to veto a Commonwealth Government decision to make a billion dollars of tax payer's money available to Adani. Adani was to build a railway line from their proposed mine site to their coal port on the World Heritage Great Barrier Reef coast.

The TAA attended rallies in Cairns and organised rallies in Atherton. For instance, there was a synchronised National, Stop Adani demonstration on Tuesday 25 July from 12 – 2 pm. outside the Commonwealth Banks (CBA)s around Australia. We set up a protest in front of the Atherton (CBA) to encourage the bank to do the right thing for the community and the planet by not funding this project. It all worked. Within two weeks of the national protests, the CBA announced that they were not funding Adani. The following story was published in the local newspaper:

The Tablelands Action Alliance supports the National Stop Adani campaign. We don't want the Commonwealth Bank to fund the Adani company's dangerous and polluting mega coal mine planned for the Galilee Basin, southwest of Bowen.
According to Stop Adani.com, twelve of the world's largest banks have already said no to Adani's mega mine. In Australia, Westpac and NAB have ruled out contributing to this destructive climate disaster.
The Adani company do not have the consent of the Wangan and Jagalingou people whose ancestral lands, water and culture would be destroyed by the mine.

Climate change puts the World Heritage Great Barrier Reef at risk. Warming waters killed 29% of shallow corals in 2016 and a similar result is expected from 2017's excessive heat. The mine would see 500 extra coal ships moving through the reefs each year risking groundings and spills.

Politicians claim the project would generate 10,000 jobs. Adani's own report projects a net average of only 1,464 employee full-time jobs. Adani's CEO claims the process would be automated from mine to port.
Adani's Carmichael mine would be the Southern Hemisphere's largest coal mine. If the project goes ahead, it would rank as the world's seventh biggest contributor of CO_2 pollution, putting more pressure on the Reef and risking 69,000 tourism jobs.

Adani has been granted unlimited free access to precious groundwater for 60 years and would extract billions of litres each year causing irreversible damage to groundwater systems. Source – Stop Adani.com.)

I felt fortunate that we had family members around for mutual support in uncertain and hostile times. There was Christmas Eve and Christmas Day at Miya and Dugan's, to share Christmas with Bella and Silas. Sara flew up from the Sunshine Coast for a couple of weeks to participate in our family celebrations. Other family members joined us on the Tablelands. Rose and I really enjoyed having our grandchildren, Bella and Silas here and they often slept over.

Old Friends Come to Visit

It was during the Easter of 2016 that our friend John Humphreys came to visit. We all spent quality time together and John took in the local haunts including the Herberton Heritage Village. Rose and I took John for a visit up to Cooktown as he wanted to explore more of Capt. James Cook. I found it a bit odd, that John was fascinated by the achievements of Captain Cook. Cook came close to losing everything when his wooden warship struck a coral reef and the crew managed to temporarily repair the gaping hole in the hull. The crew had to throw some cannons overboard in order to float the ship clear of the reef and sail into the mouth of the Endeavor River, to fix the hull. On behalf of the British Colonial Office, Captain Cook then continued his claiming of our First Nations country as he sailed up the East Coast without so much as a by your leave. We stayed in the Seaview Motel and spent a day in the old Catholic Convent - now the Cooktown Museum.

I had prepared my bikes for John's visit and later took him on a motorcycle cruise around the southern Tablelands. John handled the Norton 500 single with confidence. I took my Commando. For John, the cruise around the elevated tropical southern Tablelands, on a 1949 classic Norton 500 single was the highlight of his Australian visit. We all stayed at Ellis Beach north of Cairns for his last night before his departure.

Friends Pia and Franz from Switzerland came during the second week of John's stay and we enjoyed good times together. A swing and African American blues music night, in the moonlight, amidst the shadows of the rainforest by the fire marked Pia and Franz's departure. Darby and Lyn arrived soon after.

Darby, the childhood friend whom I've already talked about, came for a visit in mid-October 2017. Darby and his wife Lyn had been running a small supermarket in the remote town of Swifts Creek in Northeastern Victoria, since the 1970s. Darby maintained a lifelong interest in gold and small-scale gold mining. They stayed with us for five days and Lyn was pleased to be able to catch up with her old friend, my sister, Judith, who wasn't well and now a resident in Atherton. In her capacity as Civil Celebrant, Rose conducted a Renewal of Vows ceremony for Darby and Lyn, and I took pictures of the occasion for them. This time with photos of the event.

Family Matters

My sister Judith's daughter Gabi and her family had recently moved to the Tablelands from Melbourne. I was increasingly concerned for Judith's welfare and continued to encourage her to relocate to the Far North where she could be closer to family. Here is a letter I wrote to Judith, back in 2012.

Dear Judith,
As usual, it was good to talk with you on the phone the other day and I'm relieved to hear that you've had further tests. I understand that you've had a pretty rough time lately and also glad to hear that while you're still very tired, you're on the mend, if not entirely out of the woods. I write to share my concerns with you and please understand that it's not my intention to offend or upset you.

We've all lived separate and very different lives. My life experience has taught me to value my family above all else. Our parents and the Yapa and Yolngu people we got to know, more than anything else have informed the development of such values and world views. Among other things, my current concerns are that my grandchildren grow to enjoy life in a healthy and sustainable future. This presents the greatest challenge I've ever been faced with.

On a more personal level, as I begin to come to terms with my own mortality, my vision for the future is about consolidation. Part of this vision is where we're able to maintain strength in rallying together to provide comfort and security for each other in the face of an increasingly uncertain and hostile world. Let me say something as an example of this vision.

We're a powerful family. Sara's returned to the North, you and Elaine are here on a visit, spending time with us and we share the simple pleasure of telling our stories over a nice cup of tea by the fire. We gather and listen to you play on Dad's piano, familiar songs heard in childhood – perhaps, songs without words. I'm making progress with your help with some learning strategies on the piano. There is an ongoing discussion as we view early photos. Our writing is progressing at a good pace. We share gardening, the production of veggies and have many meals together. We share life. Mum and Dad and Grandpa find great pleasure in this.

Judith, I'm sure that Gabby and your little nephews, as they approach adolescence, would benefit from seeing more of you. Certainly, Miya and Sara, would love to be part of our family tradition by learning, among other things how you create those wonderful characters in knitted wool. Bella and Silas would also love to have another Grandma to pass on all that knowledge and skills that would otherwise be lost to the family. I'm sure that you would find great pleasure and satisfaction in being part of their growth and development through childhood to becoming young, well-grounded and informed adults who will in turn pass on this gift that you've bestowed on them. I could go on, but I'm sure you get my drift here. Everyone stands to benefit.

I'm sure that like me, you have considered these things as we approach a turning point in our lives, I'm 67 and you're 70. I understand that you're currently in a state of recovery from a severe bout of pneumonia and possible heart attack – a life-threatening condition and very tired or perhaps exhausted. I also understand that you are a foster parent caring for other people's children who suffer from severe trauma.

Please forgive me for thinking that this is unsustainable, that the chances of your remaining fully functional for much longer are diminishing and unless you're able to make a transition while you can and while other family members are fit enough to help, we may not even see each other again. I understand that Elaine and John are committed to moving to the Tablelands. Should you decide to make the transition and move to the North, I'm prepared to help with that and I'm sure the rest of the family would do the same. At the end of the day, we all tend to do the best we can in life. You can make this transition. It's doable.
Love from
Alan

Perhaps I should have written earlier. Judith did eventually make the move up North and bought a duplex in Atherton. But soon, by the end of January 2018, Judith, now 75, her health had deteriorated to the extent that she could no longer live independently.

Judith moved into the Carinya nursing home and had a stint in the medical ward at Atherton Hospital. She was suffering from recurring episodes of lung infection. Rose was working at Community Services Tablelands and gave help with services, and aged care needs.

Progressive politics was always on the horizon and in the interest of maximising the effectiveness of campaign work, over the coming weeks into 2018, I engaged in some research towards a better understanding of global apathy towards the modern crises. George Monbiot, 2017 'Out of the Wreckage – A New Politics for an Age of Crisis' and Naomi Klein's 2017 'This Changes Everything' and 'No is Not Enough,' served as my starting point.

Politics in the Pub

It was on Saturday 31st of March 2018 that the TAA and the Cairns branch of the Socialist Alliance held a Politics in the Pub weekend at a popular hotel on the main street in town. The pub was sometimes referred to as 'your thinking man's pub' and we made a point of supporting the pub by bringing friends for a good meal, a Guinness on tap, or a function.

I set up the Tablelands Action Alliance banner along with STOPADANI and other relevant printed information in the main entrance foyer. The session was all about engaging with people who shared progressive politics and various related concerns. The session went well.

It was also at this time that the STOPADANI movement was gathering pace and we brought printed materials and signs to the markets and held info nights with documentary screenings at cafés in Atherton, Yungaburra, Malanda, and Herberton.

It was early that year when Judith's doctor and family made the decision for Judith not to transfer yet again to the hospital for further treatment because of physical and emotional distress. The doctor would provide care for Judith at the nursing home.

Judith has Passed Away

Judith passed away on 23rd of April 2018. We held a family wake for her with a fireside gathering to celebrate her life. I played Mendelssohn and Bach, Rachmaninov, and her other piano favourites. I'd prepared a simple shrine for her in the form of a large candle-lit photo of Judith and Mum in happier times in the backyard at Ringwood during the early 1960s. Judith's children, Victor and Nikki flew up from Melbourne to attend the occasion.

By the middle of 2018 a trend had developed where the TAA was also represented in Cairns-based campaigns on Refugee Rights, Union activity, and other events as well as our Tableland events such as ongoing screenings market stalls, and other public events.

More Campaigning

A Climate rally at Atherton TRC office in support of the Victorian bushfire victims. 2019. Photographer unknown.

By mid-March in 2019 with the Federal elections only nine weeks away, campaign work was gathering pace. The focus was on Adani, Climate, and Refugee Rights. I organised an information stall at Yungaburra markets. The TAA attended the Australian Marine Conservation Society's Climate Election launch in Cairns.

Friday 15th of March saw TAA members taking part in a student lead street-march in Cairns and a rally in Atherton. At Atherton State High School, students were restricted to marching around the school oval. A pointless exercise I thought, but a start, and with some commitment and organisation, we would get out on the street next time.

The 10th of April the same year, saw the TAA taking part in the ACTU Union National Change the Rules campaign protest for fair wage rises, and better job security - "Change the Rules – Change the Government". The rally was held outside the front of local Federal MP Warren Entsch's office in Mulgrave Street Cairns. We scheduled our Atherton Climate Roadshow for 3.30 pm on 7th of May, using the Land Rover for displaying signs mounted on the back. We took a short break for a trip south to visit friends.

Rose and I flew to Adelaide on 15th of April to visit friends and then catch the Indian Pacific to Broken Hill and on to Sydney to visit Werner and Lisa at Wagstaffe. Then we took a train to Tamworth to visit Bruce and Kate, next on to Toowoomba to visit Anne and Errol, and Brisbane to Rose's sister Lily and finally home.

A New Allegiance

For me, the anti-capitalist movement was making sense in the context of relentless social and environmental destruction. We got to know members of the Cairns branch of the Socialist Alliance (SA) and I was inspired by them. Rose and I found ourselves participating in SA public street marches, rallies, and meetings as part of the national and global movement for Refugee and Asylum Seeker Rights, the #STOPADANI movement, and the Climate Crisis. The SA and supporters reciprocated by coming to the Tablelands to join the TAA in similar actions, online and in the streets. We were all actively supporting progressive Unions as well.

By mid-June, we were preparing for another trip to see Parry in Darwin and Yapa at Lajamanu. Sara and her partner Dave came as well. Miya, Dugan, Bella, and Silas had left earlier on a road trip across to the Kimberleys. We met them at the crossing at Kalkaringi (Wave Hill) and camped overnight. We all drove south to Lajamanu the following morning.

Apart from catching up with past students and the Warlpiri families we knew, we were concerned about the impacts of the Howard Government's racist Intervention policy and the threat of fracking. I understood that in practice, the Intervention policy made vast tracts of Warlpiri and other First Nations land available to transnational mining interests.

I spent time with the staff at the Learning Centre and a lot of time with Neil Cook Jupurrula, who was working in the local Warnayaka Arts Centre with Louisa and local artists producing traditional stories on canvas for distribution and sale. We also caught up with Neil's brother Albert, their father, Henry, and others we had known in the past. The opportunity for Bella and Silas to meet the Warlpiri people was valuable.

We drove out to Emu waterhole with Neil the following day – I'd never seen it before.

I visited the staff at the Central Land Council (CLC) office and initially, they seemed friendly enough. That was, until, I mentioned I was planning a public screening outside the Art Centre, of an anti-fracking documentary along with historic images of life at Lajamanu during the early 1970s. The CLC staff seemed suspicious and took it upon themselves to attend our screening. On the night, no Yapa turned up – only the three CLC people.

I began the session with images of the 1970s slide show of past students engaged in school activities. The CLC staff soon left. Soon after, when the Warlpiri mob turned up, we switched over to the documentary – Brendan Shoebridge's, "The Bentley Effect", which we recently screened in Cairns and on the Tablelands. They enjoyed the documentary and Warlpiri Elder Jerry Jangala hit the nail on the head when he commented on the film being essentially about "people power".

While it was a small attendance at the screening, I was pleased with the response and level of understanding of the threat of fracking in the Northern Territory. When we got home I wasted no time in contacting filmmaker, Brendan Shoebridge for more copies for Neil, Jerry and others to distribute among the Yapa, from Lajamanu in the North to Yuendumu in the South. We ran a fundraiser for Brendan to help pay for his amazing and inspiring production.

Once home again it was back into campaign work, consciousness-raising at the Yungaburra market stall, and continued public screenings of the Bentley Effect and other documentaries.

TAA Yungaburra Market stall, 2019. Photographer unknown.

A couple of examples of the wording for signage used in our street marches, rallies, community screenings, and fundraisers were *Our Capitalist System – Incompatible with Life on Earth* and *Corporate Greed = Climate Disaster.* It was also during this period that we had begun making adaptations to the already changing climate.

I was painting the house an off-white colour which deflected much of the heat from the western side of the house. I also had insulation installed in the roof cavity. I installed roller screens, designed using aluminium agricultural pipe from the farm across the creek and 80% shade mesh at the back of the house. We installed an air conditioner the following year. All this made the house more comfortable during the increasingly hot and humid days of November to April. For me, the days of sleeping under a doona during the summer months were pretty much a thing of the past. A new and powerful movement was emerging.

School Strike for Climate (SS4C)

Danish school student, Greta Thunberg built a global climate movement under the slogan of #SCHOOLSTRIKE4CLIMATE. (SS4C) A global action was scheduled for 20th September, and it was on that day that the TAA organised its first SS4C public rally. About thirty TAA members turned up at the Atherton roundabout armed with a TAA banner and powerful and colourful signs and chants demanding climate action. SA members from Cairns also joined us. Local high school students attended. The ETU, local left-wing Labor Party members and the Greens Party participated. In all, about 60 people turned up to join the students. The support from passing motorists was encouraging - some motorists drove around the roundabout twice with thumbs up out the window to show their support, while others sounded their horns in support. We gained full front-page coverage in the local Tablelander newspaper. Our chanted message to governments was clear - *"Climate Action Now", "Fund our future, not fossil fuels"* and *"When our planet's under attack, what do we do? Stand up Fight back"* and #STOPADANI.

It was about this time that Sara bought a big mobile kitchen, fully equipped with a pizza oven and other processing machines and equipment, fully fitted inside in food-grade stainless steel. Sara's partner, Dave, helped with the towing of the food van. Their first regular engagement was at the Humpy – a popular roadside fruit and veg shop selling local produce. After Dave left, Rose and I filled the gap, helping with preparation, sales orders and so on. Bella also helped in the food van. Sara developed her own web page and sold pizzas and other delicious food for social and community events.

Rose and I flew down to Brisbane and on to Toowoomba to visit Anne and Errol Klibbe. Anne had retired from her nursing job in Oakey sometime before. She was suffering from an aggressive form of Parkinson's disease along with other complications and we were shocked to see her in such a state. She was stooped almost at right angles and could scarcely walk. Anne passed away in late May 2019. Errol had been a full-time carer for her and was now recovering from grief and loss. We spent a few days with Errol and his family including his son Henry and his wife, Angela. I helped Errol with the pruning of his fruit trees in his backyard.

By mid-November, we were planning a School Strike for Climate (SS4C) public event – a first, for Atherton and the Tablelands.

It was on 29th November when over 60 TAA supporters turned up for our Sit-In at the Atherton Silo shopping centre, in solidarity with all those who were affected by the climate-induced, catastrophic bushfires in Victoria and NSW earlier in the year. Following the Sit In was a march and rally outside the Tablelands Regional Council (TRC) office and the presentation of a Climate Action letter to the Council.

Christmas for us was quality time with the family. Our policy was not to travel during this time of the year because of the risks involved with the hot weather, cyclones and so on. Sara was home and we picked Rose's sister Lily up from the train at Gordonvale. We had a swim in the Little Mulgrave River on the way home up the Gillies range. Sara was getting catering contracts for her mobile kitchen.

Miya was on time off, having enjoyed a successful work year as she transitioned towards her private consultancy. Grandchildren, Silas and Bella, were also in transition from homeschooling back to school and the classroom culture.

The following year – 2020 was dogged by the Covid 19 pandemic and the impacts of Climate change. There was a tide of Climate and Covid refugees escaping from the coast and the southern states with the hope of a tree change and a future in the Far North. During this time, there was a transformation of the landscape occurring here on the Tablelands and it has had a negative impact on our quality of life. It could be described as a corporate frontier, characterised by an incoming tide of thousands of disconnected souls in a desperate struggle for basic quality of life no longer possible in the major southern urban centres.

The small rural town of Atherton was being smothered by runaway urban development, putting pressure on local services. Small family businesses were being consumed by the juggernauts. Harvey Norman, KFC, Dominoes, McDonald's, Bunnings, Supercheap, Big W, IGA and further expansion of Toyota and other car yards have sprung up, seemingly out of nowhere. There are new parking lots and road upgrades with concrete refuges like bunkers in the middle of the road for pedestrians but no new pedestrian crossings. Local roads are no longer safe because of reckless driving and the increase in cars and trucking.

Atherton in particular is being hit hard with low-cost housing development and other development. The rapid increase in population is most evident in the build-up of traffic in the town.

Extensive high-density concrete block housing estates are spreading like cancer across prime agricultural land on the outskirts of the town. Beyond the town limits, other more insidious changes are playing out. Traditional small-scale dairy and cropping are disappearing in the wake of large-scale agribusiness involving avocadoes and blueberries, among other things. Due largely to state deregulation, remaining local farmers are forced to find employment outside the farm and lease out their land to large-scale monocropping. The State fast-tracks development. Is anyone concerned? Does anyone care?

It was at around this period that the dominant Murdoch press was closing down its regional newspapers and we lost the support of our local journalist and the Tablelander print news outlet. Cairns media outlets found it too arduous to take the trip up the range leaving us at the mercy of social media.

Miya's help and support were critical at this point in the Climate campaign. Miya and Rose helped with the editing of letters, emails and other correspondence and Miya developed a PowerPoint presentation for a local council meeting prior to the local government elections adding a powerful and professional approach.

It was also during this time that we were organising public screenings of the Greenpeace production – Dirty Power – a powerful expose' of dodgy dealings between the State and the fossil fuel industry. Screenings were held in cafés and public venues across the southern Tablelands. But it was the street marches and rallies that had the most impact on the public. The Tablelands community had no past experience with grassroots democracy in action. Responses were varied but generally supportive

The National School Strike for Climate (#SS4C) event, planned for the 22nd of February would be a three-pronged approach focusing on the Tablelands Regional Council's (TRC) inaction on climate. We met at the old RSL building. We were covered by the Peaceful Assemblies Act and local police were supportive. There was a march up the Main Street of Atherton, a U-turn at the police station, and a return via Jack Street, and Railway Lane, down into the park and roundabout for a rally, with live music and guest speakers. It was drizzling on the day when the police arrived, providing an escort front and rear of the procession.

TAA SS4C March up along Main Street Atherton, 2020.
Photograph courtesy of Greg Sorenson.

Following on from the success of this event, another public demonstration was planned for 15th May but had to be cancelled due to Covid restrictions.

On Saturday 25 July, a public march and rally were held, compliant with COVID-19 safety requirements. There was positive feedback from all in attendance and a high level of support for stronger action on climate at the local level. We hand-delivered the following letter to the Tablelands Regional Council (TRC) as part of the campaign.

On behalf of the Tablelands Action Alliance (TAA) I wanted to thank you for your support to date with our collective efforts to progress meaningful action on climate change. I also want to take this opportunity to provide you with a brief update on the campaign so far and since our presentation to TRC on 28 May 2020.

As you are aware, on Saturday 25 July, a rally was held, compliant with COVID-19 safety requirements and the provisions of the Peaceful Assembly Act 1992 (Qld). There was very positive feedback from all in attendance and a high level of support for stronger action on climate at the local level.
A number of guest speakers presented, including Peter Valentine, Adjunct Professor, at James Cook University, and Elise Springett from the Australian Marine Conservation Society. Youth were well represented at the rally, with students, Tessa and Shizuki presenting a powerful case for action on climate to protect the fundamental human rights of children and future generations.

I am also pleased to provide you with a copy of and link to a recent petition calling for TRC to take action on climate change, including:
1. participating in the free Climate Resilient Councils initiative, and
2. leading the development of a Climate Resilience Strategy to reduce local greenhouse gas emissions and facilitate adaptation to the impacts of climate change.

The petition has so far attracted over 520 signatures and further demonstrates to Council the strong levels of community concern about climate change, and the importance of a climate-safe future for our communities, children, and natural environment.

The call to action is consistent with TAA's correspondence to TRC Councillors and staff late in 2019, to prospective candidates, and with our recent presentation to TRC. It is also consistent with TRC's obligations and good governance requirements and will ensure TRC is well-placed to proactively manage the impacts of climate change in all its planning, decision-making and operations.

I would be grateful for your advice as to how we can most effectively deliver this petition to Council, and if any further assistance might be required on our part to ensure it is taken into account and that things are progressed accordingly.

As you are aware, taking action to address climate change has the potential to reduce energy expenditures, improve food and water security, build community health and well-being, and stimulate local job creation and economic recovery.

As a minimum, we would hope to see TRC join most of the local governments across Queensland, including its neighbouring Councils, taking part in the Climate Resilient Councils initiative, as a matter of priority. This initiative will help to ensure that Council is acting from an informed basis moving forward.

A Climate Resilience Strategy is also imperative to help Council and the community to mitigate and adapt to climate change impacts. In the interim, as a minimum, we would hope that climate considerations are included as key themes in the revised Corporate Plan and Community Plan.

We look forward to collaborating further with TRC, to progress these important priorities for Council, the community and the Tablelands as a region.

Yours sincerely,
Alan Isherwood

The TAA was actively supported in the Climate campaign by the Cairns branch of the Socialist Alliance (SA) and its supporters. The SA brought the Cairns Climate Choir for the marches to maximise impact. As it happens, the TRC did eventually join the Climate Resilient Councils program but was not under any obligation to progress to any community action and simply adopted a business-as-usual approach to the ongoing climate crisis. Attempts at working collaboratively with the state bureaucracy weren't working. It was time to seek out a new approach to working for change.

The Socialist Alliance (SA)

We joined the Socialist Alliance (SA) and became members of the Cairns branch after ratification in early January 2021. We registered for the online SA National Conference. I also renewed our Yungaburra market monthly information stall. We were also in touch with Frontline Action against Coal (FLAC) organisers planning a trip to the front line for the #STOPADANI campaign at Camp Binbee.

Front Line Against Coal (FLAC)

It was the 7th of April when we drove with Miya Bella and Silas down to Camp Binbee, west of Bowen. We were representing the TAA and friends from Cairns and the Tablelands. We arrived late in the afternoon at the homestead and outbuildings set in a picturesque open forest. Camp Binbee was a special place. We found a surprising level of sophistication in the way in which the place was organised and run on a daily basis.

As well as day-to-day arrivals and departures, semi-permanent volunteers organised rosters for orientation and training of activists, infrastructure maintenance, the kitchen and mess areas, IT and media, public relations, police liaison, toilets, showers, maintenance workshop, veggie gardens, accommodation, and camping ground. Volunteers were rostered onto tasks like painting banners, drafting press releases, and other printed materials.

There was also a place, under-cover, dedicated to meetings where planning decisions were made and activists planned their actions against the Adani coal mine and its infrastructure. For example, activists would nominate themselves for direct involvement and others would have a support role for a particular action, be it a lock-on or blockade. We nominated for upcoming direct action.

Bella and I volunteered to participate in the blockade of the work site of the contractors building the Adani coal railway line. Specific tasks were allocated, such as who was driving, food and drinks, internal communication, media, photography, who would be arrested or fined, and so on. In all, there were about 15 activists involved.

On the FLAC Blockade April 2021. Photographer unknown.

In view of our limited experience, we were allocated minor roles like erecting the gazebo, helping put up banners, making food and drinks available, and joining the chants.

It all seemed to run like clockwork. The call to action, in the form of a large suspended oxy-acetylene bottle, rang out precisely at 2.45 am. Activists had finished breakfast and were ready to go at 3.15 am. I travelled in the troop carrier and Bella was on the bus. It was a bumpy ride along the rough, dusty, dirt road through the remote bush. We arrived at the rail construction site just before daybreak, having been followed for the last 10 kilometres by Adani security agents.

Workers' vehicles were blocked from entering the construction site as they arrived. Security workers took videos of the proceedings to hand over to police as evidence when the police arrived from Collinsville some hours later.

We set up the gazebo and fixed our colourful anti-Adani banners along the high mesh fence. A Cairns activist was set up about 50 metres inside the compound with a banner across the road to block the workers' access to the site. We sang protest songs and chants, took pictures and videos for the media and chatted with the workers. You could see that the workers and security people were now accustomed to the routine and were quite friendly – even voicing concern about the welfare of the activists working with limited protection against the heat of the day and so on.

Police arrived around 10 am, established their authority and began the routine process of making arrests and issuing fines. It was close to midday before the activist was processed, loaded into the back of the police wagon and driven off, back to the Collinsville police station for further processing. We were to pick her up on the way back after she was released. Processing at the police station took a couple of hours and while we were waiting we had a walk around the streets of this coal-mining town. While out on the street, I was directed to turn my #STOPADANI t-shirt inside out to avoid coming under attack or other hostility from the coal miners in the town.

We all returned safely to Camp Binbee late in the afternoon for the debriefing and unpacking and the next day we made the trip back home.

On reflection, the most bizarre thing that happened at the blockade was that as part of one of their last tasks on site, the police confiscated most of the banners from the fence, on the grounds that we had our fingers inside the compound in order to tie and secure the banners to the mesh fence. That constituted trespassing. There was a standard fee for the return of the banners. Our TAA banner was saved only because by pure chance, it had been used to block the workers' vehicles at the entrance and I didn't bother putting it back up on the fence.

It was a valuable experience for us. I thought of it as a normalised ritual procedure – a media stunt – the action was remote and too long a distance for the media to come, leaving Facebook as the main conduit to the public. These actions against the fossil fuel industry have been going on for years with seemingly limited success. Perhaps the delays caused by the actions are simply factored into Adani's operational budget. The National #STOP ADANI campaigns did have a measure of success in that the company changed its brand name.

According to Marxist theory, and how it applies to the modern crises, in relation to FLAC blockades, lock-ons and other actions are ultra-leftist tactics and not designed to reach the public. Such blockades are an attempt to influence the ruling elite and appeal to a perceived better nature of the dominant capitalists and the people that represent them in the parliament. On reflection, the Adani blockade we participated in, was just that - a game plan to the letter, from the moment the security people, workers, and police showed up to act out their roles as if part of a one-act play. Perhaps we need a revolution.

Below is a media release covering our latest climate action event.
Students Hold Mass Strike to Protest PM Morrison Throwing Cash at Gas.
Friday, May 21st - school students in Atherton will join tens of thousands of students and supporters nationwide as part of the first national school strike since Covid-19, demanding that the Morrison Government says no to funding dangerous gas and coal projects, and instead invests in clean renewable energy, secure jobs and First Nations solutions to protect Country.

Today's National Strike marks the biggest climate protest since Covid-19, with dozens of strikes taking place *in capital cities, regional centres and country towns across the continent. The day is being organised by the School Strike 4 Climate network, with support from First Nations communities, unions, parents, and everyday Australians.*

Federal government subsidies to fossil fuel corporations reached $10.3 billion last financial year. *That's $19,686 a minute, spent on fossil fuel subsidies. (Australia Institute. 27th April 2021) and if the new Federal budget is anything to go on, it looks like more of the same.*

Spokesperson, Alan Isherwood said "The Morrison Government could be protecting our climate, land and water, and creating thousands of new jobs by growing Australia's renewable energy sector and backing First Nations solutions to protect Country. Instead, they are lining the pockets of multinational gas companies, which are fueling the climate crisis, devastating our land and water, wrecking our health and creating very few jobs. We're striking to tell the Morrison Government that if they care about our future, they must stop throwing money at gas."

You are invited to join the action for photo, video and interview at 4 pm on 21st May in Atherton's Main Street and at the Parklands next to the Cook Street roundabout, Atherton.
Media enquiries: Alan Isherwood.
More info: Visit the national day of action website: SS4C.info/May21.

There was no response from the local media.

*School Strike for Climate march, Main Street Atherton, May 2021.
Photograph courtesy of Paul Gobert.*

It was late in November that we held an SA event at our property. It was a fireside get-together to welcome new members from Cairns and the Tablelands and raise campaign funds for the upcoming Federal election.

Sara sold pizzas and I organised recorded music by the fire out the back, amidst the rainforest. Here is an extract from my address to new members.

On behalf of all present here today, I pay my respect to the traditional custodians of this land, the Wadjanbarra and Yidinji, and elders, past, present and emerging. I acknowledge that this land was stolen and their struggles for justice continue. Their connections and contributions to the identity and wellbeing for country continue. Always was, always will be, Aboriginal land.

I joined the Socialist Alliance early this year and I'm enthusiastic about supporting Renee Lees, our candidate running for the Senate in Qld. in the upcoming Federal election.

I joined the Socialist Alliance because it's made up of people like me and you -people who are fed up with life under the shadow of warmongers, racists, union bashers, greedy corporations and their dodgy representatives in the parliament.
For example, the corporate bungling of Covid 19 and the government's shameful dereliction of duty in the disastrous UN COP26 Climate Summit

serve as a stark reminder of the greed and incompetence of those currently in control.
They're also trying to deregister small progressive parties like the Socialist Alliance, by raising the membership threshold from 500 to 1,500 members.

Well, they've done us a favour because people like you have rallied. Our Cairns branch membership has risen 10 fold, to 80 members - and nationally we're currently up around 2300 members - *all this within the last couple of months or so.*

We support socialism based on these 5 principals:
Solidarity and Collaboration – *not dog eat dog competition;*
Environmental Sustainability & Eco-socialism – *not environmental degradation & destruction that hits the poor the hardest;*
Participatory Democracy – *where workers and communities make decisions directly and representatives are accountable and recallable;*
A Social and Democratic Economy – *where people's needs come before profits; and*
Equality - *between peoples, nations, religions, genders and sexualities.*

We understand that a society based on these principles is absolutely realistic, and necessary if our children and grandchildren are to enjoy a safe, sustainable and harmonious future.
We understand that in order to bring about such a society, we have to replace the institutions that protect and defend the billionaires – their Parliamentary system, their bureaucracy, their police and their military, and take back ownership of the economy.
Our goal is to replace them with institutions under our control - In other words, we need nothing short of revolutionary change, a transformation, brought about by organised actions taken by the public.
Since 2001, Socialist Alliance has campaigned for workers' rights, women's rights, against fracking, environmental protection, justice, civil liberties, justice for First Nation peoples, for refugees and against racism, for the rights of gays, lesbians, trans and intersex people, for equal marriage rights, and for international solidarity with all people who are struggling with exploitation and oppression. Socialist Alliance members are recognised leaders in many of these movements.
Socialist Alliance is a registered political Party with three elected local councillors, Sam Wainwright in Fremantle (WA), Sue Bolton in Moreland (Vic.) and Rob Pyne here in Cairns (Qld.)

Socialist Alliance stands candidates to give a voice to people like us – a voice to people grappling with, unemployment, insecure jobs, environmental destruction, poverty, domestic violence and homelessness - and to meet the need for our political representation.

Socialist Alliance representatives use their positions to oppose rotten policies, initiate and support community campaigns, and social movements, and promote the mass campaigns that can defeat the attacks on jobs and living standards. Socialist Alliance members who are elected to political office only accept the wage of an average worker.

Under capitalism, young people face special discrimination and political exclusion. Socialist Alliance seeks to involve young people and encourage them to lead the movement for change.

We understand that the majority of people, by acting in their workplaces, on their campuses, in their communities, and on the streets, can develop the power to create a just and environmentally sustainable alternative to the tyranny of profit-driven capitalism.

We can do this.
Welcome to the Socialist Alliance.

Christmas 2021

Here is a family Christmas message I wrote for 2021...

Well it's hard to believe, but 2021 – is almost finished – and what a year it's been – yet another year of life under the crises of Covid, Climate change, desperate lack of housing affordability and escalating homelessness and other unnecessary hardships for people, as our government and opposition combine to prepare for another election in the new year – what a shambles to have to deal with.

Despite all that, unlike most, we haven't done too badly. There are advantages to living in the remote far North. To date, we've avoided the worst impacts of the current disastrous situation. Our family have been able to generally get on with life by adopting a flexible and resilient approach to life on a daily basis.

Through the year, in the face of severe Covid restrictions, Rose and Alan have been able to continue climate campaign work in the form of organising rallies and street marches in support of the global #SCHOOLSTRIKE4CLIMATE,- never previously seen in Atherton - with family involvement and support.

We've also joined the Socialist Alliance – a small but progressive left national political Party with a branch in Cairns. The general idea is to work towards a total replacement of the current unsustainable Capitalist system with that of a democratic system based on the principles of Eco-socialism – and sooner rather than later. Our last activity was a welcoming of new members and introduction of our local regional candidate, running for the Senate in the upcoming Federal elections. There were 42 members and supporters from Cairns and the Tablelands in attendance at the fireside event at our place where Sara sold pizzas from her mobile kitchen and we sold drinks to raise funds, all complete with blues, rock and roll, Melbourne Ska and swing music – a great night, only last weekend.

From left – Grandchildren Bella, Silas, my daughter, Miya, and her partner, Dugan. 2021.

We managed a trip to see Kirk and Bronwin Smith and family at Charters Towers and out at Dreghorn cattle station. Other trips down to the beach, Chillagoe, Cairns and other local haunts have been good too. We've also had visits from Kirk and Bron, Werner and family, as well as other friends from Cairns and FNQ.

Miya and her family are all fully occupied and keeping well. Miya has established her home-based environmental consultancy and is doing a lot of work that aligns with her purpose and values. Dugan continues his full-time work. Bella is in year nine next year at Malanda High School. Silas will be in year four at Malanda primary school.

Sara and Rose operating the mobile food van, 2021.

Sara and her new partner Jeff are living here in the flat. They work in the mobile kitchen selling curries, pizzas and do general catering. They were at the Malanda Christmas Street Festival last Saturday. Sara is also developing an arts business. With Jeff's help, she is working towards an independent, multi-focused community service enterprise.

In these uncertain times, as a family, we tend to stay put, especially during this festive season.

We wish you and yours a Merry Christmas and a safe and happy 2022. Alan and Rose

I was really feeling the impacts of runaway climate change with high temperatures and relentless humidity. With increased episodes of hay fever, itchy skin rash and fatigue. Sometimes I think I may not survive another wet season. The elections were likely in May.

Federal Elections

The SA was in campaign mode, and for the first time, running two candidates, Pat O'Shane for the seat of Leichhardt and Renee Lees for the Queensland Senate.

Here's an extract from my MC notes for the Atherton Senate launch, Friday 3rd May, 5-6 pm, reflecting the Tablelands approach to the elections. The program included a rally at the roundabout, presentations, an open forum and dinner at the Thai restaurant afterwards.

"This event is part of a planned series of Qld. Senate launches offering a vibrant, progressive alternative to the dull, uninspiring, business as usual, corporate claptrap, dished up, yet again, by the major parties here on the Tablelands and beyond.

I want a safe and sustainable future for my grandkids and their generation. Why should they have to struggle through life under the rule of profit-driven corporations, warmongers, racists, union-bashers, and their dodgy, representatives in the parliament who have time and again, shown a callous disregard for the common good – common decency and pretty much everything we stand for.

Government bungling of Covid 19 and the shameful dereliction of duty in the UN COP26 Climate Summit, and their lack of support for those who lost everything in the bushfires. Continued atrocities are being committed against First Nations people, Afghanistan, refugees and asylum seekers, blatant inaction on women's rights, and so on.
No way - Not in my name!
I'm going to support Renee Lees, our Socialist Alliance candidate running for the Senate in Qld. in the upcoming Federal elections. I've worked alongside Renee as an activist and know her to be a person of substance and integrity, a good listener, a mum, a community lawyer, and totally committed to working towards a fair and sustainable future – an eco-socialist future – where people and planet are put before profit."

On polling day, our small but formidable Tablelands team managed to cover Atherton, Tolga, Malanda, Yungaburra, Herberton, Ravenshoe and Mareeba booths. We started out with 50 corflutes and finished with 25 – some still in the Daintree, Townsville and with volunteers yet to be collected. On the southern Tablelands – two corflutes were mowed over by TRC mowing contractors at Malanda, and others were torn from the stake, and disappeared, In Atherton two were repeatedly thrown into Prior Creek from the bridge. I collected the Atherton ones before dark and hammered them back in on the nature strip early in the mornings to catch the passing traffic and it worked well.

The Senate first preference vote for SA in Leichhardt was 1.5%; up to 3% in Cairns booths; and as much as 8% in Torres Strait. We pulled close to 1% in the Southern Tablelands. The first preference vote for O'Shane across Leichhardt was 4.07%. This was despite a record field of 11 candidates. The Greens attracted 10%, ensuring the overall progressive vote expanded while the far-right vote declined. (Source: Jonathan Strauss).

Election campaign - Yungaburra market stall, 23rd April 2022.

Other market stallholders always anchored their gazebos to the ground to avoid sudden wind gusts blowing them over. I was often concerned about it too, having recently suffered some damage. Let me share a vivid dream I had, the night before the April markets.

We had set up the Yungaburra market stall and were relaxing in between public engagements when a strong gust of wind lifted the gazebo off the ground. I called out to Rose and Renee to hang on to the frame with me, inside, to hold it down. Like an earlier trip in a hot-air balloon, we were airborne. It was at about a thousand feet when we passed over the township of Yungaburra, and drifted west North-west, lost altitude, and thankfully, had a smooth landing in one of Gabi's paddocks just off Thomas road. It was then that I woke up, and from then on, made sure that our gazebo was safely secured.

As a protest against an unregulated funeral industry seeking profit from grief and loss, Rose and I arranged to donate our bodies to the James Cook University medical laboratory. Just incidentally, there was another recent flying experience that I'd like to share.

At 77 I was left with hardly any cartilage in my right knee. In an effort to avoid invasive knee replacement surgery, I took up riding my pushbike on a daily basis, early in the morning, from home, five kilometres through Atherton to Platypus Park and back. I was on the return trip, down Golf Links road, at speed, when the front wheel slid through a small mud puddle on the side of the road, just as I was turning into our road. I was thrown over the handlebars. After an initial involuntary summersault, I was flying, inverted. I saw the bike cartwheeling across the sky – there were clouds too.

For the moment, it was slow motion and I was enjoying the experience, until my impact with the bitumen road. The first thing I felt was a severe jarring sensation as the back of my head hit the road. The impact broke the helmet and I thought my brain had separated from its meninges.

Lying in the middle of the road, in shock, my system then went into pilot mode to avoid further danger. I got on my bike and rode the short distance home. I was sitting at the kitchen table when Rose noticed the blood on the floor. My left leg must have caught the peddle as I came off the bike, leaving a large bloody wound.

As the shock subsided, I felt pain in my right elbow and wrist. After a visit to my doctor and x-rays, it was discovered I had suffered a fracture of the scaphoid bone just above the radius. I made a quick recovery and in a couple of months, I was back on the bike.

Conclusion

I began work on this autobiography on Friday 28th of November 2003 when I was fifty-eight. It was a sporadic affair with gaps of months and years between episodes of enthusiasm between concerns with the more pressing aspects of life. I have attempted to present my identity and connection to the past four hundred years to John Bradshaw and the English Revolution, to Colonial Australia, to our contemporary times through my Mum and Dad.

Through this book, I simply wanted to share my story - a celebration of life with my extraordinary family and friends and the wider society.

I hope that this book might also serve as an inspiration to those who have a passion for exploring the big picture and the big questions of why things are the way they are, on the positive side and occasionally the not-so-positive.

It's April 2023 and nearly half a million women are homeless. Public Housing is being sold off to private developers for profit. Adani's Carmichael coal mine is operating and fossil fuel projects expanding. There is still no justice for First Nations people and Refugees. Our Governments are disengaged from the social and environmental responsibility we would normally expect. We're told that there's not enough money for Health, Education and other essential public services. And Governments spend hundreds of billions of our taxpayer money on subsidies for fossil fuel companies and the purchase of nuclear submarines.

'Isherwood's Australia,' I hope, will show our children and grandchildren, and future generations, the importance of being connected to nature. I also wanted to show that a safe future is possible.

I wanted to convey that it's all right to stand up and be counted. It's all right to get involved in politics, and it's all right to question authority. In other words, it's all right to exercise our democratic rights and fight for what we believe in - a just, caring and ecologically sustainable society. I'm seventy-eight, still campaigning for a better world, and ready to prepare for a revolution.

My family have created and defended our sanctuary on the Tablelands in Far North Queensland. A wander in quiet solitude under our rainforest canopy and my conversation with the trees renew my strength and remind me of the triviality of human endeavours compared to the transcendental power of a 180 million years old ecosystem. We are indeed custodians passing through. By the way, I spotted a green possum in the rainforest near the front gate last night.

Thank you for sharing my journey.

Acknowledgements

To all who have directly and indirectly contributed to this work.

I remain indebted to you, Mum and Dad for being my devoted parents and for your efforts in establishing who I am. And Grandpa, Judith and Elaine for providing those important snippets in the recall of childhood days. Rose, thanks for being such a loving, imperturbable, and understanding lifelong friend. Thanks for providing support and the triggers, Rose, during my struggles to recall important events and the hours you devoted to proofreading. Sara, thanks for providing professional advice and help in navigating Windows. Miya, for alerting me to cultural protocols and professional advice. Melanie Smith for putting a map of Australia together with First Nations place names for inclusion in the book. Thanks to Crystal Leonardi of Bowerbird Publishing for her patience and understanding of my idiosyncracies and professional support. Thanks to all those who gave their permission to be included in my stories.

I acknowledge Australia's First Nations Peoples – as the Traditional Owners and Custodians of this land. I acknowledge that this land was stolen and sovereignty was never ceded. I acknowledge that their connection to land and culture continues. I give respect to Elders – past and present – and through them to all Australian Aboriginal and Torres Strait Islander people.

Thank you to my Yapa and Yolngu friends from Central Australia and North East Arnhem Land. Especially Henry Cook and sons Jupurrula jarra, Albert and Neil Cook, Lionel and Joe James, Morris and Agnes Luther, Marritngu, Djiniyini Gondarra OAM, Widji, Yungalama Yinyindjurr, Wirilma and many others.

Thanks to Jonatani Rika, David Holt, Jeff Hulcome, Terry and Sue Parry, Alistair Burns, Bruce Mercer, Richard and Lyn Darby, Klaus Wieneroider (Hoyte), Kirk and Bronwin Smith, Mark Hollands, Werner Sattmann-Frese, Jim Varghese, and John and Marie Woodley for your companionship and solidarity through the years. And thanks to Billy Marshall Stoneking, writer and fellow teacher during my days at remote Papunya, who, with author Christopher Isherwood in mind, provided encouragement by suggesting a title for my book – 'Isherwood's Australia.'

To all my other friends who have shared my journey and may not have been included in this acknowledgement, thank you.

About the Author

Alan Isherwood was born in Kew Victoria and spent his early years in Hawthorn and Ringwood, Victoria. He has lived and worked in diverse roles, all over Australia, from remote and isolated First Nations communities in North East Arnhem Land and Central Desert to Cape York and Torres Strait, and Guadalcanal. Alan and his family have enjoyed their permanent base on the Atherton Tablelands since 1989. Alan spent time in China, USA, Denmark, Central Switzerland and the UK. Alan and Rose introduced their daughters, Miya and Sara to their ancestral homes in Derbyshire and Sar Chung.

Photograph courtesy of Ian Poke Photography, Cairns.

Alan contested the seat of Kennedy in the 1998 Federal elections and again as an independent candidate for the 2001 Queensland State Elections. Alan founded the community group, Tablelands Action Alliance or TAA in 2014. The TAA is still operating today.

After some years of experience as front-line activists, Alan and Rose joined the Socialist Alliance. More recent campaigns include the NOT4SALE campaign, #STOPADANI, and #SCHOOLSTRIKE4CLIMATE among others. Our current campaigns include confronting Government inaction on Public Housing, Refugee and Asylum Seeker rights, and Climate Change.

Alan is protective of his family home – a Queenslander set amidst the rainforest sanctuary on Mazlin Creek and can often be spotted quietly strolling under the canopy. He also enjoys long-distance swimming in solitude at Lake Eacham in the Tablelands and Etty Bay, down on the coast. He enjoys conversations with the chooks and growing organic fruit and veggies and making Cornish pasties. Music is important in his life. He shares Mendelssohn's Songs Without Words, Rachmaninov, and, at high volume, the Melbourne Ska Orchestra, 1950s Classic Rock and Roll, African American Blues, Reggae and 1940s Swing. On a dry-season evening on a cool, clear moonlit night, you're likely to find Alan out the back, by the open fire, being a DJ or in lively conversation with friends and family.

To purchase copies of 'Isherwood's Australia' go to www.crystalleonardi.com/bookshop

To contact the author or to leave a review, email: arisher45@internode.on.net

Praise for Isherwood's Australia

"This is a wonderful book about an adventurous and exciting life. The stunningly written stories give a view of various areas of Australia and other places all over the world. Alan's mind and activities are based on the deep belief to make this planet a better place."

Pia Rast - Sursee, Switzerland

"What a Life. I was amazed and impressed by all the work you have done. It was a wonderful look back over a life based on strong relationships. The passion you have for the country of your birth with all its wonders and imperfections, your love of family whether through birth, marriage or through connecting with the communities you have lived in makes for an inspiring journey."

Dr. John Humphreys - London, United Kingdom

"... I thought I would skip the early history and jump to the 1960's however, so interesting, have to read everything."

Mario Barbagallo - Sunshine Coast, Australia

"A great read full of humanity and adventure.
It resonated with me in a number of ways,
least of which were love of family and community."

Bruce Mercer - Manilla, Australia

From the Publisher

'Isherwood's Australia' is an outstanding example of how one man's individual journey, combined with a rich family tradition of sharing stories, can unite generations in a stunningly relatable and compelling way. Alan has created an intricate, emotionally sophisticated portrayal of the ensemble cast - his extended family, and friends, and the tales of 20th Century Australia and beyond.

I wish Alan all the success and happiness in his new endeavour as a published author. I have no doubt that 'Isherwood's Australia' will educate and entertain many readers around the world.

Crystal Leonardi
Bowerbird Publishing
www.crystalleonardi.com

www.ingramcontent.com/pod-product-compliance
Lightning Source LLC
Chambersburg PA
CBHW072144070526
44585CB00015B/995